Praise for
Creating a Sustainable Organization

"Peter brings together the wide-ranging aspects of present and future organizations to bolster environmental, social, and governance (ES&G) performance, presenting a clean and clear understanding of *organizational sustainability*. There are two ways to take over the world in business within the income statement and balance sheet—cash and profits! Peter presents anecdotal and factual evidence for translating typical ES&G data into financial knowledge, ultimately to decrease bad costs, optimize use of assets, and increase the profitability of revenue streams."

—**Michael R. Pisarcik**, Director, Environment & Safety Management Systems,
Sara Lee Corporation

"Peter Soyka's book *Creating a Sustainable Organization* offers an informative, comprehensive look at many foundational issues for the emerging field of sustainable business management."

—**Carol Singer Neuvelt**, Executive Director, National Association for
Environmental Management (NAEM)

"Peter Soyka is a master at bringing clarity to concepts, deconstructing the labels in vogue, and offering a multidisciplinary, grounded perspective that links socially responsible investing to corporate sustainability. He also diagnoses the changes, challenges, demands, and expectations of the paradigm shift involving the EHS/ sustainability and financial communities. This book is for organizations seeking to catalyze sustainability thinking and practice, develop a sustainability DNA, and stimulate the right conditions for value creation."

—**Donna Vincent Roa**, PhD, ABC, CSR-P, Managing Partner & Chief Strategist,
Water Sector Communication Expert, Vincent Roa Group, LLC

"Peter's message is clear: Sustainability leadership is now synonymous with business leadership. The book is a clear roadmap to leverage sustainability thinking to create shareholder value."

—**Tim Mohin**, Corporate Responsibility Director, Advanced Micro Devices;
author of *Changing Business from the Inside Out:
A Treehugger's Guide to Working in Corporations*

"I've worked with Peter for more than 25 years. This is exactly the kind of work I'd expect from him. It's a book for current and aspiring sustainability professionals, and moves the discussion from the emotional, green, crunchy granola appeal of sustainability to the argument that appeals to the brain. *Creating a Sustainable Organization* presents the theory, the evidence, and the organizational case underpinning the argument for green; it shows why caring about sustainability is good for the bottom line and the economy as well as the earth."

—**Lawrence G. Buc**, President, SLS Consulting, Inc.

"Peter Soyka conducts a full-field scan of sustainability in the marketplace as well as a full-body organizational, behavioral, and historical scan of how corporations are responding to it. In a dispassionate and thorough treatment, he makes a reasoned case that the interrelatedness and magnitude of the sustainability/ES&G issue requires an integrative corporate response. There is a sea change coming. Companies and managerial professionals need more dialogue to meet this change with a shared understanding of sustainability. Getting people to understand sustainability's interconnections is a core challenge Soyka diagnoses well through a come-let-us-reason-together approach and tone. He more than achieves his purpose of demonstrating how the complex nature of sustainability and the show-me character of the corporation can meet to mutual benefit and to societal and stakeholder gain. He achieves this not only with clarity in his arguments but with evidence from a wealth of field experience. His advice, frameworks, and approaches will help anyone serious about sustainability to promote it faster and better, and those who may not be, to become more so."

—**David J. Vidal**, Director, Center for Sustainability, The Conference Board

"With characteristic modesty, Peter Soyka says he is not a paradigm-busting pioneer or visionary. He is, on this particular, self-effacing point, simply wrong.

"By admirably pursuing the aim of bridging the conceptual and semantic gaps that divide rather than unite witting and unwitting stakeholders in the business of sustainability and the sustainability of business, he provides a template that cannot but be of inestimable value to all such stakeholders: corporate executives, managers, employees, suppliers, distributors, and customers; sustainability professionals, scholars, students, advocates, and critics; government officials and administrators; financial analysts and investors; representatives of non-governmental organizations in the environmental, safety, health, business-commerce-trade, development, human rights, public interest, and educational fields; citizens, communities, and the media; and, yes, even specialists in the field of national security, robustly conceived.

"By impressively achieving his aim, along the way heightening the sophistication of our understanding of sustainability, underscoring the essential importance of thinking and acting holistically, entreating us to assume a multidisciplinary posture, awakening us to the need for an entirely new repertoire of skills attuned to the 21st century, and advocating integrative approaches that cut across organizational, institutional, sectoral, national, and even international lines, he makes an enduring intellectual and operational contribution of truly strategic import."

—**Gregory D. Foster**, Professor of National Security Studies;
Director, Environment Industry Study,
Industrial College of the Armed Forces, National Defense University

Creating a Sustainable Organization:

Approaches for Enhancing Corporate Value
Through Sustainability

Peter A. Soyka

Vice President, Publisher: Tim Moore
Associate Publisher and Director of Marketing: Amy Neidlinger
Executive Editor: Jeanne Glasser Levine
Editorial Assistant: Pamela Boland
Development Editor: Russ Hall
Operations Specialist: Jodi Kemper
Senior Marketing Manager: Julie Phifer
Assistant Marketing Manager: Megan Graue
Cover Designer: Chuti Prasertsith
Managing Editor: Kristy Hart
Project Editor: Anne Goebel
Copy Editor: Gayle Johnson
Proofreader: Linda Seifert
Indexer: Lisa Stumpf
Senior Compositor: Gloria Schurick
Manufacturing Buyer: Dan Uhrig

© 2012 by Pearson Education, Inc.
Publishing as FT Press
Upper Saddle River, New Jersey 07458

FT Press offers excellent discounts on this book when ordered in quantity for bulk purchases or special sales. For more information, please contact U.S. Corporate and Government Sales, 1-800-382-3419, corpsales@pearsontechgroup.com. For sales outside the U.S., please contact International Sales at international@pearson.com.

Company and product names mentioned herein are the trademarks or registered trademarks of their respective owners.

Printed in the United States of America

First Printing February 2012

Pearson Education LTD.
Pearson Education Australia PTY, Limited.
Pearson Education Singapore, Pte. Ltd.
Pearson Education Asia, Ltd.
Pearson Education Canada, Ltd.
Pearson Educación de Mexico, S.A. de C.V.
Pearson Education—Japan
Pearson Education Malaysia, Pte. Ltd.

ISBN-10: 0-13-287440-7

ISBN-13: 978-0-13-287440-3

Library of Congress Cataloging-in-Publication Data

Soyka, Peter Arnim, 1958-

Creating a sustainable organization : approaches for enhancing corporate value through sustainability / Peter A. Soyka. -- 1st ed.

p. cm.

Includes bibliographical references.

ISBN 978-0-13-287440-3 (hardcover : alk. paper) 1. Organizational effectiveness. 2. Organizational change. 3. Sustainable development. 4. Investments--Environmental aspects. I. Title.

HD58.9.S675 2012

658.4'08--dc23

2011034569

For Sheri and Leeann,
and all others committed to creating a more
sustainable world

Contents

Acknowledgments

In writing this book, I summoned perspectives and experiences that extend many years into the past, to the early days of my career. I drew upon a wealth of knowledge, insights, and wisdom imparted by an array of people who have helped me grow professionally and personally over the past two decades. The available space in this book and the limitations of my long-term memory prevent me from recognizing everyone who has had a positive (or at least important) influence on my development and the formation of the ideas articulated in this book. However, I would like to recognize some of the many people who have played an important role in helping me reach this point.

I have learned a great deal since I first came to work in Washington, D.C. back in the mid-1980s. I am indebted to many former colleagues, clients, and fellow travelers for the body of knowledge I have developed over that time span. Among many others, I would particularly like to acknowledge the contributions made by a number of people who were helpful to me in developing the facts, ideas, and concepts presented in this book.

For his many contributions to my thinking about organizational sustainability in all its dimensions over the past 15 years or so, and for his ongoing (and persistent) encouragement to take on the challenge of writing a book on this topic, I want to thank my good friend and frequent colleague Ira Feldman. I am especially pleased that he was willing to share some of his expertise and perspectives for the book, which are included in several of the chapters. I also would like to thank Larry Buc, who gave me my start in the environmental consulting business some 25 years ago. He also provided major and early opportunities for me to grow professionally and served as my first (and only true) mentor in the business. He has been very generous over the years in sharing his time, knowledge, and accumulated wisdom. Many of the successful projects on which we have collaborated over the years have helped me develop a level of understanding and insight that has enabled me to address the major topics in this book in the depth they deserve.

During the past five years or so, I have been fortunate to have worked with a number of talented people on projects that have brought to light new information and insights about the relationships between corporate environmental management and sustainability behavior, performance measurement and reporting, and financial community evaluation and investment decision making, among other topics. Involvement in these projects has allowed me to both contribute and further develop my capabilities while helping clients better understand and make sound decisions about their own operations and activities. I would like to specifically acknowledge and thank Shana Harbour and Bill Hanson of the U.S. EPA, Mike Fanning of the U.S. Postal Service, and Carol Singer Neuvelt of the National Association for Environmental Management. They provided me with opportunities to contribute to the important work being done within their respective organizations and gave me the creative space I needed to develop and deploy some unconventional yet, in the end, highly effective approaches for addressing challenging issues. Many of the facts and perspectives provided in this book originated in the work performed under the direction of these people.

I also would like to thank a small number of people who are among the many thousands who are doing the work of corporate sustainability on a daily basis or are engaged in evaluating its effects. Each was kind enough to share some personal insights reflecting his or her organization and/or experience in the field. They include Mark Bateman, Alan Knight, Tim Mohin, Sandy Nessing, Mike Pisarcik, and Marcella Thompson. I particularly appreciate the candid and insightful feedback provided by Ira Feldman and Larry Buc. They carefully reviewed draft chapters and were instrumental in helping me improve them. I also would like to thank Paul Bailey, Greg Foster, Jeff Goodman, and many others within my professional circle for their support in developing my idea for a book and helping it take shape.

Developing a written work of this length and depth is an involved process that includes many steps and much painstaking review and improvement. I would like to thank my editors, Jeanne Glasser Levine, Anne Goebel, and Gayle Johnson, as well as their colleagues at FT Press/Pearson for their interest in the book, helpful suggestions, and professionalism. The finished product has benefited substantially from their involvement.

Finally, I could not have pushed through a project of this size and complexity without the active support and encouragement of my friends and family, particularly that of my wife, Sheri, and daughter, Leeann. Their love and support have kept me going during many an extended workday.

About the Author

Peter A. Soyka is an experienced and accomplished sustainability and environmental management consultant and a recognized expert working at the intersection of environment/EHS and finance. He is the founder and President of Soyka & Company, LLC, a small consultancy focused on illuminating and resolving the issues limiting sustainable business success. With 25 years of environmental management experience, he has served a wide variety of corporate, public agency, and nonprofit clients focusing on improved, cost-effective environmental and sustainability performance. Much of his recent work has involved identifying and capturing the financial and other organizational benefits of proactive environmental management and sustainability practices. During his career, Mr. Soyka has successfully designed and executed hundreds of consulting projects, including a number devoted to driving sustainability thinking and practices into client organizations at a strategic level. He has developed a substantial number of new innovations for understanding and acting upon the organizational and financial aspects of corporate sustainability issues; he brings a substantial track record of innovative thinking and success in devising creative solutions to very challenging environmental/business management problems and translating new ideas into approaches, tools, and techniques that produce real results.

1

Introduction

Over the last ten years or so, a number of books and other published works on the topic of corporate sustainability have appeared. Early on, much focus was placed on the "triple bottom line" construct developed and promoted by John Elkington in his book *Cannibals with Forks*, published in late 1999. Following a bit of a lull in the ensuing years, "greening" and more general notions of corporate sustainability have again recently come into vogue. This is in part due to increasing concerns about climate change and other global-scale environmental issues, but also because a number of large U.S. multinational corporations have mounted highly publicized campaigns to "green" their operations. Today, it seems that "green business" is a bandwagon that many people and organizations are seeking to drive or at least jump onto. Attracting less fanfare but still reflecting important developments and thinking, several recent books have addressed emerging realities in the financial world. In particular, the continued evolution of socially responsible investing (SRI) and the increasing interest in corporate sustainability shown by a number of major financial institutions and quasi-public organizations have attracted significant commentary. Few, if any, authors have sought to link these two trends and to draw out the implications for those who work on corporate sustainability issues or want to. With this book, I intend to fill this important gap.

In an attempt to address organizational sustainability as they perceive it, financial community actors, led by SRI investors, have developed the construct of environmental (and related health and safety), social, and governance (ES&G) posture and performance. This construct defines a set of behaviors that they believe is meaningful and around which investment strategies can be defined and implemented. Although it's not identical, the ES&G framework is very similar and closely related to the triple bottom line and another concept commonly used in U.S. corporations, corporate social responsibility (CSR). These terms and what they represent are still somewhat vague to many observers, but it is clear that each attempts to define a standard of behavior that is socially acceptable, accounts for all important factors (financial and nonfinancial), and, in the case of ES&G, allows a third party to make an informed judgment about the investment potential of a particular company or industry. This book attempts to bring some clarity to these different concepts and to show how and under what conditions they are most suitable for use by companies and their many stakeholders.

Professionals working in the environment, health, and safety (EHS)/sustainability field and in the financial sector perform different activities; have different perspectives, academic training, and priorities; and rarely cross paths in any regular or organized fashion. Yet increasingly they are working on different dimensions of the same issue: how the EHS and broader sustainability posture and performance of corporations affect these firms' financial performance and investment potential. A few thought leaders have noted that more integrative and complete thinking across disciplines and these discrete, disconnected "communities of practice" must occur if sustainability thinking is to be translated into action on a broad scale. What is needed, however, is a much broader and more meaningful dialog involving all the relevant actors, and a set of organizing principles and facts to both explain why greater cross-pollination is necessary and form the basis for the early conversations.

In particular, EHS and sustainability professionals, and professionals working in other functions and disciplines who have an interest in corporate sustainability, must develop a more complete understanding of how the financial community operates, what its members value, what motivates their behavior, and the basis of their growing interest in corporate sustainability. At the same time, to take advantage of the opportunities presented by corporate sustainability, financial sector actors, particularly investors and investment analysts, must develop a broader and deeper understanding of how sustainability issues affect companies' financial posture, performance, and future prospects; what types of corporate practices create the conditions required for sustainable value creation to occur; and what types of indicators may be useful in predicting which firms will benefit (and which will suffer) from evolving sustainability trends. In other words, a bridge must be built between the disparate worlds of the EHS/sustainability professional and the investor/analyst. This book begins to build this bridge.

In taking a professional path that has traversed many different sectors and disciplines, I have found it possible to take a step or two back to view the broader landscape. It is clear to me that the increasing bodies of knowledge being brought to bear in both the EHS/sustainability and financial communities, each on their separate paths, are about to converge. This will represent a major paradigm shift that I believe is already under way. To reflect and, in my own small way, help promote this shift, I have compiled, in this book, descriptions of the following:

- How sustainability issues affect the business enterprise
- The important stakeholders who influence corporate behavior, particularly as it pertains to EHS and social equity issues
- How sustainability issues can and should be managed in an organization
- What financial markets are and how they work, with particular emphasis on sustainability issues
- The ways in which investors and other financial market actors evaluate sustainability posture and performance
- The evidence showing how skillful management of EHS and broader sustainability issues can create new corporate financial value and positive investment returns
- What performance measures are most important from all important stakeholder perspectives, and how current measures could be improved
- How those interested in contributing to organizational (and global) sustainability can become more effective and influential

This book outlines a coming "sea change" and discusses its implications for professionals in the relevant fields, for corporate leaders, and, in due course, for policymakers, regulators, and the educated general public. The book will have particular import for those who would lead internal sustainability or CSR efforts—including senior managers who have recently adopted the Chief Sustainability Officer (CSO) title—and those who would provide expert services to support these individuals and their organizations. In particular, I believe that these professionals will need to expand their existing, separate paradigms and broaden (and, in some cases, deepen) their skill sets. I believe that there is ample justification for reaching this judgment.

I have seen the broad outlines of a new way of viewing corporate sustainability issues taking shape for a considerable period. Since the mid-1990s, I have pioneered some new thinking about the relationship between environmental management and corporate performance, especially in linking environmental management improvements to financial value (such as to stock price changes and durable competitive advantage). As shown in this book, the additional leverage brought about by the growing and active involvement of financial market players is moving the world of investment into alignment with many of the goals of corporate sustainability. This alignment is taking shape and gathering force more quickly than many realize. As it becomes more prominent, it will bring many changes and challenges, and this book shows both the progress to date and my thoughts on the path forward.

Major Themes and Messages in This Book

As I show in the following chapters, the past 20 years or so have witnessed the development of a substantial body of work about and understanding of how best to manage environment, health, and safety (EHS) issues. For the most part, EHS management practices and methods are well developed and widely understood within the EHS profession. The landscape, however, continues to evolve. The array of issues that are in the purview of EHS people has been expanding at an accelerating rate in recent years. In a parallel and related development, the number, diversity, and sophistication of the stakeholders having an interest in EHS management behavior and performance continues to grow. It now includes many people and entities that until recently had expressed little interest in matters involving the environment or worker health and safety, much less sustainability.

These changes necessarily place new demands and expectations on the EHS/sustainability professional.

In particular, a strong and growing impetus for corporate sustainability is emerging from an unexpected source. Influential actors in the financial sector are becoming increasingly interested in corporate environmental/EHS, social, and governance performance and in the management practices that improve it. Indeed, investments (both equity and fixed income) in firms made at least in part on the basis of EHS, social, and/or governance criteria are growing far more rapidly than their conventional, "mainstream" counterparts. Increasingly, investors and the information providers that supply them are posing a greater number of more sophisticated questions regarding not only conventional indicators of performance (such as compliance record) but also the degree of senior management involvement, the presence and effectiveness of internal systems and processes, and whether and how existing businesses may be affected by significant EHS issues (such as climate change). As I will show, these expectations are too numerous, persistent, and important for firms to ignore. I also provide evidence that these demands and, more generally, the involvement of the financial sector in corporate management of ES&G issues are very likely to increase during the coming years.

Supporting and fueling this trend is the rapidly increasing availability of information and the public scrutiny of corporate ES&G performance it enables. In the Internet age, information (and sometimes misinformation) is everywhere and available more or less instantaneously. Complicating matters is a diverse array of stakeholder values, preexisting beliefs, priorities, educational levels, and technical sophistication. Stakeholders do not, as a general rule, speak with one voice, and embracing their respective agendas may lead in divergent, even diametrically opposed, directions.

Among the types of stakeholders demanding more and higher quality EHS information are major customers, who are rightly considered "first among equals" within many companies. We are now witnessing a spate of new supply chain initiatives focused on the life cycle EHS impacts of an array of products and services. Most of the action and public attention seem to be focused on the high-profile efforts addressing consumer products sponsored/driven by major retailers (such as Walmart), although other prominent efforts are under way as well. Most of these initiatives have an explicit transparency component (they require public reporting of product/service environmental aspects), including upstream (production and transport of raw materials and components) and downstream (in-use and post-use) life cycle stages. The resulting data will make it increasingly easy for a wide array of stakeholders to identify the leadership companies (as they perceive them) and to distinguish them from the laggards, in any industry or economic sector.

Some of these major trends have been observed by other prominent participants in the EHS/sustainability field. The following sidebar describes a particularly insightful example.

Emerging Corporate Sustainability Leadership Behaviors

A keen observer of major sustainability trends is my good friend and frequent colleague Ira Feldman. He is a prominent and internationally renowned expert on environmental policy and regulation. He closely follows major developments pertaining to corporate sustainability, use of voluntary standards, climate change adaptation, sustainability investing, and a wide array of other topics. He sees several areas in which major advancements in corporate attitudes and practices have occurred in recent years. According to Ira:

- "Leaders in various industry sectors now clearly see the value of embedding sustainability in their corporate DNA."

- "Standards, toolkits, and road maps have evolved to the point where business and industry have ample guidance to embrace sustainability best practices."

- "The financial sector is finally providing a clear signal to business and industry that high performance on environment, social, and governance (ES&G) issues—another way to phrase sustainability or corporate social responsibility—will be rewarded."

- "Even if sustainability concepts are not fully understood, most companies have a greater appreciation of the need to satisfy a multiplicity of stakeholders. The multistakeholder dynamic is a hallmark of sustainability."

- "Sustainability has reached the C-suite with the advent of the Chief Sustainability Officer (CSO)."

- "Supply chain management for sustainability has made great strides, gaining widespread acceptance through visible supply chain initiatives of companies like Walmart and sector-oriented or collaborative approaches like the Sustainability Consortium."

(Feldman, 2011)

Each of these trends, along with a number of others, is discussed in depth in this book.

These and other trends make it increasingly important for those involved in sustainability issues from any angle to apply a multidisciplinary perspective and methods. It is clear that continuing to view the issues through the lens of any one professional discipline—whether EHS management, manufacturing, marketing, supply chain management/logistics, or public or investor relations—will be inadequate to fully understand how the dynamic is changing and what to do in response. From the standpoint of some of the important stakeholder groups, it seems equally clear that far more interchange of expertise, perspective, and talents will be required. As this book discusses, most investors, and even many of their specialist ESG analysts and data providers, are poorly equipped to really understand how EHS, social, and governance issues work in a corporation, how they can most effectively be managed, and how and to what extent improved practices and performance are and can be expressed in terms that are relevant to security valuation. Similarly, in the context of understanding/promoting corporate sustainability, public-sector institutions, labor unions, and even the NGO community are in many cases organized to respond to an operating environment that in large measure no longer exists, or at the least is undergoing rapid and significant change.

Unfortunately, many of the communities of practice involved with different aspects of environmental policy, EHS/sustainability management, SRI, and investment analysis/management have often worked in isolation and sometimes in conflict with one another. There are many reasons for this—some structural, some cultural, and some contextual. Regardless of the root cause(s) that apply in any particular case, I believe that the status quo will need to change for us to advance the practice of sustainability as far and as fast as external conditions require.

This book suggests some ways in which bridges can be built across these communities so that companies are encouraged by all important stakeholders to take appropriate measures to improve their ES&G performance in ways that create new financial and broader societal value. This can and should occur through implementing improved management practices; providing consistent and timely information that is relevant and actionable to financial and other stakeholders; and receiving, understanding, and acting on appropriate feedback provided by market participants.

To make this happen, two key conditions will need to be met. One is that more frequent, extensive, and meaningful dialog will take place, leading to shared understanding. The diverse constituencies and people who need to be involved in the discussion must interact and develop a much deeper and more meaningful understanding of one another's perspectives, needs, and talents than is typically the case now.

In parallel, and for this deep understanding to fully take shape, the second condition is that many of those involved will need to expand their perspective and, in many cases, their skill sets. Remaining solely within one's professional discipline or official role will be increasingly untenable for anyone who wants to meaningfully contribute to the sustainability of his or her own organization, and certainly for anyone seeking to catalyze sustainability thinking or practice in other organizations.

This book not only describes the conditions, trends, and root causes that have brought us to this point, but also provides some suggested answers. For corporate organizations and the people who lead and serve them, I recommend a number of long-term objectives and strategy elements that, if adopted, can place a company on the path toward a more sustainable future. I also recommend both immediate and short-term actions to define the direction and contours of this path, and some early stepping-stones. For those working outside the organization, whether in a consulting or other stakeholder role, I suggest a number of approaches, techniques, and tools that can be used to help focus the attention and efforts of clients and others they seek to influence on the issues and endpoints that are most important, the techniques and messages that are most effective, and, in general, how they can improve the effectiveness and impact of their work in promoting organizational sustainability.

A Few Disclosures and Caveats

I want to emphasize that, with very few exceptions, I am not proposing a new, "game-changing," paradigm-busting approach to managing ES&G issues. Accordingly, I do not view myself as a pioneer or visionary in advocating the approaches I detail in this book. At the same time, and viewed from another perspective, the ideas I promote cannot reasonably be dismissed as unrealistic, impractical, too expensive or time-consuming, or ineffective. Rather, my suggested approach is firmly grounded in the practices that have been developed within and by the EHS profession during the past 15 years or so. They have been deployed, refined, and demonstrated repeatedly by the many thousands of people who perform the work of EHS management on a daily basis. These people include corporate headquarters and plant/field staff, consultants, staff from some of the more solutions-oriented NGOs, and regulatory agency personnel. Collectively, they (including, in my own limited ways, myself) have brought us to where we are. Without their efforts, both the quality of human health and the environment as it exists today, and our ability to understand and effectively manage our EHS aspects in the future, would be significantly reduced.

This may seem self-evident (if not flagrantly self-congratulatory), but I believe that it is important to articulate this perspective for two major reasons. First, in keeping with my approach to writing this book (and my work more generally), I believe in transparency. This means making clear my point of view and biases so that you can reach your own conclusions about whether I am building my ideas on a strong foundation.

The second major reason is that I have observed many recent changes in the public perception of EHS issues (environment in particular), accompanied by a proliferation of media stories, new businesses and concepts, and general buzz on this topic. It seems that "green" and "greening" have again captured a significant portion of the public mindshare. While in some respects this is encouraging, and even gratifying, I believe that it is important not to let enthusiasm overwhelm sound judgment. Having worked in the environmental/ EHS field for 25 years, I have seen several previous "waves" of interest in the environment. Just as in the past, I will not be surprised if the recent high tide soon begins to ebb, whether due to economic conditions or in favor of some other issue.

Moreover, while the growing interest in the environment has many positive aspects, it also has promoted a trend that I find disquieting. As I discuss in detail in Chapter 8, meaningful public sustainability (or ES&G) reporting occurs to only a limited extent and has only recently begun to grow strongly. However, there has been a veritable explosion of "green" product and service claims; new greening "experts" are appearing regularly; and scores of new companies and consortia are entering the field to provide advice and assistance on green branding, marketing, communications, and advertising. To the extent that these new entrants (both ideas and those who promote them) gain traction with the public and, more troubling, with corporate executives, there is significant risk of placing undue emphasis on the message (and/or messenger) rather than on its content. Indeed, several studies have documented that unsubstantiated or potentially misleading green claims are widespread,[1] and a few particularly abusive situations have induced enforcement actions by the U.S. Federal Trade Commission (FTC).[2] Such behavior has not gone unnoticed more broadly; several recent consumer surveys indicate growing skepticism of "green" claims among the general public.[3]

In addition, it is an open secret that during the past decade or so, many companies have shed EHS staff, apparently in the belief that they had largely completed their work in this area, such that EHS management was now in more of an ongoing maintenance mode than a building mode. Ironically, these staff cuts were in many cases made by the same executives and companies that have most loudly proclaimed their commitments to sustainability. The consequences of this type of behavior can be seen most vividly in the 2010 BP disaster in the Gulf of Mexico, but they are playing out in less visible ways across American industry. It is only a matter of time before other "shocking" EHS incidents and accidents occur because of inadequate staffing and/or practices at firms esteemed for their solid management team, history of innovation, or even sustainability leadership.

I believe it is important to place the cart *behind* the horse. Indeed, in nature, and in many fields of human endeavor, form follows function. So it must be in managing ES&G issues. As discussed in Chapter 5, a sound management structure includes and is guided by corporate mission and vision and is overlain by strong governance practices. However, it also is based on the "nuts and bolts" of how EHS issues affect the business on the ground. This means that those who understand these issues, their implications, and what to do about them must be central, not peripheral, to the design, deployment, and ongoing management of the organization's ES&G/sustainability strategy, management structure, and communications. Accordingly, I believe, for example, that a company's highest-ranking sustainability executive (such as the Chief Sustainability Officer or Senior Vice President for Sustainability) should not be a public relations, marketing, communications, or investor relations professional unless there is a compelling reason for such a selection (such as earlier career experience in EHS). Nor should the sustainability (or ES&G) function be housed in or report to any of these communications-related functions.

Instead, in the context of managing for ES&G improvement or sustainability, it is critically important for organizations and those responsible for managing them to emphasize accomplishment over accolades, competence over appearances, and fundamentals over capturing favorable publicity. It starts with getting (or keeping) one's house in order. You do this by maintaining a high and improving performance level along two basic dimensions that have been with us since the dawn of the EHS field as a defined profession 40 years ago:

- Complying with the law and all applicable regulatory requirements
- Adequately protecting the health and safety of one's own employees

I would hope that you agree that these two conditions reflect the minimum EHS performance level that you would expect from any well-run organization. I would go further and suggest that any company or other organization that has not yet achieved (or that has retreated from) a high and improving level of performance along these two dimensions should dispense with any notions of, or plans to actively pursue (or, more troubling, tout their own), sustainability. Instead, the executives managing such organizations should either get back to basics or institute appropriate programs, depending on their situation, to build the required capability.

Irrespective of a particular organization's current posture or aspirations regarding sustainability, I believe that the principles and approaches outlined in this book will be of material value in helping EHS and sustainability practitioners (both internal and external to the organization) and other members of the organization. Whatever business function they perform, they will understand where they are, what they should focus on, what structures and practices will help them manage the important issues, and how they should measure and report their performance over time. I also speak to some of the important professional skills and personal attributes that will increasingly be required to achieve success in positioning your organization to achieve sustainable business success.

Endnotes

1. For example, in a recent (2010) update of an annual review of green product claims, more than half of the claims made for more than 5,000 products evaluated were either vague or unsubstantiated by evidence (Terrachoice, 2010).
2. In the U.S., advertising claims are subject to regulation by the Federal Trade Commission (FTC), pursuant to authorities provided by the Federal Trade Commission Act (FTC Act), which stipulates that a "reasonable basis" is required to support such claims. More specifically, Section 5 prohibits claims or advertising that are "unfair" or "deceptive." The FTC has issued a policy statement to clarify what is meant by "deceptive"; essentially, a claim is deceptive if it is material and

misleading to consumers who are acting reasonably. Similarly, claims are "unfair" if they are substantial, not reasonably avoidable, and impose costs in excess of their benefits to the public. The FTC recently has brought enforcement actions and levied fines. In 2009, for example, the FTC took enforcement action against three companies concerning claims that their products were "biodegradable" as well as separate actions against marketers of home insulation products. Some of these actions have been settled, and others are undergoing litigation (Federal Trade Commission, 2009).

3. For example, a recent global survey showed that only 21 percent of American respondents agreed with the statement "Companies and industries are currently working very hard to make sure that we have a clean environment in my country," while 36 percent disagreed. The remaining 43 percent were neutral. Similar levels of public skepticism were observed in many other developed countries (Globescan, 2009).

2

Background and Context

This chapter provides some important background information and context that are needed to develop a complete appreciation of this book's subject matter. The chapter begins with a brief introduction to sustainability and its importance to business. It then discusses terminology and general concepts, with the goal of establishing some clarity regarding what many of the commonly used words and phrases in the public dialog mean and how they differ. The chapter then presents my assessment of how and why sustainability as practiced in corporations has not advanced as far and as fast as some observers might have predicted. It also provides a similar diagnosis for the current status of sustainability investing. The purpose of this discussion is to help you understand some of the important barriers to sustainability thinking so that the strategies I present for formulating and implementing a sustainability program (in Chapter 5) are put into context. I then introduce some of the major factors that affect sustainability issues in a corporate setting, as well as some of the important actors and trends in this arena. The chapter closes with some observations concerning the many ways in which sustainability issues touch the corporation. They are or should be of abiding interest to anyone interested in working in or on behalf of a high-performing corporation in the years to come. This latter discussion also sets the stage for the more detailed examination of the points of intersection between the corporation and sustainability issues presented in Chapter 3.

What Is Sustainability, and Why Is It Important to Business?

"Sustainability," and its close counterpart, "sustainable development," are terms that have been in the public domain since their original formulation in the mid-1980s. "Sustainable development" was the original concept, but in recent times it increasingly has been supplanted by "sustainability." These concepts emerged from the environmental movement and reflect the recognition that major environmental issues are interrelated to economic and social justice issues. It is generally recognized that the term "sustainable development" first appeared in the 1987 report of the Brundtland Commission, titled *Our Common Future*.[1] This document presents the following widely cited and used definition:

> Sustainable development is development that meets the needs of the present without compromising the ability of future generations to meet their own needs.

The breadth of this definition has spawned many distinct interpretations of how society can (or must) adapt its behaviors and practices to enable continued growth and prosperity. However, it is generally agreed that sustainable development or sustainability reflects three interrelated dimensions: environmental quality, social equity, and economic prosperity. The impetus behind the sustainability movement has largely been provided by environmental (and, to some degree, population growth) concerns. However, there is a clear recognition within all sides of the movement that a reasonable balance among the three dimensions is a prerequisite to maintaining an organization, community, economy, or nation that is viable in the long term.

The term "sustainability" is in more common use within corporate organizations, probably because it is simpler and is not directly connected to either material consumption or development, which are major concerns to some stakeholders. Sustainability also seems more directly germane to the scale of a single organization and therefore is more useful as an organizing principle for internal business improvement initiatives.

More generally, however, the distinction between sustainable development and sustainability is not a matter of semantics, for the following reason: *Sustainable development is about helping the world's poor.* The Brundtland Commission recognized the dire circumstances in which a sizeable fraction of humanity lived (and still does), as well as the legitimacy of their aspirations for a better life and higher standard of living. They also recognized, however, that if the billions living in poverty around the world were to achieve their goal with (then) current technology, infrastructure, and relative consumption patterns, their collective actions would unleash a global environmental catastrophe. In response, the sustainable development concept postulates that the developing world and its people must receive assistance so that they can build their economies in a way that does not undermine their own natural resource base, threaten the health of their people (or that of their neighbors), or unjustly enrich a small percentage of the population at the expense of everyone else.

Sustainable development remains a worthy and important goal, but it should be distinguished from the environmental, social, and economic challenges and opportunities directly facing most U.S. organizations, particularly those in the corporate sector.

What Is Sustainability?

In my view, sustainability is a value set, philosophy, and approach rooted in the belief that organizations (corporate and otherwise) can and must materially contribute to the betterment of society. Also, successful organizations must balance their needs, aspirations, and limitations against the larger interests of the societies in which they operate. Only organizations that provide goods and/or services that are of value to people and/or society more generally, and are dedicated to excellence, interested in the full development of human potential, and committed to fairness, are likely to be durable (sustainable) over the long term. Fundamentally, sustainable organizations are purpose-driven, with the purpose being an overarching objective larger and less tangible than self-gratification or profit maximization.

Accordingly, in my formulation of the concept, sustainable organizations are

- Mission-driven
- Aware of and responsive to societal and stakeholder interests
- Responsible and ethical
- Dedicated to excellence
- Driven to meet or exceed customer/client expectations
- Disciplined, focused, and skillful

This view places the conventional emphasis on the "three legs of the stool" (economic prosperity, environmental protection, and social equity[2]) within a larger, more integrative context. It also recognizes that each is a key dimension of any coherent concept of sustainable organizations, past or present. The importance of each of the three major elements of sustainability depends on the organization's nature and purpose. Public sector and nonprofit organizations have been formed and structured specifically to provide some combination of products and services that benefit society, whether that involves forecasting the weather, teaching children, or defending the country from military threats. With the exception of agencies and non-governmental organizations (NGOs) specifically focused on some aspect of sustainability (such as the U.S. Environmental Protection Agency [EPA] or the Sierra Club), most such organizations have a primary mission to fulfill that is not directly related to either environmental protection or social equity. Nonetheless, by adopting sustainability as a guiding principle, such organizations commit themselves at the very least to ensuring that they limit any adverse impacts of their operations on the environment and treat all stakeholders fairly. As you will see in subsequent chapters, many public sector organizations, including the federal government and its many parts, have been moving decisively in recent years to institute more sustainable behavior.

Corporations are in quite a different place. They are not explicitly supported by and accountable to the American taxpayer and have not (generally) been formed to pursue a mission eligible for tax-exempt status as a nonprofit.[3] Some observers believe that in contrast to the work done by the government and nonprofit sectors, the legitimate role of business is to make money for its owners (shareholders), and the more the better. In this view of the world, time and money invested in improving environmental performance, providing safer working conditions, supporting local communities through philanthropic activity, and other such corporate social responsibility (CSR) behaviors are an unwarranted and unproductive use of the firm's assets. As discussed in this and subsequent chapters, this view, which has been held and promoted with great conviction by many in the business community and academia, is increasingly being challenged.

As I show in several places and ways throughout this book, corporate leaders should accept and, ideally, embrace the concept of sustainability, for two fundamental reasons. One is that U.S. corporations, as distinct entities holding enumerated legal rights and receiving numerous public benefits,[4] have an obligation not only to comply with all applicable laws and regulations but also to ensure that their conduct does not harm the broader societies of which they are a part and on which they depend for survival. The other is that increasingly, recognizing important sustainability issues and acting on them in an enlightened and sophisticated way has been shown to increase revenue growth and earnings and to strengthen the firm's position in terms of the factors that drive long-term financial success. In other words, the argument for embracing corporate sustainability has two elements: it is the *right* thing to do, and it is the *smart* thing to do.

What Sustainability Is Not

In addition to the distinction between sustainability and sustainable development, it is important at this juncture to highlight and clarify what I mean by sustainability and to distinguish it from several other concepts now in widespread use:

- Sustainability is not greening.
- Sustainability is not corporate social responsibility, social responsibility, corporate responsibility, or "strategic philanthropy."

Each of these other, more limited concepts has considerable merit. However, none is new or sufficient to both address the needs and interests of the broad set of stakeholders to which most organizations (at least large ones) are accountable and to position the firm to avail itself of all related opportunities.

Sustainability is often framed in the media as a campaign to "green" the world or "save the planet." I take the position that, when viewed from an appropriately broad perspective, sustainability extends beyond the currently fashionable focus on "greening." Greening is simply the latest manifestation of public interest in the environment, which has come back into vogue during the past three or four years following a multiyear hiatus. As an interested party who has watched several incarnations of a growing public/business interest in improving the environmental performance of organizations (and individuals), it is both heartening and, in some ways, disturbing to observe the eagerness with which many are now embracing everything "green." Greening sounds and feels admirable, but public interest in this topic tends to wax and wane over time. My fear is that it will again fall out of fashion, unless the renewed focus on environmental performance improvement is coupled with considerations of social equity and both are underlain by rigorous economic analysis. Sustainability, defined in this way, provides the only theoretical and practical environmental improvement framework that can be fully justified and maintained during both good and challenging economic times. Therefore, it is robust and "sustainable" enough for the long haul.

My concerns with the terms CSR and social responsibility are somewhat different. Although in most formulations they include the three "legs of the stool," they really are about delineating and acting on the obligations of the modern corporation to society at large. In contrast, and as highlighted a moment ago, I believe that it is most useful to think of sustainability as an imperative that applies to all organizations and political entities (countries, states, municipalities). Each of these is challenged to understand and address the broad conditions under which it operates and its relationships with other entities and the natural world. They also must chart a course on which they can thrive without undermining their asset base or unfairly precluding or limiting the sustainable success of others. In that context, CSR can be thought of as one element of a corporate strategy to address the sustainability imperative. Such an element can, for example, identify the concerns of external stakeholders and define and execute processes to ensure that these external interests are respected as the firm pursues its broader business goals. In other words, CSR and its analogs can be an important part of (but in any case are a subset of) an organization's approach to sustainability. In particular, CSR can, and often does, comprise an organization's efforts to respond to the imperative to promote sustainable development. Similarly, CSR can be used to appropriately target a company's philanthropic activities. Or the firm may separately deploy a strategic philanthropy campaign. But by its nature any such activity is far more narrow in scope and effect than organizational sustainability. The two should not be confused or, in my view, ever be used interchangeably.

These distinctions are not trivial. Indeed, understanding and resolving them has proven difficult for many organizations and practitioners. Regardless of what words you choose to employ, the key point is that pursuing sustainability at the organizational level is more complex, more important, and more difficult than simply greening the organization to some arbitrary but comfortable level, or becoming more attentive to particular stakeholders and their views. However, substantial rewards can accompany this greater level of difficulty. This topic is explored further next.

In this book and from this point forward, I will use the concept of *sustainability* rather than *greening* as the key objective to be pursued at the organizational level. As mentioned previously, sustainability has emerged directly from the environmental movement and is often focused on key environmental issues and challenges. However, there also are important opportunities for corporate leaders to examine social equity and economic issues in parallel with the environmental aspects of their organizations. The concept of sustainability provides an integrative framework to facilitate this thought process. Moreover, in practice, and as illustrated in many places in this book, synergies and scale economies often make it possible to address issues having both environmental and social aspects more effectively and economically than would be possible by pursuing separate, unrelated approaches.

What Is Sustainability, or ESG, Investing?

As discussed in depth in Chapters 6 and 7, an important new segment of the capital markets has taken shape during the past 30 years or so. It now represents a large and influential force. Initially constituted as practitioners of socially responsible investing (SRI), these organizations focused on identifying and selecting companies for investments that offered attributes acceptable to the subscribers, clients, or beneficiaries of the SRI firms. From its inception, the SRI community has focused on ethical issues, and early on it added environmental concerns to its evaluation practices. Today, the long-standing practices of exclusionary screening (for example, no investment in companies that produce or sell tobacco or alcohol, or participate in gambling) remain in place. But in terms of scale they have been overtaken by a broader and more sophisticated evaluation of an array of environmental, health and safety, social, and governance practices. Generally speaking, investors interested in considering sustainability endpoints use the term ESG. The acronym stands for environmental, social, and governance attributes.

In my formulation and throughout this book, I accept and use this terminology, with one small but important modification. Reflecting both the importance of the issues and the ways in which they are typically managed in companies and in the profession at large, I include health and safety considerations in my definition. Therefore, sustainability investing involves assessing a company's (or industry's) posture and performance with respect to environment, health and safety, social issues, and governance. To distinguish this treatment from that employed by others, including many sustainability investors and their data providers, *I use the acronym ES&G*, where it is understood that the E signifies the domain of environment, health, and safety (EHS).

Why Sustainability Is and Will Remain Important to U.S. Corporations

Capitalism—in particular, the entrepreneurial American brand of capitalism—emerged from the 20th century as the dominant global economic philosophy. This happened as the inevitable demise of the Soviet Union unfolded and sweeping economic liberalization took hold in formerly closed or tightly controlled economies from Eastern Europe to South Asia. The resulting growth in international trade has made the world economy ever more interconnected. We now confront the failure of multilateral efforts to further reduce international trade barriers, rising economic inequality within and across societies around the world, and the hazards posed by global environmental challenges such as climate change and access to water. Most recently, we have faced the failure of unregulated financial markets and the ensuing economic meltdown. Many people are questioning whether corporations are behaving appropriately, contributing more to solutions than problems, and, in some cases, are larger and more powerful than is appropriate for the good of society.

Concerns about the appropriate role of corporations and their behavior are hardly a new phenomenon. Yet the tenor of the debate is changing. Many more people are now openly questioning the classical position of free-market advocates that, in essence, corporations' primary or even sole responsibility is to make money for their shareholders. It is now increasingly accepted that *how* corporations make money also is vitally important, for several reasons. One is the backlash against free trade that has occurred globally (even here in the U.S.). It has become clear that although some countries, companies, and individuals have reaped enormous financial benefits from globalization, many others have been left behind or put at a severe disadvantage. Another reason is the perception of outsized and inappropriate influence exerted by major multinational corporations on national and even international public policy. Many major companies have financial resources that exceed those of national governments in developing countries. Skeptics of corporate beneficence also are not comforted by the fact that corporate leaders are not elected by the people of the countries in which they operate. The speed and severity with which the recent economic contagion spread across virtually all international markets also illustrates the pervasive influence of corporate voices in promoting the idea that less regulation stimulates or unleashes innovation, reduces overall risk, and creates and helps distribute new wealth in ways that are equitable. It can fairly be said that the events of the past three years have called each of these assertions into question.

Finally, rightly or wrongly, corporations are blamed for many of the environmental problems that increasingly are receiving public attention. Ironically, many major corporations have been leaders in developing and deploying more environmentally friendly technology over the past three decades. Often they are far more eco-efficient than smaller organizations operating in similar businesses. In many cases, companies have invested considerable time and resources in attempting to reduce their EHS footprint, and even to develop new eco-friendly products and services. Some such efforts have been successful (both in execution and in generating a positive public perception), but in other cases they have been denounced by environmental advocacy groups as "greenwashing."

Accordingly, the business climate today is challenging in ways that require new perspectives. The public in the U.S. and many other countries expects that companies will operate in compliance with the law and in ways that are environmentally sound, treat their own people and those in surrounding communities fairly, and engage with their stakeholders on issues of common interest. At the same time, the expectations of the capital markets have not changed. Publicly traded companies must grow revenues and earnings, consistently generate cash, and effectively manage risk. Balancing these sometimes conflicting imperatives requires a framework that, when applied to a specific organization, is flexible and yields an internally consistent set of values, normative behaviors, business goals, methods, and performance metrics.

Sustainability offers this framework.

Moreover, as suggested earlier, the "envelope" of expectations brought to bear by a wide array of interested parties is now wider than ever. Corporations face expectations and pressures from many sides. These include customers, suppliers, competitors, regulators, their own employees, and shareholders, to name a few. Companies that succeed in the long term will need to find ways to understand and satisfy the expectations of all of these and other important stakeholders. When and where possible, firms should seek to find and exploit opportunities to achieve financial success while creating value for one or more of these important constituencies. Given the apparent complexity of such a challenge, it is reasonable to assume that not all firms will have the vision, leadership, and skill to succeed. This suggests that solving (or at least making significant ongoing progress on) the sustainability challenge will produce durable competitive advantage.

There is evidence all around us that the need for corporate sustainability is growing significantly and at an increasing rate. Public perceptions of environmental behavior (and perceived misbehavior) already were at high levels before the Deepwater Horizon exploded and released a giant oil spill in the Gulf of Mexico in April 2010. Expectations for improved practices and acceptable behavior more generally are quite significant. These expectations will not diminish in the coming years as the magnitude and urgency of global environmental issues become more clear. Increasingly, corporations will be asked what they are doing to both protect their own operations and limit business risks and contribute to larger-scale resolution of these issues.

Two sustainability issues in particular should be in the minds of corporate senior executives in virtually any U.S. company of significant size: climate change and water availability and quality. Constraints imposed by climate change and, in the longer term, availability of water in needed quantities with adequate quality will influence myriad business decisions in the 21st century. Taking the broad-spectrum, integrative approach suggested in this book will help maximize the chances of any business making the best decisions when they need to be made.

Another factor that cannot be ignored is the growth in economic power and expectations among developing countries and the people within them. It is widely understood within the business community that expansion internationally offers many U.S. industries and companies their greatest growth prospects. Countries in the developing world often offer vital sources of raw materials. Companies will find that increasingly, the people in these countries will expect that firms that do business within their borders will show respect for their laws, customs, cultures, and the rights of indigenous people. And they will expect this whether or not in all cases the governments that (at least in theory) represent them uphold the same standards at all times. Many large U.S. companies and their senior managers are highly experienced and skilled at working under these conditions. But many others have not displayed the necessary cultural sensitivity or skill to avoid igniting controversy, resistance, and other problems. In some cases, U.S. multinationals have had to abandon major international investments and have generated extensive negative press coverage as well. I conclude that to prosper in the future, U.S. and other Western companies will need to compete on the basis of strength. Adopting the framework of sustainability to guide their plans and actions will help ensure that they are looking at investments and operations around the world through all the appropriate lenses. These issues are explored further in Chapter 4.

If you work in the EHS field within a large, advanced company, you might be wondering how much real upside potential embracing sustainability offers when your firm already has advanced EHS management practices in place. The following sections offer a few thoughts in this regard.

Sustainability Helps Demonstrate Appropriate and Effective Corporate Governance

Many stakeholders want assurance that the people at the top of the organization have thought through its important environmental and social issues and that they have developed and deployed effective programs, systems, and practices to address them. Sustainability provides an integrating structure that can both guide and explain how corporate leaders meet these expectations and do so in a way that is far more streamlined, sophisticated, and ultimately less time-consuming than would be possible otherwise.

Sustainability Serves as a Reference Point for the Organization's Values

Illegal and, increasingly, unethical behavior is not well tolerated by regulators, customers, suppliers, and other business partners. Such behavior can have severe financial consequences, both immediately and in the longer term. Understanding what is legal requires competence and vigilance on the part of one's general or outside counsel, but understanding what is ethical requires a set of organizational values and business norms. It is now widely understood that well-run companies have a core "DNA" or identity that embodies shared values and aspirations and is independent of any individual. This attribute enables the organization to remain strong and vibrant over an extended period even as people enter and depart from it. Moreover, this type of organizational identity provides many advantages under normal circumstances but is especially critical during crisis situations, when people need to know how to act as well as what to do. Sustainability can serve as a common, unifying principle to guide the thinking and behaviors of all members of the organization. This is important when different members are called on to execute their unique functions, some of which may be in conflict. Moreover, sustainability provides the needed flexibility to address the following realities:

- Environmental, social, and economic considerations must be balanced.
- The way in which they are balanced will differ according to the organization, issue, and circumstance in question.
- This balance will likely change over time.

Sustainability Helps Bring Clarity to Intrinsically Complex Issues

The complexities of and interrelationships among environmental, social, and governance (ESG) issues require a management approach that combines and considers all these disciplines. Such an approach should address all significant needs and requirements (particularly compliance), surface and resolve conflicts among them, provide consistency and predictability, and should be both effective and efficient. In other words, some sort of overarching concept and management structure is required, and sustainability provides the "umbrella" under which many organizations are now organizing their previously disparate internal functions. I am unaware of any competing or alternative concept that has been shown to be workable while providing similar benefits.

Properly Construed, Sustainability Provides the "Theory" Underlying a Value Creation Orientation

In my view, the best way to pursue sustainability is to consider the three primary determinants of value for any business enterprise:

- The revenue stream and the customer base that generates it

- Earnings or, in the case of public sector organizations, effective control of costs and management of capital
- Adequate understanding and management of risk

A sensible sustainability strategy embodies careful consideration of how new initiatives or changes to existing programs might affect all three of these determinants of value. History has shown that absent this orientation, environmental and social improvement initiatives are continually underutilized because they are not seen as contributing to core business drivers or creating financial value in any tangible way. By the same token, a properly specified sustainability approach imposes a new measure of financial discipline on both internal and external proponents of new "greening" ideas and prospective investments in projects or activities having primarily a social orientation.

Sustainability Facilitates "Mainstreaming" of Environmental, Health and Safety, and Social Equity Issues into Core Business Processes

As discussed in Chapter 3, EHS issues have in many cases been managed tactically in U.S. corporations and public sector agencies. Historically, EHS functions were often housed within and directed by the organization's legal department because the focus then was on understanding legal requirements and ensuring compliance. More recently, EHS people have reported through various administrative functions (such as human resources), facility maintenance, or manufacturing management. In short, with few exceptions, EHS has been managed primarily as a facility-based tactical function rather than as a strategic issue or source of potential broad-spectrum financial value creation. Adopting a sustainability framework can help disrupt, and may even compel, the breaking of the resulting organizational "silos" that exist in many companies. This can create the conditions needed for people across the organization to reach out to one another. They can identify and manage environmental and social issues in ways that limit risk, build brand and market value, and generate new cash flows. In an organization actively pursuing sustainability, achieving better environmental performance or more equitable dealings with stakeholders is not a task to be delegated to someone else. It is an integral part of everyone's job (if only in a small way), from the boardroom to the shop floor.

As stated in Chapter 1, the ideas presented here are not entirely new and certainly are not a radical departure from the views held within many leading U.S. companies. Indeed, a number of firms have in recent years embarked on new initiatives to pursue organizational sustainability. Unfortunately, many of those efforts have not been fully successful, for reasons that I explore in the next section.

Where We've Been and What We've Learned

Although the active pursuit of corporate sustainability is a relatively new phenomenon, it builds on the three decades or so of experience of those involved in managing EHS issues in a corporate setting. This experience, and the understanding and perspective that it has engendered, provide the principal foundation on which most of the meaningful work addressing sustainability is now occurring, notwithstanding the claims of some in the architecture, information technology, and marketing fields. Chapter 5 attempts to distill the major principles and approaches that many successful companies have used to develop and deploy highly effective EHS and sustainability management programs.

In the current context, however, I believe that it is useful to review some of the less successful experience of many firms and practitioners and provide a diagnosis of what went wrong and why. I also believe it is useful to identify some additional factors that have limited the momentum of improved EHS/sustainability behavior across the American economy. Armed with the resulting insights, you will be in a position to identify potential barriers, ineffective approaches, and unseen threats when addressing sustainability issues in your own organization. Major root causes for some of the disappointing outcomes that have been obtained up to this point are discussed in the following sections.

Situational, Bottom-Up Management of EHS Issues

As discussed previously, at the outset, new EHS requirements were imposed through regulation. They were evaluated by corporate legal staff and addressed by plant-level engineers, manufacturing personnel, and/or a new cadre of professional EHS managers and staff. Generally, field staff reported to a plant manager, and even corporate EHS staff might be housed within facilities, engineering, legal, or human resources organizations. Even today, it is not unusual to find the corporate EHS organization buried several layers down on the company organizational chart. In the early days, such arrangements made a good deal of sense. Early implementation of EHS regulations was often contentious and involved new and poorly understood legal risks, so having EHS overseen by General Counsel was in many cases a prudent approach. As EHS activities became established, they shifted into more of a routine "maintenance" mode. In many firms, much of the ongoing work was performed by custodial and plant maintenance personnel and was overseen by facilities or, commonly, the plant manager. Again, this often made sense at the time. Regardless of which box was selected to house EHS, however, the common interpretation was that EHS activities were a cost of doing business and should be controlled and minimized as much as possible. That is, they were perceived to have little or no value-creation potential. As you will see throughout much of this book, this view of the situation is no longer accurate (if it ever was). The problem, however, occurs when people within such a deeply embedded EHS function attempt to turn around the thinking in their firm; shift to a more integrative approach; and focus more on cost savings, profit growth, and generating new revenues. They often have no platform, no visibility, no access to decision makers or resources, no authority, and no clear path to reaching their goals. As discussed in Chapter 5, senior corporate executives who want to promote sustainability thinking and practices in their companies should avoid the mistake of submerging those responsible for making it happen in low-visibility, low-status positions and reporting relationships.

Tactical Approaches Driven by Crisis, Isolated Events, or Loud or Persistent Outside Voices

Many organizations have pursued EHS or sustainability ideas and initiatives in what appears to be a haphazard manner, limiting their effectiveness. Some firms seem to move from crisis to crisis and often pay what seems to be disproportionate attention to one or a small group of stakeholders who have decided to focus their attention on a particular issue at that level of the firm (such as sourcing of paper). I would not dispute that some good can come from such interchanges and the detailed examination of current practices that often results. But I do have to question whether this is the most productive and effective use of the firm's time and resources. The question in such cases is not, for example, whether a better sourcing policy resulted from intense dialog and focus. The question is what else might have been accomplished with the time and effort that were invested in them. Such questions are difficult to answer with much confidence. But I submit that putting the work into developing a comprehensive understanding of which EHS and other sustainability issues are truly important, to whom, and why is a much better investment than flying from crisis to crisis, attempting to mollify critics and possibly customers and the news media. Sustainability is simply too complex and important to be managed in such a tactical manner. Instead, it should be addressed through a formal strategy/policy formulation process. This topic also is explored at length in Chapter 5.

Frequent Lack of Corporate-Level Vision, Strategy, Commitment, Resources, and Follow-Through

Those who have worked in medium-sized or large corporations or other large organizations for any significant length of time have probably had the experience of going through at least a few reorganizations, or new mandates, programs, or initiatives. Unfortunately, all too often a new strategy or initiative is introduced with great fanfare, often by the executive leadership, and described in considerable detail. The leader makes many pronouncements about how this new way of doing things will improve effectiveness, productivity, morale, and opportunity and/or provide other benefits. The program will then be rolled out earnestly by those assigned. But within a matter of weeks or months, it will be moribund, and within a year or two, it will be all but forgotten. This rarely means that the idea of the program or initiative was invalid or did not have the potential to produce the promised benefits. Instead, failure is often a consequence of inadequate senior management forethought about how (or whether) the program would fit in with the established norms, practices, and incentives that exist in the organization. What is needed for success is a clear and compelling vision of how the proposed future state is better than the current state, from the perspective of the employees who are expected to make it happen. Often, even if there is general agreement that the proposed change would be desirable, there are no additional resources with which to perform the needed work. If we can confidently say one thing about human nature, it is that people tend not to do extra work for an employer without some type of compensation.[5] This point is examined further in a moment. Finally, and on a related point, requests for more work from the "troops" without apparent forethought about how the additional work will be accommodated along with existing demands suggests that those promoting the new approach lack true commitment to and understanding of how things actually are done in their organization. The most effective way to counteract these negative reactions is for the senior manager to demonstrate visible, active, ongoing support. This person also should throw his or her weight behind the program by ensuring that those involved feel that they are all in it together.

Absence of Alignment with Financial Value Drivers or Endpoints Considered by Financial Sector Stakeholders

For many years, as suggested by conventional economic theory, it was generally believed that EHS activities, and their associated costs, represented a "deadweight" loss to the corporation that it would have to either internalize or pass along to its customers. The idea that managing EHS (and, later, sustainability) issues adroitly could be shown to impart financial benefits was at first considered outlandish but is finding increasing favor. Even now, however, the ways in which most firms describe their EHS/sustainability activities and present their outcomes does not conform to the types and forms of information that are sought and evaluated by financial industry stakeholders. This is particularly true of investors and the analysts who serve them. This remains a major barrier inhibiting more rapid and widespread acceptance of sustainability in both the corporate sector and the investment community, as discussed at length in Chapters 6, 7, and 8.

Passive Approach to Interpreting and Enforcing SEC Disclosure Requirements

As discussed in Chapters 6 and 7, publicly traded companies in the U.S. (those that have stock or bonds traded on exchanges) are subject to public disclosure requirements. These requirements include information on environmental liabilities (from contaminated site cleanup responsibilities, for example) and must be reported at the end of the fiscal quarter in which they are discovered. For many years, both companies and the responsible federal agency, the U.S. Securities and Exchange Commission (SEC), have interpreted this rule in a way that allowed firms to not report their potential liabilities if their actual occurrence, magnitude, and/or timing was highly uncertain. As discussed in Chapter 6, recent changes in accounting standards should at least partially close this loophole. However, it is fair to say that the absence of the public scrutiny that otherwise would have occurred has enabled many companies to devote less attention to managing their environmental issues than they might have otherwise.

Inadequacy of Corporate EHS/Sustainability Reporting Practices

Despite the emergence of consensus-based sustainability guidelines more than ten years ago, the unfortunate fact remains that most U.S. companies, even the largest, generally do not issue regular EHS or sustainability reports. As discussed at length in Chapter 8, the generally accepted standard for sustainability reporting is the guidelines produced by the Global Reporting Initiative (GRI). These guidelines address several dozen indicators of a given organization's environmental, social, and economic performance. The GRI guidelines have helped promote clarity and consistency in corporate reporting, but I believe they have some important limitations. The most important is that they and the indicators embodied therein have only an unclear or limited relevance to financial endpoints and value creation. Although some investors and financial sector analysts may find much useful information in a GRI report, they will not find much, if any, data or information that they can use directly in a valuation model. And because most financial sector stakeholders don't use or particularly value GRI reports, the business case for preparing them is often weak or absent in many companies, producing the observed slow rate of uptake of the GRI guidelines among U.S. companies. This situation is particularly unfortunate, because it leads to the absence of a potentially powerful driver focusing senior management attention and convergence on a widely accepted practice—sustainability reporting. As discussed in Chapter 8, I am a proponent of corporate transparency. I hope that more interaction between corporate leaders and financial market actors on sustainability issues and their financial implications will, over time, produce more regular and meaningful information interchange, through an improved set of GRI guidelines or some other means.

Several other barriers and problems have to do with more fundamental factors that accompany all human activity. All of these issues may limit the pace and effectiveness of any new initiative(s) intended to pursue organizational sustainability or, indeed, to accomplish any other change initiative. I have seen the pernicious effects of each one during my career as a consultant.

Inertia

Physical science tells us that inertia is the intrinsic resistance of an object to disturbance from its current state of motion or rest. Overcoming inertia requires the application of force, or energy. Human behavior includes an analogous form of resistance. We are all "wired" in a way that can accommodate change, but our natural, equilibrium state is to carry out many of our daily activities in the same way at regular intervals. More generally, if a person, or organization, has developed a certain way of thinking about an issue or carrying out a particular task that is established and accepted, "energy" is required to bring about a change that will be durable. In other words, to have real effect, this change will need to alter the existing state and establish and maintain a new equilibrium rather than allow the person or organization quickly revert to the prior state. Such energy can take the form of intensive ongoing communications and/or training, deployment of additional resources, visible and consistent management commitment, and new/reworked incentives, among other tactics. Many EHS, sustainability, and other organizational change initiatives have faltered because, although they had valid goals and sensible implementation steps, they were delivered with only limited energy, or impetus. The amount of energy needed in such situations is directly proportional to the magnitude and difficulty of the change being sought. Those pursuing or considering corporate sustainability initiatives should carefully evaluate the amount of change this will entail and be prepared to expend an adequate amount of corporate "energy" to overcome the inertia that these initiatives will inevitably encounter.

The "Principal-Agent Problem"

This refers to a situation in which the employee's personal incentives are not fully in alignment with those of his or her employer. For example, a company may have established goals for recycling paper and other wastes that apply to all employees. However, suppose the responsibility for actually collecting, segregating/sorting, and separately managing this paper and other materials falls to the janitorial staff (as it often does). Suppose these staff members receive no benefits (overtime pay, recognition, a share of the cost savings) from carrying out these extra steps. All they get is extra work. In that case, no one should be surprised that such an arrangement tends to produce very little in the way of results (recycled materials or otherwise)—other than, perhaps, disgruntled employees. The key to preventing such unfortunate situations is to ensure that the incentives for the employee and employer are in alignment. So, if the employees get some type of reward for doing the extra work, they are more likely to actually perform it. In my experience and that of many organizations, the reward does not need to be large. Most people simply like to feel that they are valued. Recognition, small prizes, workplace amenities, and bonuses can go a long way toward stimulating the type of behavioral change that may be desired.

The Answer Is Two

One particularly common and insidious form of inertia found in organizations is resistance to looking at issues in new ways, including using new or unfamiliar tools and approaches to help make decisions. Advocating something new in such situations can push people out of their comfort zone and make them resistant to accepting the new approach, even if intellectually they understand that doing so is rational and may yield a better outcome.

Early in my career, I experienced this phenomenon firsthand. I was managing a project on behalf of the U.S. EPA. This involved, in part, performing field studies to characterize certain types of wastes that were being evaluated to see if more stringent regulatory controls were warranted. The wastes in question were generated by facilities in several different industries. One of the questions to be addressed was how many facilities in each industry needed to be sampled to yield data that could be quantitatively analyzed to produce statistically significant results. To resolve this issue, I consulted with a colleague who had the appropriate training (a PhD with substantial graduate study in the application of statistical methods). This person had developed a valid method that would determine the minimum number of facilities that would need to be visited and sampled in each industry. These visits would support valid conclusions about whether each industry's wastes did or did not exhibit characteristics justifying (in part) more stringent regulation.

I presented this proposed solution to the EPA decision maker and her senior staff at our next client meeting. As I began by explaining that the solution involved the use of statistical methods, I could see their expressions change and their eyes glaze over. I did my best to explain why our proposed method was the best solution, including the fact that it was scientifically defensible (an important advantage) and would limit the number of sites that needed to be visited (thereby reducing project costs). I probably could have been more effective at advancing our arguments, but it was clear almost immediately that our ideas were fundamentally in conflict with how these senior EPA managers viewed the issue and the limits of how far they were willing to stretch their existing understanding. In other words, our favored approach was doomed before I even began speaking. The meeting adjourned after a few questions, with a decision promised for the next day.

The following day we were informed that the people we had briefed had decided that we would visit two facilities in each industry, irrespective of how many facilities were in each. Small industries (some of which had only two domestic facilities) therefore would receive complete coverage in our sampling program. In larger industries we would cover only a small percentage of facilities. Accordingly, data from only two sites would be used to characterize the waste streams generated by the entire industry. I was dismayed by this outcome and concerned about the validity of the sampling results it would generate, but in time I came to understand what had undermined our proposed approach. The decision makers simply could not establish (indeed, did not even attempt to reach) a level of comfort with the concepts we presented that was sufficient to accept our proposed solution. They understood intellectually that our solution was superior to their chosen course on a technical level, but it was unfamiliar and therefore posed unknown risks from their point of view. Being good consultants, we completed our design of the sampling program as directed by our clients and carried out the program.

You might think that the behaviors described here are limited to uninformed, inexperienced, or incompetent people. But the decision maker in this case had a successful, high-profile career at the EPA and went on to serve in a number of high-level positions in the Agency.

Culture

Beyond the inertia that exists in all human endeavors, in some organizations the culture poses a significant barrier to more sustainable behavior. Many companies and other entities have a well-established way of doing things and may not welcome change or promote individual initiative. Those who would suggest a new or better way may have a large burden of proof to surmount. If they are relatively early in their careers (they didn't grow up professionally in the culture/work practices of their employer), they may be accepting significant risk by challenging the existing order, even if at the margins. Quite simply, questioning the wisdom of the existing hierarchy could be considered a career-limiting move. Corporate leaders interested in promoting sustainable business behavior can do a lot to ensure that they are projecting and, as appropriate, enforcing an attitude of openness to productive change, questioning the status quo, and, in general, promoting suggestions and feedback from their people. After all, those working on the front lines often have the best vantage point for seeing what works and what could be improved.

Inadequate Grounding in Science

Another persistent and serious problem is the capability of people within organizations to fully understand and take appropriate action on environmental/sustainability issues. The unfortunate fact is that the general level of literacy about environmental issues in the U.S. is quite low (see the following quotation). More fundamentally, scientific understanding is limited within this country's adult population—even among recent college graduates (Hartley, Wilke, et al., 2011). Furthermore, it does not appear that the next generation will make up for our collective shortcomings. Assessments of children in our elementary and secondary schools, including a recent update of *The Nation's Report Card* for science, show that the level of achievement in science is declining relative to that of many other advanced countries (National Center for Education Statistics, 2011). If we are to move decisively toward a more sustainable future, we need to correct this deficiency.

"[t]he average American adult, regardless of age, income, or level of education, mostly fails to grasp essential aspects of environmental science, important cause/effect relationships, or even basic concepts such as runoff pollution, power generation and fuel use, or water flow patterns...

"Research has shown a persistent pattern of environmental ignorance even among the most educated and influential members of society."

(Coyle, 2005)

Personal Empowerment

Finally, the notions of decentralization and "empowerment" have received great emphasis in recent years. During the past 20 years, many organizational leaders and management "experts" have extolled the virtues of placing decision-making authority in the hands of those closest to the production of the organization's goods or delivery of services. Such approaches often have been well received by the non-managerial staff to which they were directed. To be sure, nothing is wrong with giving each employee a voice or opening a communication channel that operates in both directions. Moreover, senior managers can often benefit from receiving occasional unfiltered perspectives from "where the rubber meets the road." The problem arises when an organization attempts to institute change, or even to accurately represent itself to the outside world. If divisions, regions, facilities/sites, and even employees are empowered to interpret corporate-level directives as they see fit, and to implement new programs using a "tailored" approach in accordance with local conditions, serious problems can arise. It quickly becomes unclear whether or to what extent the organization has the following attributes:

- Speaks with one voice (ideally, that of senior leadership)
- Has a defined (or definable) philosophy about or approach to a particular business practice or issue
- Is performing in accordance with expectations (if indeed this can even be ascertained)

Embracing sustainability means instituting at least some degree of organizational change. As discussed in detail in Chapter 5, such change must be guided by a consistent and uniform approach. If it is not, and employees are empowered to interpret for themselves what a sustainability initiative is and how it will be implemented, the chances of success, meaning tangible performance improvement by the organization as a whole, will be greatly diminished.

Empowered or Abandoned?

Some years ago, I was managing a substantial new project for a national-scale organization with both headquarters and regional environmental staff. The project involved developing and deploying a formal environmental management system (EMS, described in Chapter 5), along with the training and technical assistance required for the organization to implement the system nationwide. At a meeting of all the environmental staff at headquarters to kick off the project, the senior executive in charge of the organization delivered some remarks.

In his prepared statement, he told some amusing anecdotes about his days in the Army, and how much he and the other officers in the field resented the headquarters staff: "Headquarters pukes, we used to call 'em." He went on to state his admiration for the knowledge and wisdom of the regional staff in the room. He encouraged them to share these assets with their headquarters colleagues who organized the meeting, were in charge of the EMS deployment, and were my clients. He concluded his statement and walked out of the room to applause from those in attendance.

Because he left, he missed my presentation on the EMS and the benefits the organization would gain from its implementation. Much more importantly, he also missed the experience of seeing a regional representative stand up and say that she had no idea which environmental issues and needs were really important, which were not, and how to tell the difference. She also confessed that she felt somewhat lost and overwhelmed by it all and that she needed more help from (you guessed it) her headquarters and other colleagues.

By making the statements that he did, the leader of the organization, purposely or otherwise, had several effects on his audience. He undermined the authority and credibility of his headquarters staff, whom he had charged with carrying out the new initiative, which he had approved. He also implicitly encouraged the regional staff to resist the initiative, as well as create their own interpretations of how it should be carried out, thereby losing any opportunity for nationwide and organization-wide consistency. Finally, he sent a clear signal that he was out of touch with the reality on the ground in the regions. He did not care enough about the issues or the work to be done to avail himself of facts that might call into question his preconceived ideas and ideology.

Although by no means unique, this type of management by proclamation will be increasingly ineffective or even counterproductive as organizations take on the multifaceted challenges of sustainability. It also illuminates the fact that "empowerment" in the form of making the staff figure it out on their own is a poor substitute for active and informed leadership, particularly when taking on new and complex initiatives.

In terms of what happened with this client, the EMS deployment initiative was ultimately successful. But it took much sustained effort to overcome both active and passive resistance among the regional staff and management.

The good news in all of this is that although instituting sustainability is challenging, as is any other organizational change initiative, it can be done. Armed with an understanding of what can go wrong, I hope you will have greater success than some in the past in translating a sustainability vision into concrete action and in taking your organization where it needs and wants to go.

The next section returns to the other major topic presented in this book—the influence of investors on corporate EHS/sustainability behavior. As you will see, those who have been promoting the wider adoption of practices for considering sustainability endpoints in investment analysis and decision making have encountered some challenges that are unique to the financial services industry.

What ESG/Sustainability Investing Is and Why You May Never Have Heard of It

As mentioned earlier, substantial amounts of money are professionally managed using an approach that explicitly considers a firm's environmental, health and safety, social, and governance posture and performance, as well as other, more conventional operating and financial information. This type of investing is increasingly being referred to as ESG investing. It is an outgrowth of the field of socially responsible investing (SRI), a segment of the market that has existed for several decades in the U.S. and Europe. ESG investors believe that a company's ability and willingness to devote the resources needed to understand its important EHS and other sustainability issues and manage them effectively plays a meaningful role in that firm's ability to consistently grow revenues, increase earnings, and control investment risk over the long term. This idea may not seem unreasonable or controversial, but it has encountered considerable resistance within the broader investment community, and, despite its impressive growth, has been limited by a number of important factors. These are discussed in depth in Chapter 6, but I provide a synopsis here to acquaint you with ESG investing. I do this because in writing this book, I have asserted that the continued growth of ESG investing and the demands of those who participate in it will induce more rapid and extensive adoption of corporate sustainability behavior. I contend that market actors will increasingly buy and hold securities issued by firms that show they understand and are effectively managing sustainability issues at the expense of those who do not.

To reach this point, the field of ESG investing (and SRI before it) has had to overcome some rather long odds:

- One significant barrier has been stiff, even fierce, ideological opposition to the concept that choosing securities based (even in part) on ESG criteria could possibly allow an investor to outperform the market. This objection is based on conservative economic theory, including, as discussed earlier, the belief that EHS practices create only costs, not benefits, to the corporation. The limitations of this theoretical argument are examined in detail and, I believe, refuted in Chapters 3 and 6.

- Another barrier concerns fiduciary duty, which in this context essentially requires those managing investment funds on behalf of someone else to place the interests of their beneficiaries above their own. This includes not constraining investment choices (such as through applying SRI/ESG criteria) that might limit available investment returns. As discussed in Chapter 6, recent evidence and detailed analysis of fiduciary duty and national securities laws show that this concern is no longer an obstacle to the use of ESG investing by such fiduciaries as pension fund trustees.

- An additional factor limiting the advance of ESG investing is the early track record of SRI (in the 1970s through the early 1990s), during which the predominant technique was use of negative screens. Negative screens remove the stocks of firms involved in certain activities from consideration for an investment portfolio. Historically, negative screens were often applied to preclude investments in firms involved in the production or sale of tobacco, alcohol, gambling, firearms/weapons, nuclear power, and other identified issues. Unfortunately, removing such companies from the investable pool often produced substandard investment returns, and as a consequence, early SRI funds often lagged their benchmarks. Such underperformance elicited further disdain for SRI as a fringe, specialist investment activity suited only to those willing to sacrifice their money for their convictions. However, as discussed in Chapter 6 and demonstrated (with empirical evidence) in Chapter 7, ESG investing as it is practiced today is not a fringe activity, nor does its skillful use result in substandard returns. Indeed, the more sophisticated approaches to ESG investing often outperform their mainstream counterparts.

- Along the way, ESG investing practitioners and proponents in the U.S. have not been helped by the public policy climate, although conditions in Europe have been far more supportive. The SEC has generally been silent on the question of the materiality of ESG issues to corporate financial success. No U.S. national sustainability policy, statute, or set of generally agreed-upon principles exists to provide clarity to the corporate sector, investors, and the public regarding sustainability and its importance. In this policy vacuum, corporate sustainability and ESG investing have had to blaze their own (and, up until now, separate) trails.

So although ESG investing is hardly a term that is widely known and discussed in the business community at large or in the public arena, that is changing. The information in this book will help you understand what ESG investing is and how it will affect corporate behavior in the years ahead.

Major Factors, Actors, and Trends

Several other external factors, agents, and phenomena affect the need for and practice of corporate sustainability and are worthy of mention. One is the great and nearly instantaneous availability of information (and misinformation) on specific companies, EHS and social issues, product characteristics, and many other aspects of corporate behavior. There are few places to hide in an age of extraordinary and growing connectivity. We can stream video, search the Internet, and reach large numbers of people (such as through tweets) instantaneously on their cell phones virtually any time, anywhere. Companies must manage their public image and brand(s) carefully and ensure that they are aware of how they are being portrayed by others. For many, developing and deploying proactive strategies to engage key stakeholders and the public may be a sensible way to limit downside risk arising from unfavorable changes in public opinion (whether warranted by facts or otherwise), as well as to gain insights into issues that may require active management.

A second factor that should be considered by the senior management of all publicly traded companies is the emergence of activist investors. The days when investors could be relied on to simply make buy and sell decisions and leave management of the company to its board and senior executives are over. Increasingly, major institutional investors such as pension funds are asserting their rights as owners of large blocks of company stock to press for changes that they believe are needed to improve their understanding of company operations, protect the firm from business and financial risks, and/or operate the firm in a more ethical and sound manner. These investors are wielding their considerable power, both individually and in coalitions, to press for changes to the status quo in many firms. In the current context, they have been particularly interested in such issues as corporate governance, climate change, and human rights. The importance of activist investors is discussed in more depth in Chapter 6.

The past decade or so has witnessed significant advances in SRI/ESG investment theory and practice, and this field appears to be on the verge of a major leap forward. During the past five years or so, and even in the face of a global economic collapse and prolonged downturn, ESG investing has grown substantially, at far greater rates than conventional investing. This activity also has stimulated the entry of major international financial institutions into the ESG investing market space. As discussed further in Chapter 6, ESG investing and investors can be expected to exert a major influence on the practice of corporate sustainability during the next decade.

Finally, no discussion of corporate behavior and markets would be complete without addressing the role of government. Government touches virtually every aspect of commerce and finance in some way. Usually government defines and enforces boundaries within which market activity can take place and/or provides information to participants and the wider public. In the sustainability arena, however, the role of government has largely yet to be defined. As noted earlier, the U.S. has no national policy or statute on sustainability. But over time the U.S. government and several specific departments and agencies have taken leadership roles in helping organizations of all types and sizes understand and manage their environmental and social aspects. Some of these take the form of regulations required under various statutes. But increasingly, federal activity in these domains is focused on technical assistance, training, information development and dissemination, and other activities intended to move American business and other organizations to beyond-compliance, sustainability-driven behavior.

In recent years, and under several different administrations, the federal government has sought to provide environmental and sustainability leadership. This has often been done through issuing executive orders (EOs). These are directives signed by the president that require, with any stipulated exceptions, all federal departments, agencies, and locations to conduct their operations in a certain prescribed manner or to carry out certain activities. Some of these EOs provide tangible, and often comprehensive, descriptions of how an organization can better understand its current environmental/sustainability footprint and then take steps to reduce it.[6] In that respect, they, and the programs developed in response to them, can serve as models and useful sources of information for those working on sustainability issues in a corporate context.

It also is important to recognize the catalytic role of voluntary, beyond-compliance programs. Typically, these take the form of a government agency (such as the EPA or OSHA) defining a policy goal and then forming an initiative offering services, information, and other benefits to a target industry or group. Industry participants agree to analyze their operations and adopt new or modified practices where they are indicated and will be cost-effective. Post-adoption, participants measure and report changes in, for example, energy consumption, waste generation, or pollutant emissions, as well as any cost savings or other positive results. Such programs have attracted skepticism from the outset. But experience has shown that the more thoughtfully conceived and effective among them have made major contributions to reducing pollutant emissions, risks, and manufacturing costs while providing other benefits as well. Although such approaches appear to have fallen out of favor in the current political climate, those involved in sustainability activity may want to evaluate the existing program offerings for information, examples of successful projects and approaches, and ideas. This book is not oriented toward the public sector policy maker per se. But it is important to understand that cooperative/collaborative arrangements brokered by public sector entities can be a highly effective means of defining and capturing sustainability improvements across an entire industry or set of industries. Hence, they are often worthy of corporate support.

Companies have responded to these trends in a variety of ways. As is usually the case, certain companies (and industries) have chosen to exercise leadership positions and aggressively pursue new opportunities created by advances in technology, growing understanding of ES&G issues and their importance, and increasing stakeholder demands. Among leading companies, awareness of the importance of adopting a sustainable business posture has been accelerating during the past several years, as discussed in the sidebar on page 48.

ES&G Concerns as Key Requirements and Determinants of Long-Term Business Success

So far, I have established that sustainability appears to be an up-and-coming business management concept and that a substantial portion of the investment community appears to be paying increasing attention to certain ES&G issues. This section briefly highlights some of the major categories of ES&G issues that are of interest to investors and that have relatively clear connections to business outcomes that can affect corporate financial and investment performance in a material way. Growing evidence exists that in the foreseeable future, investors will enforce a high level of performance along each of these dimensions. Accordingly, it would be advisable to those working on sustainability within corporations to ensure that their program adequately and explicitly addresses each one, preferably in the program design stage.

Resource Efficiency

Simply stated, pollution and waste are nothing more than resources that a company has paid for but not put to productive use. Indeed, some of the more sophisticated firms now refer to such "nonproduct output" as a single category that is to be minimized or eliminated wherever possible. The good news is that U.S. (and many international) companies have made quantum leaps during the past few decades in (at first) preventing pollution from occurring or being generated and (now, increasingly) designing waste and emissions out of their production processes altogether. Techniques such as Lean Manufacturing and Six Sigma have been particularly useful in continuing to drive higher efficiencies and productivity. Such gains are a good example of sustainability thinking, in that they often reduce waste, pollutant emissions, energy and material use, and costs, and also may improve product quality. That is, they offer "wins" along multiple business-relevant dimensions. As discussed in Chapter 6, the more sophisticated ES&G investors already evaluate companies' resource efficiency when making their portfolio selections. Those involved in corporate sustainability (or management more generally) can expect this to become the norm in the near future.

Risk Management and Reduction

EHS management always has been about risk management and reduction. What is relatively new is a wider appreciation of the different forms that sustainability-related risks can take, how significant they can be, and how difficult they can be to detect and effectively manage. The most prominent example today of the risk to individual firms posed by an ES&G issue is climate change. It is not an exaggeration to say that climate change impacts, or the consequences of possible legal mandates imposed to address climate change (such as carbon emission constraints), could pose an existential threat to some companies. This phenomenon is widely understood within the investment community, particularly the ESG investor segment. What is less widely appreciated is that the availability of water is emerging as an issue that may be even more problematic to some firms. It is not by coincidence that the most successful initiative designed to promote corporate disclosure of climate change risk and posture is led by investors. Those working in corporations should take note. Increasingly, investors will be inquisitive about whether and to what extent their senior managers understand the risks posed to their businesses by ES&G issues. They will seek adequate assurance that effective management strategies are in place.

The View in and Around the C-Suite Is Changing Rapidly

Mike Pisarcik is Director of Sustainability, Environment, and Safety Management Systems at Sara Lee. He is one of the relatively few people of my acquaintance with extensive experience in managing both EHS issues and corporate finance. He has witnessed some significant changes at Sara Lee and in a number of other companies:

"Over the last decade there has been a transition in the treatment of the topic, from an issue that was maybe a trend or was an acute interest that 'others took care of' to something much more in the reach of every person. A lot of the change is due to expectations from a variety of places, from customers (who want to do business with responsible suppliers) to employees (who want to feel that they are working for a good employer). The result is a feeling of much more local, more personal ownership over sustainability issues. This, in turn, leads to new dynamics in the company. For example, members of senior management can now see how they can bring attention to a sustainability-related topic in ways that can introduce opportunities to get employees involved with a specific business purpose—say, bringing in new sources of revenue. This is a big change from years ago."

(Pisarcik, 2011)

Another informed observer is Tim Mohin, Director of Corporate Responsibility at AMD. I first got to know Tim when we attended graduate school together in the mid-1980s. He has gone on to hold significant environmental policy positions in the federal government and has helped catalyze sustainability thinking in a number of leading companies, including Intel, Apple, and now AMD. According to Tim:

"There has been an evolution in attitudes toward CSR over the last decade. Back when we started in this field, it was really trench warfare, with a focus on localized environmental issues. Now, globalization has taken over, and focus has broadened to supply chains. The scope of the issues has also broadened. In addition to environmental issues, CSR requires competence on labor, human rights, ethics, governance, and other issues. Another shift is that all of these issues are far more intertwined with a company's reputation and brand."

(Mohin, 2011)

Customer Expectations

Well-run companies tend to be attentive to the needs and wants of their customers and to invest ample resources in remaining abreast of emerging, even unexpressed, needs. Although many consumers may feel that they have little say over what corporations produce and how, the last few years have witnessed some substantial efforts by large multinational firms to "green" their supply chains, producing ripple effects that are being felt far and wide. New supply chain requirements may include eliminating certain materials, not sourcing materials or components from certain countries, adopting particular production or management practices, conforming to specified codes of behavior (such as human rights/labor practices), and reducing their energy use or broader environmental footprint. These expectations can have major implications for how the supplier company can operate its business and hence have nontrivial revenue and cost impacts. Investors are increasingly aware of these intercompany dynamics and are factoring the possible implications from an investment standpoint into their evaluations. In the future, those working on company sustainability efforts will need to understand what these emerging demands are, how they are likely to evolve, and what options exist for addressing them effectively and optimally.

Fair Dealing and Ethical Treatment of Stakeholders

With today's 24-hour news cycle and constant access to various forms of news media via the Internet, it is important that corporations continuously safeguard their reputations. The experience of the past 15 years or so has shown that the quickest and surest way to garner vast amounts of unflattering media coverage is to mistreat your employees or purchase from suppliers that mistreat theirs. (Just ask the folks at Walmart and Nike.) Moreover, another consequence of globalization is access to large numbers of new suppliers, along with the downward pressure on prices that this wider access brings. This means that existing commercial relationships may be put to the test, and business partners that are found not to warrant the trust of their counterparts may be supplanted by others. Even with a more competitive economic landscape, it is probably more important than ever for firms, and the managers and executives within them, to uphold a reputation for integrity and fair dealing. Such behavior becomes even more important with new scrutiny from investors who demand that the companies that they invest in be ethically managed. Despite the old saw that "business ethics" is an oxymoron, people involved in corporate sustainability efforts would be unwise to take this sentiment to heart.

Transparency

Calls for more disclosure along more dimensions of corporate behavior and performance are being heard from a variety of audiences. The public and members of the communities in which firms operate want to receive assurance (in the form of facts) that companies are being operated ethically, safely, and in a way that provides overall net benefits to society. Regulators and members of the NGO community seek evidence that firms are in compliance with all pertinent laws and regulations and that unregulated activities are being conducted in a way that does not pose unreasonable harm to the environment, workers, or communities. And, as discussed earlier, investors increasingly seek information on corporate ES&G posture and performance. Meeting these demands requires significant effort and a level of corporate transparency that may pose both cultural and practical challenges for many companies. Notwithstanding the difficulty of the task, those involved in corporate sustainability efforts should understand that demands for greater transparency and disclosure are likely to intensify in the coming years. Moreover, if, as I anticipate, ES&G investing becomes further established or, over time, the dominant form of institutional investing, much more extensive and regular disclosure will, as a practical matter, become mandatory, whether formally required by SEC rule or otherwise.

Assurance of Senior Management Control and Awareness

As suggested previoulsy and illustrated at various points throughout this book, ES&G issues can affect the performance and future prospects of companies in numerous ways. Many external stakeholders, including regulators, customers, suppliers, investors, and rating agencies, among others, have a direct and important interest in understanding whether and to what extent those managing companies at the most senior levels are aware of these issues and have taken adequate steps to ensure that they are being managed effectively. The news media (including the "green" segment thereof) tends to focus on either existing problems or new initiatives, products, and services having a sustainability orientation, but many of the most important stakeholders of companies are focused on the bigger picture. They require ongoing assurance that the firm is adequately capitalized. They also need to know that its senior management understands both the threats and possible opportunities presented by ES&G issues. Finally, management should have established structures and practices that are sufficient to adroitly manage day-to-day operations and address any possible contingencies. For this reason, some stakeholders, particularly investors, have an abiding interest in corporate governance practices, policies, management systems, programs, and involvement in activities that may produce new revenues from sustainability-oriented products and services. It is important to understand that ES&G performance data (such as energy conservation and pollutant emissions) are necessary but insufficient. As discussed in depth in Chapter 6, investors make judgments about firms' future prospects based on the evidence they have and what they can infer from current behaviors. Demonstrating senior management command of and engagement in sustainability issues is a crucial means by which companies can send the appropriate signals to the investor community. This will become increasingly important to retaining investor support during the next decade.

Implications for Sustainability Professionals and Others Working on Corporate Sustainability Issues

From the foregoing, it should be obvious that understanding and producing meaningful results in the domain of corporate sustainability is substantially more multifaceted than is commonly realized. My hope and intent are that you will find much of what you need to know to get started in earnest in this book. For now, it is perhaps useful to be mindful of the following issues as you read further:

- **Language/terms.** As illustrated in this chapter, many terms are used in the EHS and sustainability field. I have offered here my own formulation of sustainability, which I find useful and employ throughout this book. Whether you accept this formulation, adopt another, or create your own for use in your company or in those you work with, I encourage you to be clear about what you mean by "sustainability" or whatever other terms you employ. Also be consistent in how you apply them. This is the best way to avoid confusion and spending lots of unproductive time debating what specific words and phrases mean instead of solving real problems.

- **Interrelationships.** This chapter also offers a few brief glimpses of how various ES&G issues are related to one another, as well as how the interests of the corporation and many of its external stakeholders are interconnected. As you think about how to contribute to your organization's long-term sustainability, it is important to remember the presence and importance of these interrelationships. The analogy of a spider web comes to mind, in that touching one part of the web sets off vibrations that may be felt in distant, seemingly unrelated parts. Many sustainability issues have similar widespread, and often subtle, connections, and it is important to try to identify and understand them as you proceed.

- **Interdisciplinary knowledge.** By now, it is perhaps clear that actively pursuing sustainability in a company has many moving parts and that many people and business functions must be involved for substantial success to be achieved. This necessarily means that any one person's knowledge and domain expertise are likely to be inadequate to address all the necessary tasks and activities involved in operationalizing sustainability. Instead, a multidisciplinary, collaborative approach is required to ensure that all appropriate expertise and perspective are brought to bear. This is particularly true during initial planning (or periodic retooling) stages, and in defining and launching initiatives to enhance existing and introduce new products and services having a sustainability component.

- **Skill sets.** Similarly, the skills required to orchestrate and manage an internal sustainability program or initiative extend well beyond technical knowledge of the issues. They include team building, communications, facilitation, and mentoring. It also is important to bring an open mind and exhibit flexibility and a willingness to try new ways of doing things. These aspects of pursuing corporate sustainability are discussed in more depth in Chapters 5 and 9.

The next chapter delves into more specific details about how various ES&G issues can and do affect the business enterprise. As you will see, the influence of many sustainability issues is substantial—or can be under some circumstances. This means that effective management of the business requires careful consideration of the points of intersection between the company and various environmental, health and safety, social, and governance/ethical issues. Knowing what some of these influences are will help you understand the perspectives of many major stakeholder groups (profiled in Chapter 4) and will demonstrate that the formal approaches to sustainability management that I advocate and describe in Chapter 5 are both necessary and appropriate.

Endnotes

1. The Brundtland Commission (named after its chair) was formed by the United Nations in a 1983 resolution.

2. Some people and organizations are now using the phrase "people, planet, profits" as convenient shorthand for this concept.

3. Most U.S. nonprofits are organized under Section 501(c)(3) of the Internal Revenue Code, which enables them to receive monetary and other donations that are tax-deductible for the donor. Tax-exempt organizations eligible for Section 501(c)(3) status are limited to organizations formed and operated exclusively for charitable, religious, educational, scientific, literary, or other defined purposes (Internal Revenue Service, 2001).

4. Sadly, many people in the business community and press seem not to recognize how many benefits the U.S. federal and state governments provide, and how different this largesse is from the situation in many other countries. I would point out but leave aside the issue of the vast direct subsidies and tax expenditures that benefit specific industries and companies. A fair treatment would require an entire book to fully outline. A simple and partial list of the benefits provided to U.S. firms in general would include the ability to operate within secure borders; transport their goods and employees along/through advanced roads, ports, airports, secure sea lanes (protected by the U.S. Navy), and other infrastructure; have use of a reserve currency accepted (and preferred) around the world; have instant access to astounding quantities of free and valuable information; and have dedicated civil servants traversing the globe, working to open new international markets and execute trade agreements. Despite receiving these many benefits and more, some corporate representatives continue to complain about paying taxes (paying their fair share) and "excessive" regulation. Regulation in the ES&G context is discussed in more depth in Chapter 3.

5. Importantly, though, such compensation need not always be monetary. As discussed in Chapter 5, there are many different ways of motivating line employees to contribute to company goals, many of which are not particularly costly. One essential element is respect.

6. EOs can be retrieved, by number, from the U.S. National Archives at www.archives.gov/. Prominent examples of important environmental/sustainability EOs include EO 13514, *Federal Leadership in Environmental, Energy, and Economic Performance* (2009); EO 13148, *Greening the Government Through Leadership in Environmental Management* (2000); and EO 12856, *Federal Compliance with Right-to-Know Laws and Pollution Prevention Requirements* (1993).

3

ES&G Issues and How They Affect the Business Enterprise

It is widely understood, if only generally, that the system of legal and other controls that exists in the U.S. to control pollutant emissions and other environmental and safety impacts can impose costs on the affected business enterprise. In response to new requirements, the business generally must modify its operations in some way to reach and maintain compliance. It also is increasingly understood that EHS and broader ES&G/sustainability issues can affect businesses in ways and through mechanisms that are not regulatory in nature, and that these impacts can be both adverse and beneficial. This chapter describes how and why these impacts occur, what form they take, and what types of behaviors are indicated for a company that seeks to optimize its responses to ES&G issues. Developing and successfully implementing an optimized (if not optimal) response strategy is vital for firms to become more sustainable in the long term.

Environmental, Health and Safety, and Social Equity Laws and Regulations

The stimulus for the development of most mature corporate-level programs and approaches addressing EHS and broader sustainability issues is the system of laws and regulations that have been developed during the past 40 years in the U.S. The vast majority of these address various aspects of protecting the environment and, along with it, human health. An additional major federal statute addresses occupational safety and health. In contrast, managing corporate social and governance issues generally is not directly addressed by federal or state law. Accordingly, the focus of this section is limited to the legal and regulatory system addressing EHS issues.

It can safely be said that in the absence of this system, much of what we know about how to reduce the adverse EHS impacts of commercial, industrial, and broader human activity would not exist. In recent years we have witnessed the emergence of sophisticated beyond-compliance corporate behavior. However, few informed observers would seriously dispute that the legal/regulatory control system now in place remains the foundation of our society's approach to improving the quality of human health and the environment. Moreover, because this system functions to redress fundamental imbalances between the benefits and costs of commercial activity and who receives/bears them, it also helps create the conditions needed for business models and approaches that are truly sustainable in the long term.

An Abridged History

When I was a boy, things were very different than they are now. Difficult as it may be to believe, prior to 1970, there were essentially no legal controls on the discharge of pollutants into the environment, in both the U.S. and most other countries. For example, few laws could force someone polluting the air or a river or stream to stop. There were existing common-law principles, such as abating a public nuisance or suing to protect enjoyment of one's property. But no overall doctrine, certainly at the federal level, defined and enforced a set of uniform pollution control requirements. Some limited elements prevented pollutant discharges to surface waters, but their purpose and primary effect was simply to maintain access for navigation (movement of ships and other watercraft).

With the first Earth Day in 1970, however, a powerful movement began to take shape. It resulted in a panoply of major laws governing pollutant emissions to air, water, and land. It also regulated, for the first time, the manufacture and usage of pesticides and other toxic chemicals. These early laws were followed in the mid-1970s and 1980s by new statutes controlling the management of hazardous wastes, mandating the cleanup of uncontrolled hazardous waste sites, establishing controls over drinking water quality, and requiring public disclosure of toxic pollutant emissions. These statutes empowered, for the first time, the federal government to establish new standards for a wide variety of activities (managing wastes, discharging pollutants, selling and using pesticides) that would apply uniformly across the country.

It is fair to say that we have come a long way in the span of 40 years. An array of major federal statutes and implementing regulations are in place, all of which have withstood legal challenge. And analogous state statutes and regulations have been enacted across the country. Accompanying the development of this legal foundation has been the accumulation of substantial case law, which, when viewed in its entirety, shows that the system that has evolved has repeatedly passed Constitutional muster. This system has been used to establish clear standards of environmental and safety behavior on the part of regulated entities, provide for enforcement of these standards, and impose penalties (including fines, required actions, and prison sentences) for noncompliance, particularly for willful and serious violations.

Today, the regulatory control framework envisioned in the major environmental statutes has been more or less fully completed. The regular, ongoing oversight and enforcement of these laws and implementing regulations have now been delegated to individual state governments in the vast majority of cases. This has resulted in the nationwide deployment of uniform, protective standards in a way that reflects each state's characteristics and priorities, allowing for flexible, practical application at the local level. This framework has accomplished a great deal and is widely viewed as a success story. Evidence for this assertion is provided by the fact that situations in which a major environmental public health threat or uncontrolled pollutant release occurs are relatively rare and for that reason may be considered newsworthy. In parallel with these appropriate developments, the U.S. and other developed countries have witnessed a profound change in how individuals, organizations, and entire societies interact with the environment. It is now assumed and expected that organizations, particularly corporations, are in compliance with all relevant environmental and safety control regulations. It would be the rare individual who would assert that it is acceptable to pollute the environment or endanger one's employees (or neighbors) rather than take reasonable steps to manage a material safely and dispose of it properly.

At the same time, it is worth mentioning that most of the major environmental and health and safety statutes were enacted at a different time in our history. The National Environmental Policy Act (NEPA), Clean Air Act (CAA), Clean Water Act (CWA), Safe Drinking Water Act (SDWA), Resource Conservation and Recovery Act (RCRA), Toxic Substances Control Act (TSCA), Occupational Safety and Health Act (OSHA), and Federal Insecticide, Fungicide, and Rodenticide Act (FIFRA) were all passed by the U.S. Congress in the 1970s.[1] The Comprehensive Environmental Response, Compensation, and Liability Act (CERCLA), better known as "Superfund," was enacted in 1980. A number of major amendments have been added to some of these statutes, particularly during the mid-1980s and early 1990s. But it is generally recognized that the statutes and amendments to existing statutes passed during this roughly ten-year period provide the foundation of environmental, health, and safety law in the U.S. Moreover, these statutes have been used as models for a number of other countries as they too enacted national legislation to address EHS issues.

It was within the social and political crucible of the 1960s that the modern environmental movement came into being and laid the foundation for the improved environmental quality and sustainability management assets that we have today. The conditions at that time enabled the formation of a general political consensus, which included Democrats and Republicans, political liberals and staunch conservatives, that the environment on which we all depend was under assault and that strong measures needed to be taken. The publication of Rachel Carson's classic, *Silent Spring*, first brought public attention to the issue of pesticides in the environment, and the fact that *no one* had the authority at that time to limit their production, use, and misuse. Several catastrophic events (such as massive fish kills) and a continuing series of warning signs (such as the Cuyahoga River catching fire) served to elevate concerns among the public and elected officials. And the national political leadership at the time had already shown itself and the American people that it was capable of taking on difficult political issues.[2] Therefore, those who were committed to the issue of environmental protection were able to garner enough support from enough places to prevail. It probably helped their cause that at the time the specific sources of many major environmental problems were not well understood, nor were the initial costs of more benign practices.[3]

Today, of course, the political climate is very different. It is far more difficult to get any piece of legislation, let alone a major new environmental or health and safety protection statute, through the gauntlet of the entrenched interests represented in the U.S. Congress. Those of us who lament the repeated failures to enact even a rudimentary national greenhouse gas/energy policy bill by Congress can only dream of what it must have been like in the past. During those heady days, it was possible to think big and, with lots of work and coalition-building, enact a new statute to address a major unmet environmental policy need.

This attenuated discussion of recent history illustrates that the legal framework that protects the environment and worker health and safety, though in some ways incomplete and unwieldy, is the legacy of a rare time when "the planets aligned." Despite the frustrations that many people feel about some of these laws (limits on authority, lack of flexibility), we are fortunate to have them. If they had never been created, considering our current social and political culture, it is not at all clear that we would now have the wherewithal to create something equal or better.

Returning the focus to what we have rather than what might have been, there are a few important facts to take away from the foregoing discussion. One is that we have a mature and, at a general level, well-functioning legal and regulatory system to define key environmental, health, and safety issues.[4] Another is that given the political realities, it is unlikely that the current system will change markedly in the foreseeable future. Although it is true that some new chemicals and products, for example, may face more stringent controls, it is unlikely that we will see any wholesale changes to the overall approach to their regulation in the U.S. The flip side of this type of "stability," if you will, is that some of the inefficiencies, gaps, and seemingly nonsensical outcomes that arise with the current system are likely to be with us for the long term. Some of us in the environmental/EHS profession believe that we are overdue for a "stem to stern" review of our environmental and health and safety legislative and regulatory system, with the goal of filling gaps and increasing both effectiveness and efficiency. With the current state of our political culture, however, it is highly unlikely that this type of review and/or overhaul will occur anytime soon.

Along with the markedly different legal environment than the one that existed prior to 1970, a parallel and in some ways equally important change has taken place within our society. It concerns the expectations of individuals. Today, nearly everyone wants a healthy environment and feels some obligation to do his or her part to contribute toward this goal. It is generally expected that organizations will conduct their affairs in a way that does not impose undue burdens on the environment or expose their people or neighbors to hazardous conditions. At a bare minimum, companies are expected to comply with all pertinent environmental and health and safety regulations and conditions. This marks a sea change in public (and corporate) attitudes toward EHS in the span of less than two generations. It may be difficult to imagine today, but in the 1970s, the leaders of more than a few newly regulated companies openly challenged the government's ability to force them to control the untreated (and often highly hazardous) wastes that they were venting to the air or pumping into rivers, lakes, or oceans. These early challenges came in a number of different forms. At the corporate level, most of the fights occurred in the courtroom, as corporations and their trade association representatives challenged the constitutionality of most of the major statutes, or at least some of their major provisions. At a more tactical level, during their initial site visits, more than a few federal and state inspectors were welcomed at the plant gate or facility entrance by an unsmiling man brandishing a shotgun.[5] In terms of what might be considered socially acceptable attitudes, we have come a long way in a relatively short time.

At the time when most of our major environmental statutes (and OSHA) were enacted, the existing knowledge base concerning the environmental and human health effects of chemicals and other substances was quite limited. Also, the effectiveness and costs of different pollutant emission controls and alternative waste management methods, as applied on a broad scale, were largely unknown. The potential of forward-looking and integrated approaches such as pollution prevention was largely unexplored, if not undefined, during this period. Similarly, both data and depth of understanding of how natural systems work and how they are influenced by human activities, including pollution and overexploitation, were extremely limited. It is not an exaggeration to say that in the early days, the people writing the laws and, later, those who drafted the implementing regulations were literally inventing new approaches as they went along. There was little to nothing to base decisions on, beyond whatever engineering, economic, and technical studies might have been commissioned to support a particular effort, and the all-too-common "best engineering judgment."

As the new environmental and occupational safety and health laws were implemented, an interesting thing happened. Many new processes, operating practices, and capabilities were developed that enabled many organizations to greatly reduce their pollutant generation and emission and accident rates, often more rapidly and easily than had been predicted. Indeed, as the collective expertise within our society grew, many members of the regulated community discovered that they could cost-effectively reduce their negative effects on human health and the environment beyond what was strictly required by statute, regulation, or discharge permit. These successes also gave rise to the concept of "pollution prevention," which means eliminating pollution at its source rather than relying on downstream treatment or disposal. This approach is strongly preferred by regulators and leading companies, and in fact has been U.S. national policy for more than 20 years.[6] Similarly, in the field of occupational health and safety, the concept of "behavior-based" safety has been widely embraced since the mid-1990s.

Today, the regulatory, policy, and technical expertise resident within many of our public sector institutions is highly developed. So is the published literature in the fields of environmental/health and safety law, public policy, pollution control engineering, risk assessment, environmental/natural resource economics, and many others. Experience has shown which types of approaches are effective and can be deployed at reasonable cost and which are not or cannot. In 1970 there was little private sector environmental expertise, but today there is a well-developed multibillion-dollar EHS services industry (actually, a set of industries). Its members employ hundreds of thousands of consultants, engineers, scientists, and other professionals who deliver a wide array of products and services in the fields of environment, health and safety, and related fields on an ongoing basis. The mechanics of managing wastes, controlling pollutant emissions, and limiting unsafe workplace exposures and other EHS "basics" remain ongoing challenges in some operating environments. But increasingly the focus is on rethinking and redesigning business processes to make them safer and more environmentally benign, rather than focusing on end-of-pipe (point of discharge) pollution control.

It is important to celebrate the successes that environmental, health, and safety protection efforts have achieved in improving the quality of our air and water; reducing exposure to toxic chemicals; protecting high-value ecosystems and habitats; and eliminating deaths, injuries, and illness on the job. Some important residual, high-profile environmental issues still exist (such as fish kills, waste impoundment failures, stream/habitat destruction from mountaintop mining). But we no longer have healthy people killed by massive air pollution episodes, lakes devoid of plant and animal life, rivers that catch fire and burn, or routine residential exposure to high concentrations of acutely toxic and/or carcinogenic substances. And although industrial accidents, injuries, and even deaths continue to occur, particularly in some occupations, on the whole, American workplaces are far safer and more conducive to continued good health than they were a generation or two ago.

With all that has been accomplished, you might think that our society has surmounted its greatest environmental problems. That supposition would, unfortunately, be incorrect. In a sense, we have tackled the most obvious and most easily addressed problems first. If large, fixed facilities are discharging pollutants into the air or water, or are burying toxic wastes out on the "back 40," it is sensible to prohibit or tightly regulate these practices if they pose significant risks to human health and environmental quality. Indeed, this was exactly the approach taken in our initial efforts to improve the condition of the environment. We went after the major pollution sources that were in plain sight and that generally were under the direct control of an entity (such as a corporation, hospital, or local government) that could be identified and compelled to make the desired changes. These efforts were hugely successful. Total annual loadings of the highest-priority pollutants (as defined in statutes) have declined substantially, even as our population and economy have continued to expand. Moreover, these improvements have been made in ways that, contrary to the dire predictions made along the way, did not bankrupt our society or, indeed, very many (if any) companies. The plain truth is that the vast majority of environmental and health and safety laws have yielded tangible environmental quality, human health, and economic benefits. The value of these, despite the seemingly eternal complaints of their detractors, greatly exceeds their cost. This issue is discussed further in the following sidebar.

But Aren't Environmental Regulations Too Costly?

The issue of the benefits and costs of new environmental regulations has been raised repeatedly over the past 40 years or so. Studies that have been conducted at various points during this period have shown repeatedly that well-designed EHS regulations yield significant *net* societal benefits. That is, on an overall basis (benefits minus costs), *they do not cost money; they save money*. For example, the EPA recently calculated that the *overall benefits* of the Clean Air Act Amendments of 1990 and their implementation *exceeded the associated costs by a factor of more than 30. These benefits totaled $2 trillion* over the 20-year study period (USEPA, 2010). In addition, a more recent study of the economic effects of all EPA rules promulgated by the Obama administration to date (roughly two and a half years) showed that the combined annual benefits exceeded the corresponding costs by $32 billion to $142 billion per year, with a benefit/cost ratio ranging from *4-to-1 to 22-to-1* (Shapiro, 2011).

This is not to say that EHS regulations or broader ES&G expectations are "free"—at least, not to everyone. As discussed later, firms affected by new requirements generally experience some new costs as they modify their activities to come into compliance, and others as they maintain compliance over time. These expenses are properly viewed as additional costs of doing business. They are not, in most cases, the result of government overreach or the handiwork of an overzealous and misguided bureaucracy. They are instead an *intervention to correct a market failure*. The simple fact is that releasing pollution into the environment or exposing employees to unsafe working conditions imposes costs on society, which then must deal with the consequences (unhealthy air or water quality, additional burdens on social services). Economists call these costs "externalities," because by avoiding some of the adverse consequences of their behavior, firms can avoid, or externalize, some of the costs they would otherwise incur. Appropriately crafted EHS (or, more generally, ES&G) regulations force companies to accept responsibility for their externalities, thereby reducing the burden imposed by the few (the affected companies and, indirectly, their customers) on the many (the public, the instrument of the public [various agencies of government], affected employees, and/or the ambient environment).

To the extent that a newly regulated company experiences a cost increase as a consequence of new requirements, it can either bear the cost internally (reducing margins), pass along the cost to its customers in the form of a price increase, or some of each. In any event, markets then function more efficiently as the prices of goods and services more accurately reflect their true costs. A new market equilibrium is reached as the true marginal social cost of the last unit produced equals the corresponding marginal social benefit. Moreover, the affected firm is provided with a clear economic incentive to develop means of eliminating or reducing the substance (such as a regulated chemical) or activity (managing hazardous wastes on site, for example) that triggered regulation in the first place.

The nature of markets and how ES&G issues affect and are affected by markets is discussed in depth in Chapter 6. Chapter 5 discusses how regulations have influenced and shaped contemporary ES&G management practices.

What we are left with now is, increasingly, the "tough stuff"—problems that are of significant magnitude but are difficult to resolve.

Here are a few examples of the types of major EHS issues that continue to defy adequate resolution:

- Reducing greenhouse gas (GHG) emissions and limiting (or adapting to) global climate change
- Ensuring adequate water supply and quality
- Understanding and limiting the effects of endocrine-disrupting chemicals
- Appropriately controlling exposure to low/no-threshold effect compounds and mixtures
- Preventing the spread of invasive species
- Reducing line and area sources of pollution (such as roads and farm fields)

Adequately addressing these challenges and, at a more personal level, doing what we can within our own spheres of influence will require better understanding of what the environmental/sustainability issue is, how performance can be improved, and what the practical and financial consequences of action (or inaction) are at personal, organizational, and societal levels.

These issues, among others, are difficult to resolve for one or more of the following reasons:

- **Many sources of small impact.** Many remaining major pollution sources are diffuse and scattered across the country rather than centralized in one location (such as a power or chemical plant). It is fundamentally more difficult to control thousands (or millions) of pollutant sources than a few dozen or hundred.
- **Large installed infrastructure and (potentially) stranded costs.** Some issues are intimately associated with the life and work styles we have chosen and with the commercial and industrial infrastructure we have developed as a society over the past century. The most prominent example is our near-total reliance on petroleum to power our personal mobility (generally by driving a car, often alone). Most of us, myself included, must, from a practical standpoint, drive a motor vehicle to get where we need or want to go on a regular basis. These vehicles are powered by gasoline or diesel fuel that we can obtain readily from any of thousands of gas stations across the country. Replacing this hydrocarbon-based fuel source with something

more environmentally benign (hydrogen, electricity) will take substantial time and vast amounts of capital. Moreover, the suburban sprawl that continued more or less unabated for the latter half of the 20th century has significantly exacerbated our dependence on motorized personal transportation. Although some people dream of freeing ourselves from the automobile, the plain truth is that, with the exception of some urban dwellers, it will not happen soon—if ever.

- **Behavior of individuals.** In a similar vein, many important pollution and waste sources result from the individual choices we all make every day (personal automobile use, for example) or periodically (such as what products to buy, or where to live and in how large a dwelling). Such decisions are well beyond the traditional purview of government and, for that matter, most cultural institutions.

- **Transboundary.** Some environmental problems span national and other political boundaries (such as climate change). This means that finding and reaching agreement on solutions can be intrinsically difficult and time-consuming, even if there is general agreement about the source of the problem and what needs to be done.

- **Obsolete, limited authority.** Despite the profound impacts of the major EHS statutes briefly described here, any new environmental improvement efforts that rely on legal controls are limited by the boundaries and approaches established by our major environmental statutes. With only a few exceptions, these laws are all at least 20 years old.

- **Gridlock.** Recent years and events have only served to highlight some of the profound philosophical differences that exist within our political, government, and corporate institutions. The ongoing debate over climate change is only the most obvious area in which it can be difficult within our society to reach a general consensus on the nature, causes, desired improvements, and indicated approaches for resolving important environmental or other sustainability issues.

These factors are well known within the environmental policy arena. In some cases they have been overcome with concerted efforts on the part of a number of stakeholders. Examples include the Montreal Protocol process, which resulted in the coordinated international phase-out of many ozone-depleting compounds. To some degree, the

Kyoto protocol is another example. After several years following its signature by 84 nations, it was ratified by enough signatory countries to go into effect in 2005.[7]

More generally, however, it is not entirely clear that our existing statutory and institutional structure and tools will be adequate to address these challenges. This suggests that substantial improvements or even extensive retooling will be necessary at some point. A number of observers have advocated a move toward "next-generation environmental regulation" as a means by which this might be done, or at least initiated. Ira Feldman is a prominent voice and thought leader in this area. He believes that as our legislative and regulatory system evolves, it will be informed by sustainability principles rather than be driven by the risk management focus underlying our existing legal and regulatory structure:

> Any future "stem to stern" review will almost certainly be based on an appreciation of sustainability concepts and principles. In addition, there are ideas now in play that were not even part of the discussion as of the mid-1990s. These include 1) sector-specific approaches; 2) the concept of industrial ecology; 3) appreciating the nature and importance of ecosystem services and using them as part of the basis for regulatory structure and policy; and 4) shifting to more of a materials management, rather than a waste/residuals, focus. While it is unlikely that we will see any major changes in the near term due to the current political climate, at some point we will be ready to make the needed enhancements. The pendulum shift will happen, just as it always does. (Feldman, 2011)

Whether it happens quickly or, more likely, over a more extended period, our societal approach to defining mandates addressing ES&G issues will evolve. In the interim, business leaders should understand that EHS and broader ES&G laws, regulations, and expectations are firmly rooted legally, culturally, and institutionally across our country. There is ample room for streamlining, consolidation, and general improvement in how these controls are deployed. But they continue to serve an important role and are unlikely to be eliminated, regardless of recent ill-considered and largely uninformed public statements made by certain interest groups, politicians, and candidates for public office. Indeed, as explored further in a moment, leaders within most well-run companies actively support appropriate regulations. It would be unwise to assume that the business community generally would support any broad efforts to repeal or undermine our major EHS statutes and programs. Our best companies have simply invested too much time, effort, and money and have reaped too many benefits to retreat to our previous, unsustainable practices, regardless of short-term economic or political conditions.

Corporate ES&G Obligations

A complete compendium of federal and state EHS laws and implementing regulations would fill many volumes and would provide a granularity that would not be very useful to most readers. Instead, this section describes some high-level characteristics of the legal controls system that has been developed and put into place in the U.S. during the past 40 years or so. The intent is to acquaint you with the types of controls that exist, what they address and are intended to accomplish, and where their coverage ends.

What Is a Law? What Is an Environmental or Health and Safety Law?

Laws and legal requirements arise from several different places within our system. The ultimate source of authority for enacting laws in the U.S. is the Constitution. It grants specific rights to and imposes restrictions on each of the three branches of the federal government: executive, legislative, and judicial. Generally, the right to enact new laws rests with Congress, the members of which are elected by the American people. The executive branch may present legislation for consideration by Congress, but it has no direct right to impose new laws on the American people. As a practical matter, however, Congress generally confers authority by statute to the executive branch and its agencies to implement new statutes. This implementation commonly involves developing specific requirements in regulations and overseeing compliance by the regulated community. Both executive and legislative authorities are tempered by the oversight and approval function played by the judiciary (through the courts). Legislative activity may be challenged with respect to its conformance to the Constitution. Executive branch activity may be challenged and overturned if it is found to substantially diverge from congressional intent. These well-known "checks and balances" play key roles in defining how environmental, health and safety, and other regulations are developed.

Some regulations have been promulgated that may seem to defy common sense and may even reject the preferred course of action on an agency's part, but they have been crafted to reflect specific (usually well-intentioned) Congressional mandates. This often occurs following a successful court challenge to a regulation by representatives of industry, public interest groups, and/or other stakeholders, or in response to threats of litigation during regulatory deliberations. In addition, court decisions and opinions in some cases comprise part of the law when they address issues that have not been fully articulated in statutes and regulations; this is known as "case law."[8] An additional area of law is based on English common law, which is the basis of many civil actions ("torts"). Common law establishes a general duty on everyone to avoid doing harm to others, either willfully or through negligence or inaction. Finally, treaties between the U.S. and other nations (once ratified by the U.S. Senate) carry the force of law and may impose additional requirements on entities and individuals that would not exist otherwise.

National programs such as our major EHS statutes and implementing regulations are often delegated in large part to state government agencies. Typically, this occurs after a particular state has enacted legislation that parallels or is more stringent than the corresponding federal requirements and has demonstrated that it has sufficient authority and capacity to enforce the federal (and its own) requirements. Incentive to take on these programs is provided through federal grants and technical assistance. As noted earlier, virtually all major federal environmental regulatory programs are now fully delegated (or nearly so) to the states.

In the EHS arena, major programs have typically begun in the form of federal legislation crafted in response to a perceived problem or important issue. That is, the creation of most major EHS laws, particularly in the early years, has been reactive in nature. Some major statutes were passed without lengthy debate and in the absence of detailed supporting studies or analyses. In all cases, however, statutes are a product of the give and take of the political and legislative processes. Consequently, some statutory provisions have been difficult to implement; created inconsistencies and conflicts; or provided incomplete coverage across industries, pollutant sources, or other important dimensions. As discussed here, the responsible agencies are bound to implement these statutes as they are written, and generally face significant constraints on their ability to creatively interpret legislative intent. The result of this process is an overall EHS regulatory system that is perfect from no one's perspective, but is acceptable to most people. One might say it more closely resembles a patchwork quilt (with a number of large and small holes) than a tightly woven blanket.

In addition, and by design, there are some very important limitations to the regulatory powers provided to federal agencies such as the EPA. With few exceptions, environmental laws provide authority to limit potentially harmful emissions or waste management practices. But they do not extend agency jurisdiction into such crucial decisions as the selection of materials, technology, operating practices, or other portions of the core business enterprise. Indeed, regulated industry has zealously (and generally successfully) defended itself against regulatory agency intrusions into, for example, its management of in-process materials, even though such management may seem indistinguishable from waste management activities.[9] Accordingly, the EPA and other federal and state regulators generally are not empowered to compel, for example, the use of energy-efficient manufacturing equipment, recycled-content raw materials, or stewardship of land or other natural resource holdings. Although some such authority does exist within other designated public resource management agencies (such as the U.S. Bureau of Land Management, the U.S. Forest Service, and state-level analogs), it is limited in scope (to public lands) and often must be explicitly balanced with many other considerations (often local/regional economic growth, jobs, recreational use). Some important exceptions exist at the state level, particularly with the use of toxic materials, and at the international level (as discussed later). But as a general matter, environmental regulations are limited in scope to what residues (materials other than products) emerge from production processes and how they are managed, rather than what is produced and through what means.

The major EHS statutes contain articles (titles and subtitles) that address particular concerns and that direct a specific federal agency or agencies to develop detailed regulations that establish specific requirements, limits, procedures, and the like. Typically, environmental issues are referred to the U.S. Environmental Protection Agency (EPA), and health and safety issues are delegated to the Occupational Safety and Health Administration (OSHA) within the Department of Labor. That said, other entities such as the Department of Transportation (DOT), Nuclear Regulatory Commission (NRC), U.S. Army Corps of Engineers (COE), U.S. Fish and Wildlife Service, National Oceanic and Atmospheric Administration (NOAA), Council on Environmental Quality (CEQ), and other federal departments and agencies also have regulatory or advisory responsibilities with respect to certain EHS issues. The EPA, however, has primary responsibility for most environmental programs and has by far the most involvement in regulating potential impacts on the environment.

The EPA typically develops policies and regulations at its headquarters locations and provides permitting, oversight, enforcement, and technical assistance through a network of ten regional offices located across the U.S. Regional offices carry out these functions directly in states within their respective regions that have not been authorized to carry out a particular regulatory program. They also serve as a source of information and guidance to analogous state government agencies in authorized states. In many cases, these decentralized portions of the EHS regulatory structure establish (generally through permits) the specific operating conditions that will apply to a particular facility.

In addition, many state governments have developed their own programs to address pressing environmental issues in the absence of federal action. These include state-level statutes and regulations addressing oil and petroleum products, recycling, toxic materials use, air and water pollution control (including greenhouse gas emissions), hazardous waste, and other issues. Companies or company facilities located in such states are, obviously, obliged to conform to any additional requirements imposed by these state laws.

In sum, the legal landscape faced by any large company with U.S. operations will include pervasive federal EHS requirements, specific conditions stipulated by regional and/or state government officials (such as permit limits), and, in some cases, additional and perhaps profound state and/or local requirements.

Compliance Obligations

Being or becoming subject to EHS regulations imposes one or more requirements on an affected company, and these requirements vary substantially in terms of the work or other burdens imposed, and their associated costs. In many cases, an initial investment of staff time and other resources is required to come into compliance, with much lower periodic investments needed to meet ongoing program maintenance obligations. As a practical matter, corporate EHS staff (at both the corporate and facility levels) spend much of their time keeping up to date with evolving compliance obligations, ensuring that existing programs are effective at maintaining ongoing conformance, and performing some of the tasks required (such as periodic training, maintaining records, reporting). Many specifics, permutations, and combinations can apply to a particular company or facility, and every situation has unique characteristics. But it is possible to make some generalizations about the types of activities that are required by firms in the regulated community. Some general categories are described in the following sections.

Permitting

Programs developed under several of our major environmental statutes recognize that certain activities commonly result in the emission of pollutants and/or the generation of waste. Although it would be desirable for there to be no emissions of pollutants into the environment, in most cases such an outcome is not possible, at least not in the short term. Accordingly, under normal circumstances, and starting from an unregulated condition, these programs were crafted to allow regulated companies to discharge certain quantities or concentrations of defined pollutants into water or air, or the on-site management and transport of particular wastes under prescribed conditions. These conditions are specified in one or more permits that are issued by the EPA or an authorized state agency. Moreover, the statutes and implementing regulations are designed to specify that regulated discharges/waste management activities that take place without the appropriate permits are illegal and subject to legal sanctions (discussed later). This system therefore allows for and essentially confers the right to pollute, but only up to defined limits. This arrangement has generally served as an effective means of providing certainty to the regulated community and ensuring that the overall emissions of particular pollutants are within known and acceptable limits.

Pollution Control Engineering and Processes

In the early days of EHS programs, vigorous activity in companies, regulatory agencies, engineering firms, and other entities focused on a new problem. Previously, companies were left to themselves to determine how much of their material streams they would try to recover and how much they would discharge into the environment. After new emissions limits were defined, it became necessary to develop and demonstrate the effectiveness of new technologies to remove pollutants from effluent streams, reduce the volume and/or toxicity of waste streams, and otherwise limit the magnitude of the nonproduct material management side of commercial/industrial activity. The focal point of such efforts in the early days was the "end of the pipe"—the point of discharge. These efforts were highly successful and over time gave way to more of a focus on preventing pollution in the first instance ("pollution prevention," or "P2") and, more recently, "design for environment" (DfE). As discussed in Chapter 5, among the more sophisticated companies, the common perspective is that all waste and emissions are nonproduct output that must be minimized, generally through careful evaluation of product function and use, materials, production technology, sourcing, end-of-life management, and other considerations. But because the landscape continues to change, pollution control engineering remains an active field and a focus of significant effort. New engineering solutions are often needed as new products are continually being designed and brought to market, new companies are being formed, and new regulatory standards are being promulgated (albeit at a much slower pace than previously).

Moreover, as discussed in subsequent chapters, the great majority of companies, particularly small and medium-sized enterprises, have yet to establish sophisticated approaches to EHS management.

Testing/Evaluation

Many substances used in commerce can harm human health and/or the environment under certain conditions. Accordingly, a key feature of the regulatory landscape is the requirement that regulated entities carry out periodic testing and evaluation when any of a number of prescribed conditions occur. For example, certain types of waste materials are strictly regulated as hazardous wastes if they exhibit any of several physical or chemical characteristics. Companies that generate wastes are required to test them to ensure that they do not exhibit these characteristics under specified conditions. The wastes must be managed as hazardous if they do (including, for large quantity generators, obtaining a permit). Similarly, certain types of pollution control equipment must be tested at prescribed intervals to ensure that it is operating properly, so as to prevent failure that might lead to excessive pollutant releases and human/environmental exposure. And a number of methods and procedures across the EHS arena must be tested and evaluated at periodic intervals to ensure that on-site personnel can carry out all required actions, and that equipment and supplies are in place and available. Also, the existing processes and procedures must be sufficient and effective in preventing the adverse outcomes they were designed to preclude or limit.

Remediation

Prior to the enactment of federal statutes controlling the discharge and placement of waste materials on the land,[10] property owners were largely free to stockpile and/or bury virtually any material they chose. Consequently, by the 1970s, hundreds of thousands of open dumps, municipal and industrial landfills, waste piles, and unmanaged accumulations of materials were scattered across the country. Many had been (or were subsequently) shown to be releasing toxic constituents to surrounding media and posing potential human health and/or environmental threats. The EPA's new solid and hazardous waste management programs were developed to curtail the practices that lead to the formation of these sites. The "Superfund" program formed under the auspices of CERCLA created a formal process by which sites would be evaluated and, in cases in which threats were significant, cleaned up. Either the responsible party or parties or, in their absence, the EPA would perform the cleanup. Some 30 years later, despite noteworthy successes at thousands of the most contaminated sites, tens of thousands more remain to be evaluated and cleaned up. New ones are added annually to the Superfund National Priorities List (NPL). Managing such legacy sites will be a lasting feature of the EHS/sustainability profession for many decades to come. Finally, although the formation of new, large-scale hazardous waste sites is, fortunately, uncommon, ongoing accidents, spills, process upsets, containment failures, and other such episodes occur occasionally. These must also be cleaned up, often using the same types of technologies and approaches as are applied to long-standing NPL sites.

Training

Understanding the requirements of existing regulatory programs, how to carry out certain stipulated processes and methods, and what to do during emergency conditions generally requires that specific instructions and more general education be administered to operating and managerial personnel. Training is a vital part of any organization's efforts to achieve and maintain compliance, safe and healthful working conditions, and operating efficiency. Some regulatory programs have specific training requirements, including refresher training at periodic intervals (generally annually). Corporate EHS personnel often spend considerable time ensuring that their colleagues have received the training appropriate to their responsibilities and can execute their desired roles. Moreover, during the past 20 years or so, a thriving industry has taken shape that specializes in providing training courses covering various aspects of EHS compliance and management. Such offerings are available far and wide from consulting firms, for-profit training institutes, and even community colleges nationwide.

Record-Keeping

Accompanying the myriad requirements for deploying effective engineering controls, operating within certain defined parameters, ensuring that staff are appropriately trained and can carry out their assigned responsibilities, and other aspects of the regulatory control system, a common feature of many regulatory programs is the development and maintenance of detailed records. Written evidence is often required to demonstrate conformance with regulatory requirements and permit conditions. This is especially important considering the low frequency with which most regulated entities/facilities can be inspected. In this context, records provide a window into how a company/facility has been operated during a period of time preceding the inspection or site visit. They also provide a time line of sorts in understanding conditions there on an ongoing basis. More generally, records are a crucial part of any organization's management infrastructure. They not only provide a factual base for the necessary assurance of management control to regulators and other external stakeholders, but also offer valuable insights into the effectiveness of existing practices (and individuals) and areas needing additional attention. The burden created by record-keeping requirements is highly variable. Some firms and facilities operate few, if any, practices subject to detailed record-keeping requirements. Others, particularly those in resource-intensive industrial operations, typically experience substantial ongoing demands for staff time and other resources simply to create and maintain the required documentation.

Reporting

In parallel with record-keeping requirements, many regulatory programs require regular reports from the regulated entity, generally at the facility or even unit level. Reporting must be done using a prescribed format and at a specified level of detail. In recent years, many regulatory agencies have adopted electronic reporting, which often reduces the effort and time required to develop and submit required data. Reporting has been a core feature of most regulatory (and many public sector nonregulatory) programs since their inception. As discussed in subsequent chapters, however, nonregulatory reporting suggested through national and international codes of conduct, industry norms, and voluntary standards (so-called "soft law") is becoming more prominent and is increasingly in the public eye. The burdens imposed by these new expectations on companies vary widely.

Companies affected by EHS regulatory requirements are obliged to develop an understanding of the specific provisions that apply to their operations and to take whatever actions are needed to ensure compliance. In the event of noncompliance, either from lack of understanding or otherwise, the EPA and other regulatory agencies may use administrative orders to compel compliance, or may seek a civil action (through the U.S. Department of Justice). The responsible agency also may seek to have a recalcitrant company suspended or debarred, which means that the affected firm may be prohibited from contracting with the federal government. For some enterprises, such a sanction might mean very little. For others, it could pose an existential threat, and not just because the federal government is the nation's largest purchaser of goods and services. Another noteworthy feature of several major environmental statutes is that they allow individual citizens and citizens' groups to file lawsuits to compel compliance. This has directly resulted in extensive litigation focused on accelerating development of new rules, imposing more stringent standards, and otherwise adding more "teeth" to the regulatory control system. The role of major environmental advocacy groups in this regard is discussed further in Chapter 4.

Finally, it is important to understand that our major environmental statutes give regulators only limited discretion to implement regulatory requirements in ways that are not strictly uniform across all companies and facilities within a particular industry or sector. For this reason, the several dozen voluntary programs that the EPA has launched so far offer regulatory relief in a tightly constrained manner. But they typically offer public recognition, information sharing, and other benefits as well. Ira Feldman, who played a key role in formulating the EPA's audit policy and in creating some of its early voluntary programs while serving in the EPA's Office of Environmental Compliance and Enforcement, explains:

> Regulators have discretion in only three areas: 1) permitting, 2) inspections, and 3) enforcement. For this reason, all of EPA's (and OSHA's) corporate excellence programs address

one or more of these three dimensions. Examples include expedited permit reviews, fewer/lower-priority inspections, and less intensive enforcement. (Feldman, 2011)

Legal Liability

Noncompliance with environmental control or health and safety regulations can engender serious legal consequences. Most of the enabling statutes establish both criminal and civil penalties for organizations and individuals found not to be in compliance at all times. The nature and extent of the legal sanctions that may result from violating environmental and health and safety laws and rules are somewhat complex, but they fall into one of three basic categories:

- **Criminal liability** can be sought against organizations and individuals who misrepresent the facts or knowingly or negligently violate the law. Note that "knowing" of a violation does not necessarily mean that the person charged knows the requirements of the applicable law, but rather that he or she knows the relevant facts. In other words, ignorance of the law is an ineffective defense. Importantly, over time the focus of many enforcement actions has shifted from the company level to those in the management chain ultimately responsible for the firm's conduct (senior corporate officials). This shift has been supported by the courts.[11] In fact, a substantial number of senior corporate officials have received prison sentences for particularly egregious violations committed by their companies during the past decade or so.

- **Civil liability.** More commonly, civil penalties may be sought and obtained for violations of EHS laws and regulations. As a general matter, the government will seek injunctive relief—an order that the affected firm stop violating the law/regulation and/or take the required actions to become compliant. In addition, monetary penalties are usually sought based on two factors: the gravity of the violation and the economic benefit obtained by the company from noncompliance. Gravity is evaluated according to the seriousness of the consequences of the noncompliance (for example, contaminating a town's water supply is more serious than failing to submit a required report on time) and how much the observed behavior differs from the required behavior. The economic benefit component is defined as being equal to or exceeding the financial value of the lack of compliance or delayed compliance. Base penalties include both components and can be adjusted based on other factors, such as the willfulness of the violation, the degree of cooperation received from the violator (or lack thereof), and the violator's compliance history. Certain statutes (including the Clean Water Act and CERCLA) allow the EPA to act to address pollution that damages or endangers public health or the environment. The EPA can either bring a civil action or, in the case of CERCLA, abate the hazard itself and then seek recovery of damages from the responsible party.

- **Financial liability.** Civil penalties for violating most major environmental laws range from $10,000 to $50,000 per violation per day. Obviously, continued violations and/or noncompliance at multiple facilities can result in substantial fines. Although multimillion-dollar fines are not an everyday occurrence, they are levied in some cases. Moreover, if natural resources are damaged (such as the imminent hazard situation just described), the costs of abatement and restoration can easily run into the millions of dollars. In many cases, monetary fines may be reduced if the violator agrees to undertake one or more supplemental environmental projects (SEPs). SEPs typically are negotiated during enforcement actions. They may result in substantial reduction of fines for projects that are found to be beneficial to the environment and/or the public, innovative, focus on pollution prevention, and other factors.

Clearly, the existence of this framework of legal sanctions and the knowledge that it can and will be applied to companies that fail to comply with EHS requirements means that ongoing vigilance is required of all regulated firms. Indeed, EHS personnel spend much of their time ensuring that the systems and practices that they have deployed to maintain regulatory compliance are working properly. Maintaining compliance is the baseline level of performance that should be expected of any company, and it certainly is a prerequisite for any firm that wants to pursue organizational sustainability.

Stakeholder Expectations and Nonlegal Requirements

In addition to the extensive legal framework now in place establishing a variety of behavioral norms in the EHS arena, a substantial and growing array of voluntary EHS/sustainability expectations apply to companies in different industries. These expectations do not carry the force of law, but they have in many cases been established by stakeholders who can exert substantial influence on company behavior. The following sections describe a few of the more important mechanisms through which major stakeholders are influencing corporate sustainability behavior.

Industry Codes of Conduct

Over the past two decades, the members of several industry and trade organizations have developed codes of conduct and standards for managing ES&G issues. Some of these now explicitly identify sustainability as an overall industry/policy goal. Examples include the Responsible Care program, jointly operated by 53 mostly national-level chemical associations around the world (ICCA and Responsible Care, 2008), and the Sustainable Forestry Initiative (SFI) and the Forest Stewardship Council-US standards that have been adopted (one or the other, or both) throughout the U.S. forest products industry (SFI, 2010; FSC-US, 2010). These programs provide comprehensive frameworks for addressing the major environmental/sustainability issues facing their respective industries. Both reflect major advances in EHS management principles (described in Chapter 5) and are tailored to reflect industry-specific circumstances. For example, Responsible Care devotes significant attention to working with customers (chemical buyers) to ensure that members' products are being used safely and responsibly. In contrast, forest products programs focus essentially no attention on the ultimate end use of forest products. Instead, they detail the approaches to be taken to maintain long-term forest and ecosystem health and productivity. They also ensure that products carrying a program label are rigorously tracked through a detailed chain-of-custody process. A number of other, less expansive programs have been developed by other industry and trade groups, many of which focus on small to medium-sized enterprises. Examples include associations representing the print graphic industry (graphic designers and sign manufacturers), direct marketers, and many others.

Voluntary Standards

Consensus-based, internationally developed standards largely defined and developed by the business community have been a feature of the commercial landscape for many decades. Whether widely understood or otherwise, these voluntary standards and guidelines have been developed and used to define a wide range of product and process specifications. These range from the prosaic (standard thickness of plate glass) to the highly technical (laser surgery techniques). The general intent of these standards is to promote international trade and the unencumbered movement of goods and services among countries. This reflects the understanding within the business community (and among national governments) that achieving consensus on a variety of standard characteristics and approaches helps lower costs and eliminate inefficiencies and therefore is in everyone's best interest. The major source of these consensus international standards has been the International Organization for Standardization (ISO), based in Geneva, and its sister organization, the International Electrotechnical Commission (IEC). For many decades, ISO/IEC quietly went about their business, working primarily with technical experts in industry and government. In the process, they developed and disseminated many thousands of standards and guidelines across a broad span of commercial activity.[12] Beginning in the 1990s, however, ISO decided to branch out from its successful development of quality management standards[13] to address the emerging field of environmental management. The rest, as the saying goes, is history. In relatively short order, and working through its international committee structure, ISO produced an entire series of voluntary standards and guidelines addressing various aspects of environmental management. ISO standards and/or guidelines now address such issues as formal environmental management systems, auditing, product labeling, environmental performance evaluation, life cycle analysis, greenhouse gas accounting, and a variety of others. Other analogous standards exist, whether developed by ISO or by other national or international bodies, for managing health and safety (OSHAS 18000 series), greenhouse gas accounting (PAS 2050, WRI/WBCSD protocols), and even social responsibility (ISO 26000). In addition, public sector entities have developed voluntary programs that generally offer an assortment of benefits in return for attaining conformance with a set of defined standards. Examples include OSHA's Voluntary Protection Program (VPP), the EPA's Energy Star and SmartWay Transport programs, and a variety of others. The lineage of these programs dates from the mid- to late 1990s, meaning that the concepts they reflect are established and widely accepted. Although these standards are, strictly speaking, voluntary, corporate executives and managers should understand that in a variety of circumstances, conformance with one or more of them may be a condition of doing business in particular markets or with certain entities. Moreover, as discussed in Chapter 5, many of the approaches listed or recommended in these standards and guidelines have been shown to be workable, effective, and flexible in application. When used correctly and adroitly, they can help create efficiencies, improve quality, reduce costs, and confer other tangible business benefits.

Supply Chain Obligations

As discussed in several other places in this book, companies are becoming much more demanding in terms of what product, process, and company operating attributes they are willing to accept from their suppliers. Some of these requirements have emerged from new regulatory requirements from other geographies, notably Europe. Others reflect a desire among larger companies in a sector to reduce the life cycle EHS footprint of their own products and services. An early example of this occurred about ten years ago. The "Detroit three" automobile manufacturers issued individual decrees over a short span of time requiring all their primary suppliers to implement a formal environmental management system (EMS) and to obtain certification to the ISO 14001 EMS standard.[14] The consequence was that over a two-year period, hundreds of small and medium-sized companies had to develop and deploy a new way of evaluating and managing their environmental issues. For some, this was a completely new topic with which they had no experience or existing expertise. Despite the predictions of many observers, the vast majority of the affected suppliers were able to meet the new customer mandates, generally without extreme disruption or new costs.[15] The same dynamic took hold in the microelectronics industry in the 1990s, in which continued access to important European markets depended on having production facilities registered to the ISO 14001 standard.

More recently, legislative requirements have been enacted in Europe and elsewhere that require the phaseout of certain materials. The European Union (EU) issued the Restriction of Hazardous Substances (RoHS) directive in 2003, and it took effect in 2006. This directive places severe restrictions on the use of six hazardous materials[16] in the manufacture of electronic and electrical equipment. It is closely linked to the Waste Electrical and Electronic Equipment (WEEE) directive, which sets collection, recycling, and recovery targets for electrical goods and places responsibility for meeting them on the product manufacturer. These directives apply to any business that sells applicable electronic products, subassemblies, or components directly in EU countries, or that sells to resellers, distributors, or integrators that in turn sell products within EU countries. The EU also has put in place a far more sweeping environmental directive aimed at reducing risks from chemical use more generally—the Registration, Evaluation, and Authorization of Chemicals (REACH) regulation. REACH places responsibility for the safety of chemicals on manufacturers. It also seeks to develop a more extensive body of public knowledge on the more than 100,000 chemicals currently in use in European markets. Producers and importers of more than small quantities of chemicals will be required to register these substances and provide information to a new pan-European chemicals management agency. This agency has the authority to restrict chemical use in cases in which such use is found to pose a danger (European Commission, 2006).

Finally, some high-profile initiatives have begun to better understand and manage the EHS aspects of the supply chain for a variety of goods, particularly consumer products. None of these is more prominent or potentially far-reaching than the Sustainable Sourcing project sponsored by Walmart. The company uses its market power to drive behavioral change in hundreds (if not thousands) of consumer goods manufacturers and other suppliers. Walmart asks all of its more than 100,000 suppliers to complete a 15-question sustainability assessment. The company also formed a consortium to build a database with life cycle analysis results for a variety of products. Finally, Walmart developed and provides product-level information to its customers.[17] More generally, the field of life cycle analysis and the inclusion of upstream EHS considerations in evaluating the sustainability of products and services have gained substantial momentum during the past few years. As discussed in Chapter 6, sophisticated ES&G investors commonly use life cycle perspectives. Also, a growing number of multinational companies are evaluating the contributions of their supply chains to their overall EHS and social impact. These developments have been accompanied by increasing activity in the public sector (such as by the EPA) as well as the nongovernmental organization (NGO) community focused on product life cycle tools and information.

Other examples may be found in somewhat unexpected places, as described in the following sidebar.

Toward More Sustainable Utilities?

Sandy Nessing is the Managing Director of Sustainability and ESH Strategy and Design at American Electric Power (AEP). AEP is one of the nation's largest electric utility companies, as well as one its largest emitters of greenhouse gases. Sandy describes some of the recent changes in her industry, which is not often thought of as particularly dynamic or (incorrectly) particularly attentive to important environmental issues:

"Companies like AEP and PG&E in the electric utility industry are bringing industry along. These companies, and their leaders, are competitive. What we are seeing now is that industry laggards are beginning to talk with stakeholders and make other changes from long-standing behavior. This approach is affecting other industries too. We have been conducting surveys of our coal suppliers and are now seeing companies in the coal industry work on sustainability reports for the first time. Peer pressure is becoming more important in terms of sustainability expectations. At the same time, there is more collaboration. We have started a sustainability supply chain initiative involving utilities and coal suppliers."

(Nessing, 2011)

It remains to be seen what will ultimately emerge from this initiative and others like it. I believe that such collaborative efforts will be crucial to moving the needle on such important and complex issues as progressing toward a less carbon-intensive and more sustainable energy infrastructure.

Consumer Demands

Real demand for environmentally sound or beneficial products by U.S. consumers is notoriously unreliable. A variety of studies conducted over the past few decades have shown that most Americans espouse an interest in low-impact, "green," or otherwise more sustainable products. But relatively few are willing to either expend significant effort to find such products or pay more for them than for conventional alternatives. More than a few companies have stumbled or experienced disappointing results in attempting to launch new green products or brands. With that said, recent studies of consumer attitudes and behaviors seem to show growing acceptance of the idea that more environmentally sound products can be manufactured in ways that yield all the desired attributes (such as initial quality and durability) at an equivalent cost. Moreover, as the life-cycle attributes of products become more widely understood, more people are expressing a willingness to incur greater acquisition costs in return for lower operating costs over time, along with reduced environmental impacts. Recent public opinion surveys show that a large majority (more than five to one) of Americans hold corporations responsible for ensuring product quality and safety, worker health and safety, proper product disposal/recycling, human rights protection, reducing energy use and pollutant emissions, and preserving natural resources (Cone, Inc., 2010).

More specifically, a recent large, global survey conducted on behalf of the National Geographic Society (Globescan, 2009) yielded some interesting findings about prevailing attitudes and behaviors among U.S. consumers:

- A substantial majority of American respondents disagreed with the statement that "Environmentally friendly products do not work well." (55 percent disagreed or disagreed strongly, and 14 percent agreed or agreed strongly.)
- Slightly more than half indicated a willingness to pay more for an energy-saving product if it saved money over the long term.
- Twice as many agreed that they are currently trying very hard to reduce their negative impact on the environment as disagreed (42 percent versus 19 percent).
- Twenty-one percent agreed or strongly agreed that "Companies and industries are currently working very hard to make sure that we have a clean environment in my country," and 36 percent disagreed or strongly disagreed.
- A majority (61 percent) agreed or strongly agreed that American society will need to consume far less to improve the environment for future generations, and only 12 percent disagreed or strongly disagreed.
- Members of media and marketing firms are viewed skeptically. Thirty-eight percent of U.S. respondents agreed or strongly agreed that these organizations encourage environmentally irresponsible consumption, and only 24 percent disagreed or strongly disagreed.

These findings suggest that both risk and opportunity exist for firms in evaluating the EHS and broader sustainability aspects of their products and services. On one hand, there appear to be growing expectations that companies will take appropriate steps to reduce the EHS footprints of their operations (and products). Moreover, consumers appear to have some level of interest in having access to more sustainably produced goods and services. At the same time, there is a high level of wariness and even skepticism about green/sustainability marketing and claims. There also is a continuing unwillingness to either accept compromises in product quality or function or to pay substantially higher prices for perceived sustainability performance advantages.

Many of the expectations expressed through industry codes of conduct, supply chain obligations, and consumer demand have the practical effect of becoming de facto business requirements. In the case of a number of the industry codes, adopting these programs and complying with their provisions is a condition of membership in the sponsoring trade associations. Similarly, many major companies are inserting various product composition, energy efficiency, labor practice, disclosure, and other requirements into their standard vendor/ supplier contracts. This means that conformance to the customer company's sustainability requirements is a required condition for a continuing business relationship. Increasingly, larger customer-facing corporations are moving aggressively down this path, which will have the effect of propagating demands for more sustainable practices much more rapidly and widely than would be the case otherwise. Finally, American consumers en masse are not yet demanding improved sustainability performance from companies in any formal way. Nor are they demonstrating a widespread willingness to "vote with their wallets" on this issue. However, it seems clear that public attention to the issue is growing. Firms that can deliver appealing, cost-effective goods and services with an improved set of environmental and/or social attributes may find significant opportunities to capture new customers, revenues, and profits. In contrast, firms that are inattentive to sustainability issues as a major concern of their customers may be taking unnecessary risks with their brand value, pricing power, and revenue streams.

Costs and Cost Structure

The costs of complying with EHS, social, and other requirements and expectations can be significant. Many large companies have been obliged to invest substantial sums of money to bring their operations into compliance; maintain them there; and pursue additional, incremental performance improvements and initiatives focused on unregulated endpoints. In the early days of the EHS regulatory control system, as noted earlier, the prospective costs of compliance prompted no small amount of resistance from the regulated community. Over time, and as the initial upheaval associated with the new way of looking at EHS issues subsided, the prevailing view came to be that compliance was simply a cost of doing business. Viewed in that light, the issue became how to comply with regulations in the most cost-effective manner. In time, many companies and their service providers became quite skilled at developing and deploying innovative measures to reduce costs, often through a new focus on preventing pollution at the source. As discussed elsewhere in this book, this principle is now at the core of not only U.S. national policy but also the EHS management activities of most leading corporations. Nonetheless, certain obligations remain for many businesses, as do a number of additional expectations that, as discussed previously, are increasingly being brought to bear.

The point here is not to debate whether the imposition of compliance and other costs through sustainability requirements and expectations is reasonable, fair, or justified on its merits. My view is that with few exceptions, those issues have already been settled in the affirmative. Rather, the purpose here is to illustrate that EHS management and other sustainability program costs can be substantial, should be understood by those in decision-making roles within companies, and must be managed actively by those charged with overseeing and deploying corporate sustainability programs. The following discussion follows some conventions developed and articulated by one of my former colleagues, Paul Bailey, and his project team in an influential guidance document issued by the EPA in the mid-1990s (USEPA, 1995). The terms and organizational structure used in this document in many ways parallel similar industry-developed works (GEMI, 1994). These concepts have stood the test of time. To my knowledge, they have not been superseded or displaced by any alternative conceptual framework(s) in the many years since they were developed.

In the first category are *conventional costs*. These include the following:

- **Capital expenditures.** Compliance with our major pollution control and waste management regulations and, to some extent, health and safety regulations often requires the installation of new pieces of equipment to capture, segregate, treat, and/or store pollutants or wastes. Prior to regulation, facilities typically discharged these materials into the air or water, or piled them on or buried them under the land surface. Depending on its type, configuration, and scale, designing, procuring, installing, and testing this pollution control/safety equipment can cost tens of millions of dollars at a particular location. In some situations the need for such equipment cannot feasibly be avoided. But because many industrial processes invariably generate emissions, waste, and other nonproduct outputs, the focus today is on designing production processes and delivery systems with one or more of the following attributes:

- They incorporate material and energy efficiencies.

- They minimize the use of problematic (expensive-to-manage) materials.

- They recover waste or spent materials, reagents, supplies, equipment, and other production byproducts (such as waste heat).

When successfully and artfully applied, these steps yield required pollution control/safety equipment that is smaller in scale, less complex and energy/labor-intensive, safer, and less costly than it would be otherwise. Ideally, and in more than a few cases, thoughtful design and engineering may result in pollutant emission and/or waste generation rates that are below the applicable regulatory standards. In such cases, the company can not only avoid official scrutiny from one important type of stakeholder, but, as described in a moment, avoid a panoply of other costs.

- **Operating costs.** Whether or not a company is required to make substantial capital outlays for pollution control equipment or other assets, developing and maintaining effective ES&G management systems and programs requires ongoing effort and some level of investment. Operating costs can arise from a number of sources. These can range from replacing pollutant filtration media or filters, to energy and, often, water required to operate pollution control equipment, to compliance and system audits, to the firm's professional EHS staff. The magnitude of these costs and the complexity of the management challenge involved in carrying out all appropriate activities in an optimal, cost-effective manner vary widely. Nonetheless, it is fair to say that neither is trivial in most companies of significant size, even if they are not active in resource-intensive industries. This category includes materials, labor, supplies, utilities, and depreciation for structures and equipment.

A second and important but widely underrecognized general category of ongoing regular, or episodic, costs are *potentially hidden costs*. These are associated with activities that are difficult to link to a particular product line or business. Typically, these costs are accumulated in overhead accounts, where they are difficult to find, properly assign, manage, and reduce. Potentially hidden costs take several different forms:

- **Upfront costs** are expenses incurred prior to the operation of a new process or system. They include such tasks as siting, designing pollution control equipment, evaluating environmentally preferable alternatives, preparing bid specifications, qualifying suppliers, and evaluating bids. These costs may be allocated to overhead and research and development or be embedded in the installed cost of new fixed assets.

- **Regulatory and voluntary program costs.** Whether required by legal mandate or performed voluntarily, many EHS management activities require staff time and other resources. The list of such potential costs is long and includes such compliance items as notification, monitoring/testing, studies and/or modeling, site remediation, record-keeping, training, inspections, labeling, medical surveillance, emergency preparedness, EHS insurance, financial assurance (to cover hazardous waste management activities), and storm water management. Voluntary activities may include community outreach, auditing, public disclosure, habitat/wetland delineation and protection, landscaping, recycling, and research and development.

- **Back-end costs.** At the end of their productive life, pollution control and other EHS-related structures and equipment generally must be shut down or closed and dismantled. Depending on the activities taking place in and around these assets, the closure process may be regulated and may need to be conducted in a specific manner. For example, on-site laboratories, landfills, chemical storage tanks, and other production and storage units may be subject to specific requirements. A panoply of specific closure (and even post-closure care) requirements apply to on-site waste management units. During their working lives, the costs of managing such units at the end of their useful lives are prospective. With the notable exception of formal closure and post-closure care requirements in the waste management arena, such back-end costs may not be explicitly considered or factored into ongoing management decision making.

In an entirely different but nonetheless important category are *contingent costs*. These are costs associated with activities that are highly uncertain as to how extensive they may be, whether they will be required, and, if so, when. Such contingent costs depend on an unexpected and undesirable event or outcome occurring. This then requires a response from the affected company, either to comply with a regulatory or legal directive or to voluntarily take responsibility for its actions. Examples include fines and penalties for noncompliance episodes, site remediation, cleanup of spills or other unplanned releases, legal expenses, damage to natural resources, and injuries to workers and/or people in surrounding communities.

One final category in the EPA framework is worthy of mention—*image and relationship costs*. These are discussed next.

Clearly, any rational corporate decision-making process regarding EHS and broader sustainability initiatives and programs should consider the costs of the various alternatives to pursuing the firm's sustainability vision and goals. It is important in doing so to understand and evaluate current and prospective costs from all the perspectives outlined here, even in the absence of perfect or complete information. Many less-than-optimal decisions have been made over the years by well-meaning companies that have not adequately considered some of the hidden and/or contingent costs of both the *status quo* and potential options for improving their EHS posture and performance. Those involved in sustainability efforts in a corporate setting should therefore work to ensure that all the appropriate perspectives (and all the people with the required expertise) are involved in the evaluation and decision-making process.

Revenue Impacts

Given the foregoing discussion of relationships between sustainability concerns and competitive position, market access, product acceptability/appeal to customers, and many other factors, it should come as no surprise that nontrivial impacts on revenue can result if a company performs at levels that are substantially above or below the norm for its industry. Revenue impacts arise for one or more of the following reasons:

- **Market/customer access.** As discussed earlier, continuing access to certain geographic markets or customer types may be adversely affected by the absence of a particular EHS management practice (such as ISO 14001 certification), one or more product attributes (such as the presence of prohibited substance(s) or material(s) sourced from a controversial location), or company participation in a particular activity (use of animal testing, for example). In any event, loss of access to either existing or potential new customers has direct and deleterious impacts on an affected company's revenue stream in the present, the future, or both. These impacts can potentially be significant.

- **Competitive dynamics.** Increasingly, customers, suppliers, consumers, and other stakeholders are becoming aware of and attentive to which companies appear to be taking a responsible and effective stance with regard to ES&G issues and which are not. These emerging expectations may shift the competitive balance of power in some industries. Companies that may not have been thought of as best-in-class can show that they are in firm control of their sustainability issues and, therefore, worthy of respect. Others may have enjoyed a stronger position due to size, geographic reach, technology, customer relationships, or other factors, but have been slow to adapt to changing expectations in the ES&G arena. As expectations for sustainable business behavior expand further, the latter firms may increasingly find their position in the industry "pecking order" eroding in favor of the former firms.

- **Time to market/flexibility.** Experience over the past couple of decades has shown that companies taking a more progressive and sophisticated approach to managing ES&G issues often reap significant advantages relative to their competitors. This is true because their behavior confers a certain level of trust that simply is absent in the stakeholder relationships of companies that have not taken such approaches. Such firms may, for example, find that they can successfully site and build new facilities or expand existing ones more quickly than competitors that do not possess the same level of public trust. Similar considerations may apply to obtaining approvals for permit modifications (needed in some cases to substantially alter production processes/schedules) and other production/operating practices that are subject to public oversight. This topic is explored in greater depth in Chapter 4.

- **Pricing power.** In similar fashion, firms enjoying a high level of trust and perceived integrity from their customers have a greater ability to raise prices when indicated (such as to protect margins as input commodity prices increase) and to hold the line on prices during economic contractions or in response to growing competitive pressure. Corporate America is now very much focused on the value of brands. Building and protecting one's brand(s) is widely viewed as an important means of building a company that will be stable and successful (sustainable) over the long term. Moreover, strong brands have particular value in commanding higher prices for one's offerings relative to otherwise similar goods and services. This is a primary reason why Tide laundry detergent, Colgate toothpaste, Levi's jeans, and a vast array of other products sell at a price premium in comparison with store brands or generic competitors.[18] Increasingly, corporate sustainability posture and the specific ES&G attributes of individual products and product lines are being used to bolster company brands. This attracts new customers, builds loyalty among existing customers, and creates distinctions in the customer's mind that can be used to command higher prices. The recent upsurge in advertising focusing on the "green" attributes of a variety of products and services suggests that this trend will only increase in the years ahead.

Importantly, however, the forthcoming availability of far more information on the supply chain EHS attributes of many consumer products (described earlier) will help customers (both businesses and consumers) understand which firms and products have more favorable ES&G characteristics and which do not. This shift toward more of a fact-based dialog on sustainability characteristics will favor firms with the performance to back up their claims and market image and will work to the disadvantage of companies that seek to build their brands primarily through advertising and public relations. That is, substance will trump image.

Organizational Strength and Capability

A company's sustainability posture and performance have a number of effects on its ability to anticipate and effectively address business risks and opportunities as well as its resilience in the face of the inevitable surprises that characterize the business landscape. The degree to which the firm and its senior management understand and address emerging EHS, social, and governance issues can have a material impact on many of the key determinants of a company's strength and capability.

Staff Morale, Enthusiasm, and Creativity

People want to feel that they are valued, respected, and trusted. They also want to feel that the company they are working for embodies values that are familiar and not in conflict with those that govern their personal lives. One school of thought holds that employees cannot be trusted and must be managed closely if they are to reach and maintain acceptable quality and productivity levels. But my experience (and much management literature) suggests an alternative interpretation. I have found that people are far more effective, productive, and innovative if they feel that they have a stake in the company's success, are treated fairly, are allowed to operate with some autonomy (with appropriate accountability), and are part of a team. As we have shifted during the past 50 years or so from an industrial to an information economy, people and what they offer have become the principal assets of most firms. Even companies in capital-intensive industries must have the right people to succeed over time. This means that some of the policies, commitments, management approaches, and values discussed in this book (introduced in Chapter 5) are becoming increasingly necessary to leverage and obtain maximum value from the firm's most important assets—its employees. This is particularly true with the emergence of the millennial generation into the workforce. For them, traditional, hierarchical management approaches are particularly uncomfortable.

Treating your people right is not a sign of weakness or a luxury. It is a vital component of any sensible path toward the long-term success and sustainability of any organization. Behaving in a contrary fashion at the least virtually ensures that the firm (and its collective assets) will not achieve the throughput, efficiency, quality, innovation, or productivity of which it is capable. And this behavior inevitably will generate inferior financial returns over time.

Recruitment and Retention

In similar fashion, people are attracted to companies with supportive, even if challenging, working conditions. Most people are not deterred by the expectation that they will need to work hard. But they also want to know that their labors will serve a productive purpose and be recognized and appreciated. Although some people are drawn to the cutthroat environments that often exist in some lines of business (such as large law firms and brokerages), I believe most prefer an environment in which they can contribute and collaborate, both with their immediate colleagues and with the larger organization. They also like to feel pride (not embarrassment) when they tell their family and friends about the new company for which they will work. No one wants to feel that his or her employer is irresponsible; incapable of complying or unwilling to comply with the law; does not value its people, customers, business partners, or the community in which it operates; or places "the numbers" above all else when making business decisions.

People can vote with their feet. In a society with as much professional and social mobility as the U.S., it may not be difficult under normal economic conditions for a company's most valued employees to find employment alternatives if they are dissatisfied, for any reason, with their employer. Moreover, the next generation has been raised during an era in which (contrary to my own life experience) it is widely accepted that corporations have an obligation to operate in a responsible manner. Companies that offer a solid ES&G posture and evidence of strong performance may be much more attractive to graduating students and others entering or reentering the workforce than those that do not. Young people tend to be idealistic. I've encountered very few who would prefer to accept a job with a company that has proven to be recalcitrant in meeting its obligations rather than a similar job with a recognized leader in labor practices, environmental management, or sustainability. As companies increasingly compete on the basis of ideas and the quality of their people, it will become ever more important for them to be able to attract and retain the best talent on the basis of, among other factors, their ES&G posture and performance.

Staff Capability, Flexibility, and Resourcefulness

Operating a business in a market economy is an intrinsically dynamic, even unstable, undertaking. Business conditions are continually changing, as a function of general economic cycles, domestic and international political events, legislative and regulatory developments, technological change, evolving customer needs and expectations, competitive dynamics, and many other factors. This has always been true, but the rate at which changes continue to occur appears to have accelerated during the past decade or so. It has been fueled by advances in information technology, the explosive growth in developing countries (particularly the BRIC[19] nations), and dramatic expansion of international trade and finance. In this dynamic business environment, it is vitally important for businesses, and their employees, to be able to perceive and understand evolving trends, formulate appropriate response strategies, and execute action plans. As many of us who are well into our careers have experienced or witnessed firsthand, the days of the 40-year tenure with one company, and the job that is essentially the same in year 15 as it was in year 2, are over. And it is quite unlikely that they will ever return. Today's (and tomorrow's) successful professional will be able to tolerate ambiguity, move from one task or function to another quickly and smoothly, and accept and effectively respond to sudden changes in priorities. These skills will become more important as ES&G issues become increasingly prominent within a growing number of companies.

As described in subsequent chapters of this book, taking the appropriate steps to understand and actively manage the company's ES&G issues will enable the firm to enhance the perspectives and skills of key employees across a number of important business functions, thereby helping them develop two important attributes:

- Greater insight and effectiveness in responding to today's challenges

- An improved ability to recognize future developments, think expansively and creatively about how they might affect the firm, and define and execute appropriate responses

Organizational Resilience

In parallel with and based on the development of employee-level capability, companies as a whole will need to become better able to cope with sudden and substantial change. They also must be able to recover from the occasional setbacks that every firm experiences. This organizational resilience is a function of the firm's values, culture, infrastructure, and employee capability. The active pursuit of sustainability offers numerous opportunities for companies to examine their core strengths and areas for improvement through an expanded but sharper perspective. They also can take appropriate actions to ensure that the best of the organization's traditions and positive attributes are strengthened, aligned, and propagated as appropriate. Firms that view these "soft" corporate assets through the lens of ES&G issues will almost invariably discover new ways in which they can leverage who they are and what they do in response to emerging EHS, social, and governance issues. Companies, and their leaders, that do not avail themselves of this perspective may soon find themselves running organizations that seem to increasingly be one step behind the competition in addressing the expectations of major stakeholders and society at large.

Intellectual Capital

As is widely understood in the business community, a key source of competitive advantage today is the firm's ideas, methods, inventions, technologies, information, and other forms of intellectual capital. Indeed, as discussed at length in Chapter 6, intellectual capital and other "intangible" assets represent an increasingly large share of the future revenue and earnings potential of the typical firm. The emergence of ES&G issues as important drivers of business behavior may impose some constraints on the use of existing intellectual capital in some cases, but it is far more likely that these issues provide more upside potential than risk. As particular EHS and social issues become more prominent both generally and in the context of particular industries, products, and services, they can provide new opportunities for firms to distinguish themselves. Companies can become better able to mitigate any existing concerns, develop fundamentally new and improved approaches for product/service delivery, and identify and develop new customers and market segments. Firms that are skillful in applying their existing intellectual capital in response to evolving ES&G issues will be able to generate incremental cash flows (or protect existing revenue streams). Numerous opportunities also exist for companies of all types and sizes to establish new methods, approaches, products, and services that exploit new market niches formed explicitly through the emergence of these issues.

Customer and Supplier Relationships

As discussed earlier, it is widely recognized that taking care of one's customers is a vital function of any business enterprise. Increasingly, very large, influential consumer-facing businesses are becoming both more interested in their life cycle ES&G impacts and committed to reducing substantial impacts at whatever point in the life cycle they arise. At this juncture, all signs point to increasing scrutiny across the supply chain applied to the EHS, social, and governance performance of both large and small companies, both domestically and internationally. (If your firm has not yet received one or more surveys requesting information on a variety of energy usage, environmental performance, and management practices topics, you will soon.) Accordingly, executives and managers in companies of all sizes and types should become more attuned to and informed about these issues. At the least, they should do some contingency planning to address some of the more probable outcomes of the spread of new customer-generated ES&G mandates. At the same time, and as explained in detail in Chapter 5, executives in companies that seek to improve their ES&G posture and performance may want to consider examining their own supply chains. Doing so will help them gain a better understanding of the full EHS and social footprint of their firm's products and services.

Business and Financial Risks

Finally, it is vitally important for business leaders and managers to understand that today, even in the absence of new demands, disruptions, or crises, ES&G issues are imposing a substantial number of business risks and limitations that may have nontrivial financial consequences. Once again, the increasing scrutiny being applied to many of these issues magnifies and compounds these risks and increases the probability that they will occur and be of significant magnitude. It's indisputable that global human populations are still growing rapidly, many vital natural resources are threatened or under duress,[20] and, thus far, national and international institutions have not been particularly effective at alleviating the stress placed on important natural systems. Therefore, it is reasonable to expect that the operational and financial risks experienced by many types of businesses will only increase during the decades ahead. These factors are evident as we sit here today.

What is less visible and could accurately be described as the "tip of the iceberg" is the full impact of the changes in the global climate that will almost certainly unfold during the coming decades. These changes are already beginning to exert documented and often severe impacts. As temperature changes continue, we can expect to experience a substantial increase in sea level; regional and global shifts in agricultural productivity (and, hence, future production), water availability, and, eventually, human populations; and changes in weather patterns, among many other impacts. By and large, corporations are just now beginning to consider the implications of these scenarios and how they will both adapt to the physical changes occurring in their host countries and communities and succeed in a carbon-constrained economy. Company executives and managers would be well-advised to devote some attention and resources to examining these issues, if they have not done so already.

Among others, the following types of business risks appear to be prominent, given recent events and current trends.

Supply Interruptions

Periodic disruptions of key supplies, subassemblies, raw materials, and other production inputs are a fact of life in many manufacturing and industrial operations. Most larger companies have developed sophisticated procurement, inventory control, quality, and related processes to minimize these disruptions. Many firms have built supplier networks offering redundant capacity to alleviate any discontinuity in receiving what they need when they need it. What is changing, however, is that many materials that have been widely, if not universally, available at low or no cost are becoming more scarce. For the first time, company executives in a number of industries are beginning to confront the possibility that vital resources that they have always taken for granted may not be available for their firm's use. No resource used by business (or humankind generally) is more universally used or more important than water. Yet companies are increasingly confronting the reality that their access to sufficient quantities of water of acceptable quality is in doubt, particularly as they contemplate expansion into countries in the developing world. Already, firms in industries ranging from electric power generation to soft drink manufacturing are carefully considering their options for addressing this challenge. As suggested before, this is merely the tip of a rather large iceberg.

Material Price Shocks

In similar fashion, prices for key production inputs can rise and fall precipitously as a function of rapidly changing supply and demand conditions.[21] Many companies use derivatives and other means of hedging to blunt the impact of possible sudden price changes in key inputs. But the possibility, even likelihood, of new, previously unrecognized sources of price volatility should give pause to business executives and managers across a wide swath of industries. As supply constraints develop and ease across a growing array of key commodities and production inputs, it stands to reason that those involved in procurement and supply chain management might want to remain vigilant. A steep and sudden rise in key input prices can leave a company with a challenging dilemma. It can pay the higher price, which can crimp or eliminate its margins on a given set of products (unless it can raise its own prices). Or it can step down production until less-costly supplies (or alternative inputs) can be found or developed, thereby possibly foregoing sales and market share. As we have moved decisively to more of a just-in-time orientation across the entire U.S. economy, the impacts of input material price volatility have become more pronounced. As mentioned previously, because supplies of a substantial number of inputs provided by the ambient environment are becoming increasingly constrained, we can expect that their prices will inexorably rise and become more volatile. Accordingly, business executives in many industries will need to become much more knowledgeable of and attuned to their firms' ES&G exposures. They will have to take appropriate actions to ensure that their companies are positioned appropriately and have the necessary internal capability to address these trends.

Political Instability

To lesser and greater extents, the world has always been a dangerous place. The U.S. has enjoyed roughly 65 years of political stability and dominance in international affairs, but the situation in many other countries has been far more unsettled. During the past few decades, we have witnessed, for example, the demise of the Soviet Union and, on a smaller but far more violent scale, Yugoslavia. We have seen the advent and growth of international, stateless terrorism and the failure of entire societies (Afghanistan, Somalia). Most recently, the Arab Spring has deposed long-serving, autocratic leaders in several Middle Eastern countries. This type of instability generally is not conducive to conducting business, with certain notable exceptions.[22] There is no particular reason to believe, however, that the recent volatility we have observed will diminish, given the existence and aggressiveness of several rogue states (Iran, North Korea), the continuing and dramatic economic growth and accompanying desire for power and influence in many developing countries, and the changing awareness and expectations of people around the world. In particular, the world's poor and their advocates are increasingly demanding a place at the table (politically and economically) and, in an encouraging development, democracy and self-determination. In other words, as discussed in Chapter 2, *sustainable development* remains an important unmet need. We can expect, and senior executives in well-run companies should plan for, continual, sporadic political unrest as the supply and quality of critical natural resource-based commodities becomes more constrained in the years ahead. Already, there have been massive protests in many developing countries over increases in food prices (some of which were triggered, or at least exacerbated, by diversion of corn to ethanol production for use as motor vehicle fuel). Such unrest will likely be a consistent feature of the business landscape in developing countries during the next few decades. This may trigger political instability in countries that to this point have been friendly to U.S.-based multinationals and their interests. Concerns over natural resources and food are likely to be a primary concern. Indeed, no one should be surprised if a war erupts during the next 50 years over water—either over control of a discrete water resource or in response to mass migrations of people in search of an adequate supply. The best defense against the unanticipated, adverse business impacts of such developments is to ensure that your firm understands and is taking adequate steps to manage its risks (and opportunities) related to natural resource-related and broader ES&G issues.

Fixed Asset Impairment

Finally, on a different note, many companies operating in businesses in which capital investment requirements are substantial may face a number of unanticipated risks from evolving ES&G expectations. In many industrial and manufacturing operations, production equipment and other fixed assets are physically large; expensive to design, build, install, and commission; long-lived (a useful life of decades); and impractical to move. Examples include metal smelters, iron and steel mills, cement plants, pulp/paper mills, and chemical plants. Many of these industrial facilities, being highly resource- and energy-intensive, are already highly regulated. That is, their pollutant emission, waste management, and occupational safety practices typically are subject to permit conditions and/or requirements stipulating particular operating practices. As discussed earlier, the system of EHS regulations that we have developed during the past few decades is largely complete. This does not mean, however, that this system is completely static. New regulations continue to be promulgated, both to address gaps in the existing system and to revisit existing standards to ensure that they are achieving the desired ends.[23] Achieving compliance with some of these new standards (which, if history is any guide, will be more stringent than current requirements) may require the installation of new pollution control equipment that may be costly. Of greater concern is the possibility that for older plants and production technologies, the costs of compliance (such as achieving the required control efficiency or pollutant emission rate) may simply be impossible in a cost-effective way.[24] This outcome could render the entire plant noneconomic, meaning that the company could then have a major, immovable, essentially valueless asset and tens or hundreds of millions of dollars in stranded costs.

The implication is that leaders and managers in companies with any significant fixed asset base should be attentive to growing expectations for improved ES&G performance. They should not be surprised if and as these expectations become mandates. In particular, the issue that is front and center in this regard is climate change and the possibility that we will be transitioning to a carbon-constrained economy in the foreseeable future. The current political situation in the U.S. makes the enactment of a climate change law unlikely during the next few years. But corporate executives would be unwise to believe (much less stake a company's future on) that establishing a market price for greenhouse gas emissions is either inappropriate or anything less than inevitable. The simple truth is that the issue is too important and the need for substantial, uniform, nationwide public policy too great and urgent for delays in taking action to continue for much longer. Many business leaders are positioning their firms for a world in which careful management of greenhouse gas emissions and their principal source, fossil fuel consumption, is essential for success. It is worth noting that the leaders of many companies in energy-intensive businesses such as electric power production, cement manufacturing, and metals production are among them. They have provided examples that many others would be wise to follow.

This chapter has articulated, at a general level, some of the many ways in which ES&G issues can affect companies' business prospects, organizational strength, revenues, cash flows, and earnings potential. It also has illustrated how such impacts will become more likely to occur and grow in magnitude in the years ahead. The next chapter examines the source of many of the growing expectations for more sustainable corporate behavior. It describes the major stakeholders that have an interest in corporate ES&G management behavior and performance and their primary concerns.

Endnotes

1. Technically, some of these laws took the form of major amendments to previously enacted laws, most of which had been shown to have little effect. In some cases, these preexisting statutes were renamed to more fully capture their expanded intent and scope.

2. For example, just a few years earlier, momentous civil rights legislation in the form of the Civil Rights Act and Voting Rights Act had been enacted.

3. Indeed, in some of the major statutes, the implementing agency (EPA) was explicitly prohibited from considering costs when deciding what to regulate or how stringent to make the associated controls.

4. With that said, the system has some widely recognized problems, among them numerous organizational "silos"; substantial, even excessive bureaucracy; and, in recent years, serious budget constraints. All of these factors limit the effectiveness and efficiency of our public sector institutions charged with protecting human health and the environment.

5. Such challenges fell away within a few years. In relatively short order, the major statutes and the authority applied by EPA, OSHA, and other newly created agencies to impose and enforce regulations were upheld by the courts. And to address the occasional recalcitrant site owner or manager, inspectors and other regulatory agency personnel were helped by law enforcement personnel (such as federal marshals) as required. Such assistance is rarely required today.

6. As explicitly stated in the *Pollution Prevention Act of 1990* (PL 101-508) at Sec. 6602(b), "Policy.—The congress hereby declares it the national policy of the United States that pollution should be prevented or reduced at the source whenever feasible..."

7. Although it did not produce the ultimate outcome that it was designed to accomplish, Kyoto did motivate governments and industries in many countries around the world to focus on and reduce their greenhouse gas emissions. The treaty and its terms will officially expire at the end of 2012. The post-Kyoto regime has yet to be defined.

8. Conversely, when and where a statute addressing a particular issue is in place, there is no opportunity for case law to supersede it. This principle is known as "displacement" or "preemption."

9. Historically, the "line" between waste and in-process materials established by the EPA has been that materials that are inherently "waste-like," that are used in a manner constituting disposal, or that are burned for energy recovery are considered (and regulated as) wastes. Indeed, these distinctions have been retained in a relatively recent rule designed to promote greater recycling and recovery of hazardous secondary materials (73 *FR* 211:64667–64716. 30 October 2008).

10. The Resource Conservation and Recovery Act (RCRA) of 1976 and the Comprehensive Environmental Response, Compensation, and Liability Act (CERCLA), enacted in 1980, as amended provided new and sweeping authority for the EPA to regulate the management of solid and hazardous wastes and compel the cleanup of contaminated waste sites posing a threat to human health and the environment.

11. Indeed, the discussion within many companies in the 1990s in response to these enforcement trends was who was to become the "designated defendant" if an environmental enforcement action were to be taken.

12. ISO remains quite active, publishing more than 1,000 new or revised standards every year. See www.iso.org/iso/iso_catalogue.htm for further information.

13. ISO published the widely used ISO 9000 series of standards addressing quality in 1987. The ISO 9001 standard for quality management systems has been revised three times since, most recently in 2008.

14. ISO 14001 and EMS are described in depth in Chapter 5.

15. I had the interesting experience of performing ISO 14001 registration audits at a company responding to this mandate. I observed that the process helped them better understand their operations and control potential risks and costs. Existing staff people needed to assume some new roles and expand their existing knowledge. But they found that the new system was not unduly complex or burdensome, even in a firm with no dedicated environmental staff and 46 employees, the vast majority of which were hourly assembly line workers.

16. Specifically, the heavy metals lead, cadmium, mercury, and hexavalent chromium, and the organic flame retardants polybrominated biphenyls and polybrominated diphenyl ether.

17. See http://walmartstores.com/sustainability/9292.aspx for further information.

18. With that said, I recognize that many very strong brands enjoy the reputation that they have precisely because they are discernibly better in terms of customer-relevant attributes than competing offerings.

19. Brazil, Russia, India, and China, which now collectively account for a major share of global economic output, growth, and exports.

20. The Millennium Ecosystem Assessment (MEA) is a multilateral research effort sponsored by the United Nations focused on characterizing the condition of the world's natural systems. According to the MEA, rapidly growing demands for

food, freshwater, timber, fiber, and fuel have resulted in a substantial and largely irreversible loss in the diversity of life on Earth. In addition, MEA researchers found that approximately 60 percent (15 out of 24) of the ecosystem services it examined are being degraded or used unsustainably, including freshwater, capture fisheries, air and water purification, and the regulation of regional and local climate, natural hazards, and pests. See www.maweb.org/en/Condition.aspx for details.

21. Such dramatic price swings also can be exacerbated by the pernicious effects of speculators and traders, thereby undermining one of the great benefits of our established commodity markets: relative price stability.

22. Conflict, particularly the armed conflict and focus on (arguably, obsession with) security in the U.S. that have ensued since 9/11, has yielded a veritable bonanza for weapons producers, security and military services contractors, manufacturers and suppliers of goods used in bulk by the armed services (such as uniforms and motor vehicles), and a variety of other businesses.

23. Those who may be skeptical of the motives of regulators seeking to establish or tighten EHS regulations should understand that the designated agencies are required by statute to periodically reexamine the effectiveness of previously established standards at defined intervals. As discussed earlier in this chapter, if the agency fails to do so, it is virtually certain that it will be sued by an environmental advocacy organization, which will seek a court-imposed mandate compelling action.

24. Under the provisions of most of our major environmental statutes and perhaps contrary to popular belief, regulators do not have the authority to establish pollutant emission controls by fiat or whim. Controls must instead be based on technology that has proven to be effective and that is economically achievable (specific terms and definitions vary by statute). That said, the test for economic viability generally is based on the best-performing plants in each regulated industry or sector, which may use different technologies or methods than other, particularly older, plants. Because newer technology is nearly always more efficient and less polluting than older technology, tighter emission controls may put older plants at a significant disadvantage in terms of the difficulty and cost of attaining compliance.

4

Stakeholder Interests and Influences and the Social License to Operate

As suggested in the previous chapters, the expectations of a number of parties and constituencies regarding appropriate corporate ES&G behaviors have evolved considerably during the past few decades. New expectations concerning particular issues continue to emerge periodically. This chapter begins with a discussion of how leading companies are choosing to define their relationship with the communities in which they operate—the concept of the social license to operate. The chapter continues by identifying the major types of constituencies involved in the continuing debate about corporate ES&G behaviors and describes their influence at a general level. The chapter concludes with a more in-depth examination of the ES&G issues that typically are of greatest interest to each major stakeholder group and the types of influences applied by these stakeholders when their concerns are not adequately addressed.

As described later, in the early years, substantial demands for improved corporate EHS, social, and governance practices generally were issued almost solely from two types of entities. Both of them, in theory, represent the American people. One was the various agencies of government, which operated through the processes described in the preceding chapter. The other was a loose network of nongovernmental organizations (NGOs), many of which came into being during the formative years of the environmental movement. These organizations focused on either broad-spectrum environmental protection or on particular aspects of the natural world (such as wildlife or rain forests). Because most of these NGOs were and are legally organized as nonprofit corporations, they are obliged to operate in a manner that supports certain defined public policy goals, as discussed in Chapter

2. Most of the other types of company stakeholders that are now actively engaged with companies on ES&G issues were largely absent from the debates on these issues. Accordingly, for many years, the public agenda concerning environmental issues was primarily defined by NGOs clamoring for more controls and mandates on one side; corporations and their trade associations resisting new restrictions on the other side; and the EPA, other federal agencies, and Congress in the middle. Our elected representatives and, operating under Congressional directives, executive branch agencies invested vast amounts of time and effort attempting to determine the facts and institute public policies that appropriately protected human health and the environment and also were technically and economically viable and sensible. More often than not, it seemed, the outcomes of this process represented a compromise between two more or less diametrically opposed points of view. This situation largely prevailed through the 1970s and 1980s.

Since that period, however, the picture has become vastly more complicated, with the involvement of many more participants addressing more issues through multiple means. With the advent of socially responsible investing (SRI), which really coalesced into a meaningful industry and force in the 1990s, another set of voices was added to the debate. It focused on the financial aspects of improved corporate EHS, social, and governance performance. In addition, community-based organizations took form across the country and brought attention to the disparities thought to exist in environmental conditions, health status, and the presence of threats to both in communities of color and poverty relative to more affluent areas. These concerns gave rise to the concept of "environmental justice." This is the principle that no group of people in the U.S. should be subjected to disproportionate exposure to pollution, a degraded local environment, or other conditions that pose threats to their health and well-being. Over the course of the last 15 years or so, through inclusion in several federal executive orders, the principle of environmental justice has become more broadly accepted. It has been integrated into rulemaking processes across the federal government. More generally, focus on the community level also has helped empower citizens across the board to understand environmental and health issues more directly and tangibly. Using a number of new tools that exploit the dramatic increase in the available information on corporate environmental performance, people across the country have unprecedented access to what is happening inside the fence line of many thousands of facilities and companies in their communities and beyond.[1] Moreover, as discussed in the preceding chapter, company employees and customers have become far more discerning and demanding in terms of the ES&G posture and performance that they view as acceptable, as have investors and even suppliers.

This greatly expanded set of stakeholders who care about ES&G issues precludes the effective management of such issues through limited, tactical, fragmented, and reactive approaches. Such approaches were common in the early days of EHS management in companies. As discussed in depth in Chapter 5, what is required today in response to growing and more diverse stakeholder expectations is an integrated approach that is strategic, coherent, systematic, inclusive, and tailored toward individual constituencies and their concerns. These constituencies are identified and profiled later in this chapter.

First, however, it is important to be clear about why companies should engage with and take seriously the concerns and issues of their stakeholders. Some observers might think this is obvious or self-evident. But I believe that it is fair to question this presumption and provide an answer that is responsive to the expectations of the financially focused executive or manager as well as the skeptical reader.

The Social License to Operate

A greater number and diversity of stakeholders have become involved in the discussion about acceptable and expected corporate behavior in terms of environmental, health and safety, social, and governance issues. One major consequence is a fundamental rethinking of the relationship between the corporation and the society in which it operates. More than a few business leaders, economists, and politicians continue to espouse the view that companies are beholden only to their shareholders and that focusing only on creating new wealth for shareholders is the primary or sole appropriate focus for company leadership.[2] However, more and more corporate executives are accepting and embracing a broader concept that reflects the realities of today's business environment. They have come around to the view that only by understanding and responding to the expectations of all important stakeholders can they create the conditions needed for continuing (or continuous) business success and long-term sustainability. Notably, this idea also has been embraced and is starting to be promoted by other voices with both credibility and influence in the business community.[3]

Although this more expansive and inclusive view of corporate responsibilities can be expressed in a number of ways, I am inclined to favor the notion of the "social license to operate" as a starting point. There are several reasons for this. One is that it more accurately reflects the dynamics at play between a company and the broader society in which it operates. As shown in Chapter 3, numerous important external influences on the corporation have an interest in ES&G posture and performance. It is increasingly clear that many influential stakeholders will be dissatisfied with blithe assertions that if the company maintains a singular focus on profits, benefits (utility) to shareholders and society at large will be maximized. Indeed, firms that ignore stakeholder concerns in pursuit of profit risk relationships that are vital to securing and retaining future customers, sources of financing, key employees and business partners, and other assets and inputs needed to maintain and grow revenues and earnings and limit operational and financial risks. (The reasons are described in Chapter 3 and demonstrated by empirical evidence presented in Chapters 6 and 7.) Sustainable companies don't burn bridges that they will or might need, nor do they eat their seed corn because they are hungry today.

Another, and perhaps more unique, characteristic of the social license to operate is that the concept has been adopted and found to be effective in helping companies deal with complex stakeholder relations challenges in the context of managing some significant ES&G issues. In other words, this concept has been "battle tested" in the business world and has been found to be effective. By way of background, the social license to operate is a term first articulated and used extensively ten to 15 years ago in several extraction-intensive industries operating in different parts of the developing world. These companies wanted to gain (or maintain) access to valuable mineral, timber, or petroleum reserves that had been found in developing countries, often located in rural, even remote, areas. Many of these companies had won competitively awarded concessions or licenses to develop and extract these natural resources (that is, they had the legal right to occupy the site, develop the resource, and extract and remove valuable materials). Nevertheless, they encountered stiff local resistance from the indigenous populations in the area, as well as criticism from environmental NGOs and others concerned about both adverse environmental impact and the social equity aspects of the contractual arrangement. Through a sometimes-protracted process of trial and error, the affected firms came to realize that their ultimate success in maintaining their access to and benefits from their resource development projects depended on being accepted and trusted by the people on the ground who would be most directly affected by these projects. In a relatively short period of time, principles and best practices came to be defined and understood and are now in widespread use within the multinational minerals industry and several others.

The "social license" concept has been applied primarily at the project level. However, companies with prominent and potentially sensitive operations in the developing world are increasingly taking the sensible position that they need a consistent set of policies and approaches for how they conduct their operations globally. The importance of such consistency is discussed in greater depth in Chapter 5. An example is provided by Newmont Mining Company, a U.S.-based multinational minerals company operating mines, concentrators, and smelters in a variety of developed and developing countries around the world:Newmont has defined [social license to operate] as "the acceptance and belief by society, and specifically, our local communities, in the value creation of our activities, such that we can continue to access and extract mineral resources." (Smith and Feldman, 2009)

More generally, there is widespread recognition in the minerals industry[4] and beyond that the social license to operate is a valid concept that reflects legitimate concerns. Also, it is in the business and financial interests of companies to secure and carefully safeguard such a license. Finally, having this type of intangible asset allows a firm to operate in ways and in places that would not be feasible otherwise. Since the advent of this concept more than ten years ago and its application to a substantial number of specific projects and contexts, it has obtained a bit of a life of its own and is now used informally by a variety of companies and stakeholders. With that said, several attributes are worth considering as one contemplates whether a social license to operate is needed for a particular business enterprise and, if so, what is required to obtain and maintain such a license. These attributes include the following:[5]

- **Social legitimacy.** The company's activities, either at a particular site or more generally, yield an overall net benefit for its stakeholders and society in general. Unavoidable adverse impacts may be associated with certain commercial activities (examples include loss of forest cover during rural mine development, and air pollutant emissions from electric power generation). But these impacts can be tolerated as long as corresponding benefits are greater in magnitude and are shared equitably among the company's stakeholders.

- **Credibility.** The firm has demonstrated that it understands the concerns of its stakeholders, has the technical and managerial capability to manage its ES&G aspects, and is willing and able to both make and uphold commitments.

- **Trust.** This is the desired outcome and the most valuable intangible component of the social license. It can be obtained only by demonstrating both social legitimacy and credibility, and it generally requires years to establish.

Most companies do not face the daunting physical, technical, and managerial challenges of developing and extracting major mineral deposits from remote areas of developing countries. But I contend that the concepts and approaches developed in the crucible of such projects provide a useful model. As defined here, the social license to operate is a workable, business-focused concept that can be vitally important for companies seeking to understand and proactively manage the issues and concerns of their major stakeholders. For reasons discussed in the previous chapters (and the following ones), it will be ever more important in the future for companies, particularly large ones, to know what their stakeholders think, what is important to them, what they expect of the firm, how they want to be engaged, and what they are (or may be) willing to contribute to the firm and its success. As long as companies bear in mind the issues of social legitimacy, credibility, and trust, they are unlikely to go wrong (or very wrong) as they consider how best to address the concerns of their stakeholders. They must do this in the context of both long-range and day-to-day business opportunities and challenges.

The next section describes each of the major stakeholder constituencies that collectively determine whether and to what extent a company has earned and maintained its implicit social license to operate, and their unique roles and interests in defining and tracking important firm-level sustainability issues.

Major Company Stakeholders

Companies of even moderate size have a substantial number of different stakeholders who require attention and may have an interest in ES&G issues. Each of these constituencies brings a different perspective, has one or more primary roles in or relationships with the company, and has unique obligations and/or expectations. Although every firm and its influences are unique, most firms should be mindful of at least the constituencies described in the following sections.

Employees

Experience and a good deal of management literature support the idea that a firm's employees and their talents are among its most valuable assets. Unlike most other corporate assets, however, the firm does not own its employees. With certain exceptions,[6] they are free to take their talents elsewhere whenever they choose. Accordingly, it is reasonable and appropriate to be mindful of employee concerns in the ES&G arena, particularly as such issues receive more public scrutiny and senior management attention. Some firms, as a matter of principle, don't consider their employees to be "stakeholders" in the conventional sense. Instead, these companies prefer to send the message that all members of the organization are responsible for understanding and addressing all important business issues, including those pertaining to sustainability. In other words, they are an integral part of interpreting and responding to the concerns of stakeholders and are not stakeholders themselves. Regardless of what conventions are adopted for internal messaging and management, the fact remains that addressing sustainability in an effective and coherent manner begins with dialog with the members of the organization. They are the people closest to the issues that may pose environmental, health and safety, social, and even governance issues. They often can identify subtleties in the competitive landscape that may affect the firm's ideal approach to managing these issues. And they are the ones who in the final analysis will need to carry out the indicated actions and live with their outcomes and consequences. As suggested in the next chapter, I view active, inclusive engagement with the firm's employees as a crucial enabler of an approach to sustainability that will be responsive to all important factors and effective in the long run.

Customers

In today's globally connected and competitive economy, the need to keep customers satisfied with what they receive from a firm is of paramount importance. Quite simply, a lack of customers means no revenue and therefore no business. Conversely, attracting new customers, retaining existing ones, and selling more goods and services to both is the clearest and surest pathway to revenue growth, opportunity, and a thriving enterprise. As discussed at length in Chapter 3, a substantial number of large and influential customers are now becoming more demanding and more vocal in establishing ES&G expectations of their business partners and vendors. This is particularly true in consumer-facing businesses. For this reason alone, one could likely justify establishing a new program or initiative to pursue sustainability at the corporate level. It would be short-sighted and possibly self-defeating to build a company's approach to sustainability solely on customer desires and expectations. But for virtually any type of business, the customer's voice is an important influence.

Suppliers

The other side of the value chain is made up of the enterprises that supply goods and services to the firm. They may number from a few to many hundreds or thousands, depending on the firm's nature and scale. Suppliers can influence the company's ES&G posture and public perception. This is particularly true if they supply manufactured goods (such as garments, footwear, and other low-technology products that have been more or less entirely offshored to developing countries in the Pacific Rim); conduct facility or major equipment design, construction, and/or operating and maintenance (O&M) services; or provide extensive transportation services. The consequences of inadequate attention paid to supplier capability and operating practices can be severe (as attested to by the experience of companies such as Nike and BP). Therefore, vigilance toward and active management of supplier ES&G posture and performance are certainly warranted as part of any comprehensive approach to corporate sustainability.[7] Moreover, suppliers and their ES&G impacts will almost certainly become more publicly prominent as the shift toward a more expansive examination of these impacts, through life-cycle analysis, becomes more established during the next few years. Companies, and the executives and managers who run them, would be well-advised to invest in developing a greater understanding of the current status and capability of their suppliers relative to ES&G issues, if they have not done so already.

Communities

Local communities provide much of the supporting infrastructure used by the companies that choose to locate within them and, often, many of their employees. These companies, in turn, provide employment opportunities to people within the host community as well as tax revenue, and may provide philanthropic and other support as well. Consequently, a symbiotic relationship exists (or should) between the firm and its host community, with both receiving benefits from the relationship that they would not enjoy otherwise. The nature and terms of these company-community relationships have been tested over the past few decades, as issues such as safe and reasonable working conditions, environmental issues such as pollutant emissions and waste management, participation in community affairs, and financial issues (such as tax relief in exchange for locating/maintaining a plant, or payment for new infrastructure) have become more prominent.

These issues have made the relationships more complex and multi-faceted and have often broadened the continuing discussion between elected officials and company representatives. In addition, the rate of formation and activity level of community-based groups appears to have increased significantly in recent years. It has been powered by a combination of the public access provisions of major laws (environmental laws in particular), the availability of information, and the emergence and recognition of environmental justice as an appropriate element of public policy in many jurisdictions across the U.S., as well as at the federal level.[8] These trends, taken as a whole, mean that the days in which companies could wield substantial power and achieve their ends simply by virtue of their size and/or by cultivating good relationships with a few elected officials are over in many places. Today, and increasingly in the future, firms will need to develop and maintain relationships with a broader array of actors in the communities of which they are a part. They also must recognize that the discussion around any particular ES&G issue or set of issues is likely to be broader, and that reaching a conclusive outcome may be more time-consuming and difficult than in the past. Finally, and importantly, the community level is where a firm's social license to operate is obtained and where it can most easily be lost.

Regulators

As discussed in Chapter 3, regulatory agencies are charged with interpreting and carrying out legislative intent; establishing specific requirements; and overseeing and, where necessary, enforcing compliance. As a matter of course, they also provide technical assistance, training, and other services to the regulated community, and collect, analyze, and report information to the public. Thus, regulators and other public sector entities have ongoing relationships with representatives of many companies. As a practical matter, virtually all firms of substantial size must regularly interact with regulators at some level. The primary responsibility of regulatory agency personnel is ensuring that every firm and facility that is subject to a given regulatory requirement is in compliance, so the nature of the relationship is necessarily somewhat adversarial.

With that said, a great many executives and staff within these agencies recognize that regulation has practical limits. They also understand that if you truly care about improving environmental, health and safety, and/or social performance, finding ways to bring this about through nonregulatory means (such as through voluntary, beyond-compliance actions) is a practical necessity. Indeed, as discussed in Chapters 5 and 6, a substantial number of voluntary partnership programs have been established by the EPA, OSHA, the DOT, and other federal agencies and their state-level counterparts that target and involve both regulated and largely unregulated companies and industries. Although their record of accomplishments varies, there can be no doubt that well-designed voluntary programs can yield substantial benefits for all participants. One collateral benefit of the experience gained from operating these programs over the past 15 years or so is that for many companies, the level of mutual understanding, credibility, and trust between the firm and the regulator has increased markedly. This type of enhanced relationship is an asset that some companies have employed very effectively. It probably could be developed and used productively by many more firms and their leaders. We should always remember, however, that such relationships are based and contingent upon maintaining an effective program of full and continuous compliance with the law and all regulatory requirements.

The Media

There was a time in the not-so-distant past when the news media was focused on just that—reporting news and current events. This was accomplished through the work of large networks of correspondents posted in different locations around the world, supplemented by reporters with specialized knowledge of important topics. Generally, the expectation on all sides was that the media's job was to unearth facts, perform some limited analysis, and report the results of these activities to their readers or viewers without embellishment or reshaping to fit any particular ideology or agenda. I believe that most people would agree that this situation no longer exists in the U.S. The media today, which is increasingly dominated on the commercial side by an oligopoly of large media companies, is as much about entertaining audiences as informing them. Today's media is segmented so that a person at any given point on the ideological and political spectrum can find "news" that is tailored to his or her view of the world.

Irrespective of what you think about the state of today's news media, it is important to understand what the media does and how it works. For an issue or event to be considered "news" and therefore worthy of coverage, it must be recent, or "new," and offer one of the "three Cs"—crisis, conflict, or controversy.[9] Stories not meeting any of these criteria might occasionally be pursued and published/broadcast (such as human-interest items). But the news agenda always will be dominated by events meeting one, or preferably more than one, of the three Cs.[10] Traditionally, this orientation has placed environmental and safety issues in the spotlight every so often. It is fair to say that media attention during the formative years of the environmental movement was enormously helpful in spreading public awareness of these issues and indirectly building public support and pressure for new laws. Unfortunately, however, many or most of our remaining problems are complex and cannot be easily reduced to a short television spot or newspaper article. Also, they do not involve an immediate crisis that can be captured visually (by a film crew or photographer), and they require some existing level of knowledge to fully understand and/or appreciate. Therefore, they tend not to make very compelling news items. Typically, the best we can expect is a general description of the issue or problem, preceded by the requisite story of a person and his or her experience with the issue. These are accompanied by two generally opposed points of view about what the issue or problem really is, its root cause, and what needs to be done about it and by whom. This serves the important function of bringing the issue to the attention of the public, but you could reasonably question whether it is enough for the reader/viewer to fully understand the issue. Moreover, as discussed in Chapter 2, the level of literacy in this country regarding ES&G issues and, more fundamentally, scientific principles, is quite low. This imposes some severe limitations on the extent to which the means of communication and the business model used by conventional media are or ever will be adequate to relay all relevant facts and perspectives to the American public.

As anyone involved in commerce or active in society more generally knows, the last few years have witnessed an explosion in the growth of social media. Enabled by rapid advances in information technology, creative thinking, and aggressive entrepreneurship, social media enterprises have sprung up far and wide and have given rise to modes of communication that did not exist a few years ago. As the ability to write personalized web logs (blogs) became widespread a few years ago, it opened entirely new channels. People could communicate and share "news" and opinion without the intervention of the established media, thereby democratizing the sharing of facts and opinion. More recently, phenomena such as, "friending" and "tweeting" have come from nowhere to the point where they are practiced by hundreds of millions of people around the world. The speed with which these developments have occurred is, to an outside observer, shocking. Importantly, these practices, and the companies that promote and impel them, are changing the rules for businesses of all sizes along multiple dimensions, presenting both risks and opportunities. Along with the ability of bloggers and tweeters to say what they want, when they want, to whomever they want, we have the absence of any mechanism to ensure that any statements or claims made are factual, or at least reasonable. Although the "old" media imposed many limitations on who could reach a sizeable audience, it also placed standards of conduct on its reporters and editors. It also promoted a high degree of professionalism and personal responsibility among its news correspondents. These largely self-imposed restrictions and sense of duty to the news profession seem more or less absent within the social media world of today. The exception is organizations and people who are attempting to migrate from the old media to the new.

Companies and their leaders and managers must be vigilant about their public image. Nowhere is their exposure greater than with respect to such issues as environmental performance, employee/supplier safety, labor conditions, executive compensation and other governance issues, and the like. In other words, ES&G issues and *perceived* company performance can quickly devolve into a story that meets one of the three Cs and can be transmitted instantaneously to millions of people before anyone at the company is even aware of them. In response, many companies are assigning corporate communications and other appropriate staff to monitor the blogosphere, "follow" organizations and people with an interest in the company/ industry on Twitter, and take other measures to ensure that they remain up to date in real time on what others are saying about the firm. Other people, including senior corporate managers involved in corporate EHS management, are taking proactive measures to "inoculate" their firms against negative messaging by writing their own blogs about what the company is doing to improve its EHS performance. They also issue tweets as appropriate to point followers to pertinent web sites, company reports, and data, and to respond to claims made by others. Corporate leaders and managers interested in pursuing sustainability should pay close attention to ongoing developments in the social media domain. They should consider carefully how social media should be incorporated into company sustainability strategy moving forward.

The NGO Community

As discussed in Chapter 3, the formation of the environmental movement in the late 1960s and early 1970s both promoted and was driven by the growth and emergence of a number of nongovernmental organizations (NGOs). They were dedicated to the cause of protecting the environment or particular aspects of it. These groups achieved prominence during this period through two basic strategies that remain with us today. The first was to mobilize public support (political and financial) for their positions on major environmental issues, which generally took the form of additional requirements or limiting access to particular natural resources. Support was engendered through mailing campaigns and was supplemented in recent decades by telephone calls and e-mail messages to members and other supporters.[11] The second strategy was to bring lawsuits against companies and the cognizant regulatory agencies, as appropriate, to compel action(s) that the NGO(s) believed were needed to adequately protect the environment and/or human health. These lawsuits were enabled by the public participation provisions of our major environmental statutes, which were upheld in several early tests of the constitutionality and limits of these newly enacted laws. The NGOs were deemed to represent the public and the public interest and thus were granted the "standing" that is required to file lawsuits in a court of law.

Although this may seem like an arcane or minor point, it is not. It is through their legal standing and the associated ability of these groups to file lawsuits on behalf of the public that organizations such as the Sierra Club, Natural Resources Defense Council, Environmental Defense Fund, and a number of others could assert with at least some credibility that their positions on environmental (and, by extension, broader ES&G) issues and their actions reflect the will and preferences of American society. Those of us who have been involved in the EHS profession for some time have witnessed how these NGOs have repeatedly invoked the interests of the country in taking various positions on policy and regulatory issues. They have routinely and repeatedly asserted that they, rather than elected representatives or those appointed by them, have both the best interests of the people at heart and a well-formed and accurate interpretation of what the people really want in terms of U.S. public policy. Interestingly, however, few if any of these organizations take the views of their members or even their major supporters into account when formulating positions and desired policy interventions on particular issues. Instead, they rely on their own leaders and internal staff to decide which issues are important, what should be done about them, and what action(s) should be taken to alleviate a perceived threat or change the behavior of some set of third parties (generally, industries or companies using particular technologies, carrying out certain activities, or seeking access to publicly owned resources). The function of the membership is to provide money and, in some cases, to participate in campaigns to garner support for their position with members of Congress or the White House (such as through petitions, mailings, and/or phone calls). Having been a dues-paying member of several of these organizations, I can report that none ever solicited my opinion about any issue, whether pertaining to policy choices, organizational priorities, or internal governance. The only member access or control that is available in most of these groups is periodic elections for national board members and, in some cases, participation in state/local chapters or affiliates. In other words, despite their frequent calls for greater transparency and a more open public policy process, many of these NGOs take a highly paternalistic and even patronizing stance toward their own members in formulating their positions on important ES&G issues that are of general interest to the public.

The foregoing discussion may seem like "sour grapes" or, at the least, a bit off-topic. But it is important for corporate executives and managers to have an informed and clear-eyed perspective on NGOs when considering whether and to what extent they will be considered important stakeholders of their companies. Within the context of a particular firm, you can be virtually assured that more than a few environmental and labor NGOs would unequivocally assert the following:

- They represent the views of "civil society."
- Accordingly, their views on a company's operations and performance are legitimate and significant and are essential inputs to its deliberations on ES&G issues.
- As a consequence, it is imperative that you open and maintain a respectful dialog with them concerning these issues, and understand and carefully consider their views when making important internal policy and management decisions.

In my view, the leadership within every company should make an explicit judgment about the validity of each of these assertions and choose the appropriate level and type of engagement, if any. I have great respect for the accomplishments of many major environmental, EHS, and social NGOs and the contributions they have made to better the world. But I believe that, from the perspective of a corporate executive, a good deal of skepticism on the appropriate relationship with NGOs going forward is in order.

Investors and Analysts

As highlighted previously, investors and the analysts that serve them are becoming increasingly interested in corporate ES&G posture and performance. Briefly, this interest stems from a desire to understand and control sources of investment risk that arise from compliance obligations, legal/financial liabilities, restrictions on the use of materials and manufacturing methods, reputational issues, and many others. Conversely, a growing number of investors are very interested in various aspects of ES&G management as a means of identifying firms likely to outperform their peers, either through capturing opportunities to grow share in existing markets or through developing new products, services, and markets having an environmental, health and safety, or social equity element. As stated in several places throughout this book, investor behavior is a powerful new force that is affecting corporate appreciation and management of ES&G issues. It will be increasingly important during the next five to ten years for corporate executives to understand and actively manage their firms' activities in a way that is responsive to these growing investor expectations. The perspectives, needs, and expectations of investors relative to ES&G issues are discussed in much greater depth in Chapters 6 and 7.

The General Public

People in the U.S. exhibit some interesting opinions and behavior patterns concerning the environment and related sustainability issues. On the one hand, public opinion surveys conducted over decades show convincingly that a majority of Americans believe that protecting the environment is important or very important. In fact, until the recent and ongoing severe economic downturn, public opinion polling showed that most people, if they had to choose, would favor environmental protection over economic growth. For more than 30 years, the Gallup Organization has conducted a survey asking Americans whether they are more concerned with the environment or the economy. Figure 4-1 shows the responses to this question over the past 26 years (Jones, 2011).

Current results show that almost 40 percent of the public still supports protecting the environment even at the risk of curbing economic growth. This is true despite the continuing effects of the worst economy since the Great Depression and even though, for the first time since the survey was initiated, a greater percentage of people favor economic growth rather than environmental protection. With that said, it appears that public support for the environment has been tempered by the length and depth of the recession. In its release of the most recent survey data, Gallup concludes:

> Over the past decade, Americans have dramatically reevaluated their priorities when considering the trade-offs of economic growth and environmental protection. As recently as four

years ago, Americans maintained a strong preference for environmental protection. By 2009, those priorities flipped, and pro-economy attitudes have grown since then, apart from the temporary movement back toward the environment after the Gulf of Mexico oil spill. These changes illustrate that Americans' opinions on environmental protection are dynamic and responsive to what is happening in the real world. Based on the historical trend, Americans seem to value environmental protection but appear willing to de-emphasize that goal when more immediate, everyday concerns like the economy need attention. (Jones, 2011)

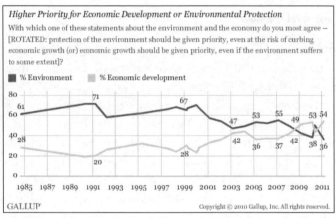

Figure 4-1 Changes in whether Americans value the environment or economic growth

In addition, more in-depth polling results show significant recent erosion in public attitudes and beliefs regarding some key environmental issues, and a growing divide along political lines. The decline in the percentage of people favoring environment over economy is strongest among self-identified conservatives and Republicans and weakest among liberals and Democrats. Similarly, support for and belief in the positive impact of the environmental movement has eroded significantly among Republicans and to a far lesser degree among Democrats (Dunlap, 2010).

This trend also can be seen regarding what is certainly the most pressing and important environmental issue—global climate change. For example, in recent polls, positive responses to the question "How serious of a threat is global warming to you and your family?" declined by ten percentage points (from 63 percent to 53 percent) from 2007–2008 to 2010 among U.S. respondents (Ray and Pugliese, 2011a). This was one of the largest percentage declines worldwide. The percentage who believe that rising temperatures are a result of human activity (34 percent) versus natural causes (47 percent), or are a result of both (14 percent), also showed a pronounced decline over the past three years or so. In the 2007–2008 poll, 60 percent of U.S. respondents attributed global warming to human activity or human activity and natural causes. In the more recent (2010) results, only 48 percent did so. Moreover, the U.S. is now the only developed country worldwide in which more people believe that global warming is due to natural causes rather than to human activity (Ray and Pugliese, 2011b).

Public concern about a number of other environmental issues remains strong, with a clear majority of Americans concerned a great deal or a fair amount about such problems as contamination by toxic waste, surface water and air pollution, maintenance of freshwater supplies, and extinction of plant and animal species. Loss of open space and global warming rank last on a list of ten such issues, however. In addition, the percentages of U.S. respondents who are concerned about these issues have declined for every issue, decreasing from 6 to 13 percent, depending on the issue (Saad, 2011).

Despite the declines in the overall level of support among some segments of the American public for strong public policies focusing on the environment, in recent years a substantial and stable majority has stated that they have made changes in their personal lives to live a more "green" life. About 90 percent report that they recycle, and 85 percent have reduced household energy use. Moreover, the percentage buying a product based on environmental attributes has increased 3 percentage points during the past ten years, from 73 percent to 76 percent (Dunlap, 2010). This suggests that opportunities remain for companies that can effectively understand and respond to the challenges posed by ES&G issues while meeting consumer expectations.

A recent survey of influential people in 23 countries[12] conducted by the global public relations firm Edelman shows that the expectation of ethical conduct and operating businesses in a way that benefits society is firmly rooted in the U.S. and every other country surveyed. More specifically, the survey found that substantial majorities in each country (85 percent in the U.S.) believe that corporations should create shareholder value in a way that aligns with society's interests, even if that means sacrificing shareholder value. In most of these countries (including the U.S.), the majority also believe that government should regulate corporations' activities to ensure that they behave responsibly. Globally, the level of trust[13] that these people have in a variety of institutions, including business, has increased slightly during the past year. With that said, the level of trust in the U.S. of business, which already was on the low end of the range, declined further, from 54 percent to 46 percent. A similar decline could be observed for trust in government, and trust in the media declined precipitously, from 38 percent to 27 percent. (Globally, people in the more developed markets are the most distrustful of the media.) In contrast, the relatively high level of trust in NGOs in the U.S. increased from 59 percent to 63 percent. Overall, the U.S. was the only country studied in which the overall level of trust in institutions fell between 2008 and 2011. Looking more specifically at the business community, the level of trust in banking, insurance, and general financial services suffered the steepest decline during this period, while trust in technology firms remained high. Companies in the automotive sector experienced a substantial jump in trust, from 32 percent to 49 percent from 2009 to 2011. Interestingly, the factors identified most often as important in determining corporate reputation by survey respondents were quality, transparency, trust, and employee welfare. The factors ranked least important were admired leadership and financial returns to investors. This suggests that being attentive to ES&G issues is an important means of building and maintaining the firm's overall reputation. Finally, the results of this survey validate the idea that trust has a protective effect on the firm's reputation among the educated public. If negative information about a company is heard once or twice, 57 percent of respondents believe it if the company is distrusted, but only 25 percent believe it if the firm is trusted. Conversely, positive news has a limited impact on a company that is not trusted. Upon hearing positive news once or twice, 51 percent believe it if the company is trusted, but only 15 percent believe it if the firm is not trusted. The authors of this study conclude that the old corporate public relations framework based on controlling information, protecting the brand, and keeping a tight focus on profit must be replaced with a new architecture based on engagement, transparency, and the pursuit of profit with a purpose (Edelman, 2011).

To summarize, companies have a number of important stakeholders, each of which has its own characteristics, objectives, priorities, and expectations. Each of the major types of stakeholders is developing a stronger interest in ES&G issues and in how specific industries and companies are addressing them. The next section discusses in a bit more specificity how these different stakeholders tend to become involved in influencing corporate ES&G behavior and what issues tend to be of greatest interest to them.

Typical Stakeholder Involvement in and Influence on Corporate Behavior

Because of their different types of relationships with individual firms, as well as their varying interests and priorities, stakeholders typically have different degrees of involvement with corporate decision making regarding ES&G issues, and widely varying levels of influence. Understanding that every company-stakeholder relationship is unique in some fashion, it is reasonable to offer the following general observations.

Employees

More than in any other stakeholder relationship, the interactions between a firm and its leadership and employees are personal, numerous, and multidimensional. As discussed in previous sections and chapters, employees are what make firms work. Their competence, professionalism, diligence, and willingness to sacrifice their short-term interests on behalf of the firm (or the lack thereof) are a key determinant of the success of any company in the long term. The power and influence wielded by employees varies widely on the basis of company culture, leadership style, the presence and aggressiveness of labor unions, and other factors. In some firms, a culture of personal accountability and common cause is manifest, and senior management takes very seriously the concerns of people throughout the company. In others, a more arms-length and even adversarial relationship exists between various levels of executive leadership, management, and rank-and-file employees.

This latter management model was prevalent during the century or so during and following the Industrial Revolution. It emerged from an industrial, mechanistic construct of how firms create value. Under this construct, capital goods and labor are largely interchangeable inputs, and the manager's job is to determine the optimal mix between the two and to limit the overall costs of production as much as possible. In an information-driven economy, however, this model for managing the firm presents some serious limitations, because people are not inanimate inputs to the production process. The primary task of management today is to create the conditions needed for employees to contribute their best efforts, not to deploy them like objects, much less intimidate or subjugate them. Certainly, a basic duty of senior management is to ensure the continued health and safety of their employees while they are on the job, as illustrated in the following sidebar.

Are You Really OK with That?

Some years ago, I had the good fortune to work with an enlightened and talented executive, Joe Smith. We collaborated on a successful project to develop and deploy an integrated EHS management system (described in Chapter 5) for his company, which manufactures plastics of various kinds. During our kickoff meeting, he described his initial interaction with his new boss, a CEO who had been recruited from a different but related industry (petrochemicals). When my client proudly related that the company had achieved dramatic reductions in worker injury and fatality rates and was approaching best-in-class status, the CEO reacted in an unexpected way.

Rather than congratulating his EHS executive on his accomplishments and those of his team, the CEO said, "So you're telling me that this year two or three of our people are likely to be killed on the job. Are you really OK with that?"

My client reported that although he was a bit stunned by this reaction, he knew that the new company leader understood the importance of effectively managing EHS issues, eliminating workplace hazards, promoting safe behavior, and not tolerating lapses that could result in serious injuries or deaths. He also believed that his new boss would be a strong supporter of his efforts to implement more systematic, effective, and cost-effective approaches to limiting adverse EHS impacts.

The beliefs and attitudes of this particular CEO were somewhat unconventional then, and even now in some quarters, but they do illustrate the type of mindset that will be needed to successfully manage complex ES&G issues over time. Leaders will need to be committed to the safety and well-being of their employees and impatient with conventional, self-limited thinking about how to attain their goals and commitments.

Regardless of the current approach taken to interacting with the firm's employees, senior executives would be well advised to ensure that they understand any concerns regarding ES&G issues felt by their employees. These are likely to include but are not limited to hazards and unhealthful conditions on the job, including ergonomic issues; labor and human rights issues, particularly in off-shore locations; EHS performance of the company's products and services in use; and any major disparities in compensation, benefits, and advancement and professional development opportunities provided to employees on the basis of anything other than merit. One of the core principles of sustainability is social equity—fairness. Fair dealing with stakeholders begins with and must include equitable treatment of the company's members.

Even if it were unnecessary to maintaining the credibility of any organizational sustainability initiative or program, there are sound business reasons for ensuring that one's employees believe they have a stake in the firm's success. One is that they are the people who will make sustainable business behavior, improved practices, and better performance happen, or will not. They are the company's ambassadors and public face. In many ways large and small, they communicate with the outside world what the company is about, whether it can be trusted, and, accordingly, whether it is a worthy employer and business partner. In the aggregate, they also know how everything works, where the problems are, (often) how they might be resolved, and where new untapped opportunities may exist.

In short, company employees may or may not be in a position to strongly influence its policies, direction, and priorities, but they should be the focus of any serious effort to pursue corporate sustainability. Much can be gained from understanding and addressing the ES&G concerns of employees and securing their involvement in charting a course and working toward a more sustainable posture. At the same time, much can be lost by ignoring employee concerns and involvement regarding ES&G issues. As these issues become more prominent in the future, it will become increasingly evident which companies are leveraging this key set of resources more effectively and which are not.

Customers and Suppliers

As discussed earlier, today the customer is king. Depending on the size and nature of the company-customer relationship, the customer's influence can be minimal or it can be powerful—even pervasive. Many customers are seeking to understand their own life cycle environmental aspects. This means that the ES&G posture and performance of their suppliers, at least the major ones, is becoming a topic of growing interest. Such life cycle evaluation often surfaces facts and perspectives that are somewhat surprising and thought-provoking. Accordingly, firms that are in the position of being a major account to other firms can exert substantial influence on the decision making that takes place in these firms. To the extent that a company is interested in becoming more sustainable, wielding this influence in a positive and productive way can pay dividends by reducing the company's organizational EHS footprint, improving its credibility, and reducing its operating and reputational risk. It also may help reduce the company's input costs over time as suppliers take steps to improve the efficiency and reduce the adverse EHS impacts of their operations.

In addition, customers, including consumers, have shown that they are concerned about labor rights abuses and other social equity issues. Tolerance among sophisticated corporations and informed consumers of abusive labor practices, both domestically and internationally, is very low. Experience over the past 20 years has shown repeatedly that U.S. companies seeking to reduce costs by outsourcing and offshoring their production operations must be vigilant about the behavior of their subcontractors, particularly those supplying goods produced with very low-wage labor. To ignore or tacitly condone abusive labor practices is to accept significant reputational risk and the possibility of both consumer boycotts and termination of previously productive relationships with major retailers and other crucial distribution channels. In addition, as a broader array of labor, social equity, and other ES&G issues receives greater scrutiny from a growing number of end-use customers and major intermediaries, it will be increasingly important for companies of all types and sizes to ensure that they have clear policies, sound practices, and a performance record that they would not be reticent to discuss in a public forum. In other words, customers today feel empowered. In today's operating environment of instantly available information and rising expectations, they expect their trusted suppliers to anticipate and respond to their preferences.

In response to such demands, companies will face the choice of either meeting these expectations or being prepared to replace customers who decide to take their business elsewhere. I submit that in most cases, the first choice will be easier to implement and explain and will provide a more robust foundation for continued, sustainable growth.

Communities

In contrast to many other types of stakeholders, the influence of communities is felt primarily at the local level, around the firm's headquarters and facilities. Generally, the official representatives of host communities tend to be very supportive of businesses. They provide employment for residents and (generally) make important contributions to funding local governments through payroll, business, and real estate tax payments. Indeed, this country has a long history of major companies playing important roles in local civic activities and politics in the communities in which they operate. Relationships with community residents may be more varied. Some will be company employees and have a direct economic relationship with the firm, but others will have no such connection. In situations in which the firm and its actions do not provoke any concerns about ES&G issues, they are likely to be viewed positively by members of the community. Where such concerns exist, however, the relationship can become tense and even adversarial. Community concerns tend to involve issues that are tangible and that may have a direct effect on residents. Here are some examples of ES&G issues that are particularly likely to evoke concerns:

- **Environmental aspects.** Visible air or water pollutant emissions, noise, odors, and accumulations of waste

- **Workplace safety and health.** Exposure to physical hazards or chemicals, use of processes or agents that pose a great intrinsic hazard (such as explosives and radioactive materials), and inadequate processes and practices to control unsafe conditions or materials

- **Labor relations.** Aggressive efforts to prevent unionization, perceptions of punitive responses to worker assertiveness, or, in general, a dictatorial approach to company-employee relations

- **Unusual public-private sector arrangements.** Provision of dedicated publicly financed infrastructure, reduced or foregone tax collections, or perception of undue corporate influence

Community concerns often develop over an extended period. Minor issues may accumulate and fester for many years before they reach a point, or an event, that causes them to erupt suddenly and forcefully. Company executives may be surprised by the nature of the reaction they receive and the vehemence with which their behavior and motives are questioned. It is easy to take for granted the firm's relationships with host communities, but doing so risks maintaining the social license to operate, which, as discussed earlier, really has its basis in these relationships. The consequences of an erosion in the trust between a company and the community, and with it the strength of the social license to operate, may not manifest themselves immediately. But they will be felt directly and dramatically under certain rather predictable conditions.

Community concerns rarely rise to the level at which a company's normal operations are disrupted, but the outlook can change dramatically if the firm wants to make a major change in the status quo. Such changes may include expanding production operations and/or a facility's physical footprint, initiating the use of certain new technologies or equipment, using significantly more of a natural resource (particularly water), or bringing new materials on site. Generally, major changes such as these require the issuance or renewal of one or more permits by state or local authorities. In addition, certain types of activities require permit renewal, regardless of whether substantial changers are being made or proposed, at regular intervals. In either case, because these permitting activities usually involve a public participation component (such as public hearings), they give members of the community access to the decision-making process. These activities also empower people to influence the public officials (whom they may have elected) who are responsible for making the permitting decision. In this way, community members can gain access to information that they may never receive otherwise, publicly state their concerns with the proposed change(s) and the company's past behavior, propose alternatives, and voice support or opposition to permit issuance/renewal.

Company executives would be unwise, based on the experience of many others,[14] to assume that community-level opposition is unimportant or inconsequential to continued operations at existing locations. They also should not assume that the support of the political leadership of either an existing or potential new host community is sufficient to obtain and maintain the social license to operate in that community. That said, this is an area in which risk and reward are highly asymmetrical. Quantifiable benefits from strong community-level relationships may be modest or negligible, but downside risk can be large and consequential. Moreover, along with maintaining a strong and positive set of relationships with company employees, it is difficult to see how any firm that would seek to become a sustainability leader would be either effective or credible in this regard if it did not recognize and respond to community-level concerns. The most effective way to establish the necessary credibility, earn the social license to operate, and mitigate risks is to invest time and effort in building and maintaining respectful and informed relationships with host communities. Ideally, these relationships operate through multiple channels. This ensures that the company's story is told in a way that does not hide or shy away from possible community concerns on the one hand while collecting and reporting any such concerns to appropriate parties in the management chain on the other.

Expelled by the Principal

Many years ago, a former colleague of mine was managing a project to site a new composting facility in a rural community. He and his project team reviewed the plans for the site. They considered the technical aspects of the proposed facility, legal requirements that would apply, and the anticipated arrangements for both supplying the incoming material (yard wastes and other organic materials) and selling the finished product (compost). Everything seemed to be in order, including project financing, and the project appeared to be on a smooth and short-duration course toward approval and ground breaking.

Then everything changed. What my colleague did not know at the outset was that the selected project site was right across the road from an elementary school. When the school principal found out about the project, he immediately became a staunch opponent and launched an attempt to rouse community opposition to its development. Very quickly, a project that seemed to be on the fast track and that would offer both environmental benefits and community employment was in serious trouble.

The project sponsor attempted to reason, and even negotiate, with the principal regarding the placement of the planned facility, but without success. Nor was this individual swayed by the findings of the technical evaluation (including a risk assessment) of the prospective composting facility prepared by my colleague and his team. The principal simply did not want anything resembling a waste-handling facility anywhere near his school and its children.

In the end, the sponsor withdrew its permit application, and the project was terminated. Even though he had no official role in providing or withholding public approval of this facility, and despite questionable credentials for making any such decision, the principal effectively vetoed its approval and construction. At the time, this type of outcome was unusual, and I found it intriguing for that reason.

I realized later that this incident was a harbinger of things to come. Communities across the country have become increasingly assertive, as discussed in this chapter.

Regulators

As discussed earlier, regulatory agency personnel are responsible for helping members of the regulated community understand and comply with their obligations. First they provide outreach, technical assistance, training, permit review, and other support. Then they provide oversight and enforcement, including inspections, report review, response to citizen complaints and concerns, and initiating enforcement actions where appropriate. Accordingly, the primary focus of management and staff within these agencies is ensuring that entities (corporate and otherwise) that are subject to the laws and regulations that have been put in place are in compliance at all times.

With that said, it would be incorrect to assume that regulators have no further interest in how companies are approaching ES&G issues. It is widely understood within federal and state agencies charged with environmental, health and safety, energy, transportation, and other regulatory responsibilities that laws and regulations can induce improved practices to a substantial extent. It is also understood that such mandates have natural limits, beyond which they become overly complex, unwieldy, inefficient, and prone to producing perverse outcomes. In response, a wide array of voluntary, beyond-compliance programs have been developed and deployed during the past 15 years or so at all levels of government. Many of these programs are well-known and respected (such as Energy Star), and many more have achieved noteworthy results.

The existence and success of these programs highlight some key attributes of regulatory agencies and those who work within them. First, these organizations are not monolithic and may not speak with one voice. Frequently, individual subunits are responsible for compliance assurance and voluntary programs, and the management and staff within each may have very different priorities and views on a particular ES&G issue. Accordingly, it is important to understand with which part of the organization you are dealing and to correctly interpret their mission, major activities, and likely priorities. Another attribute is that regulatory agencies are staffed with people who believe in the mission, often fervently. Far from being faceless, disinterested bureaucrats, most management and line staff in regulatory agencies have made affirmative choices to work for their employer, often for compensation that lags that of their corporate counterparts. Generally, they have chosen to work in government not because they had no other career options but because they want to contribute to a better future. Perhaps they want to improve the quality of the nation's waters through writing wastewater discharge permits, or provide technical assistance to small generators of hazardous waste, or inspect safety conditions on the factory floor.[15] Many if not most of these people have an abiding interest in improving the quality of the environment, reducing hazards to human health, and promoting a more sustainable society. Consequently, they are often willing to consider ideas for reaching these goals that do not necessarily fit neatly within the confines of existing regulatory (and even nonregulatory) programs. They may be willing to offer informal feedback, provide technical information/guidance, identify or make introductions to executive-level agency representatives or others with decision-making authority, and otherwise serve as valuable resources to companies having an interest in pursuing sustainability in new and creative ways. Such people often have valuable perspectives and will offer them willingly if asked.

In my experience, however, regulatory agency staff, and even senior managers, are often reluctant to advocate active involvement of their organizations in the workings of private sector entities. Accordingly, they may be hesitant to offer their own judgments about what approaches are preferred, what distinguishes "good" environmental or ES&G performers from otherwise similar firms, or what form or level of performance would be considered desirable, beyond articulating some general principles. This is unfortunate, because corporate managers often don't understand (and sometimes are frustrated by) what regulators expect of them. Generally, corporate executives and managers value clarity and predictability above many other considerations, not least because complying with past EHS regulations often has required the commitment of substantial capital. Outside the arena of explicit regulatory limits, however, such clarity has often been absent, because regulators may be placed in a quasi-advisory role in which many feel ambivalent or uncomfortable. As the concept of sustainability becomes more widely accepted and adopted by U.S. businesses, it would be appropriate for environmental regulators to overcome some of their reticence, offer more of their talents and accumulated judgment and expertise, and demonstrate real leadership. Until this happens, corporate leaders may want to consider initiating some conversations with regulators having a particular interest in sustainability issues that are important in some way to their continued business success.

The Media

As suggested earlier, it is difficult to view today's news/communications media on the whole as objective purveyors of facts and analysis intended to inform our citizenry. Although it is somewhat uncertain whether our "Fourth Estate" ever fully met this description, in the recent past people with some means who lived in or near a major metropolitan area had access to multiple media outlets staffed by professional journalists and newscasters. Major cities often had multiple independently owned daily newspapers as well as numerous television and radio stations. Competitive forces and the professional ethics of the newspeople kept most of the coverage and media accounts reasonably objective and well balanced. Today, the power in media has shifted to the polar extremes.

Occupying one pole is a small number of media conglomerates[16] that own a large percentage of the major daily newspapers, which tend to define the news agenda, as well as the major commercial television broadcast and cable networks. As a consequence, the notion that our mass media is in any respect "independent" seems more quaint and unrealistic with each passing year.

On the other pole are a proliferation of blogs, tweets, viral videos, and other contributions authored and transmitted, with little or no oversight or filtering, by millions of people around the world. This "democratized" media has been growing exponentially and has sapped the strength and threatened the viability of traditional media (particularly newspapers) in major markets across the U.S. and internationally. In particular, advertising revenue has declined precipitously as advertising spend has migrated to more effective channels (mostly online). These developments have had many positive implications, such as giving more people access to more information more quickly. They also have decimated the finances of news organizations that until recently may have employed hundreds of professional journalists around the world. These correspondents could be counted on to remain current with developments in their areas and to report news-worthy happenings on a daily basis. These jobs, and the people who filled them, are disappearing rapidly. In their place are local bloggers and self-appointed correspondents who may or may not meet tradi-tional standards in terms of general understanding and knowledge, lack of clear biases, quality and depth of reporting (including verifying information), and professional integrity.

Unfortunately, the ground that would ideally occupy the mid-dle part of the spectrum between these two extremes appears to be increasingly barren. Midsize (or even large) independent daily news-papers, radio stations, television networks, and other sources of infor-mation of interest to the public are increasingly scarce. It is unclear whether or when this situation will change appreciably, though there is hope that at least some newspapers and their news-gathering and analysis functions will successfully transition to a more fully digital world. This will require that they develop and apply business models that generate sufficient revenue and are more resistant to disruption than was print media.

In the current context, the important point to remember is that today, media takes many different forms. It is fed by traditional report-ing by professionals as well as both spontaneous and planned develop-ment of "content" by a diverse array of nontraditional sources who are not bound by traditional codes of conduct and may have a variety of agendas. This situation has several implications for corporate execu-tives and managers. One is that vigilance is important, because com-panies no longer control the message as they once did, and because negative information, whether accurate or not, can circulate and be widely accepted quickly. ES&G issues are a particularly potent source of potential perception risk. For this reason, senior executives of firms with prominent ES&G issues may want to ensure that a member of their communications staff regularly monitors the blogosphere, major NGO web sites, and message traffic on Twitter. Another implication is that a firm's degree of transparency becomes more of a strategic issue than in the past. Because the potential impact of ES&G disclo-sure is greater than in the past, company senior executives will want to think carefully and make definitive decisions about what type(s) of company information to release publicly, in what formats and forums, and with what frequency. On a related note, it is becoming more important for senior executives and company spokespersons to become more conversant with ES&G issues so that they can more effectively respond to routine questions from the media and to crises, should they arise. Accordingly, these executives should ensure that they are briefed regularly on ES&G status, trends, and performance. They also need to establish (or maintain) an internal communication process to ensure that they are alerted to any ES&G-related incidents or events (whether positive or negative) that may induce media coverage.

NGOs

The NGO community invested in ES&G issues is quite large and diverse. Different organizations may have vastly different constituencies, agendas, knowledge of the issues, major activities, business/funding models, and major tactics. Many of the old-line environmental NGOs are organized as national (even international) membership organizations supported by individual member dues, foundation grants, and donations. These organizations all populate particular niches, but most have a broad range of interests oriented toward environmental protection and improvement. Others are more narrowly focused in terms of what they seek to protect (such as wildlife, rain forests, or community health), how they carry out their respective missions (lobbying, public policy advocacy, analysis, land acquisition, standard-setting, partnerships, services delivery), or whom they seek to influence. (A partial list might include legislators, corporations, neighborhood residents, and the public at large.) Other types of NGOs represent professionals or people interested in the environment, worker health and safety, human and/or labor rights, and other issues. Such organizations tend to focus on helping their members understand relevant ES&G issues, developing effective approaches, disseminating best practices, maintaining appropriate standards of the profession, and other activities. This great diversity makes it difficult to characterize the NGO community in terms of its overall focus and level of influence.

With that said, it is possible to offer a few general observations:

- It is important to identify the NGOs that have a specific interest in your company, its industry and major lines of business, and/or its more prominent ES&G issues. Insights about which organizations are active and may have an interest in your firm probably can be obtained from your firm's EHS staff (for environmental and safety issues), plant/facility managers (for community-based issues), investor relations staff (for investor and analyst concerns (discussed further later)), and communications or public relations personnel (for issues of general interest to the business community, the media, or the public).

- As suggested previously, it would be prudent to think about, before any crisis or confrontation, what type and level of engagement the firm would consider for any particular type of NGO. It is perfectly reasonable to reject the contention of any NGO that it is an important stakeholder deserving of company time and attention based on the merits (or lack thereof). It is far easier to make and defend such a decision in any particular case if some criteria or rules have been established in advance and are applied uniformly across the firm. In practice, such criteria often come down to the same issues that frame any business relationship. In other words, what are the benefits if we do engage with them, and what are the risks if we don't? Business leaders should not be surprised if the answers to these questions, as applied to a particular set of NGOs, are not directly in line with the aggressiveness with which a relationship is sought, or with the stridency of any accompanying message(s).

- Company decision makers should be clear on what they hope to get from any NGO engagement or other type of relationship. They should insist on a clear statement of objectives from each counterparty. Clarity on and honesty about objectives will make any such interactions more productive and help avoid disagreements or confrontation. Many companies large and small regularly engage with NGOs as part of their philanthropic activities. This is admirable, but it's quite different from a situation in which the corporate-NGO relationship ostensibly is about a different set of goals and activities. Everyone should be clear at the outset (or shortly thereafter) why an engagement or collaboration is taking place, what each party will contribute, what outcomes are being sought, and what indicators will be used to measure progress.

The following sidebar describes how companies can deal effectively with increasing stakeholder expectations.

> ## Actively Managing the Stakeholder Relationship
>
> Marcella Thompson is Director of Sustainability, Environment, Health and Safety at ConAgra, a major producer of consumer and commercial food products. She is one of an emerging generation of younger EHS professionals who are transitioning into new roles managing broader sustainability issues in leading companies. She was hired about four years ago to fill her newly created position. Her description of how ConAgra addresses stakeholder requests is illuminating:
>
> "There are so many issues that can fall under the umbrella of corporate responsibility that it can be hard for an organization to keep focus. We have made the conscious decision to center our attention on where we have the most impact and can make a difference. Rather than redirecting efforts in response to the wide variety of external inquiries we receive, we respond in the context of our overall strategy and materiality assessment. We are clear on what we want to work on and why, and feel more confident about not changing our priorities to include the flavor of the month. At the same time, we are also now much more proactive in tracking emerging issues to determine how they may fit into our overall strategy. This approach enables us to have an open dialogue with our stakeholders, and overall, I think they understand and respect us for this. Of course, that's not to say that navigating differences in priorities isn't challenging."
>
> (Thompson, 2011)

Investors and Analysts

Perhaps more than any other stakeholder group, investors, particularly large institutions, have direct access to companies' senior management. Major shareholders enjoy this access simply because they have a financial stake in the company's future success. If their share of ownership is substantial, they can actually drive up the share price by buying a larger number of shares or drive down the price by selling some or all of their stake. In addition, investment analysts, who (typically) evaluate companies within specific industries, make it their business to develop intimate knowledge of the workings of the firms they follow. They frequently pose probing questions of company senior management and investor relations representatives when given the opportunity. The ability of major investors and influential analysts to literally move markets makes them a force to be reckoned with. To the extent that these stakeholders want to engage with corporate executives on ES&G issues and concerns, these desires generally are accommodated.

Furthermore, certain investors are becoming far more activist in their orientation than in the past. Led by major SRI investors and investor-led coalitions, they are pursuing a variety of strategies to ensure that their concerns about particular ES&G issues are understood and being acted on by a wide array of companies. These strategies include intensive consultations, shareholder resolutions, public information and awareness-raising campaigns, and other measures that generally advocate behavioral change on the company's part. Such changes often involve corporate governance structures and practices, transparency (public disclosure), conducting business in certain countries (such as Sudan and Burma), or positions on or preparedness for particular ES&G issues, the most prominent of which is climate change. These activities are meeting with considerable success, in that many companies have acceded to the demands made by these investors and coalitions. These successes, in turn, appear to be fueling even more shareholder-driven activism and involvement in corporate affairs. Accordingly, executives and managers in all publicly traded firms should be aware of and prepared for the possibility that investor involvement in your company's management of its major (and even minor) ES&G issues may be coming, if it has not arrived already. These issues are explored in greater depth in Chapters 6 and 8.

The Public

The general public and its members have few opportunities to directly influence corporate behavior. But public opinion, expressed both as the views of people at large and as consumer behavior, often has a significant impact on how companies are perceived, what attributes are associated with them, and, consequently, their brand identities and values. Public opinion also can have a substantial effect on other stakeholders, particularly regulatory agencies, the media, and NGOs.

In terms of the types of ES&G issues that are of the most interest, the public tends to focus on performance outcomes, particularly when they are adverse and unexpected (such as, spills and deaths/injuries). Not coincidentally, as suggested earlier, these are the types of events that tend to attract the most media interest and news coverage. With that said, the public appears to be increasingly interested in corporate performance along some more subtle dimensions, particularly energy use/greenhouse gas emissions, use of recycled materials, and production of "cleaner" products.[17] And as always, our citizens (and those in many other countries) tend to be skeptical of corporate claims regarding environmental and other ES&G improvements, product attributes, and behaviors. These changing expectations are not going unnoticed by attentive sustainability professionals in leading companies. According to Tim Mohin of AMD:

> A big factor [in the emergence of sustainability] has been changing expectations. In particular, young people care much more about corporate behavior than did previous generations. This may be a reaction to the rise of the corporation as the dominant social institution of our time. We now live in an age when the reach and power of corporations exceeds many nation-states. Increasingly, people, especially young people, believe that with this growing power comes the responsibility to do the right thing. (Mohin, 2011)

Despite these recent trends, however, the long-predicted dawn of an era of widespread public environmental awareness and sustainability-driven behavior has yet to appear, at least as manifested by either consistent consumer attitudes and purchasing patterns[18] or in the beliefs and stated priorities of the public at large. I am somewhat skeptical that we will see such an era any time soon, particularly given the persistence of a low rate of economic growth and the "jobless recovery" that has taken hold in the U.S. economy. This is not to suggest, however, that corporate leaders should ignore public opinions and beliefs about either ES&G issues generally or in the specific context of their firms. Continued vigilance on these issues and public perceptions about one's firm and industry is certainly warranted. Being trusted by stakeholders is an important asset to any company. For consumer-facing firms, establishing and maintaining trust with the public is a key component of brand value. Indeed, as has been pointed out by others (such as Martin, 2011), one important limitation of "green" marketing efforts to date has been a lack of trust among many consumers and members of the public caused by the perceived absence of credible ES&G behavior and performance by many corporations. Overcoming this hurdle may be difficult. But it is reasonable to assert that the leadership of any company should invest time and resources in at least maintaining, if not enhancing, the firm's credibility, trust, and brand strength as a sustainable business in the future.

In summary, companies have a broad array of important stakeholders with disparate interests, priorities, and specific concerns about how the firm approaches its environmental, health and safety, social, and governance issues. Executives and managers who would seek to position their firms as sustainability leaders would be well advised to invest the time and effort needed to identify their important stakeholders, understand their expectations and concerns, formulate and execute one or more engagement strategies or a set of principles for doing so, and actively manage their relationship with each important stakeholder or group. Making this investment is the best way to secure and maintain the firm's social license to operate, manage several important sources of business and financial risk, and leverage some of the company's principal intangible assets.

The next chapter builds on the foundation established in this and the previous chapters. It shows how executives and managers within companies of all sizes and types can effectively respond to and actively manage the ES&G issues that are being brought to bear by their stakeholders and American society at large.

Endnotes

1. For example, an EPA web portal to a number of databases containing company/ facility information listed by zip code may be found at www.epa.gov/epahome/ commsearch.htm. Using these databases, you can find information (including maps) on pollutant emissions, hazardous waste sites, toxic chemical releases, facility inspections and enforcement actions, and a variety of other topics.

2. Chapter 6 discusses this issue extensively.

3. This includes not only think tanks and NGOs but also highly influential management "gurus" such as, Michael Porter. See White (Ed.), 2009 for a good example of the former. See Porter and Kramer, 2011 for details on the latter—in particular, Porter's notion of "shared value."

4. For an exhaustive examination of this issue and the broader sustainability challenges and opportunities facing the global mining and minerals industry, see Mining, Minerals, and Sustainable Development Project (MMSD), 2002.

5. This discussion is adapted from concepts presented on the web site www. socialicense.com/definition.html.

6. It is not uncommon for certain named executives and other key company employees to have legally binding employment agreements precisely because their departure could pose grave competitive threats to the firm's continued success.

7. In fact, this type of approach is increasingly becoming the norm in many industries and among leading companies. Certain minimal standards regarding EHS management practices, use (or absence) of certain materials, regular performance reporting, and other requirements are increasingly finding their way into the standard contracts used (and insisted on) by many leading companies.

8. These phenomena were discussed at length in Chapter 3.

9. My understanding of these phenomena was greatly enriched by media trainer and consultant Norm Hartman, whom I hired several years ago to provide executive media training for a client.

10. If you are skeptical about this claim, watch the nightly news on television some evening and count how many stories meet the criteria and how many do not. Or consider how often we hear of a plane/train/bus/ship crash or armed conflict with many fatalities in some faraway place, and ask yourself what we, the readers/ viewers, are supposed to do with this information and how it will affect our lives or interests.

11. As discussed in Chapter 3, most of these organizations are legally organized as nonprofit organizations under IRC 501(c)(3). More specifically, nearly all the major national environmental NGOs are organized as nonprofit membership organizations, which both charge annual dues and periodically ask for supplemental (and tax-deductible) cash contributions.

12. Specifically, college-educated people ages 25 to 64 in the top 25 percent of household incomes in their age group in each country.

13. As reflected by responses to the following question: "How much do you trust [institution] to do what is right?"

14. The experience of companies in the international minerals development industry offers some important cautionary tales in this regard. Most businesses do not face the extreme challenges of the companies in this industry, but the same principles apply, irrespective of whether one's company faces a crisis situation.

15. I feel confident in making this statement because I have worked on behalf of or with scores of such people during my career and have had at least some interaction with hundreds more. At least in the realm of EHS policy and management, I have found that by and large, public agency people are just as dedicated and competent as their corporate counterparts.

16. These include firms primarily involved in news (CBS, News Corporation, Thomson Reuters), entertainment (Disney), distribution (Comcast), and a number of other enterprises.

17. By "cleaner" products, I mean the considerable and expanding supply of goods labeled or promoted as "green," "organic," "natural," and the like.

18. Indeed, some longtime observers have suggested that "green marketing" has outlived its usefulness and should be abandoned in favor of greater emphasis on determining life cycle characteristics and improved transparency. (See Makower, 2011 for further perspective on this issue.)

5

Managing ES&G Issues Within the Organization

This chapter describes how sustainability issues can and should be managed within an organization. Building on the background presented in the previous chapters, it should be apparent that, as shown in Chapter 3, the many ways in which ES&G issues affect businesses are complex, interrelated, and often of significant magnitude. Moreover, as demonstrated in Chapter 4, there is a growing understanding of the power held by stakeholders of the organization, their increasing interest in ES&G issues, and their willingness to exert their influence in pursuit of their goals. The good news in all of this is that there is now widespread (though by no means universal) understanding of the types of management strategies and practices that provide an effective means of dealing with the challenges inherent in these increasing ES&G-related demands.

This chapter begins by examining the many ways in which ES&G issues are related to one another. It suggests that in any organization of significant size, it is far more efficacious and efficient to manage these issues in an integrated fashion than in isolation. I then describe and discuss the types of management structures, policies, and behaviors that experience has shown to be effective responses to the challenges posed by ES&G issues. These structures and practices are in widespread use among leading firms in the U.S. and internationally. I conclude with some thoughts on some of the personal attributes and behaviors that I believe, based on my professional experience, are helpful in promoting the types of behavioral change that are required to move companies to a more sustainable path.

Relationships Among and Between EHS, Social, and Governance Issues

One of the major challenges inherent in developing an effective corporate sustainability program is that EHS, social, governance, and financial issues are commonly managed by different functions within the organization and by people with different educational and professional backgrounds, perspectives, and priorities. Accordingly, an important part of implementing sustainability in an organization is getting people to understand the interconnections among the issues and to make decisions that are in the best long-term interests of the enterprise.

Historically, most people inside and outside of business have viewed the domains of environment, health and safety, operations management, labor relations, finance, community development, and economics as distinct and separate fields. Indeed, each has its own educational foundation, with the academic programs used to teach entering professionals the required knowledge and skills often being housed within different schools or in different colleges in a university setting. Each has its own programs of study, academic and/or professional degrees, certificates, and other credentials. There is often little or no regular contact between these schools, except on administrative matters. And each has its particular methods, techniques, tools, and, as noted in Chapter 2, set of beliefs and lexicon. This is one major reason why the organizational "stovepipes" that are so often cited as barriers to collaboration and improved performance are so pervasive.

I believe that a coherent ES&G or sustainability program can and should help build bridges between the disparate functional domains that exist in most companies. Indeed, for any sustainability program to reach its potential, establishing these connections is a necessity. A key leverage point for doing so is common interest in many of the endpoints that are of concern to professionals working in these different fields and functions. The most obvious example is the duality of many EHS issues. For example, common operations such as chemical and other material use, pollution control, and waste generation and management have both environmental and health and safety aspects. And it is often the case that focusing on a performance improvement in one area achieves a gain in the other as well. (For example, reducing material use through a process efficiency improvement generally results in lower worker exposure as well as reduced waste generation.) These types of "win-win" situations are commonly encountered in the EHS arena. Such outcomes also have helped lead to the confluence of environmental and health and safety functions over the past couple of decades in many corporations and within the EHS profession itself. So this is old news, at least to some involved in the sustainability conversation within and about many companies.

In a similar vein but to a lesser extent, the general domain of pollution prevention and its many offshoots has produced hundreds of successful examples of situations in which a firm reduced its environmental and/or health and safety (H&S) footprint and also reduced its costs (captured a financial benefit). The magnitude of these initiatives and their EHS and financial impacts varies widely. But there can be no doubt that well-chosen investments in material use reduction, pollution control efficiency, waste reduction/recovery, and other strategies to reduce adverse environmental impact often create net financial value. Perhaps the most prominent of these approaches, at least among the general public and in certain professions, is energy efficiency. Here the idea is to install equipment and/or building components that may have higher initial procurement and installation costs[1] but also have lower operating costs. This saves money and energy and offers the collateral benefit of reducing direct and/or indirect (from electricity production) pollutant emissions. These approaches have proven to be effective under a wide range of conditions and have become established to the point that they are now components of U.S. national environmental and energy policy.[2]

Nonetheless, such approaches are often viewed as highly situational and of limited overall impact to the organization's operational and financial success. Consequently, they tend to be tactically managed and deployed within most firms. I address this issue, and the barriers that it places in the path of sustainability efforts, in the final section of this chapter.

This brings us back to governance. Historically, management of EHS issues has been viewed as strictly a tactical issue. There are several reasons for this, the most important of which have their roots in the belief that EHS issues confer risk, liability, and costs rather than opportunity. And because costs and liabilities are undesirable features of the corporate landscape that are to be minimized as much as possible, there is little opportunity for substantial, ongoing value creation by focusing on them. This belief is rational, or at least it was in the early days of environmental and health and safety regulation. Recall that prior to 1970, no law (at least on the U.S. national level) precluded or prohibited the emission of pollutants into the air or water or the disposal of virtually any type of waste material on the land wherever local zoning ordinances would allow these activities. Therefore, the initial wave of regulations limiting these releases and disposal practices had the immediate effect of internalizing what had always been an externality. Costs to comply with the new regulations were in many cases significant.

The situation today, however, is vastly different. All major companies now are generally subject to waste management, pollution control, disclosure, and other requirements,[3] as discussed in Chapter 3. In response to the implementation of these new requirements over the past several decades, business has done what it always does— adapted and innovated. Right behind or alongside the deployment of new requirements came the entry of new companies. They offered expertise to not only meet the new constraints, but, over time, to redesign and retool production processes so that they emitted fewer pollutants and less waste and/or generated effluents at lower rates or that required less treatment. In some cases, they found ways to help their clients exit the regulatory system altogether by bringing the level of a regulated activity below the applicable threshold. From that point, it was simply a matter of time before firms came into being to help other companies outsource many of their environmental and/or H&S management functions, automate and streamline their regulatory reporting processes, and assume other "non-value-adding" tasks. Such new enterprises and services proliferated during the 1990s and are now a stable feature of the EHS management landscape.

Currently, we appear to be on the front edge of a dawning awareness that there is an upside to a more sophisticated view of EHS issues and their influence on the business enterprise. Interestingly, this change is being driven by both investors (discussed in depth in Chapters 6 and 7) and consumers. Increasingly, managers of consumer-facing businesses are learning that their customers care about the content of the products they buy, how and where they are made, and the behavior of the companies with which they do business. We also must recognize the influence of major intermediaries, none of which is currently more prominent than Walmart. This company has established the goal of sustainability for itself, taken the life-cycle perspective I advocate here, engaged with its stakeholders up and down the value chain, and focused on its role and competitive advantage in the retail market space. By doing these things, Walmart is using its market power to drive behavioral change in hundreds (if not thousands) of consumer goods manufacturers and other suppliers. Although this example is unusual in both its nature and significance, it illustrates the growing expectations of American society, the scrutiny applied to business, the nearly universal and instantaneous access to information (and misinformation), and the importance placed on branding. All these issues affect company revenues, or the "top line" of business, which is a subject of abiding interest to any CEO or other corporate leader.

As discussed in some detail in Chapter 3, companies and many other noncorporate entities have both episodic and ongoing obligations (formal or otherwise) to conduct certain ES&G activities and/or achieve specified levels of performance. In many cases, these obligations are multilayered. That is, they may have a legal basis (in whole or in part) and an additional component that expresses a societal need or expectation. In many cases (and there are seemingly more every day), customer, supply chain, or other commercial influences may be felt as well. On the flip side, which in my view receives too little emphasis, these issues and evolving expectations also confer opportunity. Adroit management of one or more ES&G issues can materially improve the chances of attracting new customers (from competitors), increasing margins, and, in some cases, developing entirely new segments, categories, or markets. Thus, ES&G issues should be viewed fundamentally as having a *dual nature*. This implies that a close examination of each issue or set of issues is warranted prior to forming any firm conclusions about whether an ES&G expectation or trend is a threat or an opportunity. Moreover, because of the multifaceted nature of these issues, it is important to recognize that their relevance may be greater than is generally recognized and that their magnitude and importance to the organization's fortunes may be unexpectedly large, particularly in the medium to long term.

The importance of and interconnections among the issues and, hence, magnitude of the challenges inherent in effectively managing them is directly proportional to the organization's size and complexity. Very small businesses and nonprofits may have few if any truly significant ES&G issues that require substantial senior management attention or formal management structures. More commonly, however, and certainly for publicly traded U.S. companies and sizeable government agencies, a more formal and consistent approach is required. With that said, even small organizations can benefit from many of the principles and approaches described next.[4]

Regardless of organizational size or complexity, what is needed to sort out the nature of complex ES&G issues and their organizational implications is clarity, structure, and discipline. These attributes can and, I believe, should be expressed through establishing and operating a number of well-defined and widely accepted management structures and practices that have been developed and implemented by those in the EHS field during the past 15 years or so. This is the focus of the next section. Although in my experience these practices have largely been applied to the active management of EHS issues, they touch a number of significant social issues (such as labor relations and relationships with surrounding communities and other stakeholders) and also have a strong governance component. Accordingly, I believe that they offer the best and most comprehensive approach to managing ES&G issues in a coherent and seamless manner.

Effective ES&G Management Structures and Practices

This section describes the components and workings of an integrated and effective system of managing ES&G issues. I begin at the top—the level of organizational strategy—and then work through implementing systems and processes. I conclude with a discussion of measuring and reporting (as appropriate) performance, internal review, and course corrections. You might detect a distinct management systems orientation to the approach I suggest. This is not by happenstance. I am a long-standing advocate of the use of formal management system principles and practices to address EHS issues and challenges. I have seen through my work over the years that such approaches help provide the clarity and support needed to grasp and control all the disparate threads that influence organizational sustainability (or lead to its absence).

Vision and Strategy

Most organizations, and certainly most companies, do not exist for the express purpose of improving environmental quality, creating healthier workers, promoting more equitable societies, or other commonly shared components of what most people think of as sustainability. Instead, most organizations exist for other, more specific purposes. Perhaps they collect and efficiently distribute investment capital (operate as a bank), provide telecommunications services, manufacture and sell finished wood and paper products, or provide pre-K–12 education for the children of a particular community. Consequently, sustainability strategies (and implementing internal groups or teams) need to support and invigorate the organization's fundamental purpose, rather than constrain or detract from it. This, of course, is easier said than done. Nonetheless, my work over the years, and that of many others in the field, demonstrates that it is possible. Value, in both a financial and broader social welfare sense, can be created through implementing well-crafted sustainability strategies, structures, and practices. But it is vital to frame the issues and the organizational approach in the appropriate way for this to occur.

So prior to embarking on any initiative to pursue sustainability, it is important to view ES&G issues through the lens of each organization's basic purpose for being, defined mission, vision for the future, objectives and commitments, and strategy. As suggested in Chapter 2, many organizations and teams within them have started their sustainability efforts with a collection of ES&G issues and priorities that may have impelled action or otherwise were viewed as being of the highest priority. I would not take issue with the importance of remaining responsive to both stakeholder concerns and business-relevant events that may occur unexpectedly. But I believe that a much more effective approach is to adopt a broader perspective in which the tactical ES&G issues of the day are set into a more expansive framework. If constructed appropriately, this framework flows from rather than conflicts with the organization's existing strategy, priorities, and values.

Accordingly, rather than starting with an examination of specific ES&G issues or how they can be managed more effectively in a coordinated way, I suggest the opposite approach. Assuming that they exist, I advocate starting with the organization's mission statement, core values, long-range objectives, and business strategy and then mapping the ES&G issues into them (fitting the specifics into the bigger picture). If these types of documents do not exist, a new dialog around sustainability could offer an excellent opportunity to formalize the organization's existing norms and work practices and to begin charting the course toward its desired future. Using this type of top-down approach provides an opportunity to identify the ES&G issues that speak to or are aligned with core operational issues (such as water supply/quality to a manufacturer of soft drinks) and to develop an early sense of their relative magnitude compared to other large-scale organizational issues. This also may help illuminate more subtle trends that may have a significant impact on the organization in the future, such as customer concerns about the life cycle environmental impact of the firm's products. Thus, one thing that drops out of such an analysis are the ES&G issues that may pose the biggest opportunities and threats to the organization and that are worthy of further evaluation.[5] At the least, implementing the approach I suggest helps ensure that the sustainability strategy and implementing structures and activities are in harmony with the overall direction of the firm or agency and hence are more likely to be embraced up and down the organization.

Having developed (or assembled) and reviewed the organization's overall aspirations and plans and evaluated the most visible ES&G issues within that context, the next logical step is to develop (or refine) an organization-wide sustainability strategy. A coherent and comprehensive strategy (along with an ES&G or sustainability policy) is the road map that should guide any internal sustainability program or initiative. Without a good strategy, goal-setting and improvement programs are likely to be misdirected or, at best, not reach their full potential. I emphasize here that the sustainability strategy must be an organic extension of the overall organizational business strategy. It must be based on the firm's or agency's mission, vision, and business culture as well as an informed understanding of the interests of its stakeholders (as discussed in the preceding chapter). I have found this approach to be far more effective than trying to divine or distill overall principles from a bottom-up synthesis of the organization's EHS or stakeholder issues, or other commonly used approaches.

In addition, I strongly encourage a formulation that is appropriate to the nature of the enterprise. For corporations, the sustainability strategy should emphasize long-term financial value creation as the core precept around which environmental and social objectives are addressed. (The following sidebar describes an interesting example.) For public sector organizations, effectiveness in achieving the mission and financial stability and predictability are more appropriate objectives. This is particularly true in light of the budgetary crisis that afflicts many federal, state, and municipal organizations. Related funding limits are likely to impose significant limitations for the foreseeable future.

Executive-Driven But Inclusive Sustainability Strategy Formulation

3M, a large, well-known manufacturing firm, provides a useful example of how corporate leaders can drive the formulation of an appropriate, business-focused sustainability strategy. In 2008, 3M retooled its sustainability approach around three strategic principles, focusing on the pursuit of customer satisfaction and commercial success within a framework of environmental, social, and economic values. 3M's new Sustainability Principles are as follows:

- **Economic success.** Build lasting customer relationships by developing differentiated, practical, and ingenious solutions to their sustainability challenges.

- **Environmental protection.** Provide practical and effective solutions and products to address environmental challenges for ourselves and our customers.

- **Social responsibility.** Engage key stakeholders in dialogue and take action to improve 3M's sustainability performance.

In other words, the new strategy is not limited to meeting growing expectations about corporate governance and ES&G performance. Instead, it involves using the company's strengths to develop new products, services, and solutions that solve customer challenges having a sustainability dimension. This differentiates 3M from its competitors and earns it new customers and market share.

According to the company, this process was driven by corporate leadership, beginning with the formation of an internal strategic planning team with representatives from environmental operations, corporate communications, strategic planning, and 3M businesses. This team used feedback from 3M's external stakeholders, including customers, nongovernmental organizations, governments, investors, and others to develop a set of draft principles. Then, over a three-month period, the team held nearly 50 internal feedback sessions with 3M employees across the globe to get their input. Finally, the revised principles were reviewed and endorsed by 3M's corporate operating committee, which includes the Chairman, President and Chief Executive Officer, and other executive officers.

(Source: 3M company web site and documents. See http://solutions.3m.com/wps/portal/3M/en_US/3M-Sustainability/Global/Resources/Downloads/)

Policies and Goals

To give life and motive force to the strategy, any organization pursuing sustainability must have some additional structure. The appropriate degree of formality for these structures varies depending on the organization's nature, size, and ES&G maturity. But I believe that the concepts underlying these components are important to understand and deploy in virtually every situation. In my view, structure appropriately starts with defining what the organization stands for and what it seeks to accomplish.

Policy

Regardless of formal structural or cultural considerations, a crucial component of any organizational ES&G/sustainability program is the overall corporate-level environmental, EHS, or sustainability policy or policies.[6] In combination with the strategy, a coherent and comprehensive sustainability policy provides the road map that should guide all internal sustainability programs or initiatives.[7] The policy is the cornerstone of effective organizational programs and establishes the position, aspirations, and commitments of the organization and all its members. Importantly, and as discussed in a subsequent chapter, the presence or absence of such policies is a key indicator of any company's ability to understand and effectively manage its EHS and broader sustainability issues across the entire enterprise.

The absence of a comprehensive, coherent policy has hindered the development of many well-intentioned EHS improvement initiatives. To avoid such disappointments and optimize the use of the organization's human and other resources, the responsible executives/managers should move decisively to establish a simple, clear statement of principles and commitments regarding ES&G issues or sustainability if one is absent. Organizations that have one or more existing policies should review their provisions every few years. They should make refinements, as appropriate, to reflect operating experience and lessons learned, accommodate new business goals and priorities, and address emerging ES&G issues and concerns.

As a general matter, corporate policies should be concise, drafted in language that is understandable to all (literate) members of the organization, and unambiguous. Policy statements may include long-range aspirations and strategic objectives, but it is generally best to leave specific goals and milestones to implementing strategies and tactical plans.

In terms of policy content, there is a broad continuum of belief and practice regarding what should or should not be included in a sustainability policy. I believe it reasonable to assert that a good ES&G policy contains a number of key elements that, individually and in combination, provide assurance that the company is motivated to develop and maintain a comprehensive understanding of how and in what ways ES&G issues may affect the enterprise. Furthermore, the policy should focus on appropriate ES&G effects. Finally, all employees should be involved in and capable of contributing to improving the firm's ES&G performance.

To meet these conditions, I suggest some principles that I believe are a minimum set of policy elements to support the notion that an organization is committed to the pursuit of sustainability. Just as with my description of the overall sustainability management framework suggested in this chapter, the elements listed next are widely recognized principles and practices that are in place in many hundreds of organizations around the world,[8] many of which are quite small. I believe that including these elements will yield a solid and workable policy that can maintain or gain the rapid support of virtually any organization's members and its other stakeholders:

- Comply with the law and the organization's own commitments.
- Determine and control the organization's *significant* EHS effects.
- Prevent pollution at the source where *possible*.
- Conserve resources where *feasible*.
- Protect the organization's members from harm on the job.
- Support the protection of internationally recognized human rights, and ensure that the organization is not complicit in human rights abuses.[9]
- Uphold the freedom of association.
- Avoid and prevent all forms of forced, compulsory, and child labor in work performed by or on behalf of the organization.
- Practice nondiscrimination in employment and in providing ongoing professional opportunities.
- Check progress and improve over time.
- Address stakeholder input and transparency.

Note that none of these principles requires the organization to address sustainability issues that do not apply or to which the organization does not meaningfully contribute. They also don't require the organization to invest resources to reduce or eliminate ES&G effects unless doing so is both an effective response and financially feasible. Taken together, these provisions simply mean that the organization will develop an understanding of its EHS impacts; take appropriate steps to maintain the health, safety, and rights of its members while on the job; and do what it reasonably can to improve. The organization also will check status and progress periodically and decide whether and how it will engage its stakeholders in matters concerning the environment and the well-being of its workers and other members of the community.

At the same time, these policy elements send a clear signal that the organization understands that the environment, health and safety, and other social issues are important. The organization accepts responsibility for improving their condition and will determine what aspects of its operations pose significant effects and risks, if any. Then, any improvement efforts will be evaluated and implemented where they are sensible and cost-effective. Finally, improved EHS and broader sustainability performance over time is expected.

Several other important provisions should speak to policy application and implementation:

- The policy applies to all employees and locations.
- The policy is overseen, enforced, and periodically reviewed and improved, as appropriate, by the Board of Directors or analogous senior management.
- In evaluating the ES&G significance of the organization's activities, the policy considers all life cycle stages of the products, materials, and services it uses and provides.

I believe that it is important to apply policy requirements to all company operations and employees. The purpose of any policy, from the perspective of those who develop and issue it, is to enable (and, in some cases, enforce) the types of behavioral changes that result in meaningful improvement over time. Ensuring that policy provisions apply to all members of the organization is important. Doing so helps distribute any associated burdens fairly and also, in the current context, helps promote collaboration and the types of multidisciplinary cooperation needed to effectively address ES&G and sustainability issues across the organization. As discussed in the next section, senior management oversight and direction are crucial to securing and maintaining support throughout the organization for the investments of time and other resources and behavioral changes that are required to adopt more sustainable behavior. Many are the environmental and sustainability initiatives that began with great fanfare but then died on the vine months or a few years later when it turned out that senior management had other or higher priorities. Senior management support for and involvement in any sustainability program or initiative must continue to be tangible and visible as the sometimes-difficult work of implementing new ways of doing things proceeds during the crucial early months and years. The simplest and clearest signal of continuing support that can be sent throughout the organization is that the senior management is involved in and cares about the work being done and its ultimate result. Finally, life cycle perspectives are increasingly being applied in a wide variety of contexts, ranging from consumer goods production to "big box" retailing to ESG investing. I believe that for an organization to take a full and honest look at its ES&G footprint, it must consider both upstream and downstream aspects. In other words, it should consider the EHS aspects of the materials, goods, and services it procures, and the labor and social practices of its suppliers. It also should consider the energy, environmental, and health/safety aspects of its own products and services as they are used by its customers.

Organizations that are well along the maturity path or that want to make more rapid progress can consider some additional policy provisions and features. These may be included in the policy statement itself or articulated in implementing plans or other supporting documents:

- The organization has a senior-level officer responsible for ES&G/sustainability policy implementation.
- As appropriate, the policy scope is global, such that operations outside the U.S. are subject to the same requirements as those in the U.S. (the firm goes beyond compliance with local laws).

The first indicator provides a link back to senior management. It helps ensure that governance practices are effective and that the policy remains a "living" document that can be adapted in response to changing business conditions. The second indicator reflects an approach common in sophisticated companies, where it is recognized that the most cost-effective way to maintain compliance, product quality, and cost control is to have a common set of practices that are carried out globally.

Policy commitments also are important indicators of an organization's overall direction and the degree to which it can be expected to seek meaningful performance improvement. An organization can go in many different directions. The appropriate choices are a function of its culture, business and sustainability objectives, and program sophistication (capability/capacity). Here are a few examples of policy commitments used by a number of leading companies:

- Public reporting of ES&G/sustainability results
- Stakeholder involvement in formulating/revising the ES&G/ sustainability policy
- Auditing (internal, independent third party, or both) of ES&G results

The first two commitments speak to the degree to which the organization and its management recognize the legitimate role of external stakeholders in understanding and reacting to the firm's ES&G posture and trends, and in providing input where appropriate and helpful. Although ES&G reporting currently is not required by law or regulation in the U.S., interest in corporate ES&G/sustainability performance information has been increasing. This interest is manifested in several distinct and important trends and events.[10] The degree to which a company considers (or even solicits) external input when evaluating components of or refinements to its policy generally is a function of how it views its relationship to particular (or all) stakeholders, as well as its internal culture. Some firms are simply more internally focused, and others cultivate a deep, continuing relationship with customers. There is no "right" answer here, other than the decision about whether or how to factor stakeholder concerns and issues into the policy should be consistent with what the firm is and, more importantly, what it aspires to be in the future. The third attribute reflects the principle that periodic auditing is a necessary component of any compliance program or management system. It also reflects the growing expectation on the part of many stakeholders that ES&G data released by the firm be credible and verifiable, in keeping with the growing importance of this information.

In some situations, a corporate-wide environmental, EHS, or sustainability policy provides the general principles needed to make clear the organization's beliefs, intentions, and commitments. But it may not be fully adequate to address rapidly evolving conditions on the ground. In such cases, it may be helpful to develop subsidiary documents or tools to augment the corporate policy and meet the needs of decision makers in a particular business or geography. The sidebar on the following page provides an example of how this can be done.

Goals

Finally, complete policies or subsidiary documents identify at least the major EHS issues that are relevant to the organization's lines of business and activities. Where appropriate, it is also desirable for the organization to establish improvement targets, although not necessarily in the policy itself. Given their prominence and importance across a wide array of sectors of the economy, I believe that good sustainability policies should address as many of the following as appropriate, subject to each organization's particular circumstances:

- Climate change and/or greenhouse gas emissions
- Air and/or water pollutant emissions
- Solid and/or hazardous waste generation and disposal
- Energy use/conservation
- Water use/conservation
- Material recovery
- Worker injuries and illnesses

I believe that it is appropriate for all sustainability policies to address specific ES&G endpoints, because it is now widely understood that all business (and other) organizations have an ES&G footprint, and all have at least some ability to reduce its magnitude. In keeping with the themes of this book, I have emphasized the goals just listed because they have the clearest relationship to financial performance. For example, it has been repeatedly demonstrated that activities that reduce energy or water consumption often produce direct, tangible financial benefits (cost savings) in addition to their positive environmental impacts. The same applies to health and safety improvements, particularly workplace ergonomics. This is not to say that there might not be valid reasons to specify additional endpoints, such as philanthropy or diversity, along with those just outlined. It is simply more difficult to make the case that there is a direct cause-and-effect relationship between investing in these areas and creating new financial value.

One Policy, Many Issues

Some years ago, I was retained by a major publicly traded electric power producer that operated both regulated utility and unregulated power businesses to review a draft environmental policy document. This company had a strong regional base and was in the process of expanding into a number of new markets across the country. In doing so, however, its executives had encountered a large number of environmental concerns and issues that were new to them, some of which were local in nature. By creating a corporate-level environmental policy document, they hoped to provide consistent and clear guidance to business unit managers across the country on a wide range of issues, from renewable portfolio standards to protection of sensitive habitats.

As requested, I performed a review of the 20-page document, which took the form of some narrative along with a matrix describing in some detail the nature of certain key issues. When I met with the client's representatives, who included an environmental policy manager and a business unit executive, I provided my feedback. I told them that although their document provided much useful background information and was well written, it suffered from several limitations. It was not written to the needs and perspectives of the intended audience (nonenvironmental executives), who had limited knowledge of and interest in the details of environmental issues. It also was too detailed and lengthy. Most importantly, it was completely disconnected from the company's business and strategy. This outcome, I explained, was fairly typical. Well-meaning environmental staff often try to educate and persuade businesspeople of the importance of effective environmental management practices by sharing a communication that tries to do too much and does not speak to the audience's needs (and constraints).

I then unveiled my suggested alternative. After reviewing and identifying the strengths and weaknesses of the existing document,

I had performed some quick research. This helped me identify the firm's major lines of business, long-term objectives, specific goals, major strategies, and corporate values. Using this information and an understanding of how policies should be formulated, I then created a flexible policy-setting framework that could be applied and adapted as needed to meet local conditions across the country. The framework combined the company's mission, core business strategy and major business objectives, values, environmental commitments and goals, and key strengths with a set of considerations that took into account important external conditions and stakeholders, which varied widely according to the situation. These considerations included the local (generally state-level) regulatory environment, stakeholder interests and concerns, the specific environmental issue(s) in question, short-term business/financial goals, and partnership arrangements, among others. Thus, the framework had both fixed, corporate-level aspects and highly flexible and adaptable components that could readily be applied to address conditions on the ground in any company subsidiary and in any U.S. location.

My alternative solution was greeted with great enthusiasm by the clients, particularly the business unit executive, who asked me to fully develop it and present it to her corporate environmental management team. Subsequently, I facilitated discussions involving the company's senior environmental staff in two meetings. This culminated in the corporate VP for EHS recommending the approach, with minor improvements made during the meetings, to his colleagues on the firm's Board of Directors. Following their approval, the framework was adopted and deployed across the company. In this way, company senior management could be assured that their people were making policy decisions that were consistent with company objectives and commitments while being responsive to local conditions, including both constraints and opportunities.

Whatever issues and long-range objectives are established as a matter of policy, it is vital for the organization to define specific targets and milestones as part of any active pursuit of ES&G excellence or sustainability.[11] Articulating specific goals reflects a certain level of commitment by the firm and provides a benchmark against which efforts and success (or lack thereof) can be measured and evaluated, by both company senior management and external stakeholders. In short, goals provide evidence that the firm's performance is expected to improve over time.

I believe in "stretch" goals. This is a level of performance that requires new effort beyond the status quo. It pushes people out of their comfort zones and may even require new ways of thinking about the issue at hand. In other words, goal setting can be used as a spur for internal innovation. Indeed, this type of approach has been used successfully by a substantial number of major companies to catalyze nonlinear, or quantum, leaps in EHS performance.[12]

Whether or not a particular organization chooses to push the envelope by setting aggressive performance targets, it is nonetheless important for it to commit itself and its people to goals and then work to reach them. In the absence of explicit goals (and accompanying time frames), policy objectives can devolve rapidly into wishful thinking and unfocused, undisciplined activities that accomplish little of substance and undermine the credibility of the organization's sustainability efforts.

Management Systems

Sustained performance improvement in a large organization does not occur by itself or through the uncoordinated, spontaneous efforts of individuals, regardless of their level of commitment. Moreover, EHS and other sustainability issues in any organization of substantial size are too numerous and complex to manage in isolation. What is required instead is a formalized, systematic approach: a management system. A management system is a set of defined and coherent systems, programs, and practices. Formal environmental management systems (EMSs) have come into widespread use during the past 15 years. Many organizations have experienced greater efficiencies, improved regulatory compliance and environmental performance, and reduced costs and liabilities by deploying EMSs in their organizations. Furthermore, my work in the EHS arena over more than two decades leads to the conclusion that the presence of a fully developed EMS is a key indicator of the extent to which a company's senior management is truly in a position to understand and actively manage its environmental (and broader sustainability) issues in a comprehensive fashion.

The features and elements of the EMSs used by most U.S. companies are listed in the ISO 14001 standard, which can be readily obtained for a small fee. Some companies have instead used industry-specific variants (such as programs developed by the chemical and forest products industries for their members) that are patterned on the same concepts, as discussed in Chapter 3. Because a substantial volume of guidance on implementing EMSs in various types of organizations already exists, I will not devote space here to weighing in on how to implement an EMS in organizations that don't have one. I will just make a few key suggestions concerning how to go about the EMS design and deployment process.

Set (or Reset) the Focus

Although the international standard (ISO 14001) defining the components of EMSs emphasizes their use as a business-driven, flexible, consensus-based solution, many EMSs have been deployed using a "compliance-plus" orientation. Using this approach, the EMS and its provisions simply impose a new layer of requirements. This is unfortunate, because as discussed later, designing and implementing an EMS provides a unique opportunity for the organization to take a step back from business as usual to truly understand and optimize its interactions with the environment. Moreover, I believe that this process provides a convenient and effective vehicle through which to identify and begin characterizing opportunities to create financial value in addition to managing EHS risks and liabilities.

To make this happen, it is important to take the EMS framework and fit it into the company's existing structures and practices. I suggest applying a deft touch, using the management system concepts as they were intended. Link existing processes that work well, improve the ones that do not, fill the gaps as needed, and get everyone in the organization to accept an appropriate share of the responsibility for making the organization more sustainable. The end result should be a system that creates less work, not more, for the EHS staff and provides opportunity and empowerment for people across the organization.

More importantly, this approach enables the organization to continually improve its EHS and social performance over time, identify and capture opportunities to reduce costs and risks, and maintain and enhance revenue streams, thereby driving long-term sustainability.

Accordingly, those managing any EMS deployment process should ensure that the management system does not follow the conventional path, where it is applied using a "brute force" mentality or shaped into a compliance tool. Instead, those in charge should ensure that at key points in the EMS design and deployment process, the appropriate business-level focus is applied and maintained. These key points are identified and discussed next. All are in the planning and policy phases—that is, on the front end. If these elements are configured appropriately, the standard management system components should produce the desired outcomes if they are implemented and maintained correctly.

Policy

I have discussed the ES&G/sustainability policy at length. In the context of the EMS, it is important to make clear that the corporate policy applies, and if any additional provisions apply (such as, at a divisional or site level), they should be stated.

Aspects Analysis

This is the linchpin of the entire management system. The aspects analysis is where all the points of intersection between the organization and the surrounding environment (broadly defined) are identified, rated/ranked, and sorted as being "significant" or otherwise. Significant aspects are then addressed through specific targets and management programs by which these newly established goals will be attained. To this point, the aspects analysis used in most EMSs has been limited in scope to waste, emissions, energy and water use, and other, mostly obvious, interactions with the environment. Some organizations add worker safety endpoints as well. To help impel the organization toward a sustainable future, however, the aspects analysis must be applied broadly so that it considers the following:

- Not only environmental, but also an array of health and safety,[13] social equity, and economic endpoints
- Upstream and downstream impacts of products and services

Moreover, the tests of *significance* should include possible effects on employee health and well-being, possible impacts on stakeholder relationships (particularly with customers), and long-range financial considerations. Other tests also may be of interest, depending on the organization's circumstances. The key is to make an affirmative decision about the criteria rather than simply adopting without further thought the more narrow conventional approach.

Finally, I believe that it is important to focus on *opportunities*. In virtually every EMS I have seen, the sole focus is reducing or preventing harm. Although this is crucial, I believe this focus is incomplete and limits the utility of the management system to drive productive change. In contrast, the ISO EMS standard takes a more neutral stance.[14] Quite simply, if an organization wants a management system to help it capture value in all its dimensions, it has to design and operate the system so that it identifies and properly evaluates upside potential as well as downside risk. This brings us to the next topic.

Objectives and Targets

A properly designed and implemented system helps produce the outcomes on which it is focused. Therefore, if an organization wants to capture new revenue-producing opportunities by improving its ES&G performance, it should build objectives and targets that reflect those aspirations into its management system. For example, rather than expressing a waste reduction target simply in quantitative terms, an alternative might be to improve material efficiency by a stated percentage and/or reduce unit material (or overall variable) cost by some other percentage.

The management system's objectives and targets can be pointed in numerous different directions. The important thing is to carefully consider what ES&G and business outcomes are desired, and to orient the management system explicitly and in an integrated fashion toward their attainment.

Structures, Roles, and Responsibilities

I believe that for an organization to make substantial and durable gains in its sustainability posture and performance, it must establish appropriate management structures, define roles and responsibilities, and design and deploy programs in pursuit of its goals. I have great respect for the efficacy and accomplishments of some of the informal networks and "skunkworks" that have taken shape in organizations of all sizes during the past few decades. But I believe that such approaches are unsuitable for pursuing organizational sustainability. Instead, my experience suggests that to achieve the organization-scale change required, it is essential to establish clarity on how things will run, who is in charge and accountable, and what the priorities are.

It starts, as (almost) always, at the top. It is important that the organization's most senior executives are responsible for and involved in establishing its posture toward ES&G/sustainability. In a corporation, these responsibilities rest with the members of the Board of Directors and the senior company executives charged with operating the company (typically, the Chief Executive Officer, Chief Operating Officer, and Chief Financial Officer). Historically, the senior management within many companies and industries has not viewed EHS issues as being of strategic import, preferring to delegate their management to line managers and executives. In recent years, however, this position has begun to change in fundamental ways. The possible business impacts of global environmental issues, such as climate change, have become more clear. And shareholder and other stakeholder demands for more extensive and effective ES&G policies, practices, and disclosure have increased.

Accordingly, I recommend that organizations establish the following responsibilities and lines of authority and accountability at their most senior levels:

- A Board Committee with responsibility for ES&G/sustainability issues, or at least a responsible Board member with oversight responsibility for an executive-level committee with responsibility for these issues
- A "C-level" executive (CEO, COO, and so on) responsible for ES&G/sustainability issues

Noncorporate organizations should establish parallel structures involving their senior management and owner/member/stakeholder representatives.

These arrangements are of crucial importance and are the very heart of governance—the G in ES&G.

These indicators address the extent to which sustainability issues are directly overseen by the representatives of the firm's owners (shareholders) and are directly managed by people holding positions of authority for setting overall corporate direction, establishing objectives, and deploying resources. Only in this way can interested parties inside and outside the organization be assured that sustainability issues are being treated in a fully consistent and strategic manner across the entire organization and that they are viewed as being of sufficient importance to be overseen and managed like other core business issues.

Another key role is explicit responsibility for giving life to the ES&G/sustainability policy. Some organizations have a long-standing environmental or health and safety program (such as in heavily regulated, resource-intensive industries). Such a firm may have a general understanding of who is responsible for interpreting the policy or its pertinent parts and defining and executing activities to give the policy (or portions thereof) full effect. In organizations without a fully formed EHS function, responsibility may be much more diffuse. In either case, I believe that it is important for any organization either developing a sustainability program *de novo* or expanding the scope of one or more existing programs to assign clear responsibility for implementing the ES&G/sustainability policy to a defined department or staff function. This is important to provide both internal accountability and credibility and assurance to important external stakeholders that senior management expects that policy provisions will be driven throughout the organization. Absent such assurance, they may conclude that even the most comprehensive policy is simply a collection of aspirational statements that may or may not affect day-to-day operations.

In any event, making sustainability happen in a meaningful way across an entire organization requires that all its members understand and accept that they have a role to play. Leading companies are putting in place structures, policies, and incentives to provide the clarity of purpose and support necessary to bring about the required level of awareness, support, and enthusiasm. The following sidebar discusses one example.

Propagating Organizational Change

"Sustainable development has been an important issue for ConAgra Foods for many years. For example, the company held its first Sustainable Development Awards program in 1992. Early on, sustainability initiatives were being managed and implemented by our many independent operating companies, but we didn't have line of sight to our corporate sustainability performance. Now it is difficult to imagine running our business without these performance indicators. Over time, sustainability has evolved from being the 'right thing to do' to part of our core business strategy. Our senior leadership team recently unveiled a five-year strategic plan that includes corporate citizenship as one of five key business ambitions. To help focus our efforts and provide a more robust cross-functional governance structure, the company is creating a Corporate Responsibility Steering Council. Chaired by a member of our senior leadership team and composed of vice presidents representing key functional areas, the council will develop a holistic strategy for our 'Good for You, Good for the Community, and Good for the Planet' platform.

"I've witnessed a heightened level of personal engagement around sustainability across all levels of the company. Increasingly, employees outside of the core sustainable development team are taking ownership for sustainability and building it into how they do everyday work. We've recently begun including sustainability criteria in our performance evaluation process. For example, our operations leadership and plant managers are evaluated on whether they meet specific greenhouse gas and water reduction targets. The criteria vary by function and area of influence, as appropriate for what impact an individual can have on the organization. This has enhanced the sense of ownership and accountability related to sustainability and, in my opinion, is critical in positioning the company to meet our sustainability goals."

—Marcella Thompson, ConAgra Foods

Performance Improvement Programs

As suggested previously, I believe that the most efficient and effective way in which to manage the many activities affecting organizational sustainability, and certainly to achieve ambitious goals, is to establish or retool programs to focus on their attainment. To be effective, programs must include within their scope the activities that give rise to the organization's ES&G aspects and be focused on achieving continual performance improvement over time. Recognizing the findings of behavioral economics and reflecting my own experience working in and on behalf of major corporations and other large organizations, I believe that incentives have a powerful effect on people's willingness to change existing behaviors. Such behavioral change, even if relatively simple and painless, is much more likely to occur if the organization's people are motivated out of self-interest to adopt the new and preferred practices. Quite simply, providing appropriate incentives for the behaviors that are required to attain goals is a crucial determinant of success.

Accordingly, organizations pursuing sustainability should carefully consider formulating or modifying formal programs to ensure that they have the following attributes:

- Address direct outputs of operating the enterprise as applicable (waste, emissions, energy and water use, worker exposure to chemicals or hazardous conditions)
- Account for upstream ES&G aspects (material content, packaging, transport distance, sourcing from sensitive areas/resources)
- Consider downstream ES&G aspects (energy use and pollutant emissions in use, ease of collection/disassembly, possible community-level exposure to product/component-related emissions, material recovery post-use)
- Have a focus on eco-efficiency[15]
- Incorporate training components as appropriate (particularly for material use/waste reduction, quality, workplace safety, ergonomics, and wellness)
- Include performance appraisal elements (including incentive compensation) for responsible managers and executives
- Incorporate the use of incentives given to nonmanagerial employees (individuals or teams) for meeting company goals

I emphasize that environmental and worker health and safety concerns should be addressed with a unified approach when and where possible. This already occurs in many companies, but to the extent that these issues are managed separately, reframing programs to focus on sustainability provides a good opportunity to look carefully for synergies and efficiencies. There are at least two compelling reasons to do so. One is that safety programs, although not strictly speaking environmental in nature, often address issues having an environmental/human health component. The other is that the past several decades of industrial experience have shown that substantial overlap often exists between efforts to reduce pollutant emissions and to improve worker safety and health.

Finally, I'm a strong believer in the power and efficiency of markets and in the internal discipline required to manage a business enterprise effectively (see the next two chapters). Accordingly, I believe that it is important for any investments made in the pursuit of ES&G performance improvement be financially tenable and sensible.[16] Accordingly, objectives, targets, and ES&G management programs should include financial data and be expressed in financial terms wherever possible. This enables the organization to make informed decisions about what to do and in what order. I cannot overemphasize the importance of using this approach, for the following two reasons:

- Investing in ES&G improvements that are noneconomic destroys the firm's capital. Fundamentally, sustainability involves finding the appropriate balance among EHS, social, and economic issues and imperatives, so consistently devoting resources to activities that destroy value *undermines the organization's long-term sustainability*.

- Because no company, other entity, or country has unlimited financial resources, investing in noneconomic activities to achieve EHS or social improvements leaves less financial capital available to pursue other activities that would provide both EHS/social and economic benefits. Consequently, such behavior *produces less EHS or social benefit* than could be produced with a more rational approach. If you're moved by splashy corporate public relations campaigns touting purchases of (or subsidies for) hybrid vehicles, philanthropic activities, and other sorts of feel-good activities, consider this point carefully.[17]

Not every idea or opportunity can be expressed in monetary terms, or even quantified. But it is essential that those who would lead internal sustainability efforts develop fact-based analysis and be prepared to support their recommendations and ongoing activities with solid numbers wherever possible. Much of my work in recent years has followed exactly this approach. The result has been that client organizations have been able to clear away existing confusion and controversy over the importance of particular issues, make decisions about priorities, and capture opportunities. Businesses that are truly sustainable for the long term will need to exhibit this type of behavior on a continual, if not continuous, basis.

Measuring and Reporting Results

Defining milestones and measuring progress toward their attainment is a necessary component of any rational strategy, including a drive toward organizational sustainability. Propelling and sustaining any such drive should be performance metrics and timetables that reflect meaningful advances in sustainability, that are challenging but realistic, and that are appropriate to the organization's principal business lines and scale. Where existing measurement processes are insufficient to monitor progress, new procedures must be developed and deployed and integrated throughout the organization. In parallel with this activity, it is important to ensure that a robust and effective corrective action process is in place and to develop and deploy one if it is absent in the organization. Only in this way can the organization's leaders and stakeholders be assured that good intentions are acted on, improvement initiatives are carried out effectively, and timely and appropriate course corrections are made when and where needed. These steps often require work and some additional investment of time and other resources. But they are necessary to ensure that any organization's new sustainability-driven initiative does not join the existing (and growing) multitude of programs that begin with great fanfare and enthusiasm but then either fail to take root or founder after an initial period of success. Such failures often produce internal disillusionment and cynicism, which then undermine any future improvement efforts.

Another key aspect of effective corporate sustainability management is reporting of results. Regular reporting of management actions and performance results over time assures stakeholders (internal and external) that the company's ES&G policies are being carried out, goals are being attained, and the management system, if one exists, is functioning as intended.

The importance of this activity has been reemphasized by recent events. One clear lesson of the recent turmoil in the global financial markets is the need for improved transparency. Even before the events of the recent past, momentum was building for greater disclosure of companies' (and industries') material ES&G posture. In response, many firms and trade associations now publicly espouse disclosure of their ES&G programs and performance. I believe that this is a healthy development.

To do this effectively, organizations must determine what types, format(s), content, and timing of public performance reporting are appropriate for their particular situation. Although this may sound simple, in practice it is anything but. I suggest an approach that parallels that of my strategy development guidance, in that it begins with an examination of organizational mission, objectives, and business strategy but involves intense focus on stakeholder concerns. Stakeholders typically include owners (such as, stock and bond holders), major customers/constituents, regulators, employees, suppliers, public interest groups, the general public, and, in some cases, competitors. It may be wise to survey or otherwise develop an understanding of the perspectives of each major stakeholder group. Armed with these insights, the responsible executive(s) can then decide how best to address all major concerns and desires. They also can work to develop, organize, and present the relevant information in a way that is clear, informative, and appropriate to its intended audience. As a general matter, organizations would be well advised to adopt general conformance with widely accepted organizational sustainability reporting guidelines (such as the Global Reporting Initiative) in cases in which formal public reporting is indicated.

Chapter 8 examines the topic of ES&G performance measurement and reporting in much greater depth.

Integrating Sustainability into the Company's "Organizational DNA"

Actively pursuing sustainability as a core principle represents a paradigm shift. In my work spanning more than two decades, I have encountered no organization that could easily accommodate adoption of sustainability as a component of its "corporate DNA" without undergoing major behavioral, and even cultural, change. Accordingly, those who seek to catalyze such a transformation should bring a healthy respect for the power of ingrained ways of viewing the world, an individual's role within it, and how to carry out day-to-day activities, as discussed in Chapter 2. The simple fact is that people don't change established ways of thinking and acting easily or without good reason.

Chapter 2 highlighted the importance of sustainable business behavior and some of the real and persistent barriers that inhibit more rapid and complete migration to a sustainable business model. Therefore, before actively proceeding with the launch of an organizational sustainability program, it is important to have clarity on the desired changes and what they imply, and active and engaged senior management leadership. At an early stage of the deployment process, it also is important to understand and remove structural impediments.

However, a number of cultural considerations also should be evaluated carefully and addressed as part of the program. As stated earlier, to have real and lasting impact, sustainability must become an integral part of the organization's culture, and it necessarily must involve all the organization's people. Accordingly, any sustainability program must address the views and interests of these parties, meaning that their representatives must be actively engaged in the process, ideally from the beginning. To be effective, a sustainability program must cut across the organization and be directed by individuals with the perspective and authority to ensure that the appropriate talents and resources are brought to bear. Hence, a corporate sustainability program will likely not be a small, compartmentalized, or short-duration initiative. Rather, it will represent a substantial organizational commitment and investment.

With the vision and broad outlines of a sustainability program or initiative in place, the next question is how to go about translating vision into reality. Based on my experience in working with a substantial number of large and small organizations, I believe that several important attributes characterize entities that successfully implement sustainability and other initiatives involving organizational change.

As noted previously, the first is that to be effective—indeed, to get out of the starting gate—the program must be led by and have the strong support of senior management. This support must be genuine, visible, clear, and continuous. Many of the tasks and activities required to plan and execute a sustainability program can be delegated to senior managers and working groups. But the formation of the initial high-level team (described next), eventual rollout of the program to the organization, and a number of activities in between and following need to be led by "C-level" executives if possible. Visible support from the top is often needed to overcome initial skepticism, resistance to new ideas and ways of doing things, and the frustrations that arise when inevitable conflicts arise among important business priorities. Many well-intentioned organizational improvement programs have foundered due to a lack of ongoing senior management support and involvement, most frequently after the initial excitement fades and the real work must be performed.

> "Management support is most critical. When senior management speaks, everyone jumps."
> —Sandy Nessing, AEP

In further examining the sustainability issue or launching a program, among the most productive first steps that a company's senior management can take is to form and maintain a high-level, cross-functional sustainability planning and implementation team or steering committee. For sustainability as a value-oriented concept to take root and reach full flower, it is essential that the organization resist the common impulse to place the responsibility for and ownership of the sustainability issue solely within a single organizational unit (most commonly, the environmental or EHS department).[18] Doing so practically ensures that the sustainability initiative will break little, if any, new ground. Instead, I recommend that the initial business case analysis of, planning for, and execution of any corporate sustainability program be directed by a team composed of director/executive-level managers representing, if possible, the following disciplines: strategic planning, environmental management/compliance, health and safety, energy, marketing, operations, finance and/or risk management, investor and/or public relations, facilities, supply chain management/purchasing, and human resources. If the workforce or significant portions thereof is represented by one or more labor unions, it is important that their input be included as well. Recognizing that the effectiveness of teams often declines in direct proportion to their size, a smaller group of senior managers might be warranted. However, it is important to represent all the functions identified here in some way on the team.

I suggest that the early work of the sustainability team focus on two parallel sets of activities—one externally focused and the other internally focused. Using his or her specific expertise, each team member should be expected to lead or participate in a subgroup focused on one or more facets of the following:

- A more complete understanding of stakeholder needs, expectations, constraints, and preferences
- Organizational risks and opportunities, particularly those related to environment, employee well-being and development, infrastructure, and management structure and practices

For example, senior marketing/sales representatives would presumably lead efforts to more fully understand the perspective of major customers relative to the sustainability issue. A subgroup composed of the representatives of operations and/or facilities, energy, and environment (as well as the labor union(s), if applicable) would lead the collection and analysis of data on environmental and energy efficiency improvement opportunities and risks associated with plant and other physical assets. The information and insights gained thereby should be of great value not only for informing the nature and emphasis of a possible sustainability program, but also more immediately for identifying and capturing short-term opportunities to create new business value.

In carrying out its work, it is essential that the sustainability team or steering committee ensure that it and its members model the behaviors that are required of a truly sustainable organization. Although I would not presume to dictate to an organization or its senior managers how to behave, I would observe that becoming a sustainable organization almost certainly will require new ideas, approaches, and ways of doing business. Based on my experience, I submit that embodying the principles discussed next in their dealings with one another and with the larger organization will greatly enhance the likelihood that the team will accomplish some real breakthroughs and create the conditions required for sustainable business success.

Business Value Orientation

As briefly highlighted previously, I believe that a consistent focus on revenue, costs, and risks provides the most compelling results and, over the long term, secures the most support for continuing a sustainability program. Many companies have started (and, in some cases, ended) with environmental and energy issues as the organizing principle for their sustainability programs. As indicated in the previous section, I believe that a higher-level, organization-wide perspective is more effective in moving the organization to the next level. Accordingly, existing thinking and methods for evaluating risk, liabilities, costs, and benefits might need to be expanded or modified to fit the sustainability paradigm.

Respect and Trust

The leaders of most sophisticated organizations, even those in capital-intensive industries, now recognize that their internal human capital is among their most valuable resources. I believe that organizations realize their highest returns from their human capital when people are treated with respect, regardless of their functional discipline or seniority level. Given that a sustainability program will absolutely require new ideas and ways of looking at existing business processes, it is essential that a climate of trust prevail. If sustainability team members believe that their "turf" or other parochial interests are at risk, they will be less than forthcoming, and the program will, at best, not fulfill its potential. Company senior management must set and maintain the tone here so that participants in the process believe throughout that they will not have to sacrifice their own interests to further those of someone else or of the organization at large.

Honesty

In a similar vein, team members can demonstrate their respect for one another and the work before them by being candid about what the perceived challenges and opportunities are, where in the organization they reside, and how they might best be addressed. For the team to succeed, its members must be honest about the organization's strengths and limitations (including staff capabilities and behaviors), past experiences, and readiness to look at ES&G issues in a new light. In addition, members should be willing to state their assumptions and underlying values and perspectives, and, more generally, address any preconceived notions or "baggage" that may hinder the effective functioning of the team and its progress.

Openness and Flexibility

A meaningful sustainability program will yield a variety of new ideas and ways of thinking and doing things. Open-mindedness toward new ideas is essential to both the discovery and evaluation of possible organizational improvements. Moreover, a willingness to set aside existing habits and preferences in the interests of observation, experimentation, and critical, objective evaluation helps ensure that any new sustainability push yields new, useful insights, more effective and efficient processes, and more collective ownership of business process improvements. On the other hand, a lack of flexibility will likely yield more limited, incremental thinking and business improvements.

Inclusiveness

Leading organizations recognize the importance of their employee base, as well as the contributions made and potential offered by each individual. In the context of a sustainability initiative, this cultural attribute can be of great value. Employees up and down the line often have the greatest knowledge of how things currently are done and, potentially, how they can be done in a more sustainable manner. I recommend that the sustainability team periodically avail itself of the knowledge and insights of selected members of the workforce who are deployed on the organization's most important production operations. This might be done by forming ad hoc teams to evaluate ideas, perform pilot tests and measurements, and generally help provide "reality checks" on concepts and processes developed or received by the sustainability team. More generally, the team can regularly solicit suggestions from across the organization and invite employees who offer promising ideas to participate in discussions with the team or subgroup to further develop and evaluate them. In this way, the team can capture and leverage the institutional and operational knowledge extant in the organization, empower members of the workforce, create more of a positive buzz around the sustainability program, and, most importantly, identify and capture organizational improvements that will work as intended and yield new (or protect existing) revenues, reduce costs, and control business risks.

Transparency

A real distinction exists between sustainability and the earlier generation of programs directed toward environmental quality and health and safety. Sustainability is based on the idea that the organization is accountable to a variety of stakeholders and is expected to deal with them openly, honestly, and regularly. This implies that if the organization decides to move down the sustainability path, it will be expected not only to respond to the expectations of a variety of stakeholders, but also make clear how it is doing so. Regular reports of progress; posting of performance data on the corporate web site; and participation in conferences, forums, councils, and other public dialogs will be among the standard tactics for meeting these expectations. If the organization decides to pursue a sustainability program, these activities should be accompanied (or, ideally, preceded) by public statements about the sustainability program, its purpose, central thrusts, and goals, and even decision-making criteria. These investments in outreach to the organization's stakeholders will be, in the current context, vital to maintaining transparency and credibility.

Optimism

Finally, the sustainability concept offers the mechanism and the opportunity to collect and examine all the important things the organization does, and the positive and negative impacts of those activities. Accordingly, it is as much about finding and exploiting opportunities as it is about solving problems and reducing liabilities. This type of balanced approach frees the organization (and, potentially, a sustainability team) to focus its energies where they will do the most good for the organization. By taking a thorough inventory and carefully evaluating it using appropriate sustainability criteria, the team can develop a clear list of priorities. Many of these would not otherwise be obvious, and some might depart significantly from the usual lists of compliance, safety, efficiency, and other "problems" that tend to fill the days and work lives of environmental, health and safety, energy management, and similar personnel. Given this unusual opportunity to discover and unlock new sources of value, I believe it important that the members of the sustainability team bring a spirit of optimism to their work. This will help them reach their own potential and begin to infuse this spirit in their colleagues throughout the organization.

By "walking the talk" in the way suggested here, those leading (and, hopefully, catalyzing) the internal sustainability effort will communicate that the firm and its senior management are committed to business behaviors that are sustainable in the long term. They also will demonstrate that it really is possible to fundamentally improve the organization's capabilities and performance along multiple dimensions. Finally, they will create the conditions needed for individuals throughout the company to contribute their time and talents toward the firm's success.

Firms that can harness and channel the talents of their people in this manner can reap significant competitive and financial benefits. This topic is explored in some depth in the next two chapters.

Endnotes

1. Energy-efficiency initiatives also frequently involve early retrofits, in which new, energy-efficient equipment or components are installed to replace existing equipment that is in acceptable working order and not in immediate need of replacement.

2. See, for example, the National Action Plan for Energy Efficiency—Vision for 2025: A Framework for Change (USEPA/USDOE, 2008) and Executive Order 13514—Federal Leadership in Environmental, Energy, and Economic Performance, issued in 2009. It stipulates dramatic improvements in the energy efficiency of federal government building space operation, motor vehicle use, and other agency activities (Federal Register, 2009).

3. I note here that there are numerous exceptions, the most extensive of which are the common exemptions afforded to small businesses and, to a major extent, agricultural operations. In addition, the regulations contain thousands of general and specific exceptions for particular types of industrial operations and materials. Nonetheless, it is generally understood that controlling pollutants and waste is required of all businesses and most other organizations.

4. See Soyka, Peter A., 2010. "Governing Green: Enabling the Sustainable Organization." *Board Member*, vol. 19, no. 3. Pp. 10–14. May–June, for a brief discussion of how small organizations can take some important steps on this path.

5. Note that the same issue may offer opportunities in some respects and pose threats in others, or do so under an alternative set of conditions.

6. Given the evolution of corporate EHS and sustainability programs over time, some organizations maintain separate environmental, health and safety, climate change, and/or sustainability policies. But during the next few years, it is reasonable to expect that in most organizations, consolidation will occur.

7. To continue the analogy, the policy provides the location of the roads and other features that form the landscape between the current position and the desired destination, and the strategy represents the chosen route to reach that destination. The policy illustrates the available and desirable routes as well as constraints that limit the available choices.

8. Indeed, several of these provisions are policy requirements of the ISO 14001 standard for environmental management systems. ISO 14001 has been implemented at thousands of corporate, small business, government, and other organizations worldwide. Other provisions are derived from the United Nations Global Compact, which is discussed further in Chapter 6.

9. Note that this principle and the three that follow are most relevant in jurisdictions outside the U.S. but are prominent concerns for U.S.-based multinational corporations.

10. Examples span a wide range and include both long-standing efforts such as the Global Reporting Initiative and more targeted investor-led initiatives such as the

disclosure campaigns of the Carbon Disclosure Project and Investor Network on Climate Risk.

11. Note that for a number of the suggested policy objectives (such as compliance and no use of compulsory or child labor), many companies have an explicit goal of zero. So any occurrences are treated as exceptions to acceptable operating practice, with appropriate corrective action taken when and where they take place.

12. Not so many years ago, companies such as DuPont established the then-outlandish goal of "zero waste." This induced radical rethinking of the firm's activities and led to a number of innovations that might not have occurred otherwise. Although neither DuPont nor anyone else has attained zero waste at a corporate level, ongoing experience and sharing of best practices have enabled many organizations to achieve no net waste at one or more locations.

13. I acknowledge that a significant number of companies operate either dedicated health and safety management systems (often certified to OSHAS 18000) or integrated EHS management systems. My point is that an approach that considers all dimensions of how the organization views "sustainability" is fundamental to designing a management system that will produce the desired results.

14. The ISO standard makes clear that an *environmental impact* is "any change to the environment, whether adverse or *beneficial*, wholly or partially resulting from an organization's environmental aspects." (ISO, 2004 at 2) (emphasis added) The standard goes on to say that the purpose of the EMS is to manage these [adverse and beneficial] aspects and implement its environmental policy, which must include a commitment to continual improvement.

15. For our purposes here, I use the working definition of eco-efficiency refined and articulated by the World Business Council for Sustainable Development (WBCSD). The WBCSD has identified seven success factors for eco-efficiency: 1) reduce the material intensity of goods and services, 2) reduce the energy intensity of goods and services, 3) reduce toxic dispersion, 4) enhance material recyclability, 5) maximize sustainable use of renewable resources, 6) reduce material durability, and 7) increase the service intensity of goods and services (WBCSD/UNEP, 1996).

16. I do recognize that there may be circumstances in which an investment required for regulatory compliance purposes may not meet typical corporate investment criteria but must be made regardless.

17. For an example from my previous work illustrating this phenomenon, see Buc and Soyka, 2009.

18. Note that in my earlier commentary, I advocated a clear leadership role in driving sustainability for the EHS function rather than any of the communications-related functions. I emphasize here that all are important, all have crucial expertise and perspective to offer, and all should be represented on the implementation team. That said, I believe that it is crucial that the subject matter knowledge of the EHS representatives be given significant weight in the group's deliberations and actions.

6

Investors and the Power of Markets

The preceding chapter outlined a framework and set of principles and practices that an organization, particularly a public corporation, can use to effectively manage its ES&G issues and activities. This chapter suggests that implementing this approach, while entailing considerable effort, can be justified. It has been shown to be effective, and it creates the conditions required for the firm to create new financial value. More specifically, I delve into the workings of our capital markets, and I develop and explore one of the major themes of this book: capital markets are reshaping how companies are approaching sustainability. They will drive corporate America toward a more sustainable future, whether or not it is ready to go there. To further support this argument, and particularly for your benefit if you remain unconvinced of the value proposition presented by sustainable business practices, Chapter 7 reviews the established empirical evidence that addresses this issue.

This chapter explores in depth why investors might have an interest in corporate sustainability behavior. It also looks at whether financial market actors appear to consider sustainability endpoints and, if so, how and to what degree. This chapter also explores how market forces appear to be shaping interest in and the practice of corporate sustainability activities. I will show that financial community actors are playing a substantial and growing role. I also will offer some suggestions for appropriate responses on the part of those working in and for companies on sustainability issues.

To begin, I will review some basic information about the financial markets, including their size and prominence, and the primary interests of market participants, focusing on those who play the most pivotal role—investors. This perspective is supplemented by a brief discussion of the evidence that suggests that financial market actors are paying increasing attention to corporate sustainability issues. (This discussion is expanded on in Chapter 7.) I will then examine some of the important requirements and constraints that apply to professional investors and to companies that offer financial securities to investors. This discussion takes place at both a general level and, more specifically, with regard to ES&G considerations. With this foundation, I then describe some of the major evaluation methods investors use. This discussion is followed by a delineation of the major information providers and other intermediaries that serve investors. I also review some important recent developments and major trends that may influence the behavior of both companies and investors with regard to ES&G issues during the next few years. The chapter closes with a summary and discussion of the implications of financial market involvement for those working on sustainability practices both within and outside of the firm.

Market Theory and Underlying Assumptions

For our purposes, I define markets as venues in which buyers and sellers of defined commodities can conduct transactions (purchases and sales) in which there is a high degree of certainty that all parties will honor the agreed-upon terms. Participating sellers using markets receive continual feedback on which products and services are of interest to others, what terms and price(s) are acceptable to buyers, and other information that is crucial to making sound decisions about what to produce and offer for sale, when and where, and under what terms. By participating in markets, buyers receive access to goods and services that they might not otherwise be able to obtain or make/perform. They also can make informed decisions about what to produce internally and what to procure from outside the organization. Indeed, it is widely accepted that well-functioning, competitive markets generally offer the greatest array of products and services at the lowest prices. It is also accepted that the "unseen hand" of the marketplace induces producers to deliver the goods and services consumers want in the appropriate quantities. It also creates "consumer surplus" that increases societal well-being and, over time, leads to the most efficient allocation of investment capital.

These points are elementary and well-known (at least intuitively) to most people. What is less well-understood and often forgotten is that the generally accepted theory of how markets can and do work is based on a number of important assumptions. If these assumptions are violated, it becomes far less clear that markets, even "free" markets, will deliver what their advocates promise.[1] In the current context, the more important of these assumptions include the following:

- The market is fully competitive (no monopoly sellers or buyers).
- All participants have perfect information (about prices, availability, product/service features, and so on).
- There are no transaction costs.
- All participants maximize their personal utility (and, presumably, that of their organizations).

If examined closely, each of these assumptions is of dubious validity—at least under conditions that are quite common in a large and diversified economy such as that in the U.S. Competitiveness varies greatly among industries, in some cases because of structural factors and in others as a function of industry maturity. It is widely known that certain types of activities, particularly those that have significant economies of scale, tend to become natural monopolies (or their close cousin, oligopolies). This is why, to promote economic efficiency and societal welfare, we have regulated monopolies to provide such basic goods and services as electric power, natural gas, and other utilities in many parts of the country. Monopolies also can take shape on their own over time. As an industry matures and competitive forces produce stronger and weaker firms and, in turn, growing consolidation (the stronger overcoming [and often buying] the weaker), a smaller number of companies have increasing market power. Recognizing the adverse impacts of increasing industry concentration on consumer choice and prices and more generally on social well-being, U.S. lawmakers enacted federal antitrust laws nearly 100 years ago. This happened precisely because *markets cannot be relied on* to continuously produce full, open, and fair competition among all participants.

There may be a diversity of views on whether U.S. antitrust laws have been enforced adequately or are fully effective. However, I believe that there can be little doubt that they have provided a useful control mechanism for curbing egregious, self-serving corporate behavior and limiting volatility in the supply and price of many goods and services.

It may seem a bit odd to contemplate the availability of information in 2011, more than a decade into the Internet age, when it seems that information is all around us. Nonetheless, it is worthwhile to consider how much of what we see and hear through the Internet and various other media channels is truly useful. In the context of participating in one or more markets, information asymmetry has always existed between and among various buyers, sellers, and intermediaries. Moreover, I believe that most people understand and are comfortable with the fact that some people and organizations work harder and more skillfully to develop facts and insights than others. These attributes allow them to engage in commerce more successfully. In fact, the ability to benefit from one's own diligence and talents is a major component of our "cultural DNA." The results of these diverse efforts demonstrate that not all relevant information is instantly available to all market participants, and this evidence is all around us. Indeed, you need look no further than the countless commercial databases, industry-specific publications, membership organizations, books (such as this one), and training courses and seminars available online, in print, and in person. These and other offerings enable the purchaser to obtain insights that he or she did not possess previously and either could not develop independently or could not obtain cost-effectively (make/buy considerations). Many billions of dollars change hands in this country every year to try to correct existing information asymmetries and gain competitive advantage. If anything, such activity is increasing rather than diminishing as information technology advances. Later in this chapter I will return to this topic as it applies to ES&G management and investing.

Given the foregoing, the notion that market transactions are costless seems particularly unrealistic. Yet it is commonly accepted by many people, at least informally. Many transactions between buyers and sellers do not have any definable fees or explicit costs. But in other cases (including purchases of many securities), selling or, more commonly, buying through an intermediary involves a payment or markup. If we then consider the indirect costs of participating in a transaction, such as, purchasing information, time spent performing research/evaluation, travel, shipping, and taxes, it becomes clear that the "friction" surrounding many sales and purchases of goods and services in our economy is not zero. In fact, it may be quite significant.

Finally, one of the cornerstones of market theory is the idea that people are rational and always act to maximize their personal utility. A commonly stated and important corollary is that personal utility means wealth. In other words, people continuously seek greater wealth. In terms of our discussion here, another important implication is that people working in organizations also are rational, informed, utility-maximizing agents who in all cases make optimal decisions to benefit (increase the wealth of) their employer. As noted in Chapter 2, this book doesn't have enough space to discuss all the flaws in and counter-examples to these related theories of human behavior.

In the context of this chapter, what is most relevant is the notion that people always (or at least routinely) make rational decisions that are in the best interests of their organization. Until the last 15 years or so, this idea had been accepted (indeed, embedded) widely and deeply in the business community. So ingrained was this belief that it was difficult to even have a conversation about advanced ES&G practices with certain constituencies, or to induce public sector entities to entertain the possibility that they could be doing more to promote sustainable business behavior. The emergence of the field of behavioral economics has illuminated the factors that really drive human thinking, decision-making, and behavior. Even so, deep skepticism remains in some quarters that any intervention into the workings of markets or individual companies to promote sustainability or other desirable practices is either necessary or desirable. Such skeptics still voice concerns about whether, for example, an array of public sector programs and partnerships are necessary. They seem unconvinced that these programs produce any significant net benefits and are worthy of support.[2] This is true despite the success of initiatives such as the myriad voluntary pollution-prevention programs operated at the state level and the federal Energy Star program, which addresses the energy efficiency of a variety of building types, building components, appliances, electronics, and other goods. These diverse programs share at least one common feature: they provide information and, often, tools and other assistance to companies to help them make environmental and/or health and safety performance improvements in a cost-effective manner. That is, they help produce win-win outcomes by reducing energy use, pollutant emissions, waste, unsafe working conditions, and/or other undesirable aspects in a way that saves money, net of investment cost. They do so by creating open access[3] (no competitive barriers), overcoming information asymmetry, reducing transaction costs, and demonstrating, in tangible ways, that the partnering organization may *not* presently be maximizing its utility. In other words, these programs have proven that there actually are lots of "$20 dollar bills lying on the sidewalk" waiting to be picked up.

Although some of this discussion may seem a bit esoteric, it provides an important foundation for the treatment of capital market (and corporate) behavior that is presented later in this chapter.

Capital Markets

Among the many types of markets that exist in the U.S. and around the world, perhaps the most influential in many respects are the capital markets. Individual entities within the capital markets provide a wide array of financial products, including company equity and debt securities (stocks and bonds, respectively), loans, notes, and insurance policies. Those that are most relevant to the current context are those used by companies to raise capital, either by selling portions of company ownership (stocks) or by issuing tradeable promises to repay invested capital at a specified future time, along with periodic interest payments in the interim (bonds). Because these securities can be traded on organized markets (security exchanges), they can be purchased by and delivered to the buyer quickly at a clear price. They also are highly "liquid," meaning that an investor can (generally) sell them quickly and receive the sale proceeds without undue delay. These features have helped the financial markets attract investment capital from far and wide, greatly increasing the pool of financial resources available to firms seeking to grow. The continual and often rapid growth of companies using this invested capital has, in turn, greatly accelerated gains in general economic activity and the standard of living in countries with well-functioning financial markets.

Markets for financial securities (such as stocks, bonds, and options) are highly developed and efficient in the U.S. and in many other economically advanced countries. Generally, these securities are traded on exchanges that establish rules concerning how trades are to be made and executed, and they provide guarantees that the promises made by buyer and seller are fulfilled.[4] At this point in time, and enabled by the great advances in information technology that have occurred during the past 20 years (including growth of the Internet), it is fair to say that, at any time, one or more stock markets are open and operating somewhere. The importance of international investors to sustainability thinking and practice is discussed later in this chapter.

Companies that participate in these markets compete with one another, offering their bonds or stock as one investment option available among thousands. To be successful in this competitive environment, they must be able to demonstrate a sound business model and "financials" warranting the trust of the investing public.[5] Both debt and equity investors are looking for value. Debt, or fixed income, investors obtain value by receiving a predetermined income stream (typically a fixed percentage of the stated value of the debt security) in exchange for a given and generally well-characterized level of risk.[6] Equity investors receive no assurance of a positive return on investment but also face no limit on its upside potential. Importantly, under both investment scenarios, it is incumbent upon companies to demonstrate the efficacy and worth of their business models (including ES&G activities and programs, if any) to their investors. Sustainability improvements, just as with any other investment of the firm's capital, must contribute, if even in an indirect way, to revenue growth, improved profitability, and/or risk reduction. As discussed next, the practice of sustainability investing involves determining the financial value that each firm's ES&G activities creates (or destroys) and evaluating this net impact along with many other criteria of various kinds.

Who Investors Are and What They Care About

Those who have worked in the environmental, health and safety, and/or sustainability field for any length of time have doubtless heard (and perhaps stated) the proposition that discretionary ES&G initiatives or programs within an organization "add value." Commonly, value is not defined formally, but it may include such perceived benefits as greater efficiency, improved safety, a more highly skilled and motivated workforce, lower emissions, and the like. I believe that it is appropriate to both consider and seek to obtain such benefits through improved ES&G management practices, as discussed in depth in Chapter 5.

It is vital to understand, however, that such benefits do not comprise "value" to an investor. Instead, value is created through one or more of three distinct means, as illustrated in the following sidebar. This chapter identifies the major types of investors in corporate and other securities and describes how these securities differ from one another. First, however, I review a few fundamentals about how investors think and behave. This foundation is integral to an understanding of whether and under what circumstances an investor might show an interest in ES&G management practices and performance.

What Comprises "Value" to an Investor?

Investors commit funds to make money. They will make money only if the securities they buy are worth more in the future than when they were purchased, and/or pay a cash dividend stream, and are honored by the issuer (default does not occur). Accordingly, only the following three measures are fundamentally of interest to investors:

- Revenue (must grow)
- Earnings (also must grow)
- Risk (must decline or remain steady)

For investors to perceive any "value creation" message as meaningful and credible, it must address at least one of these criteria.

Investing is about making money and intrinsically involves making a prediction about the *future*. No rational investor buys an equity security unless he or she expects that it will be worth more in the future, or unless it yields a stream of dividends that are adequate to offset the absence of a share price increase. Assuming that the market for such securities is *efficient* and that *all relevant information is available* to motivated market participants, the market price today reflects the consensus judgment of all buyers and sellers as to any given security's true worth. Similarly, a rational purchaser of a bond expects that the yield (periodic payments) he or she receives is adequate to compensate for the lack of access to his or her capital for the holding period and to offset the risk of default by the bond issuer. Yield is determined by a bond rating, with riskier securities requiring a higher yield (interest rate) than less-risky securities. Bonds can either be held to maturity, when the original investment amount is repaid, or sold through an exchange on the secondary market, much like a stock. Because most bonds are issued with a fixed yield, changes in interest rates (or riskiness of the issuing entity) induce changes in the bond's market price. Again, a bond's market price reflects what the market overall believes is an accurate value, based on the current interest rate climate, company position, and perceived trends.

This means that any information on corporate ES&G posture, activities, and/or performance must tell the investor something about the future. Information on past performance is of interest only to the extent that it helps the investor make an informed judgment about the company's future. More specifically, such information must be relevant to the prediction of the firm's future revenues, earnings, cash flow,[7] or risk. The extent to which conventional ES&G data responds to these needs is discussed in depth in a subsequent chapter.

Professional investors evaluate these major financial endpoints at several levels.[8] First, they generally decide how to invest their capital among the different available asset classes. These include cash and very short-term investments, fixed income (bonds), stocks, options, commodities, and even real estate. Because we are primarily interested in corporate behavior here, I will focus on stocks and bonds. The investor then filters his or her investment choices for whatever capital is to be invested in stocks and bonds by assessing which economic sectors appear to offer the most favorable characteristics. This choice is based on such factors as the current stage of the economic cycle, the interest rate environment, and other macroeconomic characteristics. Finally, within the sectors chosen for investment, the focus turns to individual companies.

Investors maintain a diversified portfolio. That is, they don't hold a few securities at a time, but rather dozens to hundreds. This is because, as demonstrated by both investment theory and empirical evidence, adding securities to an investment portfolio, at least to a certain point, reduces volatility in returns (risk) without adversely affecting its expected overall return. As discussed further later, the principle of diversification is so widely accepted that it has been adopted as a component of securities law across the U.S.

As discussed previously, investors, even individual investors, often diversify across asset classes. These classes can range from those that pose little or no risk (U.S. government securities) to those that pose minimal to moderate risk (corporate bonds, from "investment grade" to "junk") to stocks and, finally (in some cases), futures and options. Assuming that markets are working efficiently and assets are not mispriced, in every case, and for every component of the portfolio, there is a direct relationship between the risk it poses and the potential reward it offers. In other words, the higher the risk, the higher the potential reward, and vice versa. So government bonds pose little or no risk but also do not offer a high potential payoff. Stocks pose a substantial risk, up to and including the loss of your entire investment, but they also offer an unlimited upside that is difficult to replicate using less-risky investment options.

In the context of relating ES&G issues to investing, a key point to consider is how a sector, industry, or company's ES&G posture and trends may affect future revenues, earnings, and risk to either the organization itself or future cash flows. Another point to consider is whether the current valuation fully and accurately accounts for all important facts, *including* ES&G issues. Additional returns (above what can be obtained through investing in broad indexes) may be generated by identifying sources of hidden value and investing aggressively in the firms positioned to capture it. Returns also may be generated by identifying underappreciated sources of risk to future returns that result in securities that are currently overvalued. In the latter case, the investor can both divest any securities owned and invest more aggressively by "shorting" the relevant stock(s).[9]

As you will see shortly, a substantial and growing segment of the investor community is examining specifically how ES&G issues and criteria can help them identify such opportunities to outperform both their competitors and standard investment industry benchmarks.

Size and Composition of U.S. Capital Markets

Notwithstanding the vast trade imbalances and budget deficits of recent years, the U.S. is still by a wide margin the world's largest capital market. As shown in Table 6-1, as of 2006, the total value of U.S. financial assets was substantially greater than that of the next-largest economy (the Euro Zone). In fact, the U.S. was comparable in size to the Euro Zone and its next-largest competitor (Japan) combined. In recent years, the picture has changed markedly due to the near-collapse of the global financial system in 2008–2009 and significant funds flows, particularly between the U.S. and China. But most of the basic relationships shown in Table 6-1 still hold. Of particular relevance here are the size and prominence of the U.S. markets for equity and private (corporate) debt securities. Quite simply, the U.S. is and is likely to remain the world's dominant investment market for stocks and bonds for some time.

Table 6-1 Global Financial Assets by Region for 2006 (in Trillions of Dollars)
Source: Adapted from McKinsey Global Institute, 2008. Pg. 9.

	U.S.	Latin America	Euro Zone	U.K.	Russia	Eastern Europe	Japan	China	India	Emerging Asia
Equity Securities	$19.60	$1.40	$8.60	$3.80	$1.10	$0.40	$4.70	$2.40	$0.80	$1.40
Private Debt Securities	$20.20	$0.50	$12.00	$2.50	$0.10	$0.00	$2.00	$0.40	$0.00	$0.80
Government Debt Securities	$6.20	$1.10	$6.40	$0.80	$0.10	$0.40	$6.80	$0.80	$0.30	$0.70
Bank Deposits	$10.10	$1.20	$10.20	$2.90	$0.40	$0.60	$6.00	$4.50	$0.60	$1.30
Total Financial Assets	$56.10	$4.20	$37.20	$10.00	$1.70	$1.40	$19.50	$8.10	$1.70	$4.20

To purchase these debt and equity securities, money managers collect financial capital from a wide array of sources, including public and private (corporate) pension funds, insurance companies, and individuals and trusts. Firms that collect, deploy, and manage this invested capital include commercial and investment banks, private equity firms, hedge funds, and mutual fund companies. A number of intermediary and supporting organizations also play important roles in supporting the functioning of our financial markets. These include the following:

- Stock, bond, and commodity exchanges, on which securities are traded
- Numerous data and research providers, who support investment analysis and decision making by providing crucial data, projections, and other information and tools
- Bond rating agencies, which evaluate the business prospects and risks of organizations issuing debt securities
- Analysts, who evaluate securities and their issuers—some from the standpoint of the issuing companies ("sell side"), and some from the point of view of the prospective investor in the securities ("buy side")

Finally, several types of organizations play important regulatory roles in ensuring that our capital markets function effectively, efficiently, and transparently. These include the U.S. Securities and Exchange Commission at the federal level; state-level securities commissions that exist in every U.S. state; and several voluntary, self-regulatory bodies representing some of the market participants, the most prominent of which is the National Association of Securities Dealers (NASD). Table 6-2 summarizes the major types of entities involved in the capital markets and their respective roles.

Table 6-2 Major Capital Market Participants and Their Roles

Providers of Capital	Money Managers	Intermediaries
Pension funds	Banks	Stock and bond exchanges
Private	Savings	Data and research providers
Public	Commercial	Bond rating agencies
Insurance companies	Investment	Analysts
Individuals, trusts	Private equity firms	**Regulators**
	Hedge funds	SEC
	Mutual funds	State securities commissions
	Sovereign wealth funds	NASD

Most of the empirical work linking ES&G improvements and financial value is focused on equities (stocks). In fact, most of the current activity in the ES&G investing space is focused on equity securities. Table 6-3 shows the value and ownership of the U.S. equity market as of mid-2010.

Table 6-3 Value (in Billions of Dollars) and Ownership of U.S. Equity Securities

	Value	Percent of Total Value
Household sector	$6,768	36.3%
Rest of the world	$2,278	12.2%
Mutual and closed-end funds, ETFs	$4,545	24.4%
Private pension funds	$1,674	9.0%
Public retirement funds	$1,566	8.4%
Insurance companies	$1,452	7.8%
Federal and state governments	$157	0.8%
Brokers and dealers	$96	0.5%
Banks and savings institutions	$95	0.5%
Totals	**$18,629**	**100.0%**

Note: Total equity value of $18.629 trillion includes $3.5 trillion in foreign issues (such as ADRs).

Source: U.S. Federal Reserve, 2011, Table L.213

This table shows that despite the strong recovery of U.S. (and other) equity markets since mid-2009, the total value of U.S. equities still has not reached even 2006 levels, much less the precrash peak of

$25.6 trillion observed in 2007. U.S. households directly own about 36 percent of U.S. shares (by value), and mutual and closed-end funds own nearly one-quarter. Together, private and public pension and retirement funds own more than 17 percent, and insurance companies account for an additional 8 percent or so. Governments, brokers and dealers, and banks together account for less than 2 percent of the total. Interestingly, nearly $2.3 trillion in U.S. equity securities, or 12 percent of the total, is owned by investors outside the U.S. Notwithstanding the fiscal and economic difficulties faced by our country, particularly in the long term, the U.S. remains a popular and highly regarded place in which to invest.

Disclosure

As discussed previously, investing in equity or fixed income securities involves finding sources of value through collecting and evaluating relevant information on particular firms' businesses, capabilities, future prospects, and ability to perform at or beyond anticipated levels. To make such determinations, investors require information, which in many cases can be provided only by the company issuing the securities itself.

Required Disclosure

Because the disclosure of financial and certain operating information is so critical, as a matter of public policy the U.S. and most other advanced economies have established requirements that mandate regular disclosure by all firms that have issued either equity or debt securities that are sold to the investing public. U.S. companies fitting this description are subject to regulations established by the SEC.[10] These regulations stipulate that such companies issue every quarter a 10-Q report, as well as an annual report and accompanying 10-K report following the close of each company fiscal year. These documents must include three basic financial statements: the balance sheet, income statement, and cash flow statement. The balance sheet is focused on "stock" measures, and the other two statements are focused on "flow" measures.

Fundamentally, the balance sheet is an end-of-period snapshot. It lists and quantifies what the company owns and what it owes. It provides financial values for the various pieces of the business. This includes both liquid (short-term) assets such as cash on hand, accounts receivable, and inventory, and long-term assets such as land and plant and equipment. On the other side of the balance sheet are listed the firm's liabilities (what it owes), again subdivided by short- and long-term obligations. Accounts payable, interest owed, and the like are listed here. The difference between the total value of assets and the total value of liabilities is equal, by definition, to the value of shareholders' equity, or the net value of the business. Healthy businesses have substantial positive net equity. The balance sheet incorporates many assumptions and conventions that have been developed within the accounting profession over the years and commonly includes many explanatory notes. Review and analysis of these notes is a key activity in investment analysis.

The balance sheet also is where any ES&G liabilities are supposed to be identified and quantified. These generally are listed in the Long-Term Debt and Other Obligations category (with the exception of the current portion, if any) and are explained in notes. Such obligations may include responsibility for cleanup of contaminated sites and other liabilities that can be reasonably quantified. As discussed in Chapter 7, however, such liabilities have been chronically underreported by U.S. companies to this point. To address this problem, several years ago the standards organization of the public accounting profession issued guidance. It made clear that firms were required to analyze and report their contingent liabilities from retired assets (such as idled, potentially contaminated plants and sites) using specified methods. Although it is still early in the process, it does not appear that disclosure of such liabilities in financial statements has increased markedly. I discuss this issue in more depth later.

The income statement quantitatively describes the firm's activities from an economic perspective. It addresses, in order, revenues (sales), the costs of producing these revenues (labor, materials), the more general costs of operating the firm, and the difference between revenues and costs, which is income (earnings) or loss. Finally, any earnings may be distributed in various ways, including in the form of payments to shareholders through dividends. In contrast with the balance sheet, the income statement considers the period (year or quarter) as a whole. It also commonly includes many explanatory notes.

In similar fashion, the cash flow statement describes the firm's activities in terms of their cash impacts on the business. These activities are organized into the following categories: Operating activities (conducting the firm's main business[es]); investment activities, such as purchasing new land, equipment, or other firms; and financing activities, including securing the funds needed to operate the firm, such as through obtaining bank loans or issuing bonds or stock. The cash flow statement collects and tallies all these sources and uses of cash into and out of the firm and again considers the period as a whole.

On a yearly basis, the 10-K versions of these financial statements are incorporated into the firm's annual report, which also must include a written management discussion and analysis (MD&A). The MD&A often includes crucial information about and insight into the company's recent experience, future plans, significant challenges, and likely responses. Company senior management is expected to acknowledge and adequately discuss any and all issues that may exert a significant influence (positive or negative) on the firm's future performance. This includes ES&G issues. Unfortunately, however, again this is an area of relatively clear regulatory coverage that historically has been widely downplayed or ignored.

Together, the three financial statements, along with the annual report, provide much of the key information investors require to make informed decisions about a particular company's existing businesses, ability to compete successfully and accomplish stated goals and commitments, and prospects for the future. As you will see a bit later, the adequacy of this information to satisfy the needs of all investors, particularly those focused on or interested in ES&G issues, is far from clear. This fact has had several important implications.

Despite clear signs that there were gaps in the coverage and/or enforcement of existing SEC disclosure rules, the requirements just described provided the basic road map for developing and reporting corporate financial information for many decades. Generally, it appeared that most investors were satisfied with the types and depth of information they were provided at quarterly intervals, although some financial institutions were not. These money management firms leveraged their relationships with the senior management of certain publicly traded firms to obtain information that had not been publicly disclosed to that point. In exchange, some touted the shares of these companies over those of competing firms, or otherwise used this information to further their own interests and/or those of their clients.

These and many other abuses came to light about ten years ago in a series of major scandals and the spectacular failures of several previously high-flying firms such as, Enron, WorldCom, Adelphia, Tyco International, and Global Crossing. In the wake of these scandals, the resulting billions of dollars in losses to investors, and the ensuing recession, the U.S. Congress enacted the Sarbanes-Oxley Act of 2002 (Public Law 107—204). Sarbanes-Oxley, or "Sarbox," contains three major requirements: disclosure controls and procedures, internal control over financial reporting, and Officers' certifications of controls. More specifically, Sarbox and implementing regulations require independence of auditors and the Audit Committee of the Board of Directors and effective oversight of the auditing function by the Committee, which must include a financial expert. In addition, to comply with the certification requirement, the company Chief Executive Officer (CEO) and Chief Financial Officer (CFO) must sign a statement of responsibility. In this statement they claim ownership of the completeness and effectiveness of the firm's internal financial information systems and controls, as well as the accuracy and completeness of its regular (quarterly) financial reports. Notably, Sarbox does not apply to privately held firms. Its purpose is expressly to protect public investors from fraudulent and abusive behavior and to promote effective corporate governance in publicly traded firms. The actual costs and benefits of Sarbox are still being debated, but its enactment has brought a greater focus to information integrity and a better understanding of risks to the firm.

Certain other SEC rules[11] also apply to ES&G issues, particularly those concerning impacts on the environment and their consequences. Core SEC requirements include a complete "Description of the Business," discussion of any legal proceedings (such as for permit violations), and, in the required MD&A, delineation of any risks or opportunities that might be material to the firm's future prospects. Such risks include contingent liabilities such as possible future contaminated site cleanup responsibilities. Existing SEC rules cover three substantive areas: accrual of liabilities in financial statements, disclosure of these liabilities in financial statement footnotes and SEC filings, and estimations for both accruals and disclosures. Many of these rules apply only to matters that are "material" to the company's financial condition. Generally, a matter is understood to be material if a prudent investor would reasonably want to know about it. That said, the SEC has consistently declined to define materiality, preferring instead to rely on established case law when and where necessary. As I will demonstrate in the next chapter, in a number of clearly documented instances, one or more ES&G issues have risen to the level at which any rational investor would want to know about them, yet the required disclosure was not made.

Recognizing this problem (or at least some aspects of it), the organization representing the financial accounting profession in the U.S., the Financial Accounting Standards Board (FASB), issued a standard in 2002. It was followed by a more definitive Financial Interpretive Note (FAS 143/FIN 47) that related specifically to environmentally impaired assets and systems. FAS 143/FIN 47 explicitly rejected the generally accepted (and vague) preexisting estimation scheme and replaced it with a mandated approach consisting of a probabilistic analysis of future liability. In other words, it is no longer acceptable to, in effect, throw up your hands and say that there are too many uncertainties to estimate a liability. Rather, the owner of a contaminated property must now use quantitative analysis (such as Monte Carlo simulation modeling) to generate and evaluate probability distributions of the different possible outcomes and generate an expected value of the property's future liability. This may sound somewhat esoteric, but the net effect of this significant policy shift is to pull liability recognition forward. This may have major income statement and balance sheet implications for affected firms (Smith, 2005).

Not all corporations have contaminated property from legacy operations that is affected by these emerging requirements. Nevertheless, this issue provides a tangible example of how ES&G issues can affect a company's financial strength and capability and pose financial liabilities that may not be fully recognized or monetized. It also is emblematic of the types of concerns that have prompted interested investors to seek additional disclosure requirements addressing ES&G issues and concerns.

Indeed, pressure from certain portions of the investor community has resulted in several recent steps by the SEC. These measures are intended to compel corporate senior executives to be more forthcoming about how they are addressing ES&G issues and/or to take steps to improve their own structure and performance, particularly in the area of governance. Recent SEC activities include ongoing coordination with the EPA to review and assess conformance with existing SEC disclosure regulations, and the formation of a study group to evaluate whether ES&G disclosure should be made mandatory, as well as formal regulatory activity. In the latter category, the SEC issued proxy disclosure enhancements in December 2009.[12] It issued a memorandum "clarifying" that firms have an existing, affirmative duty to disclose the potential impacts of major environmental issues, specifically global climate change, in February 2010.[13] And it issued a final rule providing enhanced access for shareholder nominees in December 2010.[14] In addition and, in some ways, most importantly, the SEC is still considering petitions submitted by the U.S. Social Investment Forum (SIF) and the NGO CERES urging the SEC to require mandatory ES&G reporting. It seems clear that the SEC under the current presidential administration is far more focused on shareholder rights and transparency than it was during the preceding eight years. But it remains unclear whether the SEC will ultimately require comprehensive ES&G disclosure, reporting on GHG emissions and related issues only, or neither. Those interested in corporate sustainability from any and all perspectives might want to monitor this issue, because it could be a game-changer.

Voluntary Disclosure

Currently, no U.S. legal requirements compel corporations to disclose their ES&G (or component environmental or health and safety) policies, management practices, or performance. But the SEC recently made clear that it expects companies to carefully evaluate the climate change issue and how it might affect their operations. Nevertheless, a number of current and emerging requirements for public reporting affect at least some companies. More generally, participation in voluntary sustainability reporting initiatives is growing both in the U.S. and internationally.

As discussed in Chapter 3, over the past two decades, the members of several industry and trade organizations have developed codes of conduct and standards for managing ES&G issues. Most of them now include provisions for at least limited reporting of results. An example is the global chemicals industry's Responsible Care program (ICCA and Responsible Care, 2008). Another example is the Sustainable Forestry Initiative (SFI) and the Forest Stewardship Council-US standards that have been adopted throughout much of the U.S. forest products industry (SFI, 2010; FSC-US, 2010).

At a more general level, corporate reporting of ES&G performance has been promoted by a range of organizations during the past 20 years or so. Over time, these efforts have consolidated into a small number of prominent and active programs that are now organized as nonprofits. At the same time, the scope of the issues they address has expanded, at least in some respects, to cover not only environmental issues, but also health and safety, social/equity, and economic issues. That is, they now directly take on the issue of corporate sustainability. The most prominent among these are the Global Reporting Initiative (GRI), the United Nations Global Compact (UNGC), and the Carbon Disclosure Project (CDP). Table 6-4 describes major features of these programs and how they compare and contrast.

The GRI and the UNGC are intended to reflect the interests of society at large. They seek to stimulate the adoption of more comprehensive and aggressive management, tracking, and reporting of company responses to a variety of ES&G issues. Both reflect a heavy emphasis on labor rights and the interests of organized labor generally, but they also speak to a number of important EHS issues. The CDP, in contrast, is fundamentally about investments and investors, although its goals similarly are given effect mainly through the use of principles and/or a reporting template.

The GRI, UNGC, and CDP all are targeted at and seek to directly change the behavior of corporations.[15] But nominally they have relevance to and can be adopted by other types of organizations as well.

Table 6-4 Comparison of Major Third-Party Programs Influencing Corporate ES&G Disclosure

Entity	GRI	UNGC	CDP
Represents...	Multiple stakeholders	World governments/people	Institutional investors
Addresses...	ES&G issues reporting (management)	ES&G issues management	GHG management
Through the use of...	Reporting guidelines	Principles	Reporting template
Targeted at...	Corporations	Corporations	Corporations
To produce the following response(s):	Regular, consistent, comparable ES&G disclosure	Adoption, implementation of enhanced governance practices	More extensive, sophisticated GHG management and disclosure
With the ultimate intended result(s) of:	Stronger corporate governance; improved ES&G performance	More ethical, humane global corporate behavior	Clarity as to effective corporate GHG management; reduced investment risk

A key feature of each initiative is required (or strongly suggested) corporate reporting. This reflects a shared belief that more consistent, regular, expansive, and meaningful reporting will accomplish the following:

- Offer an impetus for companies to institute stronger and more effective governance practices
- Improve companies' ES&G management capabilities and performance
- Provide more convincing assurance to investors and other external stakeholders that the firm is upholding its responsibilities and is effectively managing risks and capitalizing on opportunities

This is true despite the disparate goals of the three initiatives.

These initiatives have been highly influential. A strong correlation exists between the indicators suggested by these programs and the information that is actually reported by companies that disclose ES&G data. A few points illustrate this influence:

- The CDP now represents 534 institutional investors with assets of $64 trillion under management. It solicits disclosure of investment-relevant information concerning the greenhouse gas emissions of 3,700 of the largest companies in the world. As of the most recent full report (2008), the CDP had obtained 2,204 responses covering 82 percent of the *Financial Times* (FT) 500.

- The GRI has grown from a program of an environmental NGO to a stand-alone international organization based in Amsterdam. As of 2008, its members included 507 SRI investors/analysts, NGOs, companies, labor organizations, academics, consultants, and individuals drawn from 55 countries. Reporting guidelines have been in effect for 12 years and have been revised twice. Reporting organizations have increased steadily, although only about 10 percent of these are U.S. companies or other entities. In 2010, 164 U.S. organizations submitted GRI reports; the worldwide total was 1485.[16]

- As of mid-2009, the UNGC claimed 8,000 participants, including more than 5,300 businesses in 130 countries around the world. U.S. participants numbered 438 as of early 2011, of which 247 were businesses. Interestingly, the UNGC recently expelled 2,048 of its members (about one-quarter) for failing to meet their periodic public reporting obligations (UNGC, 2011). (This type of rigorous enforcement of commitments is quite rare among voluntary ES&G initiatives and perhaps is a harbinger of things to come.)

A subsequent chapter will explore the suitability of the information generated at the behest of these initiatives to investment analysis and decision making. For now, the important point is that, in combination with SEC requirements and conformance to any industry-specific codes of conduct, the GRI, UNGC, and CDP largely define the information developed and reported by companies that is available for use by investors. The following sections examine what types of information are of interest and how it is used to make investment decisions. But first, here are some "rules of the road."

Institutional Investors and Fiduciary Duty

Having briefly reviewed the landscape of corporate ES&G disclosure and how it does or might inform investor behavior, I now shift the focus back to the types of review and evaluation that investors and analysts perform. I begin by examining some of the constraints and obligations that guide the behavior of these parties, emphasizing particular issues that have some bearing on corporate ES&G behavior and its implications.

Organizations or individuals that manage money on behalf of others have certain obligations under the law. They are defined as "fiduciaries" and, as such, assume an obligation to act in the best interests of the party or parties they represent. Fiduciary duty exists whenever a client relationship involves special trust, confidence, and/or reliance. Fiduciaries are obligated to exercise the duties of using all available skill, care, and diligence when performing their work, and they must maintain a high standard of honesty and full disclosure with their client(s) at all times. They are precluded from obtaining any personal benefit at a client's expense. That is, in the discharge of their responsibilities, they must always put the client's interests above their own.

Fiduciary duty is important in the current context because it is the foundation of securities law in the U.S. and many other countries. For example, pension fund trustees have a fiduciary duty to their members and any other beneficiaries to manage the funds entrusted to them with the utmost care and to invest them prudently using all their available skills and effort.

Professional investor behavior also is heavily influenced by the Modern Prudent Investor Rule, which is a fundamental principle of securities law in all or essentially all U.S. states.[17] Under this doctrine, investors must do or observe the following:

- They must deploy the assets with which they have been entrusted as if they were their own.
- They must avoid excessive risk. (As a practical matter, this means developing or maintaining a portfolio rather than a single asset or a small number of assets.)
- They must avoid excessive costs.
- Although there is no duty to maximize returns, investors must implement a rational and appropriate investment strategy.
- The portfolio must be diversified unless doing so would be imprudent.
- Prudence and decisions generally are to be judged at the time of investment.

The clear intent here is to ensure that fiduciaries such as money managers understand and abide by a set of behaviors that ensure that the risks taken in investing client funds are reasonable, given the client's investment objectives and risk tolerance. At the same time, the absence of detailed guidance or more specific requirements gives the professional investor wide latitude in determining the appropriate range of options to consider for a particular client and in choosing the best course of action.

Unfortunately, over time, some common interpretations emerged and received widespread acceptance to the point where they stood largely unchallenged for many years. One such interpretation was that the duty of loyalty owed to the client implied that the money manager was compelled to attempt to maximize returns. This way of thinking became particularly pronounced during the great "bull run" from 1982 through the bursting of the Internet bubble in 1999 and to some degree since. During this period, many individual and other investors became convinced that making money in stocks and, to a lesser extent, bonds was easy and that the markets had only one overall direction—up. In such an environment, investment risk seemed muted. To many, it appeared that the biggest risk was to get left behind as stock prices climbed inexorably higher.

A related factor was an interpretation of modern portfolio theory that held that because diversification lowered investment risk, more diversification (owning more different stocks in a portfolio) always was to be preferred over less diversification. Those who favored socially responsible investing (SRI), or ES&G investing in its formative stages, therefore were confronted by great skepticism. Critics of SRI contended that the use of nonfinancial criteria (such as, environmental performance) that might restrict the number of companies the investor could consider (the "investable universe") would pose an unacceptable risk to the diversification of the overall portfolio. SRI advocates were not helped by the fact that many of the early SRI screening and evaluation methods were crude. (They often focused on exclusions according to one or a small number of criteria.) This led to the formation of investment portfolios that did not perform well on a relative basis (in comparison with a relevant market benchmark).

Thus, one of the important factors limiting the growth of ES&G investing has been an entrenched interpretation of fiduciary duty as applied to investing. It suggests that factoring environmental, health and safety, social, or broad economic considerations into investment analysis is misguided, improper, and potentially illegal. This belief has been reinforced by the available interpretations of the U.S. federal statute that governs the management of private (corporate) pension funds—the Employee Retirement Income Security Act (ERISA). Interpretations of ERISA made by the implementing government agency (U.S. Department of Labor) have allowed but not encouraged the use of SRI and similar approaches.[18]

During the past six years, however, the prevailing views on what types of factors investors can and cannot consider have changed significantly. In 2005, a detailed study of investment law in the U.S. and several other countries with advanced capital markets sponsored by the United Nations Environment Programme–Finance Initiative (UNEP-FI) provided a striking and compelling alternative view of the issue. Because the principal authors of the report were attorneys from U.K.-based law firm Freshfields Bruckhaus Deringer, the report became known as "the Freshfields Report." It analyzes the evolution of investment law from the standpoint of whether and under what circumstances matters such as environmental, social, and governance considerations may be evaluated by financial fiduciaries as they carry out their duties to responsibly manage their clients' assets. This document broke some significant new ground and provided the following major conclusions:

- Contrary to conventional wisdom, not only is it acceptable for fiduciaries to consider environmental, social, and governance issues, such issues *must* be considered when and where they are relevant to *any* aspect of investment strategy.
- Investment law in the U.S. and most other jurisdictions examined presents no barriers to integrating ES&G considerations into investment fund management activities, so long as the focus remains on the fund beneficiaries and the fund's purposes (UNEP-FI, Freshfields Bruckhaus Deringer, 2005).

As described next, this report and its conclusions have induced a sea change in how ES&G issues are perceived and managed by both

SRI investors and, increasingly, money managers and analysts in some of the world's largest mainstream financial institutions.

Recognizing these trends, and in the interests of providing more detailed guidance for institutional investors and others who want to incorporate ES&G considerations into their business models, UNEP-FI commissioned an update of the Freshfields Report. It was published in 2009. This study confirmed the findings of its predecessor and also reached a number of profound and wide-ranging conclusions, among them the following:

- Fiduciaries have a duty to consider more actively the adoption of responsible investment strategies.
- Fiduciaries must recognize that integrating ES&G issues into investment and ownership processes is part of responsible investment and is necessary when managing risk and evaluating opportunities for long-term investment.
- Fiduciaries will increasingly come to understand the materiality of ES&G issues and the systemic risk they pose, as well as the profound long-term costs of unsustainable development and its impacts on the long-term value of their investment portfolios (UNEP-FI, 2009).

Accordingly, the nature of the debate has swung from *whether* considering ES&G factors in investment decision-making is permissible or appropriate to *how* best to integrate these factors into the data collection, analysis, and investment process. What is particularly noteworthy is the implication that money managers who do not address ES&G issues may become increasingly vulnerable to charges that they have been negligent for not considering reasonably foreseeable risks that may have an adverse effect on the value of their clients' portfolios. It is probably fair to say that more than a few financial market players remain either uninformed of or unconvinced by the findings of these two reports. Nevertheless, many indicators from the markets show that their impact has been widespread and profound.

In the future, if one or more key actions by U.S. federal agencies were to be taken accepting the reasoning presented in the UNEP-FI analyses, wholesale adoption of ES&G investing in U.S. capital markets could occur quickly. One such action would be a supportive interpretation of ERISA by the U.S. Department of Labor. Another would be action(s) taken by the SEC to either require or strongly encourage regular ES&G reporting by publicly traded corporations. If either were to happen, the sea change that I (and a number of others) have observed beginning to form during the past five years could become a tidal wave.

Traditional and Emerging Security Evaluation Methods

This section briefly profiles some of the major principles and methods that have been applied to professional investing over the past several decades. The purpose here is not to train you to become an investor (or a more successful one), but instead to lay the groundwork needed to illustrate how ES&G issues are relevant to the concerns of investors. Investment theory and practice are complex and the subject of lengthy textbooks, programs of graduate and postgraduate study, and vigorous debate. I have a healthy respect for the knowledge and talents of those involved in the capital markets. Here I simply want to raise awareness of the common interests of investors and other financial market actors with those who promote more thoughtful and effective management of ES&G issues. I also seek to draw some connections between the activities and interests of those who, broadly defined, work in these two disparate worlds.

As discussed previously, investing is about appropriately perceiving risk and reward and making decisions about what (and when) to buy and sell over a period of time. Accordingly, I begin with a review of investment risk, which sounds like a simple concept but is not. I then describe some of the more commonly used techniques to identify and evaluate companies whose securities may (or may not) be appropriate candidates to add to an investment portfolio and to identify portfolio components to which investor exposure should, perhaps, be reduced or eliminated. To do this effectively, you must understand what investment risk is and be able to distinguish among different types and sources of risk to either your own capital or funds entrusted by someone else.

Risk

The value of a share of stock today is, in theory, the net present value of all the future cash flows that will be generated by the company that issued the share, divided by the number of shares. In other words, each share represents the pro rata portion of all the wealth that the company will create in the future, discounted to today. Obviously, a great many factors influence how much actual wealth any particular firm will generate through its activities. The further into the future you extend predictions about any of them, the more uncertain these estimates become.

Nevertheless, it is possible to characterize the different factors that may influence a company's fortunes and to understand how they differ. Table 6-5 shows some of the important distinctions between some of these factors and the risks they imply. Simply stated, systematic risks apply to all companies operating in an economy and include a number of aspects of the overall economic climate, such as interest rates and inflation. No individual firm can entirely escape the influence of these factors, nor can any one company change them. In contrast, nonsystematic risks are specific to a particular firm and include such factors as which lines of business the company chooses to pursue, its financing arrangements, and its management of cash. The remaining factors listed in the table have characteristics of both types of investment risk, in that they are both "macro level" concerns but also can be managed or avoided by choosing in which geographies and economies the firm operates.

Table 6-5 Sources and Types of Investment Risk

Type	Source
Systematic	Interest rates
	Market
	Inflation
Nonsystematic	Business
	Financial
	Liquidity
Elements of both	Exchange rate
	Country (political)

To mitigate these risks while seeking and exploiting opportunities to generate positive returns for investors, money managers employ a number of different methods. As discussed previously, one basic strategy fundamental to professional investing is diversification—employing the portfolio approach. Building a portfolio commonly involves diversification across several dimensions: changing the number of securities held, holding different asset classes (stocks, bonds, CDs), and adroit consideration of different economic sectors and industries to both diversify and limit risk to changing economic conditions.

In portfolio development, the investor seeks to position the investment holdings along the "efficient frontier." Investment theory holds that it is possible to optimize the relationship between risk and reward through diversification. If you were to plot risk versus reward on a line graph, the efficient frontier would be the curved line along which the maximum reward could be obtained for a given level of risk. Conversely, you would find the minimum risk required to generate a given level of reward. All the points along this line yield an identical expected value. Where a particular investor would want to position a portfolio would (or should) be based on his or her investment goals and risk tolerance. An important corollary is that all points off of the efficient frontier represent inferior solutions. This means that investing according to their locations on the graph (such as by investing solely in a small number of very high-growth companies) is likely to yield a suboptimal result. For example, you might take on too much risk in pursuit of large gains, or achieve lower returns than would be possible with an optimally constructed portfolio having the same risk exposure.

The implications of this set of relationships are profound, from the standpoint of constructing and managing an investment portfolio. Accepting the notion of an efficient frontier imposes a discipline on the investor and his or her behavior. This manifests itself in an unwillingness to pay more for a security than is justified by both its future earnings potential and risk profile. Quantitatively, the relationship between risk and reward can be expressed through the use of the Capital Asset Pricing Model. In a simplified, normalized form, it states that the required rate of return for a given security is equal to the market rate of return multiplied by a measure of the security's systematic risk (called the "beta").[19] Stocks that have higher systematic risk require a higher rate of return than those that have low systematic risk.

In addition, the efficient frontier and Modern Portfolio Theory imply that firm-specific (nonsystematic) risk can be largely removed from an investment portfolio simply by diversifying. This means that professional investors are assumed to be diversified, because by not being diversified, the investor has needlessly taken on a possibly significant source of risk. And as you saw previously, this would be viewed as a breach of fiduciary duty (and possibly state securities law) if the investor is managing funds on behalf of someone else in a fiduciary capacity. Viewed in this context, "risk" is not what we tend to think it is (losing our investment). Instead, it is *volatility in returns*. Portfolio volatility (or its inverse, stability) is an important concept that the investing public often overlooks—at least when markets are rising.

Reward (Given an Understanding of Risk)

The flip side of risk is, of course, reward. This topic captivates the public and is the focal point of most investor communication with clients. Potential reward to the investor may take one or more forms. The market prices of stocks held in the portfolio may increase, as may dividend payments over time. Bond prices may increase if and as the issuer's credit rating improves and/or interest rates more generally decline. For these pleasant developments to occur, generally speaking, the firm issuing the securities must achieve sustained improvements among one or more of the three determinants of value highlighted at the beginning of this chapter: revenue growth, earnings or cash flow growth, or risk reduction.

Most of the conventional methods for evaluating and valuing company securities involve assessing these endpoints and/or factors or conditions that have some direct relationship to them. I review some of the more commonly used methods in this section.

One basic approach is *technical analysis*. This method involves forecasting price fluctuations, focusing on supply and demand conditions that may apply to a particular security. To the technical analyst, sometimes called a "chartist," the causes of these fluctuations are unimportant. He or she is simply trying to find out whether excess supply (or demand) for a stock can be detected by analyzing patterns of price fluctuations or movement in indicators or rules. Technical analysis focuses on momentum—trends in price and/or earnings growth rather than on more fundamental factors. Because technical analysis is not based on causal factors, its relationship to the ES&G factors considered in this book is minimal, if not nonexistent, so I will not consider it further here. The important point to understand is that investors relying chiefly (or solely) on technical analysis exist, although they are likely to be a small minority. Also, the ES&G value-creation message I promote in this book (and that others share) is not likely to have *any* influence on this constituency.

The other major approach used in investing is *fundamental security analysis*. Typically, this method proceeds in steps, as discussed earlier in this chapter, beginning at the top. Analysts examine, sequentially, the economy and market conditions, major sectors and industries, and, finally, individual companies. At the level of the firm, investors and analysts apply several different types of analysis. Typically, these include net present value analysis (again, the current value of future cash flows), multiplier analysis (discussed later), and, in some cases, other techniques.

First, the overall economy and markets are evaluated. This is important because it has been shown empirically that general economic and market conditions typically account for between one-quarter and one-half of the variability in company earnings from period to period. Moreover, in many cases, stock prices have led the wider economy, particularly out of economic downturns. The state of the capital markets and investor confidence (or lack thereof) can affect the rate of return investors require to accept the risk of acquiring certain securities. This phenomenon was vividly illustrated during the recent global economic meltdown when, for example, the interest rate on high-yield corporate securities (junk bonds) soared and prices plummeted, regardless of individual issuer characteristics.

When evaluating the effect of big-picture concerns on an investment portfolio, investors consider such factors as the current stage of the economic cycle (are we in strong growth or facing a looming recession, for example), rates of inflation, interest rates, and the expected overall levels of corporate profits. Although these factors affect all companies, some of them tend to affect certain types of industries (and firms within them) more strongly than others. For example, if inflationary pressures are gathering force and interest rates are rising significantly, many investors avoid companies (and even entire economic sectors) that are sensitive to this factor, such as, residential construction and some types of banking.

The next step of the analysis is performed at the sector and industry level. Depending on the principal information sources used and their own preferences, analysts organize the firms in the economy into approximately 12 sectors, many of which contain a number of distinct industries. Table 6-6 shows commonly evaluated sectors and a sample of the major industries within each.

Table 6-6 Major Economic Sectors and Illustrative Industries

Sector	Industry
Consumer discretionary	Leisure products
	Restaurants
	Retail
Consumer staples	Food processing
	Household products: nondurables
	Retail: food
Energy	Oil and gas: integrated
Financials	Banks
	Insurance
Health care	Biotechnology
	Pharmaceuticals
Industrials	Aerospace
	Electrical components and equipment
	Freight
Information technology	Computer hardware
	Information technology
	Semiconductor equipment
Materials	Chemicals
	Construction: building materials
	Packaging
Real estate	Real estate
Services	Business support
	Education
Telecommunications services	Telecommunications: fixed line
Utilities	Utilities: electric

Again, investors will carefully consider which sectors and industries offer favorable prospects in light of macro-level factors and their particular return expectations and risk tolerance. They will evaluate, at the sector and industry level, growth opportunities (as a function of industry/market maturity and other factors), protection against economic downturns, cyclicality of revenue streams, and sensitivity to interest rates and other factors.

In particular, perceived opportunities to grow revenue in a non-linear fashion can substantially boost the appeal of a particular company or industry with investors. The huge influx of investment funds into many forms of renewable energy during the past several years is a good example. It has in many ways paralleled the growth (and pitfalls) of investing in previous "hot" technologies such as biotechnology, the Internet, and wireless communications.

It is important for those interested in promoting corporate sustainability to understand that, as shown here, investor behavior is influenced by many factors beyond whether and to what extent a particular firm has advanced sustainability management practices. With that said, whatever the circumstances of a particular sector or industry, firms in even less dynamic, slower-growing sectors can show leadership and distinguish themselves among their peers by putting in place the policies, goals, and infrastructure described in Chapter 5. In doing so, it is important that they at least consider how they can improve their performance with respect to some of the factors I will consider next—those that investors use to evaluate individual companies.

As noted previously, as an initial matter, the investor is faced with only one question when considering a particular stock, bond, or other investment for a portfolio: Should I add, remove, or hold this security? The appropriate answer to this question is influenced by two related questions:

- What is it worth?
- Is it priced correctly?

The answer to the second can be readily deduced by comparing the answer to the first (the true value) with the current price on the market, assuming that we are discussing a reasonably liquid security issued on a major market exchange. So essentially, the task (and much of investment analysis) involves determining the security's true value.

There are several ways to accomplish this. The true value is equal to the net present value of all the firm's future cash flows, discounted to today's terms using an appropriate rate. Many professional investors and, certainly, the larger information providers and money managers have detailed knowledge of company operations and sophisticated models with which to perform the necessary calculations. Such discounted cash flow (DCF) models are in common use throughout the financial services industry and in academia as well.

Another approach to both inform the development of estimates to use in DCF models and to perform screening and periodic evaluation of individual securities is to use ratio analysis. I present some commonly used ratios in Table 6-7 and then discuss them briefly.

In either case, the investor or analyst is seeking hidden value and/ or risk. Recall that the market has already rendered a judgment about the current value of any security that is liquid and frequently traded. The question then is, have market participants overlooked anything that might affect the company's future revenues, earnings, or cash flows? Or have they overlooked latent sources of risk that could jeopardize anticipated financial results? So those seeking to outperform the market are constantly looking for what is unrecognized but important, and also what might change in the future and in what ways. Those interested in corporate sustainability tend to believe that ES&G issues and how they are managed provide significant and tangible examples of some of these latent factors. And based on the published literature (discussed in depth in the next chapter), there is reason to believe that their views have been substantiated. I will introduce and discuss ES&G investing in greater depth shortly. For now, however, it is important to return to the types of endpoints that are familiar terrain for the investment analyst. In this way, as we consider new sources of value that can be created by ES&G improvements, we will be able to put them into terms that will be accessible to and valued by the professional investor.

Again, investors consider both risk and reward and try to strike a reasonable balance between them.[20] Typical reward factors include profitability, cash flow, efficiency/productivity, and growth. Risk factors include capital structure, liquidity, and cash flow (or the lack thereof).

Commonly, these factors are evaluated through the use of ratios, which compare one number (such as net profit) to another (such as sales). Most of the data required to compute traditional financial ratios is directly available from the company's financial statements (balance sheet, income statement, and cash flow statement). Because these data must be reported at regular, defined intervals, must be calculated according to certain conventions, and must be independently audited,[21] they have certain attributes that are extremely helpful to the analyst.

Specifically, financial accounting data reported by companies are provided on a timely basis and are (presumably) accurate, consistent, comparable across time periods and organizations, reliable, and meaningful within the context in which they are reported and used. Many observers have questioned whether this information set and reporting conventions (which date from the 1930s or earlier) adequately capture the current workings of a company's operations and performance or provide much insight into its future prospects. This topic is explored further in Chapter 8. In any event, there can be no doubt that having a set of independently validated data describing each company's financial results is of great utility to the financial analyst or investor.

Some commonly used ratios are listed in Table 6-7. I provide these here without significant elaboration simply to make the point that these types of basic indicators are in widespread use, are limited in number, and are not mathematically complex. Moreover, most can be readily found (already computed) on many investment company and financial web sites (such as, those of Charles Schwab, Morningstar, and the *Wall Street Journal*). These types of data are part of the common language of "Wall Street" and must be understood, at least at a general level, to address investors' concerns. In addition, some of the published literature on the relationships between ES&G issues and corporate financial results and investment returns reviewed in Chapter 7 refers specifically to these ratios.

Table 6-7 Commonly Used Financial Ratios Applied to Company-Level Analysis

Profitability	Efficiency/ Productivity Ratios	Growth	Liquidity	Others
Return on equity (ROE)	Sales/inventory	Compounded annual growth rate	Quick ratio	Debt: equity
Return on assets (ROA)	Sales/net working capital	Sales	Current ratio	Price/earnings (P/E) ratio
Return on sales (ROS)	Sales/fixed (or total) assets	Earnings	Times interest earned ratio	Bond rating
		Cash flow	Liquidity	Yield
		Price/earnings: growth (PEG)		Stock beta

Briefly, the categories listed in Table 6-7 and the ratios within each are meaningful in the following respects:

- **Profitability ratios.** Return on equity, assets, or sales provides insight into how well the company (and its management) are converting invested capital (equity), materials, plant and equipment, (assets), or funds paid by customers (sales) into profits. High profitability ratios are considered to be a good indication that the firm is converting the resources entrusted to it into profits effectively. A high ROE is particularly prized by investors.

- **Efficiency ratios.** Sales normalized by inventory, net working capital (which includes inventory), or assets tell the analyst how well and quickly the firm is converting its available resources into new sales. As discussed previously, vigorous and growing sales are the lifeblood of any business, particularly one seeking new investment capital.

- **Growth.** In a related vein, substantial return opportunity is intimately tied to company growth rates, both in an absolute sense and as indicated by certain key ratios, such as, price/earnings:growth (PEG). The PEG normalizes the P/E multiple (discussed in a moment) by the firm's growth rate. Firms with a PEG ratio less than unity (ones that are growing faster than their price-earnings multiple) are often viewed as promising investment candidates.

- **Liquidity.** Although true investors are primarily interested in long-term return prospects, it is widely understood that there will be no long term unless the firm is continuously managed properly in the short term. This includes having adequate liquid financial resources to meet the company's ongoing needs and obligations. Liquidity ratios, such as, those listed in Table 6-7, provide a quantitative measure of what sort of "cushion" of cash and other liquid assets the company has, relative to its short-term financial obligations. Generally, investors (and most lenders) like to see several times more short-term assets than short-term liabilities. This ensures that it is unlikely that the firm will run short of cash, even in the wake of an emergency or significant unexpected event.

- **Other ratios.** Several other ratios are important and are often used by analysts and investors to develop a sense of a company's position and prospects. The *debt/equity* ratio (or "leverage") quantifies how much of the firm's capital has been contributed by investors versus borrowed from lenders or secured by debt. A high debt/equity ratio (high leverage) indicates greater risk, due to the cash drain from the associated regular interest payments, which have the effect of reducing profits. The *price/ earnings* (P/E) ratio is widely followed. It indicates the multiple of a company's current earnings at which the firm's stock price (per share) is selling. Historically, the P/E for all publicly traded stocks in the U.S. has averaged about 14, but during bull markets (not to mention market bubbles) the P/E can regularly exceed 20. The *bond rating* and stock *beta* (discussed earlier) indicate the risk of a company's fixed income and equity securities, respectively. Higher bond ratings mean lower interest rates (and costs), due to lower perceived risks of default by the issuer. In contrast, a high beta means higher-than-market stock price volatility (risk), and hence, a higher required rate of return. Finally, a stock's *yield* is the value of the firm's annual dividend payment per share divided by its stock price. The average yield for U.S. stocks in recent years is about 2 percent, which is well below long-term historical averages. It is worthy of note, however, that dividend payments have represented a majority of the total return provided by U.S. stocks over the past 30 years or so.

In addition to these conventional types of financial measures, a number of alternative frameworks and methods have emerged in recent years that provide a means by which investments may be evaluated. I will briefly mention two that have attracted their own following and that may be of interest to particular types of organizations. One is Economic Value Added (EVA), which is a technique invented (and copyrighted) by the firm Stern Stewart. EVA provides a method by which a company, or a component thereof, can be rigorously evaluated according to its value-creation performance. It takes the profit or earnings produced by the company, a market segment, or even a single production line and considers (subtracts) the cost of the capital that was required to produce that profit.[22] Entities (or subunits) that have a positive result (that earned more than their cost of capital) have created value. Those with a negative result have, in effect, destroyed a portion of their organization's available capital, notwithstanding the fact that they generated positive earnings on a financial accounting basis. EVA provides some real analytical power to company and segment evaluation and is in use in a wide array of companies. Those interested in promoting corporate sustainability should be aware of this technique. Its usage involves no new endpoints or variables, but it does bring a tight focus to one of the themes of this book—value creation in a true sense.

Another approach to organizational valuation is called the balanced scorecard. The balanced scorecard is actually a strategic planning tool, but it is often used to define performance metrics and track their attainment. Its value for our purposes is that its use explicitly links financial results with some of the organizational considerations and activities that often play important but underrecognized roles in attaining the financial performance sought by senior management (and investors). The balanced scorecard combines and encourages the development of linkages among variables addressing the key dimensions of customers; internal business processes; the organization's capacity, capability, and learning; and financial performance (Rohm, 2008). As a result, proponents of this method believe that it addresses "value" in a more complete sense. It also tells a richer and more meaningful story than relying solely on the financials or on the financials plus the firm's "growth story." By explicitly considering both the desired financial results and some of the key variables that will produce them, the balanced scorecard offers more numerous and obvious linkages to ES&G endpoints than more conventional approaches. Moreover, because internal processes and employee capabilities (and, implicitly, well-being) are fundamental components, it is not unreasonable to conclude that it is closer to a true corporate sustainability concept than many other formal planning and management approaches. In addition, by working through the logic of the balanced scorecard, those interested in corporate sustainability can introduce some of the important ES&G issues discussed in previous chapters. Or, viewed from the outside, they could determine some of the issues that are most likely to confer financial risk or opportunity.

This brings us to a discussion of "intangibles." These are aspects of a company's structure and operations that confer strength and competitive advantage but that are not quantified or reflected on the firm's financial statements. The study of intangible assets has become a major focus of investment analysis and decision making during the past 20 years or so, and there is every reason to believe that this emphasis will continue.

> "As recently as the mid-1980s, financial statements captured at least 75% on average of the true market value of major corporations. In the intervening years, however, that figure has dropped to a paltry 15% on average." (Lev, 2001)

Quite simply, we have been living in a post-industrial economy in the U.S. (and other economically advanced countries) for the past 20 to 30 years. Today, the strength and future prospects of a particular firm generally have more to do with the talents and capabilities of its senior executives and workforce, intellectual capital, customer and stakeholder relationships, and other intangible factors than they do with the extent or value of their brick-and-mortar assets. Unfortunately, however, only the latter, along with the firm's financial capital, are captured in the financial statements that are released to the investing public. The following are some of the more important intangible drivers of financial value, as demonstrated by quantitative analysis (source: GEMI, 2004):

- Customers
- Leadership and strategy
- Transparency
- Brand equity

- Environmental and social reputation
- Alliance and networks
- Technology and processes
- Human capital
- Innovation
- Risk

Interestingly, ES&G factors are explicitly among those with a quantifiable impact on corporate financial performance, as is transparency. Transparency is explored in more depth in subsequent chapters.

Socially Responsible Investing (SRI) and ES&G Investing

I devote considerable attention to the topic of socially responsible investing, because it is the antecedent of ES&G investing. It is the movement and way of evaluating investments that gave rise to the trends and events that are the primary subjects of this book.

A Brief History

SRI in the U.S. had its beginnings in the 1960s as certain types of investors were motivated by issues of conscience to try to avoid investing funds in particular types of enterprises. For example, the trustees of pension funds established for the benefit of retired members of the clergy might be greatly concerned by the fact that the pension fund's assets might be invested in a broad-based stock index fund. This fund might include holdings of firms that are deeply engaged in activities that conflict with the values held by the trustees and their beneficiaries. The initial response to such concerns was to develop exclusionary screens that would remove companies from investment portfolios that engaged in activities such as, producing or selling alcoholic beverages, tobacco products, gambling, firearms and armaments, birth control devices or products, and/or pornography. In this way, the ethical concerns of particular investors could be satisfied through the new technique of "socially responsible" investing (SRI) while still allowing them to participate fully in equity and corporate fixed income investments. Before long, new companies entered the market to provide screened investment portfolios, SRI ratings of companies, and other services. Some of these new entities had their beginnings in the NGO community and later became self-standing commercial enterprises.

With the emergence of environmentalism and new environmental control laws and regulations (described in Chapter 3), the focus broadened to include a number of new indicators reflecting the expectation of legal compliance and the absence or minimization of environmental liabilities. Thus, "green" portfolio screening methods became commonplace within the SRI community and remain with us today. Over time, the focus of the more sophisticated players within this market expanded to consider resource efficiency and other indicators having a more fundamental connection to corporate value, in parallel with the maturation of environmental/EHS management practices in companies and in the public policy arena.

As I write this book in mid-2011, it is intriguing to consider how far SRI has come since my initial exposure to such "values-based" investing in the early 1990s. Despite the fact that the field has matured considerably during the past 20 years or so, it is still growing rapidly and has reached a scale at which it is difficult or impossible to ignore. According to recent data, SRI (broadly defined) now accounts for a substantial fraction (about 12 percent) of the total equity capital invested in U.S. markets. It comprises a significant, although smaller, portion of total U.S. fixed income assets as well. Accompanying and, arguably, allowing this growth has been an evolution in methods away from a "sin" emphasis and reliance on negative screens to the use of a broader and more sophisticated perspective. SRI investors and their representatives also are becoming increasingly activist. They regularly attempt to intervene in the governance of particular companies through proxy campaigns, direct interaction with company senior management, and participation in wider shareholder dialog activities. They also lobby regulatory agencies (such as the SEC) to enforce existing access and disclosure rules and institute new requirements.

Moreover, as highlighted in the next chapter, the more sophisticated users of SRI research and perspectives have shown the ability to generate investment returns that are comparable to (or better than) those of their non-SRI ("mainstream") peers. As a result, the SRI field and its practitioners now have a level of recognition and credibility among many other investors, ratings agencies, regulators, and corporate executives that would have been difficult to imagine 15 years ago.

It also seems appropriate to offer a few words about SRI and the recent financial crisis and its continuing aftermath. Many SRI practitioners see the events of 2008 and early 2009 as a vindication of their view that substantially greater attention must be focused on corporate governance and accountability (particularly on the workings of banks, insurance companies, and other financial services firms); effective internal controls (even after implementation of Sarbanes-Oxley requirements); full, consistent, and meaningful disclosure; adequate shareholder access to the boardroom; and effective regulatory controls and oversight. From where I sit, it is difficult to argue with the validity of this view or any of its constituent parts, or to downplay its public policy implications.

Given the importance of the SRI community in terms of promoting greater consideration of ES&G factors in the domain of investing, I provide some additional facts and perspectives here. Table 6-8 summarizes the growth of SRI in the U.S. during the past 15 years or so. Its contents were developed by the Social Investment Forum (SIF), the largest association of SRI practitioners and service providers in the U.S.

Table 6-8 Socially Responsible Investing in the United States 1995 to 2010 (in Billions of Dollars)

Source: Social Investment Forum Foundation, 2010

SRI Strategy Employed	1995	1997	1999	2001	2003	2005	2007	2010
ES&G incorporation	$162	$529	$1,497	$2,010	$2,143	$1,685	$2,098	$2,512
Shareholder advocacy	$473	$736	$922	$897	$448	$703	$739	$1,497
Community investing	$4	$4	$5	$8	$14	$20	$25	$42
Overlapping strategies	N/A	($84)	($265)	($592)	($441)	($117)	($151)	($981)
Totals	$639	$1,185	$2,159	$2,323	$2,164	$2,290	$2,711	$3,069

Note: Overlapping assets involved in some combination of ES&G incorporation, filing shareholder resolutions, or community investing are subtracted to avoid potential effects of double counting. Separate tracking of the overlapping strategies only began in 1997, so there is no data for 1995. Prior to 2010, assets subject to ES&G incorporation were limited to socially and environmentally screened assets.

As shown in this table, SRI has grown by a factor of almost 5 during the past 15 years and now accounts for more than $3 trillion in assets. SRI assets have grown by more than 34 percent (versus 3 percent growth for all financial assets) since 2005. Since 2007, SRI has experienced growth of more than 13 percent as opposed to 1 percent for all assets. Note that this more-recent growth has occurred in the wake of the financial crisis. According to SIF, major drivers behind this trend include new (and looming) legislative mandates, greater investor interest in clean/green technology, and increasing public awareness of sustainability issues (SIF, 2010). Interestingly, tobacco involvement has been displaced as the most commonly applied SRI criterion. This distinction now applies to company involvement in Sudan ($1.7 trillion in assets).

Most of these assets ($2.3 trillion, or 75 percent) are held by institutional investors. These institutions strongly favor a strategy of incorporating ES&G factors into investment analysis and portfolio selection; this strategy is applied to nearly 90 percent of the funds held. Shareholder advocacy is applied to about 37 percent of funds, and 25 percent are managed according to multiple strategies. This represents a major trend that has gathered strength during the past few years. According to SIF, the number of investment vehicles tracked that incorporate ES&G criteria and the associated assets under management (AUM) both nearly doubled from 2007 to 2010. The number of funds that incorporate ES&G factors in the U.S. now approaches 500. About 60 percent of these are registered investment companies such as mutual funds, exchange-traded funds (ETFs), and closed-end funds.

Interestingly, alternative investment vehicles such as hedge funds, private equity funds, and responsible property funds, which typically are available only to accredited institutional and high-net-worth investors, also are moving into the ES&G investing space. As of 2010, 177 such funds incorporated ES&G criteria, with $37.8 billion in total assets. According to SIF, this segment has grown nearly 300 percent since 2007, making it the most rapidly growing segment studied. During this same period, the AUM in these vehicles increased more than 600 percent (SIF, 2010). Much of this new money has been earmarked for investments in clean technology and/or renewable energy (thematic investing), as well as for so-called "impact" investing at the community level.

ES&G Evaluation and Investing Methods

Note that the first row of Table 6-8 speaks to one of the major themes of this book—ES&G incorporation. The entries for the past several years suggest that this is by far the dominant SRI strategy applied to funds invested with SRI money managers, which reportedly have totaled more than $2 trillion since 2001 (with the exception of 2005). It is not entirely clear what "ES&G incorporation" means in all cases. But I believe it is now widely accepted (at least within the SRI community) that the route to truly sustainable investing is to embed the consideration of ES&G factors into the fundamental research and analysis processes carried out by investment analysts and portfolio managers. Conveying this message to a broader array of market participants and convincing them of its validity is, of course, a remaining challenge. I examine the issue of ES&G integration in greater depth later.

In parallel with and enabling the growth of SRI, the past 15 years or so have witnessed significant maturation of the methods that are used to screen and evaluate companies relative to their ES&G posture and performance. One significant trend is, quite simply, better and more sophisticated analysis of not only environmental (and social) performance, but also active consideration of some of the factors that should lead to performance improvement (or the lack thereof). Thus, many SRI researchers and investors now consider such factors as the presence and provisions of a company's EHS/sustainability and/or climate change policies, the use of formal management systems, commitments and goals, and other indicia of coherent and effective ES&G management practices. These advances have been enabled by and promoted increasing demands for a greater array of ES&G metrics and data, as discussed in greater depth in the following chapters. At a more general level, given the experiences of the past couple of decades, many SRI analysts and investors understand (sometimes in excruciating detail) the strengths and limitations of the ES&G data that they use to perform their evaluations. Many of the data are collected from regulatory agency web sites and databases, or otherwise retrieved from public sources. Through experience and dialog with both companies (generally, the original source of regulatory compliance data) and regulators, SRI analysts are in general in a far better position to make appropriate decisions about which data to use and how much weight to give them than they were in the early days of green investing.

Another major change is a bit more nuanced but nevertheless is significant. Many SRI investors, and the research firms that serve them, are either deemphasizing or abandoning rigid screens, particularly negative screens, in favor of alternative approaches to identifying eligible investment candidates and making specific stock or bond selections. In some cases, positive screens are employed, such that all firms providing evidence of one or more particular attributes are screened "in," thereby becoming candidates for further evaluation and, perhaps, investment. Positive screening is commonly used to identify firms (and industries) involved in activities viewed as having favorable growth prospects (renewable energy, for example) as well as policies and practices favored by particular investors (such as significant philanthropic activity, or commitments to reduce greenhouse gas emissions). In other cases, rigid screens are not applied. Instead, ES&G factors are evaluated in various ways as components of fundamental industry or company analysis (such as, ratios developed in addition to the conventional ones discussed here). Or they are evaluated as a final "filter" following completion of the investor's established security selection methods.

In any case, use of these more-inclusive approaches yields several distinct benefits to the SRI investor. One is that it can substantially increase the pool of acceptable investment candidates, providing (potentially) greater portfolio diversification. In addition, avoiding exclusionary screens allows SRI investors to construct portfolios that closely mirror many of the mainstream stock indexes, enabling "apples-to-apples" comparisons of performance over time that are problematic otherwise. In so doing, SRI investors have overcome one of the major objections posed by critics and mainstream investors unconvinced of the value of considering ES&G endpoints: that by artificially constraining the investable "universe," SRI investors were damaging their own (and/or clients') interests by limiting access (and potential investment upside) to major and economically important segments of the market.[23] Today, most SRI investors eschew exclusionary screening in favor of a "best in class" approach that provides exposure to all economic sectors and most industries, while still reflecting active consideration of the ES&G factors that are important to them and/or their clients/beneficiaries.[24] Perhaps most importantly, as discussed in the next chapter, the published literature shows that this more nuanced and sophisticated approach to ES&G investing significantly outperforms negative screening and, in many cases, conventional investing using either market indexes or non-ES&G active investing approaches.

Another important consequence of investing in a broader array of firms is that SRI investors can apply more focus to engagement with companies, particularly those lacking the ES&G practices and/or performance they seek. Engagement with company senior management and other representatives has naturally led to greater understanding of the issues and internal workings of these companies, which is very important in evaluating future investment prospects.

Finally, and of direct relevance to the major themes of this book, as a general matter, SRI investors have shifted their emphasis in recent years. They have moved away from notions of "responsibility" and toward more comprehensive evaluations of investment risk and opportunity. In other words, increasingly investments are being made more on the basis of which companies appear best (and least) able to adroitly manage ES&G issues and less on whether and to what extent companies are "doing the right thing." I view this as a positive and, indeed, necessary development for a true alignment of corporate, investment, and societal interests and pursuit of more sustainable corporate behavior. To put this concept into effect, leading SRI analysts and investors often use or embody certain principles in their security selection processes. I will refer to such financial market participants from this point forward as ES&G analysts and investors to distinguish them from those using more traditional SRI methods. Common ES&G evaluation principles and processes include the following:

- **Long-term perspective.** In contrast to many participants in contemporary capital markets, ES&G investors often hold a long-term perspective. Among other things, this means that they can (and often do) hold individual company securities for an extended period. Therefore, they can appreciate the positive financial impacts of appropriate sustainability investments made by the companies in their investment portfolios.

- **Eco-efficiency.** As discussed in Chapter 5, this approach focuses on reducing the material and energy intensity of production and dispersion of toxic materials while promoting sustainable use and reuse of resources. Pursuing eco-efficiency criteria in a skillful way reduces costs (thereby increasing earnings), controls liabilities, and, in some cases, generates new revenue streams.

- **Life-cycle analysis.** This technique is used to evaluate the upstream ES&G (most often, environmental) aspects of a given industry sector or company's supply chain. It also evaluates the possible downstream ES&G/environmental consequences, and investing risk exposure, of the sector/company's products and services in use by the customer.

- **Risks to intangible assets.** As discussed previously, intangible assets represent the primary source of future competitive strength for most firms. Accordingly, ES&G risks, including possible impacts on brand strength/reputation and important stakeholder relationships, are often an area of focus for ES&G investors (as they are for a growing number of mainstream investors).

ES&G investors use many different approaches to constructing and maintaining their portfolios. Each brings to bear its own unique perspectives, knowledge, and beliefs in determining which assets to buy, sell, and hold. Nonetheless, I can make a few observations about the different general approaches that these investors have employed in recent years. I perceive at least three basic approaches:

- **Thematic investing.** This involves identifying high-potential technologies, companies, and/or industries and focusing investment funds on firms that allow substantial exposure to what may be perceived as rapidly growing demand (and, presumably, revenues and profits). Noteworthy examples of this approach include the many investment funds that are focused on alternative energy or "green" products.

- **"Best of the rest."** In this approach, investors evaluate the participants in established, even mature, industries and select the firms within them that they believe offer the most assurance that they are positioned to take best advantage of important ES&G factors and trends.

- **Indexing.** Much like their mainstream counterparts, some ES&G investors (and research firms) construct indexes comprising the subset of firms within a larger investable population (such as, the S&P 500) that has the most favorable ES&G profile and, as a result, the best investment prospects.

Regardless of the approach employed, the investor will either perform its ES&G evaluation internally or purchase ratings/rankings and/or data from an ES&G research firm, along with the other components of its security assessment process. Then it will construct or modify its investment portfolio accordingly. Typical evaluation criteria include the presence and coherence of ES&G policies and systems, eco-efficiency considerations, and reported or normalized indicators of ES&G performance (such as, emissions, waste, accidents, or Board composition). Depending on the investor and the indicator in question, the evaluation may take the form of pass/fail, quantitative rating, or integrated best-of-breed evaluation.

Among the more sophisticated practitioners of ES&G investing, I have been observing the logical and necessary next step toward aligning the interests of the sustainability and investor communities—real ES&G integration. Some investors, particularly in Europe, claim to have fully integrated valuation models that explicitly consider ES&G endpoints and how they affect either intangible assets (such as product quality, customer benefits, brand value, and human capital), tangible financial results (sales/margin improvement, free cash flow, capital intensity, or capital cost, for example), or both. The proprietary (and, presumably, highly valuable) nature of these methods limits the extent to which I have been able to explore their specific components and algorithms. However, I can provide a few examples of the underlying theory and types of data used to populate these emerging methods:

- The prominent U.S. investment bank Goldman Sachs (GS)[25] has developed a stock evaluation approach called GS SUSTAIN. The approach is based on the belief that companies need to perform well in five broad categories to capitalize on the opportunities of globalization while minimizing the impact from environmental and social side effects: corporate governance, leadership, employees, stakeholders, and environment. GS SUSTAIN is applied through a weighted assessment of 20 to 25 quantifiable indicators (depending on the industry), of which one-third are sector-specific. These criteria reflect, among other factors, the ten UN Global Compact criteria as well as several key environmental indicators: energy use and carbon emissions; management of water, waste, and recycling; suppliers and sourcing; and biodiversity and land use. This process yields a list of recommended companies that are provided to firm clients for investment. GS has reportedly back-tested its method, focusing on what it considers the crucial variable (cash returns on invested capital). GS found that its method outperformed both the relevant benchmarks and other SRI methods (Goldman Sachs, 2007).

- Calvert Investments operates a family of 20 mutual funds. It also offers several other investment products, such as variable insurance trusts and community investment programs, most of which are developed using ES&G criteria and research that the firm develops internally. Issues that are evaluated explicitly include governance and ethics, workplace, environment, product safety and impact, international operations and human rights, indigenous peoples' rights, and community relations. In evaluating corporate environmental posture and performance for its primary offerings ("Solution Funds"), Calvert reportedly evaluates environmental performance, responsiveness to incidents, and compliance. It favors companies that take steps to mitigate their environmental footprint, have better-than-average environmental records relative to their industry peers, and are responsive to stakeholders. They assess corporate-wide sustainability strategies, such as integrating environmental factors into product design, and corporate management and governance. Calvert seeks to invest in companies that demonstrate leadership in addressing climate change; disclose and take actions to minimize sources of environmental risk and liability; implement natural resource conservation, efficiency, and pollution prevention programs; integrate environmental sustainability into senior management decision-making; and engage stakeholders in pursuit of environmental improvement. Similarly detailed criteria are employed to evaluate the other major ES&G issues. Calvert also operates two thematic funds. One focuses on alternative energy and another on water. Another fund ("SAGE Strategies") gives investors the opportunity to support engagement with companies (some of which do not meet Calvert's standard ES&G criteria) on particular ES&G issues of interest. Calvert states that all its investment portfolios integrate its thorough assessment of environmental, social, and governance performance with a rigorous review of financial performance. But details of how this integration is performed are not readily available.

- KLD Research & Analytics (now a unit of MSCI, Inc.) is a long-standing SRI research firm (one of the pioneers, in fact) and investment fund manager. For almost two decades, it has produced what was formerly known as the Domini 400 Index (now called the FTSE KLD 400 Social Index), which for many years was the most widely known SRI index. The firm also operates nine U.S. stock indexes (Social, Sustainability, Catholic) and nine global stock indexes (Climate, Environment, Sustainability), all in conjunction with FTSE. KLD has long employed a method that yields bond-style ratings (AAA to CCC) of individual companies. The analysis considers a firm's impact on five types of "stakeholders": environment, community and society, customers, employees and supply chain, and governance and ethics. Ratings are aggregated from four levels of scoring, beginning with raw performance indicators (of which there are more than 280); going through performance ratings, impact ratings, and an overall ES&G rating for each major stakeholder; and finally a company rating. Impact ratings are weighted by industry. For example, water use may be rated more heavily for a mining company than for an insurance company. EHS issues considered include management of environmental issues, climate change, other emissions, impacts of products and services, resource management and use, employee safety, and sustainability reporting and engagement.

A substantial number of other U.S. investors claim to employ ES&G evaluation methods in constructing investment portfolios. But they have not, to this point, divulged much information to either substantiate these claims or provide details on their methods. I expect that this will change markedly during the next several years, as ES&G investing continues to take market share and as broader adoption and full implementation of the Principles for Responsible Investment (PRI) occurs. The PRI is described later.

Before departing this topic to consider the next, I want to clarify the state of play regarding SRI and avoid the appearance of making predictions that I do not expect will come to pass. Despite the emergence of sophisticated approaches to ES&G investing in recent years,

I expect that the two dominant approaches (such as ES&G integration) and more conventional SRI practices (such as negative screening) will continue to exist in parallel in both U.S. and international markets. This dichotomy reflects the distinction between values-based and risk-based investing. Because, as discussed previously, it reflects the interests of some investors to not associate with certain types of business(es), the values-based approach necessarily involves some degree of negative screening. In contrast, risk-based investing reflects a judgment that certain EHS and/or other ES&G characteristics impart differential opportunities to capture future financial returns and/or impart risks to these returns and the firm's capital. And in practice, the two approaches may be used in a complementary fashion.

Given the substantial number of values-based asset owners (such as pension funds) in the U.S., it is highly likely that the traditional forms of investing behavior that they demand will continue indefinitely, even as methods and data enable more sophisticated risk-based analysis to evolve and expand. Given this dynamic, which I view as both reasonable and healthy, it is appropriate to focus on contributing to advancements in sustainability practice and appropriate recognition of ES&G value-creation potential within the financial community, rather than suggest that negative screening is obsolete or inappropriate for all informed investors.

Barriers to ES&G Investing

In reviewing the information just presented concerning the substantial and rapid growth of ES&G investing, the progress made by its proponents and supporters, particularly during the past five years or so, seems impressive. Those who have been in the field for more than a few years, however, understand that garnering and maintaining support for ES&G investing beyond those who already practice or promote it has been a long and arduous task. So I now turn my attention to some of the factors that have limited the rate of adoption of ES&G investing and the extent to which it is actually practiced. In short, the issue has to do with why mainstream investors have not been more receptive; why so few seem willing to experiment with ES&G value concepts; and why, in 2011, use of ES&G valuation concepts occurs so rarely within major U.S. investment banks, mutual fund companies, and money managers. This section discusses some of the major reasons for what I observe versus what we might expect.

In addition to the factors discussed in Chapter 2, many of the important phenomena limiting the spread of ES&G investing are related to the entrenched beliefs and attitudes common in the investment community, as well as to certain structural arrangements:

- **Short-term perspective.** One factor that is widely bemoaned and known to most observers is a focus on the share prices of equities over a short time horizon. Consider the logic of how and why a company makes the investments necessary to put in place the ES&G management structures and programs discussed in Chapter 5 and this chapter. It seems obvious that reaping the benefits accruing from these changes would take place over a period of years. In contrast, the relevant period of performance for some analysts and investors is a maximum of one fiscal quarter and, in many cases, from one press release to the next. Indeed, enabled by today's electronic market exchanges, a sizeable cohort within the broader population of stock and bond traders operates (buys, holds, and sells) on a time horizon of *minutes*. Whether such people should even be considered investors, as opposed to traders (or speculators), is a matter of opinion. What is clear, however, is that such financial market actors do not and will not have any interest in sustainability issues.[26] These issues simply play out over a much longer time horizon than the one of interest to them.

- **ES&G significance.** Another concern has to do with the proven significance of environmental or other ES&G issues to a particular investor's evaluation model(s). In addition to those who are skeptical about the importance of ES&G impacts on asset valuation, others have either performed quantitative analysis or reviewed available studies. They have concluded that although improved ES&G performance has a statistically significant impact on one or more financial variables, or on the value of a company's securities itself, the effect is so small that it is overwhelmed by other, non-ES&G factors. In such cases, as a practical matter, it is far more tractable to collect and evaluate data on a smaller number of the most important variables concurrently for perhaps hundreds of companies than to include every variable having a marginal impact on firm value or one of its components. The problem becomes even more acute when you consider the numerous gaps in important ES&G data across large company populations, as illustrated and explored in greater depth in Chapter 8.

- **Incentives.** The ways in which money management and investment firms have been established and operated also play a role in inhibiting the spread of ES&G investing. One important factor is, as is often the case, incentives. Most firms have firmly established ways of conducting valuation analysis that have been successful over time. Those who would suggest a new or better way have a high burden of proof to surmount. If they are relatively early in their careers (they have not grown up professionally in the culture/work practices of their employer), they may be accepting significant risk by challenging the existing order, even if at the margins. Quite simply, questioning the wisdom of the existing hierarchy could often be considered a career-limiting move. In recognition of this pervasive problem, two initiatives have taken shape in recent years to provide support and, to some extent, financial incentives for firms to integrate ES&G factors into their business models and investing activities. These are the Enhanced Analytics Initiative (EAI) and the Principles for Responsible Investment (PRI). These are discussed further in a moment.

- **Capability.** The other major factor within investment firms that limits the adoption of ES&G principles and investment activity is a pronounced capability gap. The plain truth is that both established and entry-level investment analysts are woefully underprepared to truly understand ES&G issues, to formulate and develop answers to the appropriate questions, and to process whatever ES&G information they encounter so as to inform investment decision making in a sophisticated manner. The importance of this fact was highlighted several years ago in a report called "Generation Lost," issued by the World Business Council for Sustainable Development (WBCSD) and UNEP-FI (WBCSD and UNEP-FI, 2005). As the old saying goes, "Enough said." In terms of assessing important root causes of this problem, and without taking on the contentious issue of the adequacy of our public school system and educational establishment, I do believe it appropriate to point out that the general level of literacy about environmental issues and, more fundamentally, science is very low within our adult population. This is true even of recent college graduates, as discussed in Chapter 2. If we are to move decisively toward a more sustainable future, we will need to correct this deficiency. In the current context, those interested in corporate sustainability and in aligning ES&G considerations with those of the capital markets should be aware that the challenge extends beyond awareness-raising into what should more properly be considered education.

From a completely different perspective—that of the corporation seeking due credit for its ES&G advancements—additional barriers exist. A conversation about ES&G issues should be occurring between investors and analysts on the one hand and corporate senior management on the other. Unfortunately, although within most public companies these parties interact regularly, the conversation almost never includes discussion of ES&G factors. In some of my previous work (Soyka, 2009), I have documented the fact that there is almost no inclusion of environmental information in investor relations presentations or external dialog. I have no reason to believe that the situation is materially different for other ES&G issues. On the other side, corporate representatives typically state that mainstream investors *never* ask about environmental or other sustainability issues. So neither side appears to be broaching the subject of ES&G issues and their relationship to corporate success and investment quality. This is so despite the fact that both sides have an abiding interest in any issue that affects the firm's future. Unfortunately, the more things change, as I have described in this chapter, the more they stay the same. Some major findings of a study that I coauthored and published well over ten years ago are summarized in the following sidebar.

I am seeing greater investor interest in ES&G issues and data. But the fact remains that those best able to articulate the value-creation potential of (and capture from) improved ES&G practices and performance are the individuals running those organizations. Therefore, and as suggested in the earlier research, for the state of play to reach the next level, corporate senior executives will need to become much more engaged on ES&G issues. They also will need to be much more proactive in explaining to capital market participants why the firm is making investments in this area—specifically, what it expects to gain, and how the firm's enterprise value will be enhanced as a result. The good news here, if there is any, is that increasingly, corporate senior executives are beginning to become more engaged in ES&G issues and take the necessary steps to reorient their companies to at least consider the opportunities and risks posed by sustainability issues. This phenomenon is explored in greater depth in the next chapter.

Corporate and Investor Dialog Concerning Environmental Issues

"The majority of respondents indicated that they *would be willing to pay more* for equity or debt issued by a firm in response to a convincing public announcement that the firm expected to *create positive incremental cash flows through improved environmental performance.*"

"Interestingly, the *same overall response pattern* may be discerned among the managers who employ environmental screening or evaluation and those who do not."

"Several respondents indicated that they would view the firm much more favorably if presented with a compelling case that EH&S programs would create competitive advantage."

"...very few of these investors routinely ask about EH&S programs or their cash flow contribution. On the other hand ... these same investors assert that *if corporate executives believe that their EH&S management programs create value, it is the responsibility of these executives to communicate this information to the investor community, even if it is not requested.* Once again, these general rules hold both for fund managers that use and do not use environmental criteria for stock or bond selection."

(Soyka and Feldman, 1998)

And although I have great respect for the work done by the many thousands of EHS professionals deployed across corporate America, I believe that many of them need to raise the level of their game as well. In the work that I have done in recent years, I have encountered several common justifications for EHS (or ES&G) excellence.

It is simply "the right thing to do," it is "an extension of who we are as a company," or it is simply the best response to an array of potential liabilities. In my experience, EHS people, perhaps because most are engineers or scientists, tend to be skeptical of the idea that the financial benefits of ES&G can be quantified or even estimated at a general level. And for understandable reasons, they generally hold the belief that investors are disinterested in the ES&G value story. To a significant degree, we all are products of our own experience, and I understand why EHS professionals tend to not be way out in front in communicating the ES&G value proposition. I suggest, however, that they have a potentially critical role to play. They could greatly improve their effectiveness (and their influence) by devoting some additional attention to the financial aspects of the work they do and casting the associated investments and benefits in a broader organizational context. This can be done in a variety of ways. Ideally it should result in the creation of facts and messages that are pertinent to the topics discussed among company senior management and external financial community stakeholders. Mike Pisarcik of Sara Lee Corporation offers an example of the type of thinking that is needed among far more people in the EHS profession:

> One idea for doing this is that the quarterly meetings that are structured around earnings announcements could also be a good opportunity to inject the sustainability message in a way that connects it to business success. For example, the CEO or other senior executive could mention that our energy savings initiative saved $X million, or we continued our string of so many days without a lost-time injury. (Pisarcik, 2011)

As discussed earlier, some very important structural impediments to ES&G investing have only recently begun to undergo significant change. As broader acceptance of the findings of the Freshfields reports concerning fiduciary duty take hold within major investment firms and their clients, I have observed some changes that suggest that long-standing barriers are beginning to come down.

One important constituency is pension funds. As shown in Table 6-3, pension funds own about 17.5 percent of the total equity (stocks) in the U.S. Insurance companies, which invest and manage funds to produce the capital needed to pay future claims, own an additional

8 percent. These institutional investors, by their nature, operate in a conservative manner because they are accountable to their beneficiaries and must ensure that they receive the income streams or other benefits to which they are entitled. At the same time, these institutions generally invest at least some portion of the assets with which they have been entrusted in equity securities so that they can generate sufficient returns over time to pay their obligations. Generating such high returns is extremely difficult to do solely with fixed income investments. Many of these pension funds are quite large, with some exceeding $200 billion in assets. Out of necessity, such investors have their funds deployed in a wide array of investments, to such an extent that they are commonly referred to as "universal owners" because they literally hold at least a small position in *every* stock in the market. Accordingly, they tend to disfavor divestment, even in firms exhibiting behaviors that they find troubling. Instead, they often focus on engagement, with the goal of bringing about corporate behavioral and/or structural change. That is, rather than "voting with their feet," they often try to get firms to change from inside the system. Because some institutional investors hold major positions in the stock of some companies (as much as several percent of voting shares), the senior management of such companies tends to receive and be attentive to their concerns.

That said, in the past many institutional investors were content to defer judgment of whether or how best to deal with particular ES&G issues to company senior management. The general assumption has been that senior management had the specialized knowledge and expertise needed. And, in any case, performing triage and focusing attention on the most critical (and only the most critical) issues was part of senior management's job description. In similar fashion, many major institutional investors who have deployed assets into mutual funds have entrusted all major decisions to the fund managers they have chosen. Fund managers, in turn, have historically displayed a more or less completely passive attitude concerning the management of ES&G issues in the companies held by their funds. Indeed, in reviewing the proxy policies of several major mutual fund companies in the middle of the last decade (circa 2005), I was struck by how disengaged these large, sophisticated financial market players were in the conduct of important business within the firms they owned. As illustrated in Table 6-9, however, the situation has evolved considerably during the past several years.

This table is excerpted from a larger compilation. It provides a sample of some of the larger and more prominent financial services firms in the U.S., several of which now claim to be active proponents of ES&G investing. For illustrative purposes, I have selected several "household names" that appear to have taken a more activist stance, several who appear to have not, and several who occupy intermediate positions on this spectrum. Several intriguing observations can be made about the data summarized in this table. First, the fact that all but one of the firms profiled has made its proxy guidelines publicly (and often easily) available is a major improvement in the transparency of this industry and its workings. Second, all but one has guidelines that specifically mention corporate social responsibility (CSR) (as discussed in Chapter 2, the common corporate shorthand for sustainability). Several have additional proxy provisions addressing either environment or climate change or both. Finally, some of these companies have frequently thrown their support behind shareholder proposals that a particular company address climate change in some fashion.[27] Quite simply, this type of behavior on the part of major banks, investment houses, and mutual fund companies would have been inconceivable just a few years ago. I believe this is further evidence that the landscape regarding the treatment of ES&G issues is evolving in some fundamental ways.

Table 6-9 Mutual Fund Proxy Guidelines for 2010

Fund Family	Facts on Guidelines Publicly Available?	Guidelines Mention Topic as a Separate Consideration?			2009 Support for Climate-Related Resolutions
		CSR	Environment	Climate	
Wells Fargo	Yes	No	No	No	82%
TIAA-CREF	Yes	Yes	Yes	Yes	78%
Charles Schwab	Yes	Yes	Yes	Yes	77%
Goldman Sachs	Yes	Yes	No	No	53%
Blackrock	Yes	Yes	No	No	30%
T. Rowe Price	Yes	Yes	No	No	27%
AIM Invesco	Yes	Yes	No	No	18%

Fund Family	Facts on Guidelines Publicly Available?	Guidelines Mention Topic as a Separate Consideration?			2009 Support for Climate-Related Resolutions
		CSR	Environment	Climate	
American Century	Yes	Yes	No	No	13%
DWS (Deutsche Bank)	Yes	Yes	Yes	Yes	0%
Fidelity	Yes	Yes	No	No	0%
State Street	No	Yes	Yes	No	0%
Vanguard	Yes	Yes	No	No	0%

Source: Adapted from Berridge and Cook, 2010. Appendix 4.

International Situation and Trends

ES&G investing and analytics are firmly established in a number of international markets around the world, including Western Europe, Japan, and Australia/Asia. In many respects, Europe would have to be considered the world leader in ES&G investing practice by virtue of its more supportive public policy environment; extensive involvement by large, mainstream financial institutions; and its active and sophisticated research community. I provide here a few salient facts and observations.[28]

At a general level, belief in the importance of ES&G factors and issues to investment analysis and decision making among investors and asset owners appears to be substantially more widespread in Europe than in the U.S. This pattern also applies to interest in having ES&G issues integrated into mainstream investment strategies. Evidence for this observation can be seen by the active involvement of major mainstream financial institutions in Europe as well as substantial and early support for the Principles for Responsible Investment (discussed in detail a little later). Europe has, by a substantial margin, both a larger percentage of enrolled participants and participation of a larger number of major mainstream banks and other financial institutions than does the U.S.

In addition, notwithstanding the significant upswing in proxy activity in the U.S. in recent years focused on ES&G issues, it appears that trustees and managers of many European pension funds generally have a far more activist orientation on such issues than do their U.S. counterparts. Pension fund signatories to the PRI in Europe outnumber those in the U.S. by a substantial margin. Note that all U.S. pension fund PRI signatories manage funds on behalf of state government employees, teachers, clergy members, or foundations. In contrast, European pension fund signatories represent a more diverse set of organizations and constituents, including those representing employees of national governments (France, Norway) as well as several European multinational corporations (BP, BT, Storebrand). Some of these institutional investors rival the largest U.S. pension funds (such as CalPERS) in terms of total asset size, at more than $200 billion.

In terms of size and global prominence, European corporate financial institutions rival or exceed their U.S. counterparts. Of the 17 largest financial-services companies in the top 50 of the 2010 Fortune Global 500, only six are based in the U.S., and ten of the remaining 11 are based in one of seven European countries. Only one U.S. firm (Bank of America) is in the top ten (*Fortune*, 2010). This disparity also can be observed in the socially responsible investing (SRI) segment of the investment market. As of 2008, of the 30 largest self-reported SRI firms, 22 were based in Europe, and six were based in the U.S. As a group, the 30 firms managed more than $2.1 trillion, or about 16 percent of their total assets under management (AUM), according to one or more SRI criteria (Responsible Investor, 2008).

Within the European community, there is wide variation in the degree to which particular countries, and their capital markets, have embraced ES&G investing. From my vantage point, it seems clear that the U.K. and its major investment firms occupy a leadership position. That said, there is a noteworthy level of activity in more than a handful of other European countries (including France, the Netherlands, Belgium, Switzerland, and the Nordic countries) and on the part of individual financial institutions within them. Perhaps most significantly, in contrast to the U.S., where the ES&G/SRI dialog and most investing activity occur within and are driven by the SRI community, many major and venerable mainstream financial institutions in Europe are very active in the ES&G investing market space. Although several major U.S. investment houses also are moving in this direction (such as Goldman Sachs), their European counterparts seem to be significantly further down this path, at least in the aggregate.

At the level of the firm, many different approaches are being taken to consider ES&G factors in investment analysis and decision making. This reflects different investment philosophies and objectives, theoretical or empirically based beliefs about the appropriate factors to consider, legal requirements, cultural norms, and other considerations. Even with this diversity, several common themes emerge. One is the growing and widespread use of the integrated approach to consideration of ES&G factors in concert with operational and financial characteristics that I strongly advocate. Just as in U.S. capital markets, very few investors in Europe focus solely on environmental criteria.

Funds invested according to ES&G criteria in Europe are quite significant, both in absolute terms and as a percentage of the total, particularly in equity markets. Such investments exceed 2.6 trillion euros (about $3.4 trillion) and appear to approach, in the aggregate, 18 percent of total funds invested with the European asset management industry. Thus, the European ES&G total AUM exceeds that of the SRI AUM in the U.S., despite the fact that the total size of the latter is substantially greater than that of the former. In parallel, ES&G investing in Europe includes a significant number of major mainstream financial institutions. Using adherence to the PRI as a simple indicator, the distinctions between Europe and the U.S. are striking. U.S. money-manager signatories are, with a few exceptions, SRI firms and, generally, small-niche players.[29] Those based in Europe include both "traditional" SRI investors and several large, multinational, mainstream banks, such as, ABN AMRO and Robeco (Netherlands), BNP Paribas and Crédit Agricole (France), and HSBC (U.K.). These institutions are joined by a number of major European pension funds, including Fonds de Réserve pour les Retraites (FRR) in France, Dutch pension fund ABP, and Norway's Government Pension Fund, among many others, in adopting mandates that require consideration of ES&G criteria in selecting and maintaining securities within fund portfolios. In some cases, these mandates were imposed by national legislation.

A number of large European banks now offer portfolios and/or individual investments selected, at least in part, on the basis of ES&G information. These include the U.K. banks Insight Investment, Newton Investment Management, and Schroders; the Swiss banks Bank Sarasin, Pictet Asset Management, and money manager SAM Group; and, in the Netherlands, SNS Asset Management. In addition, a larger number of European financial institutions reportedly have significant ES&G/SRI assets under management but have not disclosed much in the way of supporting information. These include Dexia Asset Management (Belgium); Robeco (the Netherlands); Baillie Gifford & Co., F&C Management, Hermes Fund Managers, and KBC Asset Management (U.K.); BNP Paribas Asset Management (France); and Carlson Investment Management and Nordea Investment Management (Sweden), among many others.

Despite its clear leadership position, some barriers and limitations have prevented ES&G investing in Europe from advancing even further and faster. These include country-level legal/cultural issues and the absence of consensus (or even widespread agreement) on how best to address ES&G considerations in this rapidly changing arena. I anticipate that both will diminish in the next several years, as a function of national-level implementation of recent EU directives pertaining to ES&G disclosure and accumulated investor experience. More important is the same major factor that limits more and better integration of ES&G considerations into investment analysis and decision-making in the U.S.—the lack of sufficient meaningful, complete, comparable, and timely data on ES&G management quality and performance. The fundamental sources of information used by all providers are the same—companies themselves and government databases.[30] In the absence of much more extensive, regular, and reasonably uniform ES&G reporting of the type I advocate in this book, it is difficult to see how this limitation will be overcome.

Analysts, Rating Agencies, Data Providers, and Other Intermediaries

The focus of this book is on the beliefs and behaviors of decision makers in both corporations and the financial community as they affect and are affected by ES&G issues and performance. However, it is important to recognize that a number of other types of entities influence investment transactions and the factors that go into them. Generally, these are third-party providers of information, advice, ratings, rankings, and other investment-related products and services. In some cases, however, these entities and people may reside within money management firms themselves and provide services and expertise to internal audiences and, in some instances, to external clients as well. This section briefly profiles some of these entities and illustrates the degree to which they encourage or inhibit the active consideration of ES&G information by investors.

Equity Analysts

Many of us are familiar with the "talking heads" that inhabit cable TV news and financial shows expressing opinions and predictions about the direction of investment markets and, often, of particular stocks or other securities. They and many other less-well-known analysts are in the business of understanding companies' workings and prospects and, generally, industries, and rendering judgments about which among them will perform well in the future. As discussed previously, future outperformance as an investment will be heavily influenced by the firms' ability to grow revenue and profits and effectively manage risk and liabilities.

There is a distinction in the financial services industry between two camps, both of which may coexist in some organizations. One is the "sell" side, which involves, essentially, promoting the shares of particular companies, often those that are underwritten or otherwise supported by the firm. Sell-side analysts are a prominent feature of most investment banks. The other side is, not surprisingly, the "buy" side, which involves identifying and screening appropriate candidates for an investment portfolio. Buy-side analysts are frequently employed by mutual fund companies and other large investment firms with substantial ongoing needs to deploy new investment capital in additional shares of stock and other securities.

Sell-side analysts as a group have wielded considerable influence on investor sentiment around particular stocks, at least in the short term. As a group, they also have been decidedly skeptical of the idea that ES&G management and performance improvements can increase shareholder value. However, as discussed in the next chapter, at least some recent evidence suggests that this is beginning to change (Ioannou and Serafeim, 2010). Buy-side analysts tend to work under the direction and focus on the interests of one or more portfolio managers, who actually make the investment decisions. Regardless of which side of the transaction an analyst is working on, the degree to which he or she is motivated to evaluate and is fully capable of considering ES&G factors is a major impediment to more extensive and rapid integration of sustainability into investment analysis.

At the same time, however, the inability or unwillingness of mainstream analysts to address these factors has opened the door for others to fill the needs expressed by SRI and ES&G investors. I explore the ES&G research industry in some depth in Chapter 8.

Bond Rating Agencies

Firms that issue fixed income securities (bonds) must, as a practical matter, obtain a "bond rating" from one of several organizations that issue these ratings. In the U.S., the "big three" are Standard and Poor's, Moody's, and Fitch, although some smaller players have cropped up in recent years in an attempt to disrupt the existing oligopoly.[31] Most people are generally familiar with the standard conventions used (A+, BBB, for example) and understand that these letter-denominated labels tell us something about the quality of the bonds being offered. That quality is a function of the riskiness of the issuer. This is the probability that the issuer will make all the interest payments promised by the bond and also repay all the invested capital when the bond reaches its maturity date. Issuers that have more assets, fewer liabilities (including other bond repayment obligations), greater growth prospects, and the like offer lower repayment risk and therefore have higher bond ratings. And because their risk is lower, so is the interest rate that they have to pay to borrow money, on both loans and any debt securities (bonds) they issue.

As it happens, the factors that bond rating agencies consider include many of the same factors that equity analysts and investors evaluate. Table 6-10 lists some of the more important general considerations. These include factors that may apply at the industry level, such as, economic, market, and industry risk, as well as firm-specific variables such as, earnings, management quality, and funding and liquidity.

Table 6-10 Typical Factors Considered by Bond Rating Agencies

Business Risk	Financial Risk
Economic risk	Credit risk
Industry risk	Market risk
Market position	Funding and liquidity
Business diversification	Capitalization
Geographic dispersion	Earnings
Management	Risk management
	Financial flexibility

Source: Daicoff and Wiemken, 2005

Because bond rating agencies are charged with evaluating the ability of the bond issuer to make payments of a cash stream over an extended period (typically years), they have a fundamentally longer-term perspective than at least some components of the equity markets. Consequently, these agencies generally have at least some awareness of major ES&G issues, at least to the extent that they can be quantified. For example, on the basis of exposure to site contamination cleanup responsibilities and major ongoing waste management costs, certain industries (mining, oil and gas production) are fundamentally viewed as higher-risk than others by the bond rating firms, all else being equal. So their ratings are correspondingly lower.

It is unclear at this point how actively the major ratings agencies are tracking or actively considering a broader array of sustainability endpoints. However, it would seem that they would be naturally amenable to the financial value-creation message espoused here and might welcome the opportunity to add sophistication and new insights to their rating process. In the short term, however, the focus of these firms is likely to be on restoring their credibility following the abject failure of their evaluation processes to identify the inherent risks posed by securities underlain by low-quality residential mortgages. This failure is widely recognized as a major root cause of the 2008 global financial crisis and its aftermath.

Data and Information Providers

As discussed previously, performing investment analysis of the type and to the extent needed to create and manage diversified investment portfolios requires information, and lots of it. Investors and analysts routinely tap a number of different information sources to obtain operating and financial data, industry and company news, data about and insights into market and technological trends, and many other types of information. In parallel with the development of our capital markets, a number of information providers have stepped in to cater to the specific needs of those in the financial community. Many offer various combinations of data, news, and analysis. Some of the established players include Standard & Poor's and Dow Jones, as well as a number of others. Specialized publications focused on the investor community include *Barrons* and *Investors Business Daily*. News services such as, Reuters and Bloomberg provide continuous news feeds and articles from around the world.

However, with a few exceptions discussed next, most of the existing flow of information to investors and analysts has been distinctly lacking content addressing ES&G issues in any complete or systematic way. This gap has been filled by what is now a well-developed subsector that focuses on these issues and specifically caters to the needs and interests of the ES&G investor. This collection of entities is worthy of elaboration and is profiled in depth in Chapter 8.

Trends and Potential Game-Changers

Providing a complete and up-to-date description of the ES&G investing space is a daunting task, not least because this topic is changing so rapidly. As I write this book in the middle of 2011, many discernible trends will likely influence the direction and rate of uptake of ES&G investing practices for many years to come. I identify and discuss some of the more noteworthy issues, events, and trends here. Given the dynamic nature of this field, however, it's possible that by the time this book reaches you, some of the fundamental facts might have changed, and/or additional factors or circumstances might have arisen that are far more consequential.

Bloomberg

One of the great business success stories of the late 20th century has been the formation and rise of a company founded by Michael Bloomberg, the current mayor of New York City, the world's foremost financial capital. The primary offering of Bloomberg's eponymous company, Bloomberg L.P., is a "terminal"[32] that provides business and financial data, news, and analysis. Other providers of such information and products exist. But a few characteristics distinguish Bloomberg from its competitors. One is market penetration and scale. According to this firm's web site, more than 300,000 financial professionals in more than 100 countries use the Bloomberg product, meaning that virtually any investor or analyst in the U.S. has Bloomberg data instantaneously available to him or her. The importance of this degree of market ubiquity is magnified (and, arguably, enabled) by the firm's business model. Subscribers have full access to *all* the data generated and reported on the terminal. For one flat fee, any user can see hundreds of available data feeds, data sets, streaming news, forecasts, and other information on any company worldwide.

Recently, Bloomberg expanded the scope of its terminal to include, for the first time, a set of consistent ES&G criteria. These criteria are not only based on the GRI reporting guidelines but also include additional indicators requested by the firm's clients, yielding an information base of about 110 variables. The terminal also includes some simple screens and indexes that allow sorting and ranking by industry and firm, according to (at present) the level of completeness with which a particular company has reported GRI data. One benefit of this approach is that all the information sources are fully transparent and can be viewed by the user (for example, the full environmental/sustainability policy text can be viewed, in addition to variables indicating its conformance to certain criteria).

If you've watched the steady and sometimes slow growth of ES&G investing, this development may mark an important watershed, for the following reason. Assuming that a reasonable number of mainstream investors can be convinced to be more attentive to ES&G factors in their investment analysis, the problem remains of which data to use, and ensuring that this information is available to the investor community. As described previously, the information provider portion of the value chain is populated with many different firms, philosophies, and approaches. This creates a regrettable lack of consistency and clarity for corporate executives regarding what factors are most important to manage and report, and why. In short, additional hurdles would presumably stand in the way of the mainstream investor who wanted to broaden his or her approach to consider ES&G factors, even if that person were sufficiently motivated. With the inclusion of ES&G data (even if limited to the GRI data) on the Bloomberg terminal, this hurdle is of greatly diminished importance. Today, any analyst or investor can immediately call up a respectable array of data on emissions, waste, sustainability policy provisions, and a number of other indicators. In recent discussions with Bloomberg company representatives, I was informed that new variables are being added regularly at the request of a "critical mass" of customers, as are new analytical capabilities.

Accordingly, if and when ES&G investing truly becomes mainstream, at least some of the basic data required to implement the approach will be ready and waiting. Those working on sustainability issues in or for companies should take careful note of this development.

Principles for Responsible Investment (PRI)

The Principles for Responsible Investment (PRI) is an initiative of UNEP and a number of global financial institutions that was launched in 2006.[33] The PRI is an attempt to increase participation of financial institutions in the process of embedding corporate responsibility into mainstream investing. PRI is made up of six principles:

- Incorporating ES&G into investment analysis and decision-making processes
- Being active owners and incorporating ES&G issues into ownership policies and practices
- Seeking appropriate disclosure on ES&G issues by the companies in which members invest
- Promoting acceptance and implementation of the principles within the investment industry
- Working together to enhance members' collective effectiveness in implementing the principles
- Reporting on activities and progress toward implementing the principles

Accordingly, active participation in the PRI is a clear indicator of the types of commitments and behaviors that are consistent with those that I advocate within the investor community. Participation in this initiative is growing strongly. According to the PRI web site, as of December 2010, there were 808 signatories with $22 trillion in assets, representing a near-doubling since 2008. According to the PRI (PRI, 2010), as of 2009, $6.8 trillion worldwide was being managed using an integrated ES&G investment approach, or 7 *percent* of the global total. With this magnitude of support from institutional investors and apparent progress on the difficult task of ES&G integration, I suspect that the capital markets may be approaching an inflection point, beyond which active consideration of ES&C factors becomes the rule rather than the exception. The answer will be clear within the next few years.

High Net Worth Individuals (HNWIs)

Another emerging phenomenon concerns one of the niche segments of the investing world, albeit an important one. High net worth individuals (HNWIs) are defined as individuals, family trusts, and the like with more than $1 million in liquid assets to invest. They have long been clients of money management firms, and many have played an active role in the deployment and ongoing management of their invested funds. Interestingly, such people, who include a growing cadre of relatively young investors, are becoming significantly more interested in "green" and other forms of sustainability investing. According to a 2009 study of about 420 organizations conducted by Eurosif, the European analog of the U.S. Social Investment Forum, the 2010 European HNWI sustainable investment market was projected to be approximately 729 billion euros (about $950 billion), representing approximately 11 percent of European HNWIs' overall portfolio assets (Eurosif, 2010).

Funds invested by this market segment were one of the very few to grow during and throughout the 2008–2009 financial market downturn. In fact, it grew by 35 percent during this two-year period. This particular investor group also reportedly brings a sophisticated point of view to its sustainability investments, perceiving ES&G investing as a financial discipline rather than a specific investment style such as SRI. That is, they believe in the financial value creation thesis posited in this book, and they seek investments that offer attractive risk-adjusted investment returns as a function of their ES&G characteristics. Consequently, these investors believe that specific knowledge of ES&G issues is necessary to succeed in this market segment, as distinct from relying on simple indices and scores. As suggested at several points in this book, such knowledge is not widespread either in the general population (including the wealthy) or in the investor/ analyst community. Other interesting recent survey results include the fact that fewer than 10 percent of HNWIs report that they are filling a philanthropic need when investing sustainably. Seventy-eight percent believe that sustainable investments will increase with the generational transfer of wealth that will occur as the previous generation departs and their descendants and other beneficiaries inherit their assets (Eurosif, 2010). The lives and investing activities of such people may be (and remain) unfamiliar to many of us at a personal or professional level. However, it is important to understand that collectively, HNWIs own significant investment capital and are increasingly deploying it into what they perceive as sustainable investments. Relative to their numbers, they exert disproportionate influence on the financial markets.

Investment Consultants

Investment consultants have for many years been retained by many institutional investors to provide expertise and assistance in defining specific investment objectives and appropriate investing strategies, choosing money managers, and related activities. Generally, these individuals and firms have remained firmly within the mainstream financial services industry. However, a small number of investment consultants are either established members of the SRI community or have expanded their areas of interest and activity into the ES&G investing market space. Recently (2009), the Social Investment Forum conducted a survey of the beliefs and behaviors of U.S. investment consultants regarding ES&G investing. SIF received 41 responses to its survey, representing a range from relatively small firms (AUM of less than $100 million) to very large companies (AUM of more than $1 trillion). Responses were telling in several respects. First, most consultants reported that they perform their own ES&G evaluations of companies in-house, despite the fact that only the three largest have full-time ES&G staff with (presumably) the appropriate expertise. Fully two-thirds of these firms provide their clients with advice on ES&G-based exclusions. About one-half advise on positive selection, ES&G integration, and/or best-in-class security selection (SIF, 2009). Whether and to what extent this internally generated analysis and advice are based on the thorough, value-oriented, and rigorous evaluation of ES&G posture and performance suggested in this chapter is unclear. There may perhaps be at least some recognition of a capability gap, in that most survey respondents report a cautious approach when addressing ES&G issues. Reportedly, 71 percent of survey respondents discuss ES&G integration only when clients ask about it. Of course, this could also reflect an absence of the conviction that ES&G investing is an appropriate strategy for most of their clients.

What does seem clear, however, is that respondents to the SIF survey share the unanimous view that client interest in ES&G and responsible investing is not a passing phenomenon. No respondents (of the 41) apparently believe that client interest in this topic will decrease in the near future, and nearly 90 percent believe it will grow over the next three years. These findings suggest that ES&G investing is steadily converting the skeptics, and that an additional tipping point may be near. If investment consultants as a group develop the conviction that ES&G investing is a winning strategy and then develop the expertise necessary to do it well, another significant lever in favor of the concept will be activated.

Stock Exchange Listing Rules and Reporting Requirements

Another important emerging trend involves a portion of the overall investing infrastructure—the venues in which securities are traded. At this point there are neither ES&G listing or periodic disclosure requirements on any U.S. stock or commodity exchange, but such requirements are beginning to be seen in several international markets. For example, the Australian Stock Exchange now requires ES&G disclosure of listed firms on a "comply or explain" basis, and the Johannesburg Stock Exchange requires integrated reporting on the same basis. In addition, Malaysia (Bursa Malaysia) has established mandatory CSR reporting for listed firms (Hayles, 2010; Ciurea, 2010).

In a related development, the national stock exchanges of a number of countries have established "sustainability" indices and/or issued sustainability guidance, as shown in Table 6-11. These data reflect the situation as of mid-to-late 2010. Remember that, as with other aspects of the ES&G investing arena, events are evolving rapidly.

Interestingly, national stock exchanges on every continent (except, of course, Antarctica) have either established one or more sustainability indices or issued corporate sustainability guidance. These types of structural support for the concept of ES&G investing are especially prominent in Europe and Asia.

Table 6-11 Emerging Stock Exchange Practices in Support of Corporate Sustainability

Geography	Sustainability Index	Sustainability Guidance
Americas	Canada	Canada
	Mexico	Mexico
	Brazil	
Africa	Egypt	
	South Africa	South Africa
Europe	Turkey	France
	Germany	Switzerland
	France	Spain
	Nordic countries	Italy
	Spain	
Australasia	Indonesia	
	China (2)	China (2)
	Korea	Malaysia
	India	Singapore
		Australia
		Taiwan
		Thailand

Sources: Morales and van Tichelen, 2010; Hayles, 2010; Brooksbank, 2010

Summary and Implications

As shown in this chapter, despite skepticism that has both theoretical and practical roots, there is steadily increasing recognition of the importance of ES&G issues as a source of financial value and risk. Furthermore, more people are beginning to believe that understanding these factors is important to making appropriate investment decisions.

It is clear that there is growing interest in and capital devoted to ES&G investing, in both the U.S. and other developed capital markets. Moreover, the approaches that are being used to allocate capital to specific investments are becoming increasingly sophisticated, more directly linked to drivers of financial value, and based on facts and data rather than supposition or belief. There is every indication that these trends will continue.

Substantial barriers to more extensive and thoughtful ES&G integration have existed from the outset, and some of these remain significant. With that said, many of the more important barriers are beginning to fall away. This includes the traditional interpretation of fiduciary duty, pervasive attitudes and beliefs within the mainstream investment community, and the passive approach to proxy voting exhibited by many mutual funds and other institutional investors. Other systemic barriers remain, not the least of which are existing incentive systems and the limited capability/capacity to properly implement ES&G investing within many money management firms. I am cautiously optimistic that the PRI will help address the former, but I believe that fundamental changes in educational approach and career development will be required to move the needle on the latter.

I believe that corporate EHS/sustainability professionals have numerous opportunities to provide clarity and add value to this ongoing dialog. Such people can best understand how ES&G issues are related to important business drivers. They have a key role to play in developing, organizing, and analyzing the material facts needed to support the business case for new ES&G investments; measure the direct and indirect impacts of improved ES&G management practices; and participate in the crucial translation of enhancements in ES&G posture and performance into financially relevant terms. External to their own organizations, they can participate in dialog with the ES&G research and investor communities to better align what is measured and reported with what is valued (and truly of value).

These efforts can be supported and amplified by senior management and those playing other significant roles in the corporation—particularly those with responsibility for or influence on interactions with financial community representatives (investor relations, finance), customer interactions (marketing, customer relationship management), product/service design and production (design, engineering, operations), physical plant (facilities, maintenance), and investments in employee capability (human resources).

Similarly, there are abundant opportunities for finance/investing professionals to add value and stimulate more sustainable corporate behavior in the companies that they study and (perhaps) invest in.

These start with educating corporate EHS professionals and senior managers about their investment/value thesis and how ES&G considerations are factored in, what ES&G management practices and levels of performance they seek, and which types of investments in new organizational capability are, from the investor's point of view, most likely to create financial value.

These and other opportunities are explored in the final chapters of this book. The next chapter looks at the empirical evidence for the financial value-creation potential of ES&G management and performance improvements. This discussion is provided in the interests of supporting the ideas and recommendations presented in this book with objective facts. You can judge for yourself whether and to what extent a convincing general business case for corporate ES&G improvements has been made, as well as how solid the case for ES&G investing truly is.

Endnotes

1. An early and thought-provoking critique of these assumptions is provided in the influential book *Natural Capitalism* (Hawken, Lovins, and Lovins, 1999).

2. Unfortunately, this view is not limited to graduates of the "Chicago School" or other adherents of the teachings of Milton Friedman. Consider, for example, that the Obama Administration's EPA Administrator summarily terminated two of the EPA's most visible and successful voluntary environmental improvement programs shortly after assuming her new position.

3. Note that some programs may have performance-based entry requirements and that the newer and more carefully designed among them often require commitments to improvement goals and regular performance reporting.

4. Note that one of the main causes of the recent worldwide recession was the widespread use of credit default swaps and other exotic investment instruments that were *not* traded on exchanges. When the fundamentals underlying these securities eroded, they could not be readily valued, and they became highly illiquid.

5. The recent subprime mortgage debacle illustrates the perils of departing from this long-standing investment principle.

6. Risk levels are quantified through bond ratings. These indicate the creditworthiness of a company's debt securities as a function of many operational and financial variables, as determined (generally) by one or more of the three major bond rating agencies in the U.S.: Standard & Poor's, Moody's, and Fitch.

7. Cash flow is an important indicator and is derived from corporate earnings. Under federal securities laws, publicly traded firms in the U.S. must include a cash flow statement as part of their 10-K and 10-Q filings, along with their income statement and balance sheet. Some investors focus more on cash flow than earnings. Cash flow tends to be less volatile and is unaffected either by activities that do not require cash payments (such as depreciation) or by episodic adjustments such as asset write-downs.

8. Note that this discussion describes the typical pattern of investment. Some investors expressly follow a strictly "bottom-up" approach that focuses exclusively on finding individual company securities that meet its criteria.

9. Short-selling, or "shorting," involves selling a defined number of shares of a company's stock at a stated price that is lower than the current market price. These shares are borrowed from a broker or other entity offering this service, so the seller does not actually own them when the sale occurs. The seller receives the proceeds from the sale and then has a stated period of time in which to conclude the transaction, which involves buying the same number of shares at the then-current market price. If, as the short-seller anticipates, the market price declines, he or she reaps the price difference (minus transaction costs) as his or her profit. If instead the market price goes up and does not decline before the contract closes, the short-seller must still purchase the shares at the available price. In that case the short-seller pays more than he or she received from the short sale, thereby losing money.

10. The authority to issue these regulations, as well as the formation of the SEC itself, was provided in the Securities Exchange Act of 1934 (SEC Act). This statute brought sweeping changes, including vastly greater transparency and accountability, to public company reporting and investment company/advisor behavior. It was a direct response to the abusive, and ultimately destructive, behavior that led to the 1929 stock market crash that precipitated the Great Depression. The SEC Act remains the principal source of federal authority to regulate securities markets and corporate financial reporting.

11. See Regulation S-K, Items 101, 103, and 303, for details.

12. The final rule is published at 74 *FR* 245:68334–68367.

13. The SEC interpretive guidance is published at 75 *FR* 25:6290–6297.

14. The final rule is published at 75 *FR* 179: 56668–56793.

15. In theory (and officially), initiatives such as the GRI are intended to be suitable for use by a wide spectrum of organizations, including small businesses, public sector organizations, and nonprofits. Nonetheless, it is very clear that the major target organizations for the GRI, UNGC, and CDP are corporations—particularly large, multinational corporations.

16. The GRI is well aware of its difficulties in penetrating the U.S. market. In January 2011 it officially launched a new initiative titled "Focal Point USA" (GRI, 2011). To this point, the specific activities of this new effort to induce greater

uptake of the GRI guidelines and more extensive GRI reporting among U.S. companies have not been publicly described.

17. As noted, in the U.S., securities laws (including licensing of brokers) are administered at the state level. With respect to the Modern Prudent Investor Rule, a national model, the Uniform Prudent Investor Act (UPIA), incorporates the modern portfolio theory concept. It has been adopted by more than 45 U.S. states and the District of Columbia.

18. Doyle, R., 1998. Advisory Opinion. U.S. Department of Labor, PWBA Office of Regulations and Interpretations. 28 May.

19. As discussed in the next chapter, some alternative formulations of this relationship have emerged during the past few years. Most retain the beta as an important explanatory variable but also include one or more additional variables to provide incremental explanatory power and reduce error. These variables may include company size, leverage, intangible asset value, and price momentum.

20. As with so many other areas of human endeavor, the issue comes down to balancing fear and greed.

21. In the U.S., financial data are required to be prepared using Generally Accepted Accounting Principles (GAAP). Public companies must be audited by an independent accounting firm.

22. Further information on EVA may be obtained from the Stern Stewart web site: www.sternstewart.com/?content=proprietary&p=eva.

23. Empirical studies have shown that many "sin" stocks have performed well over time. This has caused portfolios lacking these securities to, in many cases, lag in investor returns relative to their market benchmarks, which do contain them. Indeed, a small number of "vice" mutual funds have been launched in recent years to allow investors to buy concentrated exposure to firms in such industries as gaming (casinos), liquor, tobacco, and defense/aerospace.

24. Note that this approach also provides benefits to firms in "dirty" industries and to society in general. It provides incentives for the participants in sectors with ES&G issues to improve their performance to become best-in-class, rather than simply accepting the earlier reality that certain investors would never consider buying their securities.

25. Technically, Goldman Sachs is now a "commercial bank," reflecting a registration change that it was allowed to make in the immediate aftermath of the financial crisis in late 2008. Nonetheless, with minor adjustments, Goldman has continued its principal business activities with little interference from new regulatory requirements.

26. I could, however, envision some exceptions to this general rule, such as when a company experiences some adverse publicity in connection with its ES&G behavior or in response to an incident. In such cases, the short-term trader may seek to short-sell the company's shares or take other measures to capitalize on these events.

27. With that said, I note with interest that two firms involved in some way in the ES&G market space (DWS/Deutsche Bank and State Street) supported no such resolutions in 2009. DWS operates a research unit that explicitly focuses on the investor-relevant aspects of climate change, and State Street has long operated a subsidiary that is an active member of the SRI community.

28. For further information, you could review a recent report that I coauthored along with two colleagues—one an internationally known sustainability expert, and the other a member of the U.S. ES&G research community. The report was prepared for the U.S. EPA and is available at www.epa.gov/osem/financial/reports.html.

29. I note with interest that this distinction is diminishing. When I initially performed this comparison in 2009, only one large, mainstream U.S. financial institution had signed on to the PRI. As of early 2011, it has been joined by several others, including Blackrock, CBRE Investors, JP Morgan Asset Management, Kohlberg Kravis & Roberts (KKR), and T. Rowe Price.

30. In many cases, European ES&G researchers and investors use data published by the U.S. EPA (such as Toxics Release Inventory [TRI] emissions) as a major source of environmental performance information for U.S. companies.

31. Smaller players include Egan Jones Rating Agency, and A.M. Best, which specializes in evaluating the creditworthiness of insurance companies and their fixed income securities.

32. Originally and for many years, subscribers actually had a hardware device installed in their workplaces by Bloomberg, which was then connected to a dedicated data line (and later the Internet). Today, the "terminal" is a software application installed on the subscriber's computer of choice.

33. Once established, this effort effectively superseded and ultimately absorbed the Enhanced Analytics Initiative (EAI), formed in October 2004 by a group of institutional investors, including asset managers and pension funds. The focus of the EAI was to promote integration of ES&G factors into sell-side research by requiring commitments to sequester and award incentive compensation specifically for analysts who improved the quality and utility of their research and recommendations by factoring in ES&G considerations. After attracting significant early support (28 members from the U.S. and Europe with AUM of $2.4 trillion), the initiative appeared to lose momentum in the face of the broader PRI.

7

The Financial Impact of Effective (or Ineffective) ES&G/Sustainability Management

This chapter reviews and discusses the financial impact of effective ES&G practices, from a theoretical standpoint and on the basis of what has been demonstrated through empirical, published research. This discussion builds on the concepts and terms introduced in the preceding chapter and demonstrates how financial market actors have evaluated and judged the outcomes of corporate ES&G activities. This chapter illustrates how economic and market theory and the bilateral relationships between capital markets and corporate ES&G practices have been expressed over the past 20 years or so. I explore what is believed and what is known about how making investments in ES&G improvements directly affects the firm's financial performance. I also look at how a lack of attentiveness to these issues can increase the firm's risk profile and costs and otherwise erode its competitive position and long-term sustainability. Finally, I review information on the beliefs and attitudes of market participants regarding the financial impacts of ES&G posture and performance, including increased profitability and returns to the investor.

In keeping with the approach used throughout this book (and in my consulting practice), the relationships I postulate are based on facts and empirical analysis. Numerous theories and beliefs in the expanding marketplace of ideas address the "value" created by disciplined investments in ES&G improvements. In sorting through these often competing ideas, I believe that the most rational way forward is to focus on what has been proven and/or can reasonably be inferred from evidence, rather than ascribing financial or other benefits to activities based solely on theory (or wishful thinking). Similarly, although examples and anecdotal experience can be interesting and highly relevant, it is fundamentally difficult to build a compelling case in support of a new approach intended to challenge long-standing orthodoxy, such as that practiced in many corners of the capital markets, with such evidence. Accordingly, the focus in this chapter is limited to a discussion of what has been demonstrated in the published literature—specifically, well-designed studies of multiple firms, generally examined over an extended period of time.

Insights from the Literature

During the past several years, I have had the opportunity to examine the published literature on the relationships between environment and finance on several occasions. The information presented in this section includes a synthesis of those research efforts,[1] supplemented by a review of some of the more interesting and relevant literature published recently. You are advised that this review is illustrative and meaningful, but not comprehensive. In most cases the literature reviewed here pertains specifically to one or more environmental endpoints. But given the overlaps between environmental and health and safety issues and prevailing management practices, I believe that the findings and conclusions of the studies examined could reasonably be extended to health and safety issues as well. In addition, to evaluate certain aspects of market behavior, I have included works that address a broader spectrum of ES&G/SRI issues.

My purpose here is not to provide a full literature review, as one might in a scholarly research article. Instead, I attempt to support my contention that despite long-standing and widely accepted economic theory to the contrary, it can be shown that well-conceived and -executed investments in improved ES&G management capability and related performance improvements more than pay for themselves. In fact, they create new financial value and corporate wealth. I assert that the empirical evidence is sufficiently strong to consider the matter settled, and I provide the major threads of the argument and supporting evidence in the interests of proving my case.

If you don't need to be convinced, you may choose to skip the detailed examination of the literature that makes up the bulk of this chapter and move to the final section, which briefly summarizes and discusses the implications. If you want to review the evidence, continue reading.

The literature I have selected for discussion was culled from a much larger collection of works. In evaluating each source's utility, I considered the source/sponsor of the work. I gave greater weight to studies that were produced independently of the organizations under study and their industries and that were otherwise free of any obvious potential bias or vested interest. I also considered carefully the endpoint(s) addressed by each study, favoring those examining variables that are of interest to external stakeholders (such as investors and other capital market participants). Another distinguishing characteristic was breadth; I was most impressed by studies that had a broad perspective—ideally, one that was market- or industry-wide as opposed to a collection of anecdotal examples. I also was attuned to the presence of new insights, data, and/or methods in the sources reviewed. In evaluating the importance of the material collected, I ascribed greater significance to works that offered a clear articulation of one or more research hypotheses; valid, appropriate, and sensible methods; rigorous data development and hypothesis testing; and fully supported conclusions. For clarity and ease of exposition, I present the major literature findings in the form of the most important studies organized by categories defined by the financial questions and/or endpoints addressed.

A number of interesting and relevant findings emerge from the literature review. As an initial point, it is worth noting that virtually no published literature was found addressing environmental management, risk, or performance in the context of fixed-income investing in the U.S.[2] One exception to this general pattern is described later. When and where studies have been performed, their focus has almost invariably been on internal corporate financial results or investor behavior in the equity markets.

The Accounting Perspective

Perhaps the most direct and obvious frame of reference for seeking a linkage between environmental and financial performance is to examine firm financial performance or position using familiar accounting-based measures. In doing so, we can see how these measures change as a function of environmental risks, liabilities, management practices, and/or performance. The studies described next are particularly noteworthy in that they address profitability (in either absolute terms or relative to assets or capital deployed) as a function of pollutant emissions or their reduction. The empirical results presented in each study document a positive correlation between emissions reductions and profitability.

- In their study of 127 manufacturing, mining, and other "production" firms that were members of the Standard & Poor's (S&P) 500, Hart and Ahuja (1996) found that implementing pollution prevention strategies and, consequently, reducing pollutant emissions had a positive (and statistically significant) effect on the firms' return on assets, return on sales, and return on equity. This effect was discernible within two years of implementing the firms' environmental performance improvements. Interestingly, the effects were greatest for firms with higher initial pollutant emissions.

- Similarly, Russo and Fouts (1997) reported that among a collection of 243 firms studied over a two-year period, return on assets increased as a function of improved environmental performance. These firms were placed into quintiles based on their environmental performance characteristics (emissions, compliance record). Again, firms that made greater performance gains (moving up one quintile or more during the study period) exhibited a statistically greater gain in return on assets.

- Stanwick and Stanwick (1998) examined the issue from a somewhat different perspective. They studied approximately 100 firms listed on the *Fortune* Corporate Reputation Index that also had reported Toxics Release Inventory (TRI) data in one or more of the most recent five years. In other words, the companies examined had a positive reputation for social responsibility but also were subject to regulatory controls due to significant toxic chemical use. The study authors found a positive correlation between low emissions and high profitability (net margin) among these firms.

These results support and extend the commonly held view that well-chosen pollution prevention initiatives more than pay for themselves. The results demonstrate that the same type of impact occurs at the level of the *firm*, rather than simply at the project level. In that regard, they help overcome one of the self-imposed limitations of many published P2 studies. They describe results in a form and at an organizational level that is of direct interest to investors and other financial market actors.

Two other studies focus on the balance sheet by examining prospective environmental liabilities that, argue the authors, should be recorded on the balance sheets of affected companies under existing accounting conventions and rules:

- In their study of the financial impacts of Superfund (hazardous waste site cleanup) liability, Barth and McNichols (1994) found that the average unrecognized liability (information not reported in company financial statements) was equal to 28.6 percent of the affected firms' market value.
- Similarly, Repetto and Austin (1999), in a detailed study of one industry (13 large pulp and paper companies), reported that despite the fact that many of the firms studied were projected to experience significant asset impairments and/or capital costs due to new requirements included in pending new regulations, none of these firms chose to report these prospective liabilities or costs.

These studies demonstrated that both actual and prospective environmental liabilities can be significant in magnitude, vary across firms in the same industry, and be quantified with a reasonable degree of precision. In other words, these data would probably be of interest to investors and other members of the financial community if they were made available on a widespread and consistent basis.[3] As noted in Chapter 2, existing SEC regulations would appear to require more consistent and complete disclosure of such data, and the fact that regular reporting occurs so infrequently is a major gap in the existing regulatory framework. I discuss the issue of disclosure in more depth in Chapter 8.

Intangible Asset Value

It is increasingly recognized that traditional balance sheet-based measures no longer give investors a complete and accurate view of a firm's strengths and weaknesses, future prospects, or worth in the marketplace. Instead, intangible assets, as discussed in Chapter 6, are now recognized as the principal competitive weapons and sources of future success and opportunity for most firms. Several particularly interesting studies examine the impact of environmental improvements (or lack thereof) on the value of the firm's intangible assets. These studies document the impact on a widely employed measure of intangible asset value (Tobin's Q) of more complete and far-reaching environmental management standards, pollutant emissions reductions, eco-efficiency, and improved human capital management, respectively:

- Dowell, Hart, and Yeung (2000) examined 89 S&P 500 companies with manufacturing or mining operations in developing countries. They found that firms with stringent, beyond-compliance environmental standards had significantly higher market values (10 percent, or $8.4 billion to $10.6 billion) than firms with U.S. standards only.[4]

- In their study of 321 S&P 500 manufacturing firms, Konar and Cohen (2001) found that the average "intangible asset liability" for inferior environmental performance among these companies was $380 million. This liability was greatest for firms in the chemical, primary metals, and paper industries (those with significant environmental aspects and extensive compliance obligations). In addition, the authors reported that during the study period, firms reducing emissions measurably increased their intangible asset value (hence, their value in the marketplace). On average, a 10 percent reduction in TRI emissions produced a $34 million increase in intangible asset value.

- Guenster, et al. (2006) performed an interesting analysis evaluating the financial effects of corporate eco-efficiency as reflected in both an accounting measure (return on assets) and a measure of intangible asset value (Tobin's Q). They examined all publicly traded firms evaluated by Innovest Strategic Value Advisors[5] from 1997 to 2004, using monthly returns data. Innovest produced eco-efficiency ratings using more than 60 indicators, with scores addressing five major areas: historical liabilities (such as hazardous waste sites), contemporaneous operating risk (from emissions), sustainability and eco-efficiency risk—weakening of a firm's material sources of competitiveness (from products' energy intensity, for example), managerial risk efficiency (capability/capacity), and business prospects resulting from eco-efficiency. Multiple regression analysis results showed the following:

- A positive and slightly asymmetric relationship between eco-efficiency and operating performance. Firms deemed "eco-efficient" had only a slightly better return on assets than the control group. The least eco-efficient firms, however, showed strong operational underperformance.

- A positive and time-varying relationship between eco-efficiency and firm valuation. Stronger environmental performers initially did not trade at a premium relative to weaker firms. Over time, however, the valuation differential widened substantially. The observed trend suggested that the shares of most eco-efficient firms relative to the least eco-efficient firms were initially undervalued but later experienced an upward price correction.

The authors concluded that their findings strongly disprove the notion expressed by SRI/CSR skeptics—that the benefits of adopting a strong environmental policy and practices are unlikely to outweigh the associated costs.

In all these examples, the authors found a strong positive correlation between improved, beyond-compliance, proactive environmental management practices and the firm's value. In some cases, particularly the earlier studies, data limitations did not allow for the calculation of benefit-cost relationships associated with making these environmental management and performance improvements. Nevertheless, the results demonstrated that market-relevant financial benefits may be obtained through appropriate investments in improving a firm's sustainability posture and performance. Results also suggest that such investments, which enhance the firm's intangible assets, are translated over time into increased shareholder value. As suggested elsewhere in this chapter and in Chapter 6, there is reason to believe that this phenomenon may be gathering momentum, as more investor interest is placed on (and capital is deployed on the basis of) ES&G considerations.

ES&G Impacts on the Cost of Capital

Several other noteworthy studies have evaluated stock market behavior in response to environmental and other ES&G characteristics in a somewhat different way. The earlier works focused on the cost of equity capital as reflected in individual firm beta, which is an empirical measure of stock price volatility.[6] One of these studies documented a positive impact on the beta (a lowering) as a function of enhanced environmental management or other ES&G practices and improved performance. The other showed a negative impact (higher beta) associated with being a large company in the same industry as several other firms with substantial Superfund liabilities. The more recent studies generally have employed a different dependent variable for expected rate of return, which has been expressed as a function of the company beta and several other variables.[7] They also differ with earlier approaches and among themselves in terms of the specific regression model specification(s) used. Nonetheless, each of the studies profiled here reflects a common interest on the part of the researchers to understand the incremental impact, if any, of more-advanced environmental management practices, environmental/ES&G risks, or broader ES&G characteristics on a firm's cost of equity capital.

- Feldman, Soyka, and Ameer (1997) examined 330 S&P 500 firms across two seven-year time periods. They carefully controlled for such confounding factors as capital structure, productivity, industry, and other important variables. Their results showed that improved environmental management practices (based on a 30-criterion scale) and performance (TRI emissions/fixed assets) decreased beta by several percent, suggesting a lower firm cost of capital and thus a higher stock price. In addition to being one of the first such studies to explicitly employ a management-based environmental rating methodology, it articulated a theory explaining how investors learn about and act on environmental management advances.

- Garber and Hammitt (1998) evaluated the cost of capital impacts for a set of more than 75 publicly traded chemical industry Superfund "potentially responsible parties" (PRPs) identified over a 12-year period. They included both large (23) and small (54) firms. Analytical results showed that a higher

Superfund liability for an industry subset increased the cost of capital for other large industry firms. The magnitude of this impact for 23 affected firms was an increase in annual capital costs of 0.25 to 0.4 percent over a five-year period.

- More recently, Plumlee, Brown, and Marshall (2008) evaluated the effect of environmental disclosure quality on both the cost of equity capital and the other key component of enterprise value—cash flows. They examined firms in five industries. Two were considered "environmentally sensitive" (oil and gas, chemicals), two were considered "nonenvironmentally sensitive" (food/beverage, pharmaceutical), and one was considered separately because it has characteristics of both (electrical).[8] Firms in the "environmentally sensitive" industries were presumed to have more to gain from voluntary environmental disclosure (VED) than the others. The study sample included 167 firms over a five-year period (2000–2004) to obtain a final sample of 629 firm-years. The authors developed and employed their own index for evaluating environmental disclosure quality. Their Brown Marshall Plumlee Index was based on the Global Reporting Initiative's (GRI) framework (described further in a subsequent chapter). This index included 62 individual indicators, such as absolute or relative quantities of water use, descriptions of the implementation of environmental management systems, and specific identification of the person responsible for the firm's environmental stewardship. Multiple regression analysis results showed that firm value for companies in the electrical and "sensitive" industries was primarily influenced through cost of capital associations with improved disclosures. Firm value for firms within "nonsensitive" industries was primarily influenced through expected cash flow associations with improved disclosures. In either case, firm value was enhanced, through either an equity capital cost reduction (in the former) or an increase in cash flows associated with higher-quality environmental disclosure (in the latter).

- Dhaliwal, et al. (2009) conducted a series of quantitative analyses to assess the relationships between corporate social responsibility (CSR) reporting and performance and the cost of equity capital. They assembled a sample of 196 firms representing more than 20 industries that collectively produced 679 CSR reports from 1993 to 2007. They then evaluated each firm's relative CSR performance using CSR strength ranking scores provided by ES&G research/investing firm KLD.[9] Results showed that firms with higher costs of equity capital were significantly more likely than others to release stand-alone CSR reports. Moreover, although for the overall sample the publication of a CSR report was not significantly associated with a lower future cost of equity capital, these costs did decline for firms with relatively superior social responsibility performance. This reduction in the cost of equity capital ranged from about 0.8 percent to 1.7 percent, depending on model specifications. The authors concluded that investors do not merely appreciate CSR disclosure per se but also evaluate firms' actual CSR performance. Results also showed that reporting firms with relatively superior CSR performance attracted additional dedicated institutional investment and analyst coverage and had lower analyst forecast errors and dispersion.

- Finally, El Ghoul, et al. (2010) also examined the effect of CSR on equity cost of capital. They developed a sample of 12,915 U.S. firm-year observations representing 2,809 unique firms in 48 industries between 1992 and 2007. As in the study just described, they related firm financial data with CSR strength ratings developed by KLD. They conducted an extensive series of multiple regression and sensitivity analyses and developed a number of interesting findings. Overall, they found that firms with a better CSR score exhibited lower cost of equity capital after controlling for other firm-specific variables as well as industry and year fixed effects. The mean (median) cost of equity for firms with a high CSR score was 56 (39) basis points lower than that for firms with a low CSR score. These differences were significant at the 1 percent level.[10] Using their model, you could predict that a 1 standard deviation increase in CSR score would lead a firm's equity premium to decrease, on average, by 10 basis points.[11] Moreover, the authors found that not all aspects of CSR were of equal importance. Quantitative analysis results showed that investments in improving responsible employee relations, environmental policy/performance, and product characteristics substantially contributed to reducing firms' cost of equity. Investments in several other common CSR domains, including community relations, diversity, and human rights, did not. (Although they were desirable from other points of view, they had no significant impact on equity capital costs.) The authors also demonstrated that firms involved in two "sin" business sectors—tobacco and nuclear power—appeared to observe higher equity financing costs while others (alcohol, firearms, and military products) did not. Thus, they were not perceived to affect a firm's risk profile by market participants. The authors concluded that their findings provide evidence that the cost of capital is an important channel through which the market prices CSR and support arguments in the literature that CSR enhances firm value.

The impact of ES&G management issues on the cost of debt capital (bonds and loans) has not been extensively reported on in the published literature. A small number of recent articles are the exceptions to this general rule. The most recent and comprehensive is described next:

- Bauer and Hann (2010) examined the impact on three distinct measures of credit risk to test the relevance of environmental management for bond investors: the cost of debt financing (expressed as the yield spread[12]), bond ratings, and long-term issuer ratings. They used environmental data from KLD's STATS product. "Strength" indicators included measures of pollution prevention, recycling, beneficial products and services, and clean energy. "Concern" indicators included hazardous waste, regulatory problems, substantial emissions, climate change, agricultural chemicals, and other. The authors developed a sample of 2,242 bonds that were issued by 582 firms from 1995 to 2006. Regression modeling analysis of a number of hypotheses and scenarios showed the following:
  - Corporate borrowers engaged in environmentally risky activities were charged a premium on their cost of debt financing, whereas firms with proactive environmental engagement enjoyed a lower cost of debt financing. A 1 standard deviation increase in the environmental strengths measure corresponded with a reduction in the yield spread of 6 basis points. A 1 standard deviation increase in the environmental concerns measure was associated with an increase in the yield spread of 5 basis points, equivalent to a 4.87 percent and 4.11 percent change in yield spread, respectively. The maximum impact of a combined change in the environmental performance measures on the annual cost of debt was estimated at 64 basis points, or 53 percent of the $3.6 million annual median interest expense payable in excess of the Treasury benchmark rate.

○ Firms with better environmental management capabilities or activities were more likely to receive a higher bond rating, and firms with more environmental concerns were associated with lower bond ratings. Review of marginal effects showed that an increase in environmental strengths significantly decreased the probability of receiving a bond rating of BBB or lower and increased the probability of being rated A or higher. By contrast, an increase in environmental concerns significantly decreased the probability of being rated "A" or higher and increased the probability of receiving a rating of BBB or lower.

○ Among the tested performance strengths, the categories Beneficial Products, Clean Energy, and Other Strength were statistically significant. For the performance concerns, the coefficients were significant for all categories. The categories most consistently associated with the different credit risk measures were Regulatory Problems, Substantial Emissions, and Climate Change. These results support the idea that climate change-related issues and regulatory concerns are linked to a higher expected default risk for firms.

○ The better credit standing observed for firms with proactive environmental activities was linked not only to a reduction in environmental risk exposure, but also to an improvement in cash flows.

○ Additional results suggested that the relevance of environmental management to credit risk has increased over time, particularly during the past decade, and that this increase is mainly attributable to the impact of environmental concerns.

○ The authors found no evidence to support the view that the stated relations are consistently stronger for firms in high risk industries.

The authors concluded that their findings extended earlier research by showing that the credit market not only responds to the potential misreporting of existing environmental liabilities, but also prices the environmental management characteristics of borrowing firms in anticipation of associated losses. Their results showed that the regulatory implications of climate change have sensitized lenders to the downside risk of poor environmental practices. Also, an assessment of past and ongoing corporate environmental activities enhances the accuracy of corporate bond pricing by enabling bond investors to evaluate the risk of environmental performance-related losses. The authors also believed that their findings contributed to a better understanding of how corporate environmental activities affect firms' credit standing and give risk managers an improved understanding of where to focus their attention.

What these and many other published studies show is that ES&G investments pay off if they are made wisely. Applying an accounting perspective, (examining financial statement items that might be affected by improved ES&G performance), the published literature supports the idea that firm-scale reductions in costs (increases in profitability) can be realized through adroit capture of opportunities to prevent pollution and reduce the organization's environmental footprint. Similarly, present balance sheet liabilities can be reduced or eliminated, and future liabilities and adverse earnings impacts prevented, through effective design and deployment of formal ES&G management systems and programs and appropriate due diligence of mergers and acquisitions. Some investigators also have found indicators of sophisticated environmental management practice to exhibit a statistically significant positive relationship to the firm's market value, along with leadership, brand strength, innovation, and other intangible assets. Finally, empirical evidence supports the market theory that firms that have more ES&G risk pay more for the investment capital needed to support their operations. Studies have shown that firms offering evidence that they were effectively managing their ES&G issues are less volatile and hence confer lower investment risk than their peers. Accordingly, their costs of equity and debt capital also are lower. Given the increased volatility of and turmoil within global capital markets during the past three years, the ability to show that senior management understands the challenges and opportunities facing the firm, and is in a position to both manage risks and capture opportunities, is likely to become increasingly important. It seems to me that instituting a well-conceived program in pursuit of organizational sustainability offers an excellent opportunity to take advantage of this trend.

Stock Price Impacts of Environmental and ES&G Events

Having shown that well-considered investments in the firm's ES&G capability can make a material difference to its balance sheet, intangible asset value, and financing costs, I shift from the internal to the external perspective. In this section, I discuss the evidence for market reactions to ES&G events and trends. As discussed at length in Chapter 6, most investors do not regularly seek, review, or consider environmental or ES&G information in making investment decisions. But it would be incorrect to assume that environmental and broader sustainability issues do not affect the stock market or individual company valuations. A number of studies have documented pronounced short- to medium-term stock price/market value impacts resulting from environmental or broader ES&G events, whether positive or negative. Both actual and prospective exposure to new environmental legislation have induced substantial share price declines in affected companies, as shown in the first two studies referenced here. Moreover, announcements by the U.S. EPA concerning enforcement priorities and negative news releases have been shown to induce similar effects. On the other hand, positive publicity concerning environmental performance (awards, recognition) conferred positive effects on share prices, some of which were quite substantial.

- Blacconiere and Patten (1994) examined a set of 47 publicly traded companies that obtained more than 10 percent of their revenue from the production and sale of chemicals. They reviewed the company financial disclosures (Form 10-Ks[13]) and placed the companies into one of five categories based on the extent of their environmental disclosure. The authors then evaluated stock price movements over a 200-day period to define a baseline and measured the price movements following the Bhopal tragedy in 1986.[14] Results showed that firms that were heavily dependent on chemical-related business suffered significant declines in share price returns, but those deriving less than 18 percent of their revenues from chemicals experienced no such effect. In addition, companies with the best disclosure practices were unaffected, but companies with the worst disclosure practices suffered significant negative returns.

- Hamilton (1995) examined the short-term impacts of adverse coverage of environmental issues in the media. He examined

450 publicly traded firms that reported TRI emissions and found that 58 with significant negative news coverage on the TRI release date experienced significant stock price declines. He also identified 134 other companies that experienced adverse news coverage later in the same year and found that the average decline was even larger. Interestingly, these declines were smaller if Superfund liability information had previously been disclosed.

- Bosch, et al. (1998) collected news references from the *Wall Street Journal* over a 20-year period. They identified 171 cases involving 77 firms in which an announcement had been made by the EPA concerning companies targeted for enforcement action. They examined stock price movements during a 12-day window and documented abnormal stock returns in comparison with the behavior of the overall market during the same period. Furthermore, they showed that the firms involved experienced a significant negative return following the initial announcement of enforcement action and that challenges to these enforcement actions mounted by the affected companies, even successful ones, had little or no impact. On the other hand, unsuccessful challenges appeared to induce significant negative returns (more than 1 percent loss in total value). Settlements also produced a negative, but smaller, impact.

- In their study, Blacconiere and Northcut (1997) examined 72 chemical companies during an eight-month period around SARA reauthorization.[15] They considered a three-day event window and compared the behavior of potentially affected firms to that of the overall market. They found that firms likely to be negatively affected by the new legislation suffered share price declines. These impacts were greater for firms with costs previously defined in Superfund Records of Decision and in response to actual legislative action.

- Klassen and McLaughlin (1996) began by performing a search of the Nexis database from 1985 to 1991. This search yielded 140 announcements of environmental awards to companies, as well as 22 stories about an environmental crisis caused by or involving a particular company. Firms with environmental awards increased in market value (by 0.63 percent overall), and firms with negative publicity declined in value (–0.82 percent). The authors then filtered out the effects of contemporaneous events by these firms. Revised results showed even more acute impacts (a 0.82 percent gain for positive news and –1.50 percent for stories of crisis), with an average annual gain of $80.5 million or loss in market value of $390.5 million, respectively.

- More recently, Griffin, Lont, and Sun (2010) examined the importance of greenhouse gas (GHG) emissions on shareholder returns. More specifically, they looked at whether stock market investors appear to react to news about corporate GHG emissions and, if so, in what way. They evaluated companies in both U.S. (S&P 500) and Canadian (Toronto Stock Exchange 200 (TSE)) markets. To do so, they used data on GHG emissions and disclosure quality from the Carbon Disclosure Project (CDP) for the S&P 500 for CDP reporting years 2006–2009 and large TSE companies for CDP years 2005–2009. They developed a sample of 1,083 company-year emissions observations, including 824 for the S&P 500. Their analysis indicated that the CDP response rate correlated positively with emissions and disclosure quality. Interestingly, the authors estimated missing GHG emissions data (for companies that did not report such data publicly) by estimating emissions as a linear function[16] of economic sector, total revenue, capital expenditures, intangibles, gross margin, and long-term debt to total assets. They used the resulting parameter estimates to assign GHG emissions to nondiscloser S&P companies. They then assessed valuation relevance by regressing market price as a function of actual or estimated GHG emissions and several other variables. The authors also conducted an event methodology study by collecting company news items in SEC 8-K reports from January 1, 2005 to January 1, 2010 that related to climate change, because these would, by definition, be considered material to investors.[17] This process yielded a final sample of 1,540 8-K filings, of which 1,395 contained a press release. The authors used these data to evaluate investor response as a function of emission intensity, GHG emissions, company size, disclosure quality and disclosure status, and country. They generated the following results:

  - Discloser companies generally had higher average GHG emissions within each sector and country, but discloser and nondiscloser companies were, for the most part, equally profitable.

  - In terms of market valuation, they found that higher emissions had a statistically significant and negative impact in each of 15 different regression scenarios. They concluded that GHG emissions explain market price as a negative valuation factor, along with several others. It is more negative in the case of U.S. companies (relative to Canadian firms) and for emission-intensive versus non-emission-intensive companies. Thus, investors price stocks as if higher intensities of GHG emissions will impose additional future costs.

- GHG emissions imposed significant negative valuation effects regardless of whether a company reported to the CDP. In other words, the market acts as if the CDP surveys are not the only source of information about carbon emissions (which, of course, is an accurate depiction of reality).

- In terms of short-term market reactions, 8-K news announcements showed a higher return response on the day of announcement than on other days, as well as significantly higher adjusted volume. Thus, when more attention is placed on the news via a press release, investors react more. In addition, the market response to 8-K filings with a company press release exceeded the response without a press release.

- Results showed a significant negative residual return for 8-K filings of emission-intensive companies and a significant positive residual return for 8-K filings of non-emission-intensive companies, increasing to an almost 2 percent spread after ten days. This result also held approximately equally for CDP disclosers and CDP nondisclosers. This again suggests that in an efficient market, investors rely on a broad set of information, not just disclosures made public through the CDP.

The authors concluded that their findings have implications for market reaction tests of materiality and loss causation in securities litigation. The findings showed a statistically significant stock price adjustment that is reliably attributable to a climate change disclosure not attenuated by other factors. However, the authors disclaim the idea that their results support increasing mandated disclosure, because they found the same empirical relations regardless of whether a company disclosed to the CDP.

Collectively, these studies show that stock and bond market participants do pay attention to news and events that they believe affect the present and future value of their investments in specific companies. These studies also show that the effects of both positive and negative news on company market value can be both measurable and significant. Finally, given the vintage of these studies (most date from the 1990s), it might be assumed that by now it would be well understood that a strong environmental/ES&G posture and improving performance have a real impact on company valuation in the marketplace, and that investors and other market observers should pay close attention to developments that pose environmental (or ES&G) risk or opportunity. As discussed in depth in the preceding chapter, however, this expectation would be incorrect, at least as it applies to most investors. This situation is exasperating for many in the EHS/sustainability field (myself included). But it does present value-creation opportunities both to companies that have not yet proceeded far down the sustainability path and to savvy investors who can (or who become able to) distinguish companies that can effectively manage ES&G issues from those that cannot.

Performance of Tailored Investment Portfolios

A number of published studies have appeared over the years examining the performance of investment portfolios constructed using different SRI, environmental, or sustainability criteria, or more formalized evaluation and rating methods. Generally, such studies have shown that SRI/ES&G portfolios either outperform comparable conventional investment portfolios and/or relevant market benchmarks, or they yield returns that are equivalent. This is particularly true if they are focused on EHS endpoints rather than based on exclusionary ethical criteria (such as involvement in alcohol, gambling, or armaments). Some caution is warranted in reviewing the published literature on this topic, particularly works that have been developed or sponsored by vendors of ES&G data, ratings, rankings, and/or related products. Although some of these published studies appear to be sound and quite sophisticated, we must recognize that their sponsors may have a substantial vested interest in their reported results.

Nevertheless, I have found several well-designed, independent studies that examined the performance of investment portfolios that were selected using "green," SRI, or sustainability rating/ranking tools or indices. They document the absence of any "performance penalty" associated with applying an environmental screen or weighting in constructing a portfolio, particularly one that reflects to any substantial degree the value-oriented approach I advocate in this book:

- Cohen, Fenn, and Naimon (1995) constructed several sets of investment portfolios with similar industry composition and tracked overall performance for three different time periods. They found that the environmental leaders in an industry-balanced portfolio did as well as, and sometimes better than, otherwise similar environmental laggards.

- Statman (2005) conducted an evaluation of the contents and relative performance of four widely followed SRI indexes over a 15-year period (1990–2004). Specifically, he examined the Domini 400 Social Index, the Calvert Social Index, the Citizens Index, and the U.S. portion of the Dow Jones Sustainability Index. As a basis of comparison, he used the S&P 500 index. Several interesting findings emerged from his analysis. Although the composition of each index differs, with varying emphasis on different types of criteria, each had a higher overall "social" score than the benchmark (S&P 500). The SRI indexes exhibited higher returns than the S&P 500 Index during the boom of the late 1990s but lagged it during the bust of the early 2000s. Over the entire study period, returns of the SRI indexes were generally higher than those of the S&P 500 Index, but the differences were not statistically significant. Tracking errors were, however, substantial (several percent), meaning that the SRI indexes often did not track their benchmark index well, making comparisons (such as on quarterly returns data) problematic. The author notes that this error can be reduced by using best-in-class, rather than exclusionary, screening methods to construct the portfolio. These methods were described in the preceding chapter.

- Kempf and Osthoff (2007) examined the effects of SRI screening on investor returns using a variety of screening and trading strategies. To do so, they employed KLD qualitative and exclusionary criteria to establish positive and best-in-class screens and negative screens, respectively. The qualitative screens employed included community, diversity, employee relations, environment, human rights, and product attributes. Ratings were used only for firms included in the S&P 500 and Domini Social 400 to avoid a possible bias from the steep increase in SRI coverage of stocks in (more) recent years. The authors constructed portfolios comprising these stocks and examined their performance from 1992 to 2004. They then conducted a series of comparisons of two portfolios: one composed of firms with high KLD scores, and the other with low KLD scores. These comparisons separately evaluated several investing strategies, including negative screens, positive screens, and best-in-class stock selection, as well as strategies involving buying high-rated portfolios ("going long") and selling ("shorting") low-rated portfolios. Results indicated that using SRI evaluation techniques could produce high abnormal returns. The maximum abnormal returns were observed when the authors employed the best-in-class screening approach, used a combination of several socially responsible screens at the same time, and restricted themselves to stocks with extreme socially responsible ratings. Using the long-short strategy, abnormal returns peaked at nearly 9 percent per year when strict cutoffs (the top 5 percent) of firms were applied. They decreased to about 5 percent per year for the top 10 percent cutoff and to 4 percent for the 25 percent cutoff. For the 50 percent cutoff (investing in the top half), the long-short strategy no longer yielded a significantly positive alpha. The authors concluded that investors should concentrate on the best stocks with respect to SRI screens. The positive abnormal returns obtained through using positive screens and best-in-class approaches remained statistically significant even after typical transaction costs were taken into account. Across the different approaches and significance tests conducted by the authors, in no case did negative screening (categorically excluding certain stocks) produce a statistically significant, positive investment return.

- Statman and Glushkov (2008) also compared returns of the companies in the DS 400 and S&P 500 over an extended period, from 1992 to 2007. Their focus, however, was on disaggregating the impacts of negative screens and positive attributes. For each year, they assembled a portfolio of stocks of firms that had one or more perceived strengths and/or weaknesses and ranked them within industry sectors to obtain the best-in-class firms within each. They then distributed them into three more-or-less equal groups and assembled a portfolio that was long on the top third companies and short on the bottom third. Returns were measured for each year according to several alternative model specifications, with the portfolio being reconstituted each year. The authors found statistically significant excess returns for the community, employee relations, and environment characteristics but not for the diversity and products characteristics. Excess returns for the human rights and governance characteristics were negative but statistically insignificant. These differences were magnified when the authors compared the "top overall" (in the top third on at least two characteristics and not in the bottom third on any) with the "bottom overall" (in the bottom third by two or more social responsibility characteristics and not in the top third on any). Excess annualized returns with a high degree of statistical significance (greater than 99 percent) of 5.54 and 6.12 percent were obtained, depending on the model specification. This same type of analysis was performed with "sin" versus other firms. The "sin-free"-tilted portfolio underperformed its counterpart by 2.27 to 3.34 percent per year, although the significance levels for the relationship were weaker than in the previous comparisons. The offsetting effects of the positive and negative screening steps were then observed in a portfolio that was long in the socially responsible DS 400 Index and short in the S&P 500 Index. That portfolio had a positive excess return by each of the three benchmarks. This indicated that the tilt toward stocks of companies with higher scores on social responsibility characteristics increased the relative return of the DS 400 Index relative to the S&P 500 Index by more than the exclusion of "shunned" companies from the DS 400 Index decreased it. But the excess returns of the DS400-S&P 500 long-short portfolio were smaller (on the order of 1 percent per year) and, again, not highly significant. Overall, the authors concluded, socially responsible investors can do both well and good by adopting the best-in-class method when constructing their portfolios. That method calls for tilts toward stocks of companies with high scores on social responsibility characteristics but refrains from calls to shun the stock of any company, even one that produces tobacco.

- In a recent article, Edmans (2011) evaluated the returns of a value-weighted portfolio of the *Fortune* "100 Best Companies to Work for in America" relative to a basket of otherwise similar companies. He conducted a series of multiple regression analyses, controlling for industry, factor risk, the timing of the announcements of which companies were on the list, and a broad set of other observable characteristics that might influence shareholder returns over time. He found that the 100 best firms posted excess returns (alpha) of 3.5 percent from 1984 to 2009 and posted returns that were 2.1 percent above industry-matched benchmarks. The best companies also exhibited significantly more positive earnings surprises and announcement returns. The author concluded that firms with high levels of employee satisfaction generate superior long-horizon returns. He stated that his quantitative findings have three main implications. First, employee satisfaction is positively correlated with shareholder returns and does not necessarily represent managerial slack or inefficiency. Second, the stock market does not fully value intangibles, even when independently verified by a highly public survey on large firms. Finally, certain SRI screens, such as employee welfare, may improve investment returns.

- Finally, Hoepner, Yu, and Ferguson (2010) attempted to dis-aggregate the key factors producing the apparent outperformance of SRI portfolios that has been reported in recent years. To do so, they compared the performance of the "Global 100 Most Sustainable Companies in the World" published by the Canadian CSR-focused media company Corporate Knights with a reasonable benchmark index, the MSCI World Index. Companies are selected for the Corporate Knights list based on sustainability ratings produced by Innovest Strategic Value Advisors. An unusual feature of these ratings is that they are both in the form of bond-style ratings (AAA, CCC–) and are industry-specific (so companies from different industries are not compared against one another). The authors assembled the ratings data from January 2005 to May 2008 and compiled a sample of 196 companies from 16 countries (38 from the U.S.) and ten economic sectors. In the aggregate, the sample contained 478 data points that were subjected to multiple regression analysis to evaluate the effects of SRI rating, industry, and country on investment returns. Results indicated that the overall portfolio (companies appearing at least once on the Global 100 Most Sustainable list) outperformed the overall market (alpha of 0.26 percent per month, significant at the 5 percent level). Further analysis showed, however, that at the sector level, most (seven or eight, depending on specification) of the ten CSR leader portfolios did not outperform their industry benchmarks. The authors interpreted this discrepancy as a strong sign of the heterogeneity of the CSR-corporate financial performance relationship across industries. The two industries with a significantly positive CSR effect on investment returns were consumer discretionary and health care, both of which are consumer-facing. The authors concluded that no general relationship between CSR and corporate financial performance exists and that the relationships are far more nuanced than has generally been recognized. They suggested that the value of CSR activities should be assessed in the context of the industrial business processes that exist in particular sectors and industries.

These findings do not categorically demonstrate that more environmentally advanced firms or companies that exhibit common SRI attributes (using particular index-specific criteria) necessarily outperform otherwise similar firms. But they do suggest that ES&G-oriented investment approaches that are focused on value creation tend to outperform other commonly used, comparable investment strategies. At the very least, these studies provide empirical support for overcoming what has been a significant barrier to SRI/ES&G investing: the fiduciary duty to the investor.[18] In other words, one investment theory holds that a portfolio of stocks selected on the basis of ES&G criteria must perform at a level inferior to that of a broader portfolio not constrained in this manner. But this theory appears to have been disproven by the available empirical evidence.

Surveys of Corporate and Investor Attitudes and Beliefs

Opinion surveys do not have any direct bearing on the issue of whether well-considered ES&G investments create value for the firm. Nonetheless, they can be useful in helping us understand the current state of affairs and identify potential barriers to the further integration of sustainability into core business practices that I advocate in this book. Moreover, surveys directed at investors and their service providers can provide meaningful insights into whether and to what extent they perceive the ES&G value-creation message and/or are taking steps to implement these concepts into their ongoing activities. A number of surveys and studies have been conducted about the beliefs, attitudes, and actions of the various players involved with sustainability and investing. The number of organizations that have seen fit to weigh in on this topic appears to be growing every year. The following two sections review some of the more relevant and interesting studies.

Investor Attitudes and Beliefs

A review of the more relevant findings from surveys of investors about the importance (or lack thereof) of ES&G issues to investment analysis and decision making provides some interesting insights. An early survey (1998) that a colleague and I conducted confirmed the generally held view that most investors, whether or not they use or represent environmentally screened investment products, did not routinely request information on environmental policies, management systems, performance, or other related issues. More recent studies, however, have suggested that awareness of environmental (along with other corporate social responsibility) issues has been growing and that these issues were beginning to receive more attention within the investor community. In fact, some recent survey results suggest that this interest is both growing and spreading to segments of the U.S. capital markets that historically have been indifferent to ES&G issues and their potential effects on investment returns and risks. A few of the more prominent and interesting studies are profiled here:

- In their study, Soyka and Feldman (1998) developed and administered a written survey to 45 U.S. bond and equity portfolio managers, representing both environmentally screened and "mainstream" (nonscreened) investment styles. The vast majority of portfolio managers in both groups stated that they would pay more for strong environmental performance if (and only if) they were provided with a convincing demonstration of value creation. Furthermore, although virtually no investors routinely asked for EHS program cash flow contribution, almost all expected company management to offer information on EHS value creation without prompting. In other words, investors believed it was incumbent upon company senior managers to articulate and support the value-creation message in their communications with investors, irrespective of the source of this value and whether or not the investor solicited such information.

- In its study, UNEP-FI (2004) reported on the results of its survey of 11 major international brokerage firms. Among the findings were unanimity that environmental, social, and corporate governance issues affect long-term shareholder value, and a widespread recognition that some of these impacts can be profound. Nonetheless, the authors stated that comparative analysis was difficult due to the wide range of reporting practices in use within and between countries and industries. In this regard, more clear government positions (regulations or guidance) would greatly aid financial research by establishing norms for reporting practices. The report also contained several recommendations, including that ES&G issues be addressed in corporate annual reports and financial statements, that pension funds should invest in a manner that reflects the strong links among the three areas, and that governments and regulatory bodies should update fiduciary responsibility regulations and require specific disclosure of ES&G criteria by both companies and stock exchanges. As you saw in Chapter 6, some of these steps are now being implemented in a number of different international jurisdictions and capital markets.

- Mercer Investment Consulting (2006) examined evolving interest in environmental issues based on a survey of investment managers in 157 firms that work in important markets or globally. Selected survey results are summarized in Table 7-1. These data show that, as of five years ago, many or most managers in global investment firms tended to view the issues listed as relevant to their evaluations. Within specific capital markets, however, there were some significant differences between the views held in U.S. firms and those of their counterparts in the United Kingdom (UK) and continental Europe. Similar (and large) percentages believed that issues such as globalization, corporate governance, and terrorism were relevant to investment analysis. But the percentages who believed that environmental issues such as climate change, environmental management, and water (as well as human rights) were relevant were generally two to five times lower in the U.S. than in the UK and the rest of Europe. Percentages of U.S. investment managers who believed certain other ES&G issues were relevant were intermediate between the UK and other European investors. This finding applied to health issues in emerging markets and, interestingly, sustainability.

Table 7-1 Perceived Influence of ES&G Issues on Asset Performance

	Europe Except UK	**UK**	**U.S.**	**Global**
Adherence to corporate conventions (such as the Global Compact)	8.7	15.8	0.0	19.5
Climate change	17.4	21.1	5.4	51.2
Corporate governance	65.2	68.4	56.8	46.3
Employee relations	8.7	15.8	29.7	24.4
Environmental management	21.7	15.8	8.1	41.5
Globalization	78.3	68.4	75.7	61.0
Health issues in emerging markets	4.3	15.8	10.8	36.6
Human rights	17.4	10.5	5.4	19.5
Sustainability	26.1	15.8	21.6	31.7
Terrorism	34.8	36.8	43.2	14.6
Water (use/access to clean water)	13.0	5.3	2.7	46.3

Source: Mercer Investment Consulting (2006), 2006 Fearless Forecast: Global Survey of Investment Managers, p. 14.

This "lag" in appreciating the importance of environmental issues by mainstream investors in the U.S. has been validated by primary research I have conducted in recent years and in other published work. As described further in Chapter 6, general awareness of environmental/ES&G issues is growing. But belief in the importance of these issues has not yet manifested itself in new patterns of detailed investment inquiry, analysis, and decision making that one might reasonably expect in most U.S. money management firms.

With that said, a recent study by Ioannou and Serafeim (2010) appears to break new ground. It examines the behavior of one influential component of the capital markets—sell-side analysts—that historically has been skeptical of the value of SRI and sustainability investing more generally:

- The authors reviewed analyst ratings and CSR and financial data on a large number of U.S. firms over an extended period (1992–2008). This provided both an extensive database and results that have historical depth and are relatively contemporary. The study focused on the overall impact of CSR strengths and concerns on sell-side analysts' recommendations. It also looked at how CSR information has been processed along with other types of data to affect analysts' perceptions of value creation and, therefore, their projections and recommendations. The authors set out to characterize conditions at the firm and at the analyst level that could potentially affect the perception of CSR value creation (or destruction). CSR performance data were obtained from KLD and aggregated across all areas of interest to produce one rating each for every firm's CSR strengths and concerns by year. Each strength and concern was weighted equally. The sample included 20,715 observations with available data for all variables from 1993 to 2008 and from 546 (1993) to 2,698 (2008) U.S. companies. Over the years, 4,109 unique U.S. companies were included in the sample. The authors then performed a series of multiple regression analyses using the consensus analyst recommendation as the dependent variable. Findings showed the following:

  ○ In the earlier years (1993–1997), firms' CSR strengths had a significant negative impact on analysts' recommendations, but the trend reversed, and subsequently, the impact became significantly positive. The authors stated that these results suggest a change in analysts' perceptions. As time passed, CSR strategies were perceived to be more legitimate, capable of creating value, and less likely to produce uncertainty about future cash flows and profitability.

  ○ Results did not show that the reverse was true for CSR concerns. In other words, analyst ratings did not become increasingly negative over time because of growing acceptance of CSR concerns. Empirical results showed an interesting asymmetrical effect. Analysts perceived CSR strengths as value-creating and, as such, rewarded them with more favorable recommendations. CSR concerns were not perceived as value-destroying and, as such, were not penalized with less favorable recommendations.

  ○ Results provided strong evidence that analysts of higher ability were more likely to appreciate CSR strengths and incorporate them favorably in their recommendations, suggesting that CSR strengths are perceived to be value-creating. Interestingly, the reverse was not true for CSR concerns and, therefore, CSR-weak firms. Moreover, because higher-ability analysts tend to produce more accurate evaluations and exert more influence on capital markets, the authors believe that they have documented a mechanism through which CSR strategies are perceived as value-creating and, through analyst recommendations, are translated into economic value in the capital markets.

○ Analysts perceived CSR strategies implemented by larger firms more favorably. CSR concerns were perceived to be relatively more value-destroying for higher-visibility firms.

The authors concluded that corporate executives and managers interested in implementing CSR strategies in their organizations should be aware that negative analysts' reactions, and subsequent value destruction in capital markets, is a real possibility when they initially attempt to implement such strategies. Accordingly, they suggested that managers focus on communicating the value of their CSR strategies to the investment community. In particular, highlighting short-term costs but also long-term benefits could mitigate difficulties that investors may face in understanding the value generated through such activities. It also might expedite the adjustment of analyst valuation methods to these new CSR-augmented business models.

Corporate Executive Attitudes and Beliefs

Despite some lingering skepticism and a notable gap between aspirations and reality in terms of corporate sustainability practices (discussed in depth in Chapter 8), attitudes and beliefs within the executive suite about the business value of sustainability are evolving rapidly. Several published studies presenting the results of extensive surveys of corporate senior executives over the past several years illustrate this phenomenon:

• *The Economist* Intelligence Unit and Oracle Corporation (2005) conducted an online survey in 2004 of corporate executives worldwide, as well as a separate survey of institutional investors. The study and its findings are somewhat noteworthy in part because the editors of *The Economist* had historically been highly and publicly skeptical of the business value and relevance of sustainability and corporate social responsibility. The authors received completed responses from 136 executives and 65 investors. Within this combined group, 85 percent said that CSR was central or important in making investment decisions. This was almost double the percentage responding in a similar way on another survey conducted five years previously. Among the corporate executives, the three most important aspects of CSR were ethical behavior of staff (named by 67 percent), good corporate governance (58 percent), and transparency (51 percent). The investors named the same aspects as most important, but in reverse order: transparency (68 percent), good corporate governance (63 percent), and ethical behavior of staff (46 percent). Interestingly, 84 percent responded that they believed that CSR practices could help improve a company's bottom line. The most important benefits of CSR in this regard were perceived as brand enhancement (61 percent) and better morale (67 percent). The most important obstacles were perceived as the cost implications of implementing CSR (42 percent) and its unproven benefits (40 percent). Respondents also indicated the strong belief that an internal focus was much more important than an external one in addressing CSR.

• More recently, consultants at the Boston Consulting Group published the results of a major survey effort in the *MIT Sloan Management Review*. In this study, Berns et al. (2009) received more than 2,000 responses to a 20-question electronic survey they developed based on interviews with about 50 "thought leaders" in the sustainability field. About 75 percent (1,560) of these responses were from senior executives and managers in for-profit enterprises. The remaining 462 responses were received from nonprofit executives, academics, government officials, and others. Responses from North American organizations comprised 28 percent of the total in this global survey. Survey results provided a number of interesting findings:

  ○ More than 92 percent of survey respondents said that their company was addressing sustainability in some way. Less than 25 percent of survey respondents said that their company had decreased its commitment to sustainability during the economic downturn.

- There was considerable variation in how respondents defined "sustainability." About 25 percent of respondents each applied the Brundtland Commission definition, "climate change, environmental, social, and economic issues," and "maintaining the viability of our business." Only 5 percent of respondents defined sustainability as "social responsibility issues."

- Responsibility for addressing sustainability appears to be diffuse in many companies. Thirty-six percent of respondents said "all employees" were responsible, 13 percent said it was unclear, and 7 percent said that they do not address sustainability. In contrast, 22 percent responded that a corporate or cross-functional group had the lead, and 15 percent said responsibility rested with a senior executive.

- The "business case" for sustainability remains elusive, with only 31 percent of respondents indicating that they had developed the business case or a proven value proposition. Very large companies (more than 100,000 employees) were most likely to have developed the business case.

- Interestingly, "outmoded mental models and perspectives on sustainability" was cited as the leading internal challenge (by 21 percent of respondents), followed by competing priorities and unclear business case/value proposition. More than 30 percent of those who considered their knowledge of sustainability "expert" reported that outdated models and perspectives were the most important barrier—twice as many as for any other response. Only 5 percent of respondents said that the leading challenge was lack of knowledge of the most effective ways to take action. Among North American respondents, by a wide margin, the lack of a business case was the most important factor cited.

- The leading external challenge (cited by 26 percent) was insufficient customer demand, followed by lack of clear regulatory policy for externalities (at 20 percent). This pattern was especially strong among North American respondents.

- In terms of the most important benefits of sustainability, improved company/brand image was by a wide margin the most frequently cited (at 35 percent of respondents), followed by cost savings, competitive advantage, and several others, at 10 percent or less.

- ○ Most respondents expect sustainability to pay off. Fifty-five percent believe they will obtain either incremental or material, differentiated financial returns. Only 11 percent believe that the financial impacts will be negative. Twenty-one percent stated that financial logic is not part of their decision making on sustainability.

- ○ In terms of the most important stakeholders driving sustainability in companies, senior leadership (at 40 percent) is by far the most significant across the respondent population, followed by consumers (18 percent), employees (12 percent), and government regulators (12 percent). Investors and other capital providers were selected as most important by only 8 percent. Environmental NGOs and community activists were each viewed as most important by 3 percent of respondents or less.

- ○ Finally, the most important organizational capabilities for companies cited by respondents included vision and leadership commitment (62 percent); product, service, and market innovation (43 percent); and business model or process innovation (39 percent).

The authors also reported a high correlation between the depth of a business leader's experience with sustainability and its perceived benefits. They concluded that the more people know about sustainability, the more thoughtfully they evaluate it, and the more they think it matters to how companies manage themselves and compete in the marketplace. They also concluded that sustainability will become increasingly important to business strategy and management over time, and that the risks of failing to act accordingly and decisively are growing.

- • Deloitte (Park and Pavlovsky, 2010) conducted a qualitative study in which they interviewed designated sustainability leaders at the U.S. headquarters of 48 large companies from late 2009 to early 2010. Participants represented companies from five major industry sectors: automotive, consumer products, process and industrial, technology, and telecommunications. Out of 48 respondents, all but three reported that their sustainability priorities were at least partially aligned with their organizations' business priorities. In general, respondent firms emphasized the environmental component of sustainability over social and governance issues. In fact, some respondents reportedly omitted the social side of sustainability from their definitions. Those who did report social sustainability initiatives commonly focused on improving working conditions for their own employees, although some also mentioned broader community- or region-based efforts. Sixty-five percent also discussed priorities related to improving the environmental sustainability of their products. The areas perceived as offering the greatest opportunities for becoming more sustainable included manufacturing process and operations (46 percent), brand enhancements and perception (31 percent), and supply chain (21 percent). Generally, respondents believed that a wide range of internal constituents are affected by sustainability efforts, suggesting a growing recognition of sustainability's enterprise-wide scope and impact. In addition, 66 percent of respondents reported that sustainability had or likely would have some type of impact(s) on their fundamental business model. Finally, the majority of respondents (73 percent) did not believe that sustainability would lead to the creation of a new "green collar" workforce. Instead, they believed their existing employees would need to develop new knowledge and skills, as required to meet future sustainability challenges.

- Also in 2010, *The Economist* Intelligence Unit published the results of a new and substantial survey of sustainability beliefs and behaviors within the international business community (Watts, 2010). The author of the study surveyed more than 200 senior executives in the areas of sustainability, corporate social responsibility, and finance. He also conducted ten in-depth interviews with corporate executives, academics, and industry experts. He stated that the survey findings documented that leading companies were making progress toward sustainability goals. The great majority of respondents (86 percent) agreed that sustainability will become more important over the next three years. Of these, 46 percent strongly agreed. In terms of underlying motivations, the most important reason cited for promoting sustainability policies was that it is the right thing to do ethically (56 percent), followed by complying with laws and regulations (45 percent) and improving the company's image (43 percent). On the other hand, only 24 percent of respondents agreed that a strong link exists between financial performance and commitment to sustainability in the short term. But that percentage nearly tripled (to 69 percent) when the time frame in question was the long term. In terms of emphasis, survey respondents tended to favor areas such as creating a code of ethics (51 percent) and promoting environmental protection (50 percent). This behavior appeared to be motivated by a desire to develop new corporate strategies (such as selling green products) and improving public image. The responding executives also reported efforts to embed sustainability into a variety of corporate functions, including supply chain relationships (29 percent), improving energy efficiency (38 percent), educating employees on sustainability (32 percent), and engaging employees in sustainability-related activities (30 percent). More than half (54 percent) reported that their sustainability efforts had been led by senior management. In terms of providing incentives for greater sustainability-oriented behavior, the most widely used was employee recognition programs (38 percent); only about one in five (18 percent) linked compensation to sustainability indicators. But the author reported that anecdotal evidence suggests that this practice is growing. Finally, only about half (49 percent) of the leading companies participating in the survey reported progress in meeting their environmental sustainability goals. Slightly more (53 percent) reported progress on meeting social sustainability goals. Despite this lack of complete success to this point, the respondents broadly agreed that stating goals and reporting progress toward those goals are essential components in pursuing sustainability.

Summary and Implications

In summary, the literature findings briefly reviewed here demonstrate that ES&G issues can have a meaningful impact on the firm's financial success. Comprehensive, systematic, and business-driven approaches such as those described in Chapter 5 should, accordingly, be of interest both to executives managing companies and to financially oriented external audiences, including investors. Despite the substantial and steadily mounting evidence of the ES&G-financial value connection, however, much remains to be done. Areas that deserve emphasis include the following:

- Consistently finding the sources of value in corporate ES&G management activities

- Effectively communicating these value sources and, importantly, the internal corporate conditions required to find and capture financial value to financial market audiences
- Translating the relevant measures of corporate ES&G posture and performance into financial valuation metrics
- Integrating these measures into financial valuation models

The literature reviewed in this chapter has revealed the following overall findings and insights:

- Well-chosen pollution prevention, eco-efficiency, and similar initiatives more than pay for themselves, both at the project level and, if practiced consistently and on a sufficiently broad scale, at the firm level.

- Both actual and prospective ES&G liabilities may be quite significant in magnitude, vary across firms in the same industry, and be quantified with a reasonable degree of precision. Information on these liabilities, and their magnitude and probability of occurrence, are of abiding interest to investors, bond rating agencies, and other financial market audiences. The fact that these issues have been chronically underestimated and unreported is a serious barrier to full and correct valuation of company securities. It suggests a need for more rigorous enforcement of existing disclosure rules.

- There is a strong positive correlation between improved, beyond-compliance, proactive environmental and ES&G management practices and the firm's value. Market-relevant financial benefits may be obtained through appropriate investments in improving a firm's sustainability posture and performance. Results also suggest that such investments, which enhance the firm's intangible assets, are translated over time into increased shareholder value.

- The evidence suggests that the cost of equity capital is lower for firms with relatively advanced environmental management practices or, more generally, superior sustainability performance. At the same time, however, investors do not appear to value sustainability disclosure per se but instead are interested in firms' actual performance. Moreover, some evidence exists that companies that report better sustainability performance also attract additional dedicated institutional investor and analyst coverage as well as lower analyst forecast errors (such as of future earnings).

- With that said, not all ES&G aspects appear to offer the same financial value creation potential. Empirical evidence suggests that investing in improved employee welfare/relations, environmental policy/performance, and product characteristics substantially contributes to reducing firms' cost of equity and potentially offers other financial benefits. Investments in several other common CSR domains, including community relations, diversity, and human rights, do not. In addition, firms involved in some businesses posing high ES&G risks, such as tobacco and nuclear power, appear to have higher equity financing costs, whereas others (alcohol, firearms, military products) do not.

- Such effects also can be discerned in individual company valuations. Several studies have shown that a tailored and sophisticated approach to ES&G portfolio construction can enable an investor to outperform the relevant market benchmarks. Again, the focus must be on the corporate endpoints and activities that have the most clear relationships to enhancing revenues, cash flows, and earnings and/or reducing risk. Empirical findings suggest that a focus on the best companies within a given sector offers the most favorable return prospects. They also suggest that positive screening and best-in-class approaches are far more effective than other commonly used ES&G/SRI stock selection methods. At the same time, however, the evidence is equally strong that rigid negative screening and other more crude approaches to ES&G investing do not outperform. Indeed, they may induce returns that lag the market as a whole.

- The literature on ES&G issues and the credit markets is much more limited than it is for equity markets, but it is increasingly clear that credit markets are sensitive to environmental liabilities. In particular, the key issues of climate change and regulatory concerns have been linked to firms' higher expected default risk. This leads to higher interest rates and costs for companies that have not demonstrated adequate management control over these issues.

- More generally, climate change is emerging as an issue that is being carefully evaluated by investors and other capital market participants. Robust evidence has been published showing that higher GHG emissions are viewed as a negative valuation factor, particularly in emission-intensive industries. In recent years, even in the absence of explicit carbon emission limits in the U.S., investors have begun pricing stocks as though GHG emission intensities will impose additional future costs, thereby limiting earnings and return potential.

- Several investigators have concluded that the relationships between sustainability and financial performance are heterogeneous across industries. Some have suggested that the investor or analyst should assess firms in the context of the industrial business processes extant in their industries. This implies taking a more sophisticated and nuanced approach to ES&G analysis and evaluation than is typical today.

- On a related point, as in other fields of endeavor, some research suggests that ES&G analysts who are more knowledgeable and experienced, and/or have more resources available to them, can outperform their less-experienced or -advantaged peers. This implies that for many participants in the capital markets, additional personal investment to broaden their knowledge base and competencies will be required to perform ES&G investing successfully.

- Corporate senior managers, particularly those who interact with investors and analysts, also need to more consistently and fully communicate the financial value of the investments they are making in sustainability-related activities. Empirical research has shown that participants in the capital markets uniformly believe that it is the responsibility of company senior managers to articulate and support the value-creation message in their communications with investors. This is true irrespective of the source of this value and whether or not the investor solicits such information. This is particularly important for ES&G issues, given the substantial knowledge gaps that exist in many segments of the U.S. capital markets. In this regard, explaining that ES&G policies, programs, and activities are *investments* (not expenses) that impose short-term costs in pursuit of long-term benefits could mitigate some of the remaining skepticism that exists within the mainstream investor community. In the process, helping investors understand exactly how financial value is being generated through such activities will help expedite the adjustment of analyst valuation models to new formulations that explicitly consider sustainability endpoints and provide more accurate and useful predictive power.

- For their part, corporate senior executives as a group are beginning to respond to the business imperatives posed by sustainability issues. Recent surveys of executive beliefs and behaviors indicate that the greater the depth of a business leader's knowledge of and experience with sustainability, the more likely it is that he or she will understand and value its perceived benefits. They also are increasingly coming around to the view that sustainability is or will become important to business strategy and management during the next few years, and that the risks of failing to act accordingly (and decisively) are growing.

- In terms of the specifics, it is clear that there is still no widely accepted, commonly applied definition of sustainability. Many companies are still grappling with how to address ES&G considerations at an organizational level. Among those with a more sophisticated understanding of the sustainability issue, it appears that there is a growing recognition that new ways of thinking about value creation and how best to operate the business in response to ES&G imperatives will be required. Perhaps some of the ideas offered in this book will be of value to those struggling with how best to overcome the outmoded mental models and perspectives by which they are currently constrained. Even with the many uncertainties that exist, a large and growing percentage of companies in the U.S. and around the world are embarking on new initiatives to pursue corporate sustainability. Most executives responding to recent surveys appear to believe that these efforts will produce financial benefits (will have negative costs and/or produce revenue gains). Many also recognize, as suggested in Chapter 5, that, as senior leaders, providing both vision and their personal, ongoing involvement and support will be vital if their firms are to be successful in creating new sustainability-driven value.

From the foregoing, it is clear to me that the business and financial value of well-designed and -implemented ES&G strategies, policies, and practices are no longer in doubt. Increasingly, capital market participants are aware of the ways in which industry and firm-level sustainability posture and performance affect the return potential and risk of company securities. They are beginning to factor these considerations into their valuation models and decisions. This suggests significant opportunity for companies that have not yet expanded their worldview, business strategy, and/or operations to include ES&G considerations. Although not all investments in EHS, social, governance, or community activities can be expected to yield financial benefits, it is clear that many do. Accordingly, the key task is to develop and implement the means to make rational judgments about how best to deploy the firm's financial, material, and human capital in pursuit of ES&G improvements. The evidence suggests that companies that take these steps and that can execute effectively can reap significant financial rewards.

In contrast, firms that continue to operate as they have in the past, treating EHS&G obligations and other activities solely as costs to be avoided or reduced, run the risk of being left behind and having their competitive position eroded. The published literature convincingly demonstrates that unmanaged environmental risks and liabilities can depress profitability, increase volatility, and corrode the firm's asset value (both tangible and intangible). Having worked in the environmental field for an extended period, I can accept the idea that at one time a passive, minimalist strategy toward EHS compliance and management of other sustainability issues could be justified. However, I am far less convinced that such a strategy is tenable in a world with an increasingly demanding and informed set of stakeholders and a set of well-established, proven management practices that are available for use by, essentially, anyone.[19] So the conventional excuses are becoming less convincing with each passing year.

This applies as surely to firms that may have been regarded as environmental or EHS leaders at one time but that in recent years have scaled back their commitment, management attention, and investments in EHS excellence as it does to others that could be considered laggards.[20] As I stated somewhat forcefully in Chapter 1, such companies need to address their "deferred maintenance" before they take on any new sustainability initiatives or proclaim their "greenness" or sustainability virtue to internal or external stakeholders.

This chapter and the preceding one have presented some important foundational concepts and evidence for the financial value-creation potential (and reality) of well-crafted corporate sustainability strategies, policies, and practices. The next chapter turns to a key component of both internal sustainability efforts and the evaluation of these efforts and their results by investors and other external stakeholders: performance measurement and ES&G data, knowledge, and insight.

Endnotes

1. Additional details on many of the studies profiled here and their specific findings can be found in several of my previous works, including Soyka, 2010, and USEPA, 2006.

2. Interestingly, some European institutional investors (such as the Swiss investment bank Sarasin & Co.) explicitly evaluate the environmental risks (and opportunities) associated with both corporate bonds and debt securities issued by sovereign governments.

3. As noted in Chapter 6, capital investment costs required to comply with the technology implications of new standards can be significant. Interestingly, the firms profiled in the latter study (pulp and paper mills) were faced with differential requirements from a tightening of existing standards to protect water quality-impaired streams. These requirements were established many years after the initial leap to control "end of pipe" water pollutant emissions had been made.

4. As discussed in Chapter 5, I advocate the use of such global sustainability policies, objectives, and systems to promote internal clarity, consistency, and credibility, as well as efficiency.

5. Innovest was acquired by RiskMetrics in 2009, which was in turn acquired by MSCI, Inc. the following year.

6. As discussed in Chapter 6, beta is a measure of a given company's stock price volatility over time. Higher betas imply a higher cost of equity capital (return required by the investor). A higher required return implies a lower stock price, all else being equal.

7. These variables include company size, intangible asset value, leverage, and/or stock price momentum.

8. Whether this categorization scheme is sensible and reflects the reality on the ground is a question that could be vigorously debated. Based on my past work, I believe that EIIS professionals employed in the food and beverage processing and pharmaceuticals industries would point out that their production facilities are extensively regulated and that maintaining continuous regulatory compliance, much less ongoing performance improvement, requires significant vigilance, effort, and resources.

9. As discussed in Chapter 6, KLD is now a unit of MSCI, Inc.

10. This means that there is only a 1 percent chance that the null hypothesis was true. In this case the hypothesis was that the cost of equity capital of firms with low CSR strength ratings was the same as that of firms with high CSR strength ratings. In other words, there was a 99 percent chance that the two groups were different, with the distinguishing feature between them being high and low CSR rating.

11. Basis points are commonly used in financial calculations, data, and communications. One hundred basis points equals 1 percent, so ten basis points equals one-tenth of 1 percent.

12. Yield spread is the difference between a bond's offered yield and that of a U.S. treasury-issued bond of comparable size and time to maturity.

13. As discussed in Chapter 6, form 10-K is a standard disclosure required of publicly traded companies on an annual basis by the U.S. Securities and Exchange Commission (SEC).

14. A chemical plant explosion in Bhopal, India killed hundreds and seriously injured thousands of workers and people in the surrounding community. Among the other consequences of this tragedy were the crippling and ultimate dismantling of the U.S. chemical company that owned the plant (Union Carbide) and the enactment of the Emergency Planning and Community Right to Know Act (EPCRA). The Act established mandatory reporting of releases of toxic chemicals to the environment, regardless of industry, as well as several other far-reaching provisions.

15. The Superfund Amendments and Reauthorization Act, enacted in 1986, reinforced and added several new provisions that expanded the reach of this revolutionary piece of environmental protection legislation.

16. Note that for some independent variables, the relationship was assumed to be linear in logarithmic form.

17. Under present SEC rules (adopted in 2004), an 8-K report must be filed within four days of the date of the actual event or company news release. The list of items subject to an 8-K report is extensive and covers all material items relating to financial statements not disclosed elsewhere. See the SEC's final rule at www.sec.gov/rules/final/33-8400.htm for further details.

18. Recall that in the U.S., fiduciary duty has historically been interpreted to mean that only the goal of maximizing financial return (subject to a given level of risk) may be considered by an investment trustee (such as a pension fund). All other factors, such as environmental performance, are viewed as either irrelevant or detrimental to shareholder financial interests and may not be considered. Further discussion of this issue, and recent significant events, was presented in Chapter 6.

19. In this regard, I note with some interest that courses, tools, and guidance materials on EHS compliance, quality and environmental management systems, pollution prevention, lean manufacturing, and related topics are offered by a plethora of state and local governments, community colleges, industry and trade groups, and nonprofit organizations all over the U.S.

20. Laggards or, more charitably, very late adopters are present in every sector of the economy and in virtually every major industry. Chapter 8 offers some examples and a general sense of where American industry stands in this regard.

8

Defining, Measuring, and Reporting ES&G Performance

Very few people who have worked in or around business have not heard the phrase "What gets measured gets managed." As discussed in Chapter 5, I am a firm believer in the importance of defining what outcomes are desired from a business-related activity; establishing metrics or indicators to evaluate whether those outcomes are being attained (or are likely); and collecting and periodically reviewing information to determine whether an activity, initiative, or organization is on course and likely to succeed. This chapter discusses in a bit more detail why this type of mindset and approach is important; how sustainability performance is typically defined and measured, and by and for whom; and typical reporting conventions and practices. Following this discussion, I return to the issue of how this information is received and interpreted by participants in the capital markets—in particular, ES&G investors and analysts. The chapter closes with some recommendations for how the whole process, from defining relevant performance dimensions and metrics through use in investment analysis, might be improved. As I will demonstrate, the current status quo has many deficiencies and gaps that limit companies' ability to optimize their responses to sustainability issues. These limitations also constrain investors' ability to fully appreciate and act on the factors that will increasingly separate the firms that can best adapt to sustainability challenges and opportunities from those lacking this capability.

Why Performance Measurement and Reporting Are Crucial

As discussed at length in Chapter 5, instituting a meaningful sustainability program or initiative requires at least some structure, if for no other reason than to establish clarity and internal credibility. In my experience, ideas that offer no clear potential benefits, and around which there are no defined outcomes, indicated actions, or time and resource requirements, do not tend to go far. It is essential that those who would carry out a sustainability initiative understand what they are trying to accomplish. Along the way, they must be able to distinguish short-term outcomes that indicate that progress is being made from those that may suggest a problem or needed course correction. Similarly, those who would approve an initiative and accompanying use of the organization's resources need assurance that tangible results will be sought and attained, as well as a way to monitor ongoing progress or the lack thereof. Managers also must have a way to hold the responsible people accountable for their use of the organization's resources and what they achieve as a result. None of these conditions can be met unless the following occur:

- Desired outcomes are stated either at the outset or following a brief exploratory effort.
- Appropriate interim milestones and time frames are defined.
- There is a means of regularly collecting and reporting information on what has happened (both resources used and accomplishments).
- Management has had an opportunity to either endorse the current process or make appropriate adjustments.

ES&G Data, Information, Knowledge, and Insight

In considering how best to define and measure sustainability performance in a company or other organization, it is important to distinguish between different levels of meaning, which together form a hierarchy.[1]

At the bottom is ES&G *data*. Most regulated companies (and many other entities) produce basic data on EHS performance in great quantity. Regular reporting on certain defined elements (such as waste generation, pollutant emissions, and accident rates) is an ongoing and often mandatory activity. Regulatory agencies, particularly EPA headquarters and regional offices and state regulatory agencies, are repositories of vast quantities of data addressing the regulated behavior of companies operating within their jurisdictions. Most of these data are in "raw" form, meaning that they are submitted in the required format (a number or set of numbers in defined units). Often the receiving agency does nothing more with the data than compare the numeric values received against any relevant performance standards or limits.

At the next level is ES&G *information*, which involves putting the basic data into a relevant context. Thus, when a set of data is connected with the circumstances in which it has been generated, it acquires more meaning and is more useful.

Interpreting ES&G information in a way that yields one or more conclusions produces *knowledge*, which is needed to inform decisions about which sustainability issues are important, how best to address them, whether current activities are on track, and a variety of other issues.

Finally, *wisdom*, or at least *insight*, involves applying judgment and previous experience to knowledge, which enables an understanding of the implications of ES&G issues and organizational posture and performance. Insight is required to decide how best to retool a sustainability initiative that is not attaining its goals, or how to set priorities among many seemingly important sustainability objectives.

These terms and the distinctions among them are not simply a matter of semantics or academic interest. In observing the ways in which different actors produce, use, and interpret ES&G data and information over a period of many years, I have concluded that confusion about how these levels of meaning differ often leaves participants frustrated. For example, a company's EHS staff might believe that the performance data they are conveying are suitable in the form in which they have chosen to report them. But the recipient actually requires input at a different level of the hierarchy. To me, it is obvious that in and of themselves, ES&G data tell us little about an organization's sustainability posture, performance, or future prospects. As you will see, however, this limitation has not prevented many parties that evaluate such questions from making judgments based on these indicators. Indeed, many ES&G researchers explicitly request performance data so that they can use their own internal methods to transform it into useful knowledge and insight that may be useful to their customers. Although these organizations may be using extensive intellectual capital and other resources to convert these data into knowledge and insight, in many cases, the ways in which they are doing so are unstated or unclear. This mismatch between what is reported and what is ultimately needed presents a substantial opportunity for improvements to the typical patterns of ES&G data development, reporting, and investment analysis now in widespread use. I share some recommendations on this point at the conclusion of this chapter.

Major ES&G Data Types and Sources

In evaluating an issue with as many different facets as organizational sustainability, nearly endless possibilities exist for the types of endpoints and data that may be of interest. Indeed, as discussed later in this chapter, a number of ES&G research firms routinely collect data to populate hundreds of distinct ES&G variables on each of the hundreds or thousands of companies in their research population. For our purposes, I believe that some useful distinctions and logical categories emerge, based on my consulting work in this area as well as the management approach I suggested in Chapter 5. At a general level, the categories discussed next provide an appropriate and meaningful structure.

Governance

These are factors and indicators that speak to the degree to which an organization's senior management and owner/member representatives are directly involved in the management of sustainability issues and concerns. Specific examples include defined Board of Directors and senior executive management responsibility for the organizational

EHS/sustainability policy; shareholder rights and access; and Board committee structure, composition, scope of activities, and member qualifications. Some stakeholders (including investors) also may have a particular interest in other specific ES&G issues, such as Board diversity and philanthropic activity. The sources of data/information on governance issues typically take the form of Board and committee policies, charters, organizational charts, and the like.

Policies, Commitments, and Goals

This area includes the foundational documents and other materials that define the organization's position on major sustainability issues, what it aspires to achieve, and what obligations it is willing to accept. The organization's policy or policies on such issues as environmental protection, worker health and safety, climate change, and human rights are typically spelled out in writing in relatively short documents. Specific commitments and goals may be found in lists in strategic plans, management briefings, stand-alone CSR/sustainability reports, and, sometimes, on dedicated pages of the organization's web site. These often address a variety of well-defined endpoints such as regulatory compliance; reduction of resource use, waste generation, pollutant emissions, and/or injuries and incidents; resource recovery; employee diversity; staff retention; and other goals that can be easily quantified. Less often, organizations will specify these goals in business-relevant terms, such as percentage of company revenues to be generated from sales of sustainability-oriented products or services, earnings increases from EHS performance improvements, and the like. Unfortunately, many sustainability goals tend to be stated in vague terms (improve brand strength, be perceived as an industry leader) or address outputs rather than outcomes (number of employees trained rather than new capability/productivity of staff).

Systems and Practices

In this area, one would look for information describing the use of formal management systems, programs, and practices by which the organization seeks to implement its policies and achieve its defined goals. These would include management systems based on the ISO

14001 standard (see Chapter 5); programs focused on defined sustainability goals/endpoints (pollution prevention, or design for environment, for example); and investments in new practices, technologies, and approaches (such as energy efficiency or water conservation). The presence of such defined systems and practices speaks to the organization's ability to actually deliver on any commitments made regarding reducing the EHS footprint or capturing sustainability opportunities. In contrast, the absence of any defined programs or other visible structure suggests that the organization and its management are taking a passive approach to improving their sustainability posture and performance, or may not view such improvements as important. This situation is particularly troubling if the organization also has established a policy and/or commitments addressing sustainability issues. Information on systems and programs may be somewhat difficult to find in many organizations. If a company publishes a formal CSR or sustainability report, this document may detail the systems and formalized approaches that are planned or have been put in place. Otherwise, there may be some limited references to these issues on the organization's web site, but the interested party may need to invest some time to find them.

ES&G Results

The area that tends to account for most of the data and around which much scrutiny is focused is EHS and social performance results. These are data that indicate how the firm or other organization performed, both in absolute terms and relative to any improvement goals. Typical indicators include an array of traditional EHS endpoints such as waste and emissions, accidents and injuries (or rates), compliance (fines and penalties, notices of violation), and the like. Increasingly, the focus is expanding to measures of resource usage and management—particularly consumption, conservation, and recovery of energy and water and, to a lesser extent, raw materials (in some industries). Depending on the company and the businesses in which it operates, there can be a great number of relevant indicators and much data to collect, review, and analyze. Some companies provide an extensive array of such performance results on their web sites and/or in sustainability reports. However, as discussed next, such reporting is quite limited when viewed across the entire population of U.S. businesses. Regulatory compliance data can, however, be obtained for many EHS endpoints from the agencies to which these data are submitted. Indeed, certain government-maintained databases are major sources of basic data and information used by the ES&G research industry. The EPA maintains several such large databases as well as a few "gateway" web sites that can be used to navigate among them to find the information of interest.[2] Databases of particular interest include the Toxics Release Inventory (TRI), CERCLIS (Superfund sites), and the Biennial Reporting System (BRS), which contains data on sites managing hazardous wastes. Each of these databases contains information that is unique and not available elsewhere (Minami, 2008). One major caveat is that much of the data is collected and, hence, available only at the facility level. This poses a major challenge for those (including investors) interested in the behavior and performance of the organization as a whole. And obviously, information on social issues that are not subject to regulation typically is made available only by the company or other organization itself (if it's made available at all).

Corporate/Financial Results

As suggested in several other chapters, I believe the financial implications of sustainability posture and performance are critically important, both to investors and other stakeholders. Unfortunately, companies rarely develop and disclose such data, except on an anecdotal, generally project-specific basis. To the extent that such information is available, it will be provided on the firm's web site and/or in the CSR/sustainability report, or perhaps in press releases or senior management presentations in isolated cases.

Transparency

The extent to which an organization and its management are forthcoming about all the issues just outlined is, for some interested parties, an important consideration. Transparency is widely recognized as a necessary condition for markets to function properly (as discussed in Chapter 6) and is increasingly being demanded by a wide array of corporate stakeholders, including investors. ES&G researchers and investors may make certain inferences about companies based on whether and to what extent they disclose what they are doing with respect to sustainability issues, why and with what expected result, and how their actions are (or are not) yielding the expected results. Certainly, the fact that a company can describe in detail its current situation, policy and commitments, goals, plans and actions, and results to date suggests that it has at least a reasonable grasp of the scope and magnitude of its major sustainability issues. On the other hand, the absence of such information does not mean that a firm lacks this knowledge and insight, but rather that it is impossible for an outside party to know either way. Given this uncertainty, many evaluators (particularly investors) will interpret the absence of information conservatively, such that no available information is assumed to mean that no content exists (no policy, structure, or ability to generate/summarize performance results). Accordingly, lack of transparency produces increased perceived risk, and investors will assuredly factor this uncertainty into their evaluations.

Creating Knowledge and Insight from Corporate and Industry ES&G Information

It is probably immediately obvious that transforming hundreds of specific ES&G data elements into a complete and coherent picture of any company's sustainability posture, recent performance, and future prospects is a significant challenge. Even if you adopt the structure just described to render some order among all the different types of data that may be of interest, you are still a few steps short of having the means to reach the necessary clarity. Getting all the way there requires that you examine the needs and interests of the different types of people and entities that might want to achieve this clarity. I believe that each major constituency is looking for different things and therefore will approach the issue in a somewhat different fashion. I would characterize these different perspectives and needs as described in the following sections.

Internal (Corporate) Perspective

To those inside the company, the key issues include the following:

- Whether the firm's leadership has identified all the important sustainability-related issues and has complete and coherent plans for how best to address them
- How internal staff and other resources are being deployed in pursuit of risk and cost reduction and revenue enhancement opportunities
- What results are being obtained
- How the firm's standing and performance are being evaluated by important stakeholders

In this world, apart from specific compliance-driven obligations, decisions are made on the basis of return-on-investment considerations. They are heavily influenced by competing priorities and, often, fluid market and overall economic conditions. Key performance indicators tend to be relatively few in number and speak to explicit goals/commitments or business drivers.

The "Green Metrics That Matter" is an ongoing project by the National Association for Environmental Management (NAEM), the leading professional association for the corporate EHS community. This project is focused on identifying, through use of a survey, the metrics member companies use internally to track sustainability performance. The Association's corporate members (corporate EHS/sustainability vice presidents, directors, and managers) represent approximately 70 companies that could be considered sustainability leaders. The survey addressed six categories of metrics that are typically included in a corporate EHS and sustainability management structure—Resource Consumption; Resource Conservation and Recovery; Emissions and Waste Management; Health and Safety; Compliance; and EHS/Sustainability Management Practices. The following highlights from the research (NAEM, 2011, forthcoming) illustrate the previous points concerning what types of endpoints matter most to those in the executive suite.

Content/Subject Matter

The NAEM survey instrument evaluated collection and use of the following types of indicators.

- **Resource consumption, conservation, and recovery**— The vast majority of respondents track energy, electricity (apart from total energy), and water use. Interestingly, most also have established targets (presumably, use reduction) for all three and also track quantities conserved of these three major inputs relative to targets. The recent focus on these parameters may be related to general economic conditions, in that firms usually focus on cost reduction opportunities during recessions or declines in demand that occur for other reasons. In addition, a significant majority also track consumption (or percentage) of energy use provided by renewable sources, although a smaller number and percentage of firms have established targets in this regard. Conservation and/or recovery of a number of other materials also are tracked by a substantial number of responding firms. These include metals, paper, plastic, and end-of-life electronics, among others. In general, roughly half of the firms that track these endpoints also have established corresponding performance targets for them.

- **Emissions and waste management**—A majority of the 50 or so respondents' firms track TRI emissions, greenhouse gases (GHG), and solid and hazardous waste. Regulated air and water emissions, although tracked by a majority of responding firms, are monitored by fewer firms. A compelling finding is that two distinctly unregulated metrics (greenhouse gases and solid waste) have corresponding targets at a majority of responding firms.

- **Safety**—Survey respondents clearly indicated that safety remains a primary concern and most track several different endpoints. These include injuries and fatalities, lost workday injuries, and the like as well as non-regulated issues such as near-misses, unsafe exposures, and driving safety.

- **Compliance**—Most responding companies track an array of different metrics to ensure continuing regulatory compliance and monitor possible or actual legal sanctions. These include formal notices of violation (NOVs), fines and penalties, excursions beyond permit conditions, spills and other unplanned releases, remediation costs, consent orders, and lawsuits or other legal actions.

- **EHS/sustainability management practices**—Some of these practices are established and have been widely adopted, such as deployment of formal management systems, employee training, and audit programs. Others are more forward-looking and address emerging issues. It appears that most of the responding firms use many, if not most, of these indicators, which cut across a number of different topics, from internal program execution to ES&G-related investments and savings to philanthropy and community investment. For some of the more established and readily quantifiable metrics, many or even a majority of firms have established targets. This applies to management systems deployment, auditing, training, employee and supplier diversity, and philanthropy. Others, which may be in more formative stages, such as investments in sustainability products and services or alternative energy, are being monitored by many of the responding companies but less frequently companies have accompanying targets.

Primary Use of Data

The survey results seem to suggest that the dominant uses for most of the sustainability data collected by respondent companies are accountability and decision-making. The other primary uses suggested in the survey (learning, regulatory compliance, and demonstration) appear to be less widespread for most of the EHS endpoints NAEM evaluated in the survey. Interestingly, the predominant use of some of the most common compliance metrics is for accountability, as distinct from regulatory compliance per se. Also, a significant number of firms seem to use compliance performance primarily for either decision-making or learning and organizational development. So even in the case of compliance-oriented metrics, the firms in the sample are making extensive use of the information collected in a managerial sense—to operate the business effectively and efficiently.

Level of Reporting

In one of the more intriguing findings that emerged from the survey results, it is clear that many EHS/sustainability metrics (and, presumably, performance against them over time) are being reported to the highest levels of the firm. More or less across the entire array of metrics and data types examined, results are reported to the CEO/C-suite and/or Board Committee far more often than to divisional, business unit, or subsidiary senior management or simply to the leadership of the EHS/sustainability function. It is noteworthy that sustainability performance is being reported to, and presumably scrutinized by, C-level executives and/or Board members at numerous companies and in the majority of firms represented in the survey.

Public Reporting

For most of the respondents, some or all sustainability results metrics are publicly disclosed, generally directly by the company without the need for a specific data request. That is, notwithstanding the broader pattern of only limited (or nonexistent) reporting by most companies (discussed in more specific detail later in this chapter), the firms in the NAEM survey appear to have taken a leadership position in terms of the transparency of their ES&G management activities and results.

Most Important Endpoints

Respondents also were asked to list the three to five metrics that they believe are most important and likely to add value to their organizations. Four metrics were cited far more often than the others: energy, safety metrics, water, and greenhouse gases. A number of other metrics also were mentioned, most of which address "conventional" endpoints such as waste, compliance, and audit findings. An interesting note here is that the most frequently identified "high-priority" metrics are many of the same ones that seem to be most common in current use. This lack of what could be a major "disconnect" is noteworthy as well as reassuring, because it suggests that those most familiar with the management of ES&G issues "on the ground" believe that their firms generally are tracking and managing the most important things.

External Perspectives and Expectations

In contrast to internal EHS personnel, senior managers, and others involved in corporate sustainability, the perspectives, needs, and expectations of a variety of external audiences may be oriented in a completely different way, as discussed in Chapter 4. Although each individual and organization that might be considered a stakeholder is unique, it is probably accurate to say that certain groups have some common expectations for corporate sustainability measurement and evaluation.

Regulators

In the current context, the primary function of regulatory agencies is to implement, oversee, and enforce EHS and related rules. Accordingly, agency personnel are most likely to be interested in compliance posture and evidence of the management practices that will ensure an absence of noncompliant behavior. This includes permit violations, inadequate training, missing required records, failure to report excursions above defined limits, toxic substance releases, and other ongoing disclosure requirements. To a lesser extent, in some agencies, particularly at the state level, there also is strong interest in promoting beyond-compliance behavior that is believed to promote such outcomes as improved worker health and safety, lower waste generation and emissions rates, and lower costs of compliance. Accordingly, a substantial number of award, partnership, and similar programs have come into being during the past decade or so. Generally, these programs have entrance requirements, specified performance standards, or both. They offer benefits such as free technical assistance, access to information, and public recognition. This stakeholder group has

a fundamental interest in improved ES&G (primarily EHS) performance. Therefore, it has a tendency to focus on explicit performance
endpoints and on the specific management practices it believes are
needed to improve performance over time.

The General Public

In this day and age, most people in American society expect corporations and other regulated entities to conduct their activities in
accordance with the law, operate responsibly, and attempt to limit
the adverse effects of their operations on human health and the environment. Therefore, members of the public also tend to focus on
compliance, as well as on efforts to reduce the firm's environmental footprint. Interest in social issues tends to vary based on an individual's values and circumstances. For example, some people are far
more interested in labor issues than others. People tend to be quick
to assign blame to corporations for perceived environmental or heath/
safety problems and often are skeptical of the intentions of companies
that espouse "greening" or more progressive practices. Most people
do not routinely seek hard data on corporate sustainability performance. But they may tend to believe that firms that provide evidence
that they are addressing the issue are being operated more responsibly than others.

Investors and Analysts

As discussed in depth in Chapter 6, investors and their information providers tend to be somewhat agnostic about sustainability issues
except to the degree that they believe that a company's ES&G posture
and performance present either underrecognized risks or opportunities. To evaluate this question, investors and the ES&G researchers who serve them have a consistent interest in understanding the
value drivers that may affect the firm's future prospects. Accordingly,
they are interested in performance data (waste, emissions, compliance) only to the extent that it tells them something about financial
risk (such as from legal liability) and/or potential influence on future
revenues, earnings/costs, and/or business/financial factors that affect

future financial prospects. This includes any inferences that they might make about the firm's management quality based on performance relative to industry peers. Therefore, rational investors will have far more interest in endpoints such as governance practices, management systems, responses to customer demands for sustainable products, and similar issues than they do in the more commonly discussed indicators of performance. As ES&G investing becomes more commonplace and more sophisticated during the next few years, we can expect this shift in focus (and contrast with the regulatory/public perspective) to intensify.

Key Needs and Gaps

In assembling and reviewing these somewhat different perspectives and sets of needs, several conclusions emerge. One is that although the different internal and external stakeholders who have an interest in corporate sustainability have somewhat divergent interests, there is a core set of issues around which it should not be difficult to forge agreement about the most important types of endpoints and metrics. These include the following:

- **Assurance of compliant behavior.** All stakeholders have an interest in receiving assurance that a company understands all pertinent legal and regulatory requirements and has taken effective steps to ensure that it is in compliance with them. This applies just as surely to the Board of Directors as it does to a citizens' group or regulatory agency. This type of endpoint has at least two major threads. One is evidence of current compliance, such as audit results that document conformance with all stipulated controls and limits. The other is the existence of management processes, and preferably systems, that provide some assurance that as circumstances change, the firm can adapt without undue disruption that might bring about non-compliant behavior or episodes.

- **Appropriate management approaches.** Although the connections may not be apparent to some, considerable overlap exists in some of the social concerns expressed by many NGOs and the interests of long-term investors and the general public.

As discussed in Chapters 4 and 5, viewing the organization's employees and suppliers as important assets and sources of competitive advantage rather than as components of the means of production leads naturally to management practices that are more respectful, likely to achieve productivity gains, and effective in improving retention and recruiting success over the longer term. These outcomes include building important intangible assets that can be leveraged to increase the firm's value-creation potential and hence are or should be of interest to investors. The general public also has an interest in supporting these types of behaviors, because it makes firms stronger, more stable, and a better long-term source of employment, tax revenue, and support for local communities. As discussed in Chapters 6 and 7, abundant evidence exists that disciplined investments in proactive, supportive management practices routinely produce financial benefits in excess of their costs. There also is evidence that firms taking this type of approach outperform their peers in the marketplace over time.

- **Value creation orientation.** In similar fashion, it may be unclear to a member of the public or a regulator why he or she should care whether companies optimize their financial resources in addressing ES&G issues. But if you consider the economic aspect of the sustainability concept, it is clear that companies must be economically competitive to be sustainable in the long term. As discussed in Chapter 5, choosing to not carefully consider the financial costs and benefits of ES&G activities is to make *less* and/or *less rapid* progress toward a sustainable future than would be possible otherwise. Accordingly, although most company stakeholders outside the firm and the financial sector do not presently much care about the costs of sustainability activities even if they do care about the associated benefits, they should.

These core issues have important implications for how firms and their leaders might want to structure their approaches to developing and populating metrics to document ES&G posture and performance and to report their results to external parties. It seems to me that reporting performance using metrics that address one or more of the three core issues just defined is more likely to satisfy the needs and expectations of multiple stakeholder groups with one set of disclosures than would be likely otherwise. Certainly, there is at least the potential for companies to reduce both the volume of information they need to develop and report and the effectiveness and consistency of their communications efforts. The alternative is to continue the typical practice of speaking in one voice and delivering information on one facet of sustainability with investors while using another with EHS regulators and a third with host communities, interested NGOs, and the general public.

In a number of areas there is hope that most or all company stakeholders might reach agreement about key sustainability indicators, or at least the general categories of interest. But a number of important gaps remain. This is true despite the emergence in recent years of some widely used corporate sustainability reporting frameworks. Sustainability reporting is the subject of the next section.

Sustainability Reporting: Extent of Use

At present, there are no legal requirements that corporations in the U.S. disclose their ES&G (or component environmental or health and safety) policies, management practices, or performance.[3] Nevertheless, a number of current and emerging requirements for public reporting affect at least some companies and, more generally, participation in voluntary sustainability reporting initiatives is growing both in the U.S. and internationally. The principal frameworks under which such reporting is typically performed are the Global Reporting Initiative (GRI), United Nations Global Compact (UNGC), and Carbon Disclosure Project (CDP). As discussed in Chapter 6, the GRI establishes principles and indicators for broad-spectrum sustainability reporting; the UNGC addresses primarily governance, ethical, and humanitarian issues; and the CDP focuses on greenhouse gas emissions.

Over the years, I have reviewed scores, if not hundreds, of corporate environmental, EHS, and sustainability reports produced by companies. It is fair to say that the state of the art in this regard has advanced considerably during the past 15 years or so. These reports display far more depth and uniformity in their content and organization than they did years ago. As I discuss further later, this trend is both positive and important. A principal driver and, at the same time, beneficiary of this trend toward a more consistent approach to ES&G reporting is the GRI, which has used an extensive and interactive multistakeholder process to develop and refine its reporting guidelines. These guidelines are intended to meet the needs of a wide array of organizations, ranging from small NGOs to major multinational corporations. The guidelines include a substantial number of endpoints and reporting metrics, most of which are viewed as universal and of interest to a wide array of stakeholders. At this point in time, it is fair to characterize the GRI reporting format as the de facto global standard for sustainability reporting, because it is by far the most commonly used approach and has no serious rival.

With that said, the number of U.S. corporations reporting their ES&G practices and performance in a structured GRI report is somewhat limited. A much larger number report at least some information to the CDP[4] and/or the UNGC. Many companies also issue environmental, CSR, or sustainability reports that are not prepared according to the GRI guidelines. Or they publish or post on their web sites data, documents, exhibits, and other materials that address some or all aspects of their ES&G policies, practices, and performance.

In 2009, I conducted with a colleague a review of the disclosed environmental management practices of the 1,000 largest publicly traded U.S. companies (Soyka and Bateman, 2009). The findings indicated that many firms report at least some of the types of information that would likely be of interest to external stakeholders, including investors. The great majority, however, provided either no information or insufficient information to enable a stakeholder to understand whether and to what extent the company's senior management fully understands and is actively managing the firm's environmental risks and opportunities. Specific highlights of the study include the following:

- Only 60 percent of the largest publicly traded U.S. companies have an environmental, EHS, or sustainability policy.
- Most policies lack rigor and sophistication:
  - Less than 28 percent have any two of six key policy elements, and less than 9 percent have three or more of these elements.

- Only 8 percent of firms vest oversight responsibility for ES&G issues with the Board of Directors, and only one in 18 has delegated responsibility to a "C-level" (CEO, COO, or CFO) executive.

- Two-thirds of firms with policies make clear that requirements apply to all employees and operations, but only one in four includes specifics, as opposed to general principles and/or aspirations.

- Only 13 percent have published a corporate environmental, CSR, or sustainability report.

- Twenty-seven percent have disclosed their direct GHG emissions. But only about 16 percent have a corporate climate change policy, and only 60 percent of these make clear that it applies to all company operations and employees.

- Only 11 percent of firms have disclosed their annual energy costs, and about 7 percent have disclosed their total water use and/or cost.

Given that environmental management has received focused, and often high-profile, attention for many years, you might expect environmental reporting practices to be advanced among major corporations. Hence, there is little reason to believe that broader ES&G reporting practices, the major topic of this chapter, are any more extensive or informative.

We conducted a more in-depth evaluation in 2010. We found that (again) across the 1,000 largest publicly traded U.S. companies (962 with complete data), coherent environmental (and broader ES&G) management approaches appear to be absent in most companies. The study was based on application of a new environmental rating methodology, the Governance and Environmental Management Strength (GEMS) rating. It was designed to rigorously evaluate companies' ability to anticipate and actively manage the EHS issues that pose risks to and present opportunities for their operations by assessing the presence or absence of 49 distinct indicators. These indicators and their relative importance closely parallel the recommended elements of a corporate sustainability program that I outlined in Chapter 5. Scores are normalized to a 100-point scale. In addition to generating a ranking of the companies with the strongest apparent environmental governance and management strength, this study revealed the following:

- Company scores ranged from 0 to 82, with nearly half of firms (448) earning total scores of less than 10.

- Every major economic sector had strong performers. This suggests that the means to achieving excellence in environmental management practice are widely understood and spreading from the traditional industrial base to more sectors, industries, and companies. That said, at a general level these concepts remain infrequently practiced.

- Across the 12 major sectors comprising the U.S. corporate economy, the clear leaders are the firms in the consumer staples, materials, and utilities sectors. At the other end of the spectrum, the real estate, services, and telecommunications services sectors are among those in which the typical firm has the least (and often no) disclosed environmental management expertise or activity.

- Even in sectors in which most firms have little apparent environmental management sophistication, a number of noteworthy firms stand out. For example, 17 firms have GEMS Rating scores within the top quartile of all Russell 1000 firms that also are more than *twice* those of their closest industry competitor.

- On the other hand, a significant fraction (170, or 18 percent of the total) have a total score of 0. This means that they have no disclosed environmental governance; no environmental, climate change, or health and safety policies; and no management systems or significant environmental improvement programs. Also, they do not measure and report environmental results (Soyka & Bateman, 2010).

The pattern here is clear. A limited number and relatively small percentage of U.S. companies have established leadership regarding ES&G data development and reporting practices. In so doing, the senior managers within these firms have provided significant assurance that they understand their sustainability aspects and have taken appropriate actions to ensure that their respective firms are in a position to adequately control ES&G risks and capture opportunities to create value. They have demonstrated that this can be done and have blazed a trail that others can follow. Based on the available evidence, and with the caveats just stated, it seems equally clear that the great majority of U.S. companies (publicly traded and otherwise) have substantial work to do to build their ES&G capabilities and provide the information and assurance of their sustainability posture and performance that their stakeholders are increasingly demanding.

Evaluation of Current ES&G Reporting Practices, Limitations, and Trends

At this point, it is worthwhile to take stock of the current situation. As demonstrated in Chapters 6 and 7, external stakeholders, including investors and financial sector analysts, require information to make informed decisions about where to invest funds. The principal source of such information is and will continue to be the company itself. Some of the information needed must be prepared in accordance with accepted accounting practices and disclosed in conformance with SEC regulations. At present, required disclosures do not include, with certain exceptions,[5] substantive information on a firm's ES&G posture or performance. Yet, as shown in Chapter 7, ES&G issues and how they are managed can have a material effect on a firm's competitive position, financial performance, and investment prospects. Accordingly, investors and many other stakeholders have an abiding interest in corporate ES&G behavior. This interest has manifested itself in the development of recommended sustainability reporting guidelines, as well as a healthy niche industry that collects ES&G data and develops and sells company ratings, rankings, and/or indices. This latter topic is explored further later.

Indeed, notwithstanding the limited extent of corporate ES&G reporting just documented, more and more companies are compiling and reporting information on their environmental, health and safety, social, and governance posture and performance every year. Both the number of companies reporting information and the range of indicators provided have been steadily expanding in recent years. Moreover, there has been a progression from the traditional media-focused reports (data on emissions, waste) that have been with us for the past two decades. Recent disclosures increasingly embody sustainability concepts and reflect a more comprehensive and sophisticated examination of the full range of ES&G issues and their interactions, at least among the leading companies. The following sidebar gives an example of why companies are moving in this direction and what they are increasingly experiencing as a result.

So it would seem that trends are moving in the right direction and that, at first glance, all the conditions required to stimulate widespread, high-quality corporate ES&G reporting are in place. This would suggest that it is only a matter of time before such reporting is as common as financial reporting, or nearly so. A deeper examination of the facts on the ground, however, suggests otherwise. As discussed earlier, most companies, large and small, do not provide much, if any, substantive information on their ES&G policies, goals, practices, or performance. Fewer still issue GRI or other formal sustainability reports, despite the public prominence of the GRI and persistent demands for greater corporate ES&G disclosure from the SRI community and other stakeholders. These facts suggest that in the majority of cases, corporate decision-makers have yet to be convinced that sustainability reporting is in their best interests. Even if they think it is, they may be unconvinced that such reporting is worth the investment of time and resources needed to assemble and ensure the quality of the required data and, possibly, prepare an attractive and sophisticated report. Some remarks I have heard from corporate EHS professionals over the years tend to corroborate this view. The business case for widespread reporting has yet to be presented to all corporate decision-makers in a compelling way.

Some Unexpected Benefits of Sustainability Reporting

"A lot of what is happening now is being influenced by ES&G investors and researchers, who in recent years have really stepped up efforts to collect information from companies thought to have EHS impact. I'm reminded here of the Heisenberg Uncertainty Principle: the act of observing an object induces changes in that object. In this case the scrutiny from outside parties (and collection and assembly of detailed information) has prompted companies to look at how they are doing things, which leads to new behaviors and, in some cases, steps forward. Many companies are seeing that making progress in this area presents opportunities for enhancing the company brand.

"Also, reporting can often be leveraged in a way that gives a firm greater control than it would have otherwise. Taking the initiative to report can let a firm set the stage for how it plans to address sustainability and at its own pace, create and launch new actions, and present its message how it chooses.

"Broadening the envelope beyond traditional EHS concerns also brings a little bit of adventure to the work and brings new energy to the business. Adding social and economic concerns to the mix gets EHS people to look at issues in a new light, seek input from people in the organization who have usually not been involved in EHS issues, and stimulates new ideas. So, CSR/sustainability gets people to think in new ways. One implication for us, though, is that EHS needs to communicate all the time and do so effectively, so this new energy is maintained."

—Mike Pisarcik, Sara Lee Corporation

Another point of view is presented by those who collect, analyze, and report information on corporate ES&G posture and performance, generally on behalf of professional investors. These ES&G researchers are described later. Over the past ten years or so, I have had the pleasure of working with one of the more experienced and insightful people within this small industry. He offers some interesting thoughts on where we are and what will be required to advance the current state of the art. Mark Bateman is a friend and frequent colleague who is the Director of Research for ES&G research firm IW Financial. He also recently formed a new venture, Segue Point, LLC. Previously, Mark served as Director of the Environmental Information Service and as the Vice President for Research and Operations of the Investor Responsibility Research Center (IRRC). Accordingly, he has an unusually deep understanding of the challenges and opportunities involved in ES&G reporting:

"I would offer two perspectives here:

"**Investors.** The biggest hurdle is that a lot of investors need to evaluate hundreds to thousands of companies, and be able to apply the same kind of analysis to each of them. The biggest impediment in doing so is a lack of information. We lack comprehensive disclosure across sectors and even industries, so investors often have to evaluate transparency, policy, or even be left with the transparency of a firm's policies. For example, how can someone evaluate the energy use/performance of an industry or portfolio if most firms don't disclose this information? Should you penalize a company that discloses but is not a top performer relative to a peer company that doesn't disclose at all? The good news is that today, versus ten years ago, we have a good spectrum of disclosure, so the factual basis for evaluating companies is getting stronger.

"**Corporate.** Here the issue is more related to leadership and culture. When you hear stories about companies that have really taken this on and are moving in the right direction, there is almost always a major component speaking to leadership. Sometimes this is provided by top management, and sometimes from the rank and file. More than just serving as an internal champion, the most influential people had both the skills and the 'permission' to become an external voice, create a network, and bring key voices back to the company to inform decisions."

(Bateman, 2011)

My own assessment is that there are several reasons for the absence of widespread, meaningful corporate sustainability reporting. One is that in many companies, as suggested in previous chapters, only a tenuous connection has been made between EHS and other sustainability-related practices and the determinants of value for the business. Beyond anecdotal evidence of value arising from energy efficiency and other "P2" projects, most companies have relatively little in the way of quantified results that directly show financial benefits relative to costs. In even fewer cases have company leaders made the effort to systematically quantify the costs and benefits of their ES&G activities and link them to the primary value drivers that apply to their business. As I suggest in Chapter 5 and elsewhere in this book, this orientation will need to change if corporate sustainability is to take root and flourish in as many organizations as it should.

On a related note, in many cases it is not apparent how the typical ES&G metrics that are requested, or at least collected and tracked, by ES&G researchers are related to company objectives and goals. Much tighter linkages must be established in this area so that both company employees and external stakeholders understand which particular metrics are being tracked and why. Metrics of interest to ES&G researchers and analysts that may not be tracked by companies should generate more dialogue. It should be discussed why these endpoints are of interest, what they signify to the stakeholder, and why it is in the company's best interests to collect and report information on these issues.

Another possible barrier concerns incentives and their impact on behavior. As mentioned previously, it may be somewhat unclear to corporate executives what is to be gained from regular and extensive ES&G disclosure. But it may be very clear how such practices could potentially damage the firm and its interests. Because of the high profile and emotional content of certain ES&G issues, some executives may believe that the less said about these topics, the better. Given the volatility of public opinion and the generally negative attitudes toward corporate behavior within the American general public, corporate leaders may believe that greater disclosure offers relatively little upside but significant downside potential.

Two other concerns also may inhibit greater willingness to develop and share ES&G data. One is company culture. The simple fact is that some firms by their nature tend to hold information "close to the vest," and always have. For them, openly and voluntarily reporting on a wide array of practices and performance is a somewhat alien concept and may push them well out of their comfort zone. The other potential concern, which may have more impact in the future than it does now, is competition. In contrast to many other areas of business, the world of EHS management has tended to operate in a collegial and cooperative way. Many industry initiatives and organizations have worked over the past two decades to develop and share best practices, tools, and other information. This openness and willingness to share has been of great benefit to those who have participated in these (generally) industry-led efforts, and many others as well. It is important to realize, however, that all that may change with the emergence of sustainability and the likelihood that increasingly, firms will try to leverage ES&G excellence not just to control costs but to create and capture new markets and other revenue streams. If ES&G management practices can be leveraged to capture market share and new customers, we can reasonably expect that companies will safeguard their knowledge in this domain much more aggressively than they have in the past. Accordingly, in the future, companies may be far less willing to share the specifics of their sustainability-related activities, approaches, methods, results, and lessons learned.

Finally, we must confront the fact that the prevailing framework for sustainability reporting is simply not entirely suitable or adequate to meet the information needs of some stakeholders, particularly investors and their information providers. Firms can reasonably be expected to be responsive to the interests and information demands of a variety of external stakeholders, including customers, suppliers, regulatory agencies, and the general public and organizations asserting that they represent the interests of the public (NGOs). In general, these stakeholders have an interest in ES&G posture and performance information for two reasons. First, it provides some level of accountability and assurance that the company is being operated in a responsible manner, that commitments are being upheld, and that goals are being attained. The second reason is that some stakeholders seek evidence of leadership and/or competitive advantage. Generally, in addition to evidence of responsibility, these stakeholders are interested in distinguishing among companies (or sectors) so that they can identify appropriate business partners, firms worthy of recognition, and/or sources of guidance and best practices.

The dominant existing framework for ES&G reporting, the GRI, responds to these needs quite well. The current incarnation of the GRI reporting guidelines (the so-called "G3") requests narratives on how the organization addresses each of the major "legs of the stool." It also includes a substantial number of quantitative performance indicators in such areas as waste, pollutant emissions, injury and illness rates, diversity, training, respect for human and labor rights, and many others. When augmented with the appropriate "sector supplement" for particular industries,[6] the GRI can provide a comprehensive and thought-provoking framework. Through applying this framework, a company (or other organization) can examine its operations, develop a coherent picture of its current posture and recent performance, and provide information to external stakeholders in a form that is useful, well-understood, and, increasingly, expected.

With that said, the GRI has some important limitations, some of which are particularly acute in the context of information development for use by the financial sector. First, it is clear that despite the fact that the GRI has operated a remarkably open, transparent, and inclusive process in developing and revising its reporting guidelines, in the final analysis, social considerations (the S in ES&G) dominate. The general reporting guidelines contain no less than 40 Social indicators, more than the total of the Environmental (30) and Economic (9) indicators combined. Within the general domain of Social indicators are four defined subcategories: Human Rights (9), Labor (14), Product Responsibility (9), and Society (8). Of greater consequence in the current context, however, is a far bigger issue: unclear linkages between the GRI indicators and key business endpoints. In other words, there is little or no apparent relationship between the G3 indicators and the widely used financial indicators (revenues, earnings, cash flow, capital structure) described in Chapters 6 and 7. Nor is there any substantial connection to some of the key intangible assets (such as intellectual capital, brand value, and supply chain relationships) that increasingly determine competitive advantage and the potential for long-term financial value creation.

This depiction of what the GRI is and why it is insufficient may seem like an indictment of the GRI process and those involved in it. But I want to emphasize that it is not. The GRI and its supporting organizations, and many hundreds of dedicated professionals from (literally) around the world, have invested great effort and energy working to ensure that the GRI reporting guidelines were made as complete, balanced, and meaningful as they could be. Considering that they are the product of a consensus-based, multistakeholder process and hence are no one's absolute ideal, the guidelines are remarkably thorough, focused on many of the most important sustainability issues, and accessible and relevant to a wide range of organizations. The fact that the guidelines do not adequately represent the interests of a wide range of (mainstream) investors and analysts reflects a failure—not on the part of the GRI, but on the part of the mainstream financial community. The simple fact is that during the decade or so when the guidelines were being scoped, developed, and refined, representatives of large mainstream investment companies (Wall Street, large mutual fund companies) were invited (repeatedly) to participate. But they declined to do so. As a consequence, now that many of these firms are experiencing the dawning realization that ES&G issues really do matter to securities valuation, they find themselves on the outside looking in. Unfortunately, those of us who have a natural affinity for and focus on the value-creation perspective similarly find ourselves with an incomplete set of tools with which to work when evaluating disclosed corporate sustainability data prepared according to the GRI guidelines. Because the guidelines are reviewed and revised every few years, there will be future opportunities to amend them to include all (or more) of the relevant endpoints.[7] But it is not certain that all stakeholders will agree that the financial criteria of interest to investors should be included. In any case, in the interim, the G3 guidelines will continue to serve as the standard, or baseline, for corporate sustainability reporting.

The modest market penetration of the GRI, coupled with the absence of any significant interindustry competitor, is no small matter. The limited uptake of the GRI in the U.S. constrains its utility to investors and to others interested in industry-wide or sector-level best practices or norms, or in conducting comparative analysis. Compounding the issue is the perception by some that the indicators are too backward-looking, do not provide actionable information, and/or are too focused on the agenda of key interest groups (such as orga-nized labor). However, the existence and magnitude of these issues is understood within the leadership of the GRI. The new "Focal Point USA" initiative was created to bring renewed attention to promoting more extensive use of the GRI by U.S. companies. Moreover, several planned or ongoing efforts are under way to promote "integrated" ES&G reporting, both within the GRI and by other entities.

The most prominent among these is the recent formation of an International Integrated Reporting Committee (IIRC) convened by the Accounting for Sustainability project of the Prince of Wales Charities and the GRI. The IIRC also has attracted support from and participation by representatives of the accounting profession and its standards-setting bodies, as well as a small number of companies, environmental NGOs, investors, and academics.

The IIRC seeks to promote development of an integrated report-ing framework to accomplish several related needs:

- Support the information needs of long-term investors by show-ing the broad and longer-term consequences of decision-making
- Reflect the interconnections between ES&G and financial fac-tors in decisions that affect long-term performance and status, and illuminate the link between sustainability and economic value
- Provide the necessary framework for environmental and social factors to be taken into account systematically in reporting and decision-making
- Shift the focus of performance metrics away from an undue emphasis on short-term financial performance
- Bring sustainability reporting content closer to the information used by management to run the business on a day-to-day basis (The Prince's Accounting for Sustainability Project and the Global Reporting Initiative, 2010)

It is important to understand what is implied by these goals. In the minds of some people, integration means far more than elucidat-ing the cause-and-effect relationship(s) between particular EHS and social issues, and their expression as changes in revenues, earnings, cash flow, and/or risk. I recently had an opportunity to discuss the IIRC and its goals and likely direction with a member of its Steering Committee, as discussed in the following sidebar.

"Integrated" Reporting Is More Profound Than You Might Think

Alan Knight is a friend and former colleague who now operates a small consultancy, TaylorKnight, in the UK. He is a member of the IIRC's Secretariat. In that role, he is one of about 30 experts from the investing, accounting, public interest, consulting, and academic professions who currently are defining the specific goals to be pursued by the IIRC and its likely results.

In Alan's view, the key issues involve far more than finding additional ways to monetize EHS and social impacts. Instead, he (and at least a small number of fellow Secretariat members) believes that the appropriate focus is on broadening the discussion to include not only financial capital, but also other forms of capital that exist, are used, and are frequently affected by corporate activity. These include *natural capital* (living organisms, the systems that sustain them (and us), and associated ecosystem services), *social capital* (civic, educational, religious, and cultural institutions), *human capital* (intellectual, physical, and emotional capability), and *manufactured capital* (physical assets, intellectual property, relationships). If we view a company as a value-creation mechanism, the key question is how its operations affect each type of capital. This then implies that proper sustainability reporting would reflect interactions with and impacts on each (whether positive or negative). In Alan's view, these impacts need to be captured and reported, whether or not they can be monetized (Knight, 2011).

Currently it is unclear whether this view and the paradigm shift it would induce will prevail in guiding the work of the IIRC. Business executives and managers interested in corporate sustainability should understand, however, that such issues are receiving the attention of many informed, thoughtful, and talented people. Some are openly questioning whether the assertions of free-market advocates should continue to be accepted at face value and are beginning to suggest alternatives to the traditional corporation. At the least, corporate leaders should promote and, ideally, lead efforts to define, characterize, and report their organizations' interactions with the environment and society in a way that is expansive and thoughtful.

Regardless of the specific direction taken by the IIRC, if this initiative is successful, even in part, it will help resolve at least some of the major limitations of currently used sustainability reporting approaches.

At present, only a small number of companies in the U.S. and other markets are developing and issuing integrated sustainability/annual reports. Few, if any, of these reflect the sort of intimate integration of ES&G factors into core business practices and financial results that are desired by many observers (myself included). But at least these reports represent an initial step on what will doubtless be a challenging path. As these companies gain experience, and if and as the integrated reporting movement gathers strength and support from a critical mass of key participants and stakeholders, we may see a substantial, and perhaps sudden, acceleration in the practice of integrated ES&G reporting. There are some early, encouraging signs, as discussed in the following sidebar. If you're interested in corporate sustainability and/or sustainability investing, you might want to monitor developments in this area closely.

Integrated Sustainability Reporting: A Potent New Tool for Investor Relations

American Electric Power (AEP), one of the largest electric utility companies in the U.S., was an early adopter of integrated reporting. Because of its heavy reliance on coal to produce electricity, it also is one of the nation's largest GHG emitters. AEP recently issued its second integrated annual-sustainability report, which provides an interesting model for those interested in the concept. (The report is available at http://www.aepsustainability.com/reporting/.)

In a recent conversation I had with Sandy Nessing, AEP's Managing Director of Sustainability, Environment, Safety and Health, and Strategy and Design, she described how the firm's thinking on sustainability has evolved. AEP started (about five years ago) with a desire to "be green," meaning focusing mainly on environmental issues and uplifting stories. Over time, however, this focus has evolved, and the firm now views sustainability as a part of its business strategy. According to Sandy, "this transition is a process that companies go through over time. When we started with sustainability reporting, many senior people thought it would be limited to environmental. Getting it done this way results in the responsibility landing on the desk of the compliance staff, which is not usually well equipped to play this role. This approach lives on in many companies."

Having gained much useful insight as the firm and its leadership gained experience with sustainability reporting, AEP has been able to improve both the quality and depth of its reporting. It also has captured some new and important benefits, including the types of business process integration that I and many others advocate. Sandy describes this process as follows: "At AEP, it is not just me that owns the sustainability report; it's owned across the firm. A breakthrough occurred about three to four years ago, when the corporate planning group was putting together a regular update to the strategic plan. When they were doing so, they came to me and said that the sustainability report contents needed to be included, because the report spoke to important sources of business and financial risk and described how various factors affect the whole business and our financial success."

Moreover, AEP's example shows that integrated annual-sustainability reporting can garner support from unexpected but welcome sources. Sandy continues: "In our company, it is now widely understood that everything is tied together. We report twice annually to the Board on sustainability issues and their business implications. I look at our sustainability strategy not as a passive, backward-looking document, but as a strategy and road map toward our future. In fact, our Investor Relations team now brings only our Sustainability Report to investor and analyst meetings, and not our 10-K." (Nessing, 2011)

This example shows that using integrated public reporting to demonstrate how advancements in sustainability posture and performance can protect and create value is not some fanciful idea promoted by environmental NGOs or activists. Instead, it's a well-reasoned, effective, and appropriate response to growing investor (and broader stakeholder) expectations.

Recent years have witnessed new initiatives to promote more coherent and relevant corporate sustainability reporting as well as pioneering efforts by a number of leadership firms. But for the present and the near-term future, we will continue to have patchy and incomplete information on the sustainability practices and performance of U.S. firms. To fill the needs of investors and others interested in this topic, and in response to the paucity of complete and representative information, a small industry has taken shape over the past 15 years or so, as described in the next section.

ES&G Research and Analysis Firms

With the advent and growth of socially responsible investing over the past few decades, there has been a continual need for information on the ES&G posture and performance of publicly traded companies. As discussed in Chapter 6, the existing mainstream providers of business and financial data and perspective did not and do not (with certain exceptions) collect the information necessary to meet these needs. As a result, a "cottage industry" formed to develop the information needed to implement negative screens and other SRI strategies. Some of the early players in this field were start-up ventures, nonprofits, and other small entities motivated as much as by ideology as by any clear sense of how performance along one or more ES&G criteria might influence the financial success (and investment potential) of any given company. The situation today, however, is vastly different.

Although relatively few in number, ES&G research firms are increasingly of significant scale and growing sophistication and financial strength. As shown in Table 8-1, many of the most prominent research firms (and ES&G research staffs within larger investment firms) have 50 or more professional staff, and several have 100 or more. In terms of their basic business model, the predominant use of corporate ES&G data is to support investment analysis. Therefore, virtually all the major ES&G research organizations cater exclusively (or nearly so) to investors. Most of these investors are institutional, rather than retail (individual), investors.

ES&G research is international in scope. This applies to both the firms being evaluated and the location of the major ES&G research organizations. This "industry" is centered in the Northeastern U.S. and the UK, Switzerland, and Germany, roughly corresponding to the financial center of each geography. That said, ES&G research (and investing) is quite active in several other European countries, including France, the Netherlands, and the Nordic countries.

Interestingly, and as an indicator of the dynamism of the field, market entry into the ES&G research/investing space by several large, mainstream financial institutions has unfolded during the past four years or so. Several of the leading ES&G data vendors/research firms are now subsidiaries of much larger corporations. Notable events include the acquisitions of RiskMetrics by MSCI, SAM Group by Robeco, and ASSET4 by Thomson/Reuters, as well as the launch of GS SUSTAIN by Goldman Sachs.

Table 8-1 provides some general information about the size and complexity of their evaluations of corporate sustainability. ES&G research firms generally evaluate a large number of indicators, often more than 100. In contrast, particular ES&G investors (who are not developing data or products for sale to others) may focus on a smaller number, in keeping with their particular investment thesis.

Table 8-1 ES&G Research Firm Demographics

Company Name	Subsidiary of	Headquarters Location	Other Office Locations	Number of Indicators Evaluated	Staff Size
RiskMetrics/ Innovest	MSCI	New York	20 others in North America, Europe, Asia, Australia	120+	1,000+
ASSET4	Thomson-Reuters	New York		250+	~ 240
Sustainable Asset Management (SAM) Group	Robeco	Zurich	Sydney New York	~ 110	~ 100

Company Name	Subsidiary of	Headquarters Location	Other Office Locations	Number of Indicators Evaluated	Staff Size
Jantzi-Sustain-alytics		Toronto	Boston Amsterdam Frankfurt Madrid	60 to 120, depending on industry	~ 60
KLD Research & Analytics	Risk/met-rics/MSCI	Boston	London	280+	~ 50
Ethical Investment Research Services (EIRIS)	(Not-for-profit)	London	Paris Boston	100+	~ 50
Oekom Research		Munich		~ 90	34
Trucost		London	Boston New York Rio de Janeiro		~ 30
Trillium Asset Management		Boston	Durham, NC San Francisco		~ 25
IW Financial		Portland, ME		125+	< 15
CRD Analytics		New York		~ 50	< 10
Maplecroft		London			< 10
Bloomberg		New York	100+ world-wide	~ 110	~ 5

ES&G researchers examine entire markets and multiple geographies and collect their information using different combinations of a limited set of methods. According to their web sites and publicly available documents, most major ES&G researchers routinely or continuously evaluate 3,000 to 5,000 companies and may provide more limited coverage of as many as 7,000. Virtually all publicly traded mid-cap to large-cap firms in the U.S. and Europe typically are included, as are some firms in Japan and Australasia. Coverage of companies in emerging markets is far more limited. To build baseline information on companies, most ES&G researchers (as well as ES&G investors that develop their own data) collect company data from company web sites, regulatory agency filings, and other sources of information publicly disclosed by the company. Some limit their data gathering to this step (such as IW Financial). Most, however, supplement this information with accounts presented in the news media, input from labor unions and/or NGOs, trade or industry associations, and/ or think tanks. Many also seek direct interaction with the companies in question. This may occur through administration of a survey or questionnaire (SAM Group, EIRIS) or take the form of an interview or structured dialogue (RiskMetrics, KLD, Oekom Research, Maplecroft). In addition, many firms solicit feedback on the accuracy and completeness of their preliminary research findings from the firms involved prior to the release of data and/or analytical results. Finally, a few ES&G research and/or investment firms make use of data, rankings, or ratings produced by others in the ES&G information space.

With a few exceptions, the range of issues of interest to these entities includes multiple ES&G endpoints, although the specific emphasis on and indicators used to evaluate each may vary. As discussed in Chapter 2, "ESG" has taken hold as the common terminology used by both investors and the organizations that provide information and analysis to them. This term also has been adopted by the multilateral organizations and initiatives described earlier that promote more extensive and consistent corporate disclosure, including the GRI, CDP, Investor Network on Climate Risk[8] (INCR), and United Nations (in the context of UNGC and PRI). In contrast, a few evaluators and investors have chosen to address a more limited set of issues:

- Goldman Sachs GS SUSTAIN is limited to environmental and financial criteria.
- The Trucost methodology considers only environmental emissions and related criteria, which it evaluates using an economic input-output model.

- Maplecroft has developed an evaluation method and index for one set of environmental endpoints—climate change management.

As described in Chapter 6 and in keeping with broader overall trends, the focus of ES&G evaluation has shifted during the past ten years or so away from the negative screens originally developed for traditional SRI investing practices and toward a distinct value-creation orientation. Although a few of the more established, traditional SRI firms still apply negative screens, these tend to not be absolute. Examples of ES&G research providers that still use negative screens include Jantzi-Sustainalytics and EIRIS; among ES&G investors, Calvert and Trillium do as well. Others will apply them at the request of a particular customer.

This latter point reflects a larger trend among ES&G research providers: They increasingly offer partially or entirely customized approaches to defining important ES&G criteria, establishing weighting schemes, and selecting specific asset groups. In other words, the ES&G research community is increasingly allowing its customers to make their own decisions about which ES&G factors are important (and how important) while still providing, in many cases, an evaluation/investment philosophy and recommended approach. Some have taken this approach, along with advances in information technology, to its logical conclusion by establishing subscription-based ES&G data web portals for their customers. Often, these portals allow investment portfolio screening and/or assembly, monitoring for compliance with expectations, and many other functions using the ES&G data they contain. As an added feature and to increase utility and foster ES&G integration, many also offer company financial and operating data. ES&G research firms that offer ES&G data web portals include KLD, Jantzi-Sustainalytics, EIRIS, IW Financial, and Oekom Research. Table 8-2 summarizes the major activities of and products and services offered by most of the major ES&G research/investing firms active in the U.S.

Table 8-2 Major ES&G Research Firms

Category	Company Name	Principal ES&G-Related Activities				Principal ES&G-Related Outputs			
		Data Collection	ES&G Strength/ Performance Analysis	ES&G Investment Analysis	Consulting, Proxy, and/or Advisory Services	Data Portal	Ratings	Rankings	Indexes
Companies that primarily solicit/collect and analyze EHS data and deliver data sets and/or products to investors	Bloomberg	✓				✓			✓
	CRD Analytics	✓	✓		✓		✓	✓	✓
	EIRIS	✓	✓		✓		✓		✓
	IW Financial	✓	✓		✓	✓	Custom		Custom
	Jantzi-Sustainalytics	✓	✓		✓	✓	✓	Custom	✓
	Maplecroft	✓	✓		✓	✓	✓		✓
	MSCI/ISS	✓			✓	✓	✓		
	MSCI/RiskMetrics/Innovest	✓	✓		✓		✓		
	Thomson-Reuters/ASSET4	✓	✓		✓	✓	✓		✓
	Trucost Plc	✓	✓		✓		✓	✓	

Table 8-2 continued

Category	Company Name	Principal ES&G-Related Activities				Principal ES&G-Related Outputs			
		Data Collection	ES&G Strength/ Performance Analysis	ES&G Investment Analysis	Consulting, Proxy, and/or Advisory Services	Data Portal	Ratings	Rankings	Indexes
Companies that solicit/ collect and analyze EHS data, deliver data sets, and manage investments	MSCI/KLD Research & Analytics	✓	✓	✓	✓	✓	✓	✓	✓
	Oekom Research AG	✓		✓	✓	✓	✓		Custom
	SAM Group	✓	✓	✓	✓	✓	✓		✓

As opposed to the "in or out" evaluation method commonly used by SRI practitioners in the past, most ES&G researchers now use a more nuanced ES&G assessment of firms. It tends to be on a relative rather than absolute scale, and it also may be applied at the industry/ sector level. The goal of these evaluations is to identify the best-in-class companies within each group of interest. Also, reflecting the typical or most common use of third-party corporate ES&G ratings, many of the entities producing these ratings have adopted a scoring/ rating scale that resembles that of another commonly used corporate evaluation metric: the bond rating. Using this approach, a particular company's stock (or fixed income) securities might receive a rating ranging from D– to A+ (or CCC to AAA). Firms using this type of approach include RiskMetrics, KLD, ASSET4, and Oekom Research.

Finally, and perhaps most importantly, a few firms have developed and applied a coherent theory of how ES&G improvements (or the lack thereof) affect a given company's liabilities, costs, revenue-generation opportunities, cash flows, and/or other operational or financial endpoints.

ES&G research firms have moved aggressively in recent years to raise their profile and that of their methods and products. Several ES&G research firms have established alliances with major stock exchanges and related entities to form new stock indexes, exchange traded funds (ETFs), and other products of interest to institutional and retail investors. Table 8-3 shows some examples. Among the more prominent are the Dow Jones Sustainability Index (DJSI) series developed by a venture between Dow Jones and the SAM Group.[9]

It has expanded rapidly and now consists of 46 distinct indices with coverage of companies in global (15), European (16), North American (6), Asian (6), and country-specific (3) markets. Similarly, EIRIS teamed with the *Financial Times* and the London Stock Exchange to form FTSE, which is now a separate company, and to develop and publish the FTSE4Good index, which is populated using EIRIS data and analysis. Most recently, CRD Analytics teamed with NAS-DAQ OMX to produce the CRD Global Sustainability 50 Index, and Bloomberg has developed a set of screens and ratings based on the GRI reporting criteria. As shown in Table 8-3, ES&G researchers also have collaborated with specialty and mainstream media to publicize the results of newly developed and preexisting rankings/ratings of corporate citizenship, "green" characteristics, and/or sustainability:

- *Newsweek* has enlisted the assistance of KLD and Trucost, as well as corporateregister.com, to prepare a ranking of the top 500 "green" U.S. firms.

- *Corporate Responsibility* magazine has published a CR Top 100 list assembled by IW Financial using a tailored scoring methodology for this purpose.

- For the past few years, Canadian CSR-focused media company Corporate Knights has published its Corporate Knights Global Top 100, which is based on assistance and data provided by ASSET4 and Bloomberg.

These developments have brought substantially more scrutiny from a larger set of actors to corporate ES&G behavior. This has created increasing pressure for companies to secure or maintain a place on and, ideally, at or near the top of these lists.

Table 8-3 Examples of Major External Uses of ES&G Ratings

Company Name	Use of Outputs
Bloomberg	Data displayed on Bloomberg terminals
Carbon Disclosure Project	Markit Carbon Disclosure Leadership index
CRD Analytics	NASDAQ OMX CRD Global Sustainability 50 Index
EIRIS	FTSE4Good Index
IW Financial	CRO Best Corporate Citizens
Jantzi-Sustainalytics	iShares CDN Jantzi Social Index Fund (XEN)
Maplecroft	Bloomberg-Climate Innovation Index
MSCI/KLD	*Newsweek* Green 500 Rankings
Oekom Research AG	Global Challenges Index
SAM Group	DJSI World; DJSI STOXX; 46 sustainability indexes
Thomson-Reuters/ASSET4	Corporate Knights Global Top 100
Trucost Plc	*Newsweek* Green 500 Rankings

Over the past 15 years or so, this formerly small and fragmented ES&G data and research provider community has evolved considerably. It now has the financial backing and wherewithal to provide more-or-less continuous coverage of virtually any publicly traded company that is within the reach of U.S. investors. The ES&G research community has become more flexible in terms of its philosophy and approach. It continues to adapt to client demands for greater access to underlying data, useful tools, and Internet-based access. All these developments make the ES&G data and products generated by these companies more accessible and useful to the investor. They also suggest that this industry may be moving toward more of a commodity orientation. This would mean that increasingly, companies will compete on price, further stimulating greater access to corporate ES&G data.

To conclude this discussion, and to put the ES&G research industry and its evolution into appropriate perspective, Table 8-4 summarizes its major characteristics and how they have changed over the past 20 years or so. As shown in this table, the remaining players in this field comprise an increasingly influential, well-capitalized, and aggressive community that can no longer safely be ignored by corporate senior managers. With the market entry of major multinational financial and media companies in recent years, the ongoing acquisition and/or restructuring of many of the smaller players, and an ever-increasing diversity and flexibility of offerings, ES&G researchers represent a powerful but underrecognized conduit. Using this emerging channel, a sophisticated approach to corporate sustainability management can garner additional favorable attention, improved image with the public and activist NGOs (among others), and enhanced investor support. At a minimum, sustainability professionals working both inside and on behalf of companies should be aware of what these entities are, what they do (and, to some extent, how they do it), and how their principal products and services are used.

Table 8-4 Evolution of the U.S. SRI/ES&G Research Community

Activity/Practice	Then (1970s–1990s)	Now	Current Examples
Organizations Involved			
Market structure	Cottage industry	Niche supplier to investors	
Typical type/size	NGO, small SRI firm/ supplier	Division/ subsidiary of multinational corporation	MSCI (ISS, RiskMetrics, KLD), Thomson-Reuters (ASSET4), Robeco (SAM Group)
Data Collection			
Scope of data review	U.S. only: S&P 500	Global: 3,000 to 5,000+	
Variables collected	Dozens	Hundreds	
Indicators reported	Dozens	60 to ~300	
Data Analysis and Reporting			
Analysis results	Grade/"in or out"	Bond-style rating	ASSET4, MSCI/Risk-Metrics, MSCI/KLD, Oekom Research
Availability of data	Spreadsheets	Interactive data portals	EIRIS, IW Financial, Jantzi-Sustainalytics, MSCI/KLD, Oekom Research
Use of Results			
Investment screening	Exclusionary, rigid	Risk/ opportunity-based, flexible	

Table 8-4 continued

Activity/Practice	Then (1970s–1990s)	Now	Current Examples
Investment thesis	Ethical	Growth, new businesses	CRD Analytics, Goldman Sachs GS Sustain, Hendersons, SAM Group, Trillium
		Risk management	Bank Sarasin, Calvert, MSCI/RiskMetrics, KLD, Maplecroft, PAX World, Trucost
		Efficiency/ROIC	Goldman Sachs GS Sustain, SAM Group
Publication in media	SRI, "green" press	Mainstream media	*Newsweek* Green 500

Potential Improvements

Given the foregoing discussion, we can observe that it would be desirable to have general agreement about a set of key performance indicators (KPIs) that would be useful to both corporate decision-makers and key external stakeholders, particularly financial sector actors, regulators, and policymakers. Establishing this defined set of KPIs would simplify and make far more consistent the practice of developing and reporting important ES&G information. It also would enable more consistent and productive approaches to disclosure regulation, investment analysis, and voluntary public policy initiatives related to environmental quality, health and safety, and social issues. The following discussion provides some thoughts on what needs to be done and how we can most quickly and effectively move from the status quo to the desired state.

Expand the Paradigm

As discussed in the previous sections, most current sustainability reporting practices do not address some of the fundamental needs of either businesspeople or financial sector stakeholders. To correct this deficiency, we need a broader, yet more focused, consideration of stakeholder needs. At this point, I would venture to say that most of the information needs of civil society and the representatives of certain portions thereof (environmental NGOs, labor unions) have been adequately expressed and vetted and are now embedded within the widely accepted sustainability reporting methods now in use. What is needed is more extensive and explicit consideration of companies' long-term organizational and financial sustainability. Although this topic is of direct and immediate interest to investors and the analysts who serve them, I submit that we all have an interest in promoting vibrant and sustainable companies. They are the principal mechanism through which new wealth creation and innovation occur in our society. We can hope that the work of the recently formed IIRC and its members, the experience of leadership companies, and perhaps a future new and improved "G4" version of the GRI will lead to significant advances in this area. Such advances are vital if ES&G reporting is to become more meaningful, useful, and widespread.

Stimulate and Maintain a Dialogue

To make progress in improving the quality and utility of sustainability reporting, it will be necessary to get more of the different parties who have a direct interest to talk with one another more frequently. As discussed in Chapter 6, the existing level of dialogue between senior corporate executives, or even EHS professionals, with investors and other financial stakeholders is quite limited and, on the whole, not very productive. The plain truth is that the corporate and investment people live in different worlds and, to a major extent, speak different languages. If we are to make significant headway, it will be important for EHS people and others in the corporation involved in sustainability issues to better understand the perspectives and information needs of investors. And investors must become much better acquainted with how ES&G issues are managed in large organizations, how they influence business and financial success, and what indicators are most meaningful from the standpoint of predicting investment risk and future returns. The best way to bring this about is through "cross-pollination." This means putting groups of people representing both camps in the same room to discuss their respective needs and begin building common understanding, such as through roundtables or structured dialogues. I have been fortunate enough to have participated in various roles in a few such meetings,[10] and I can testify to their effectiveness in getting even seasoned professionals to view issues within their domain of expertise in a new light. Many more examples of this type of interaction will be needed, however, to really move the needle.

Consolidate and Improve Metrics

At present, and as highlighted earlier, there is a significant disparity in the types and number of EHS and other sustainability metrics that companies collect and use to manage their businesses and those collected and used by ES&G research firms and some investors. Reporting these metrics to outside parties can consume significant staff time (as much as several full-time employees) and other resources. Collecting and managing the information needed to populate hundreds of metrics for thousands of companies imposes significant costs on ES&G researchers (and their investor clients) and also consumes substantial calendar time. This means that when data are released, in many cases they are not as timely as they might be otherwise. As suggested previously, it would be beneficial to most or all of the participants in this measurement, reporting, and use process if fewer metrics were in use and if internal senior managers and external stakeholders (including investors) were tracking and using the same measures of progress and success. As greater scrutiny is focused on identifying the sources of business and financial value accruing to companies that improve their ES&G practices, the key determinants of success should become more clear. Moreover, as investors develop and test their ideas about which metrics truly indicate sustainable business success, the workings of competitive market forces should produce clarity about which ideas are correct (or more correct). Such outcomes will stimulate movement toward a smaller and more manageable set of key performance metrics. With that said, it would be beneficial for those involved to focus on the gaps between the corporate and investor perspectives. They should keep an eye toward promoting understanding of the information needs of both sides and, potentially, identifying key issues that are of clear interest to both.

Report at the Corporate Level

The published environmental, EHS, and sustainability literature and the emerging green media are replete with anecdotal examples of ES&G initiatives and the environmental, health and safety, cost savings, brand value, revenue creation, and other benefits they have created. Unfortunately, and as discussed in Chapters 6 and 7, many if not most of these examples are limited in scope to a particular product, issue, location, or business line. They do not express the financial implications of the initiative in terms that are meaningful to the investor. Similarly, if you consider EHS performance data reported to regulatory agencies, it is nearly always submitted at a facility (or even production unit) level, because that is how most of the regulations requiring periodic reporting have been implemented. Although this focus is needed to demonstrate business feasibility and/or compliance, it is of limited relevance to investors, who are in the business of making investment decisions at a company level. The GRI and other ES&G reporting initiatives have helped stimulate the release of more data using the global/corporate-level perspective that investors need. But senior management within many companies, and the EHS and other personnel working under their direction, should put renewed focus on ensuring that they express (or re-express) their results in terms that can be fed into a company-wide assessment of wealth creation or its potential. As shown in this and the preceding chapters, information in this form already has existing consumers inside and outside the organization. Interest in obtaining results at this higher level of aggregation is likely to grow significantly in the coming years.

Apply Life-Cycle Approaches and Perspectives

With the emergence of substantial new multistakeholder initiatives focused on the ssustainability of product and company supply chains, it is becoming increasingly important for companies to understand the full life-cycle aspects of their products and services. The idea that a company is accountable only for what happens inside its four walls is encountering increasing skepticism. The danger (to brand, relationships, and company financial assets) of substandard ES&G performance in the supply chain of the products and services that a firm procures is becoming more apparent. Viewed in the other direction, it also is clear that buyers of products and services, including consumers, are becoming more sophisticated. They understand that the bulk of the significant EHS and other sustainability aspects of some types of products arise not in manufacturing, but in use following purchase and/or at end of life. Accordingly, more companies and industry sectors are working to understand the life-cycle aspects of what they buy, produce, and sell, either in isolation or as part of several consortia that have formed in recent years.[11] People working in or for companies on sustainability issues should be aware of and, as feasible, seek to integrate such life-cycle-based concepts and approaches into their ongoing work. This includes building life-cycle perspectives into defining ES&G performance metrics, measurement and data collection methods, data aggregation and analysis, and reporting.

Generate Fewer Anecdotes and More Hard Data

People love and are drawn to good stories. Indeed, the absence of context and a description of how a particular topic touches a person or group can make it difficult to effectively communicate a complex idea or concept, particularly if it is unfamiliar to the reader or listener. Storytelling permeates the news media and animates many fields of human activity, including investing (every new investing "idea" has a compelling story around it). Storytelling is an essential part of how humans receive and process information. Unfortunately, we have seen a distinct overreliance on stories, including short stories, or anecdotes, in the ES&G dialogue. I cannot count how many times I have read or heard an EHS person say that what he or she does "creates value," although with little elaboration and virtually no quantification. As I have suggested in this and previous chapters, we need to do better. Those working in the ES&G/sustainability arena shouldn't eliminate the stories they tell. But they do need to punctuate them with facts and show how the examples and anecdotes they have developed relate to the larger organizations of which they are a part. They also should explain in the appropriate terms how advances in ES&G posture and performance have resulted in financial value creation, or will do so in the future.

Establish Relevance of ES&G Activities to Business and Financial Endpoints

In a related vein, people working on any of a variety of sustainability-related activities should make every attempt to move beyond the vague and, to some, unconvincing assertions of ES&G value creation, and get more specific. This may require some effort and the active involvement of others across functions and disciplines within the company, but it is vitally important. As suggested in Chapter 5, taking this approach in crafting (or refining) the sustainability strategy, management practices and systems, and programs can yield big dividends in getting everyone to focus on the most important things while not overinvesting in activities or endpoints that are relatively unimportant. One ancillary benefit of taking such an approach is that people in the different involved business functions will develop a shared basis of understanding of whether and under what conditions ES&G issues and effective practices for managing them pose threats or opportunities or result in discernible impacts on value.

Promote "Real" ES&G/Financial Reporting Integration

As discussed earlier, at least one new and potentially significant initiative is taking shape to promote the concept of integrated sustainability and financial corporate reporting. This initiative seeks to realize the promise of an integrated approach to evaluating the organizations' interaction with the environment, stakeholders, and society at large. This has been a long-standing goal of the GRI. Integrated reporting also ties directly into the objectives and elements of the PRI. If it is successful, it will stimulate preparation and delivery of company-level management and performance information that investors could use more or less directly. While the IIRC works to develop the methods and conventions that could be used to define and carry out integrated reporting, those working on sustainability issues can and should promote thinking about how their firms or clients can use this concept to their advantage. Truly integrated thinking can illuminate new business opportunities as well as potential risks and liabilities. In any case, it should help firms identify and focus on the most important issues. At the least, sustainability professionals should remain abreast of developments in this area during the next few years.

The next and final chapter returns to and expands on this idea. It is set in the context of a broader discussion of creating sustainable value for the enterprise and what this means to those who are involved in (or who want to become involved in) the EHS/sustainability profession.

Endnotes

1. This discussion is loosely based on concepts presented in the Data-Information-Knowledge-Wisdom (DIKW) model, or pyramid, that has been developed and used in the information science field.

2. These sites include the EnviroFacts data warehouse and the recently deployed Facility Registration System (FRS).

3. A few exceptions to this general rule exist, as discussed in Chapter 6. These include the recent SEC guidance clarifying that it expects companies to carefully evaluate the climate change issue and how it might affect their operations.

4. Note that CDP reporting takes the form of responding to a questionnaire. As discussed earlier, response rates are high, particularly among larger corporations. That said, the completeness and quality of the responses vary widely, with many companies providing little if any meaningful information.

5. As discussed in Chapter 6, these include contaminated site liabilities and vulnerabilities to climate change and possible greenhouse gas emission limitations.

6. When this book was written, the GRI had published five supplements (electric utilities, financial services, food processing, mining and metals, and NGO). Five others had been tested, and five more were under development.

7. When this book was written, the GRI had announced the launch of a development effort to produce the G4 version of the guidelines, tentatively scheduled for public release in May 2013. A "call for sustainability topics" for possible inclusion in the G4 closed at the end of June 2011.

8. INCR is a program of the NGO Ceres.

9. In its original incarnation, the venture included a third partner (STOXX), which is no longer involved in the DJSI.

10. One example is a major meeting cosponsored by the U.S. EPA and the New York Society of Security Analysts held in New York City in June 2008. Another example is a workshop hosted by the National Association for Environmental Management (NAEM) in Fort Lauderdale, Florida in May 2011. It involved NAEM members and representatives of a number of ES&G research and investment firms and sustainability reporting initiatives.

11. As discussed in Chapters 3 and 4, Walmart's Supplier Sustainability Assessment is a noteworthy example (see http://walmartstores.com/Sustainability/9292.aspx).

9

Making It Happen in Your Organization

As shown in the previous chapters, the challenges involved in understanding and effectively managing the risks and opportunities inherent in pursuing corporate sustainability are numerous, complex, and interrelated. Many actors, both within and beyond the organization, play roles in and have different levels of influence on the firm, the nature and prominence of its major ES&G issues, and its ability to chart and maintain an optimal course toward long-term sustainability. Moreover, the types of issues that are becoming increasingly prominent in the minds of more organizational (and societal) stakeholders may be difficult to manage using conventional approaches, organizational structures, and behaviors. This chapter synthesizes some of the key ideas presented in this book. It outlines a thought process and approach that recognizes and addresses the important obstacles that limit progress toward a more sustainable business model in many companies. This chapter also provides key touch points for business executives and managers to refer to as they consider how best to address the crucial ES&G issues facing their own organizations. I then summarize some of the key skills and behavioral attributes that I believe will be important for those who work on sustainability issues within companies or who may seek to do so in the future. This discussion is predicated upon my belief that effective management of ES&G issues in the future will require a far more interdisciplinary and strategic approach than has generally been applied up to this point. The chapter, and this book, concludes with a few final thoughts.

Creating Sustainable Value for the Enterprise

With the growing interest and involvement of financial sector actors in the management of corporate ES&G issues, it is imperative that any company-wide initiative or program to pursue sustainability have a fundamental orientation toward creating value. It is legitimate and admirable for companies to participate in philanthropic endeavors, adopt a policy of corporate social responsibility, and undertake efforts to limit any adverse impacts of their activities on public goods and limited natural resources. But unless and until there is a fundamental redrawing of the role of the corporation in American society, it is important that business executives and managers approach sustainability issues with a consistent focus. They must concentrate on the determinants of financial value—revenue growth, earnings growth, and risk control/reduction. They must find ways to limit adverse environmental, health and safety, or social impacts and offer products and services that are more environmentally and socially benign than existing alternatives. And they must do so while also increasing efficiency and reducing costs, risks, and liabilities. This strategy is the most promising path toward long-term growth in revenues and shareholder wealth, greater stability, and organizational sustainability.

This chapter offers a generalized approach by which this can be done in virtually any company. Many of the specific activities listed here were described in Chapter 5. They are summarized here to show you how more fully considering market forces and actors and the financial implications of ES&G issues (as explored in Chapters 6, 7, and 8) suggests an alternative approach to organizational sustainability—one that is materially different from that employed in many companies to this point.

Create (or Improve) a Financial Value Orientation

As stated in several places in this book, it is logical, effective, and efficient to start with a value-creation orientation when defining a sustainability program or initiative. This makes much more sense than applying financial considerations as a final screen or hurdle to be cleared when evaluating specific ES&G-oriented projects or programs. The place to begin is with the firm's organizational mission, vision, major objectives, and strategy. Presumably, these are established and well understood by the executives and managers leading any such effort.[1] If they are not present, or are but do not appear to provide an adequate basis for establishing a sustainability program, the early work on the latter provides an excellent opportunity to reexamine and, as appropriate, retool the firm's defined mission, plans, and strategy, and/or clarify or refine its organizational values. In conjunction with reviewing these fundamental aspects of what the firm is about and what it seeks to accomplish, those leading any sustainability effort should consider the major financial goals that have been established by senior management. They should begin thinking, in general terms, about how various aspects of the sustainability program or initiative can support or advance attainment of these goals.

Once the key organizational objectives, plans, and financial goals have been assembled, three substantial fact-finding and analysis steps should be carried out. The first is to conduct a business position assessment that considers current economic conditions and the stage of the overall business cycle; the nature, risk profile, and prospects of the company's industry;[2] and the firm's recent performance and visible opportunities and threats. The second step is to map the firm's major business activities (both current and planned) to all relevant major ES&G endpoints. Conceptually, this process can work much like the environmental aspects analysis described in Chapter 5. The exception is that it considers both the organization's ongoing activities, products, and services and prospective new ones. In the current context, however, it is especially important that in evaluating the significance of each ES&G aspect, stakeholder and financial criteria should be explicitly included, even if only indirectly or partially. This assessment should focus on the metrics that really count (such as those directly related to company strategic goals, sources of competitive advantage, or investor concerns), rather than standard financial statement items or commonly used ratios. The final major step is to assemble the firm's relevant ES&G, operating, and financial data. This information should be organized by key financial endpoints— revenue growth, profitability, and risk management, and/or the intangible assets that are most important within the firm's industry. To the extent possible, the team should attempt to quantify and tabulate data on resources (including, man-hours and funds) invested in existing EHS or sustainability programs. The team also should outline both existing and potential linkages between these programs and core business management processes.

With the foregoing information developed and assembled in this way, the involved executives and managers can then evaluate and compare the quantified benefits of their existing activities to their associated costs. They also can better understand how these activities contribute to building the firm's intangible assets and the capabilities and attributes needed to execute its value-creation strategy, thus providing a portion of the foundation that will generate future revenues. In addition, the data will enable the team to identify and rank high-payoff ES&G-focused activities and distinguish them from others that are costly and/or that provide limited or no appreciable financial benefits. The resulting information can then be used to identify and address gaps in current metrics and/or measurement practices and make appropriate adjustments in priorities, approaches, staffing, and funding.

The final activity is to develop capture plans for and compile a portfolio of the most promising opportunities.[3] This involves defining value-creation objectives and, for each, a range of target values to be attained over time. For each opportunity, the team should develop a management program that defines methods, processes, responsibilities, required resources (money and staff), time frames, and performance measures. The management program also should address the risks and required analysis/documentation, if any, that would accompany a process change associated with pursuing the opportunity. The resulting set of capture plans can then be assembled into a portfolio of high-priority opportunities that would be presented to the relevant company senior management for consideration.

This approach to pursuing organizational sustainability offers several advantages over the more commonly used tactical, issue-driven alternative. First, it allows the team and the company to identify, manage, improve, measure, and report what really matters. They don't have to expend valuable resources on issues to which the firm can contribute relatively little and/or that offer no opportunity to create new financial value. Another advantage is that this approach allows the firm to develop and articulate a compelling value proposition to all stakeholders, including investors and other financial community entities that, as discussed in previous chapters, are increasingly engaged with ES&G issues. By taking this approach, companies also can surface, articulate, and discuss any policy/legal risks and stakeholder concerns in advance, rather than reacting to (perhaps unanticipated) developments after they occur. On a related note, by using this approach, the firm attains and maintains greater control over its messaging, image, and brand strength while offering greater transparency and credibility.[4] By proactively addressing important (and only important) ES&G issues and stakeholder concerns, improving clarity and transparency, and focusing explicitly and skillfully on creating stable but continually growing financial value, companies can achieve durable competitive advantage.

Secure and Maintain Senior Management Commitment and Ongoing Involvement

The issues involved in actively pursuing sustainability are important, will affect many different people housed within different functions, and are likely to change any number of existing beliefs and work practices. Therefore, it is vital for any substantive initiative or program devoted to sustainability to include tangible senior management commitment and visible involvement. As discussed in previous chapters, there are simply too many human foibles and entrenched behavior patterns to overcome, and too much opportunity for the effort to be sidetracked, marginalized, or "captured" by one internal group, to the detriment of the firm as a whole, for any other senior management posture to be either effective or sensible.

Forge Constructive Relationships with Important External Stakeholders

It should be clear by now that company stakeholders are growing more numerous, more interested and engaged, and more assertive regarding ES&G issues. It also should be apparent that many, if not most, of the concerns being raised by the more important corporate stakeholders are legitimate and worthy of consideration. Executives contemplating beginning or building on existing sustainability program efforts should ensure the following:

- An explicit effort to identify the firm's important stakeholders is conducted (or updated)
- A process exists for determining which stakeholders (or types) are considered significant and appropriate for engagement
- Stakeholder relationships are established (or improved upon), with a clear understanding of the roles and expectations of all parties
- These relationships receive the attention and resources they need to produce the desired outcomes

Forewarned is forearmed!

Define an ES&G Mission, Vision, and Explicit Linkages to the Overall Corporate Strategy

Regardless of whether a particular organization and its leadership choose to undertake the activities just described (adopting a value-creation orientation), it is important to explicitly define a few points. You must spell out what is to be accomplished through any sustainability program or initiative, what the desired end state would represent, and how ES&G performance-improvement activities are related to the major elements of the overall company strategy to maintain and grow its business. Absent such linkages, it may be difficult or impossible to attract or maintain support within senior management and across the organization. It also will become more likely that priorities and decisions will be made on the basis of personal preference, past practice, or other factors not directly related to creating new financial value.

Formulate ES&G/Sustainability Objectives

Any rational program or initiative has one or more objectives that represent a desired outcome. Outcomes may be defined only in general terms, be difficult to attain, and require a number of years to reach. Nonetheless, such longer-term objectives must be defined and receive at least the endorsement of company senior management. Otherwise, it may be difficult for the sustainability program or initiative to achieve more than incremental improvements over the status quo, demonstrate to internal and external stakeholders that it has a purpose and is worthy of support, and attract the participation and enthusiasm of people across the organization needed for it to succeed.

Strengthen Organization-Wide Policies, Goals, and Performance Metrics

To attain program objectives, the firm needs to establish (or enhance existing) policies regarding environmental protection, worker health and safety, human and labor rights, other social issues, and governance. Alternatively, it could consolidate its position and aspirations regarding these topics into either a smaller number of combinations or a single sustainability policy. As discussed earlier in this book, coherent policies that apply to all parts of the firm provide an essential point of reference both for any sustainability team and for all other members of the organization. Specific goals are required to render long-term objectives workable, tangible, and immediate. A ten-year objective without accompanying shorter-term goals (such as for this year) invites delay and may signal (correctly or incorrectly) the absence of a serious commitment on the part of senior management. Finally, the bookend to defining program objectives (and more specific goals) is a set of performance metrics that are populated and reported up the management chain at regular intervals. Metrics provide a feedback mechanism that is essential to ensuring that the effort is on course or, alternatively, that corrective measures are required.

Deploy Necessary Infrastructure

Actively pursuing sustainability goals, which generally requires at least some organizational change, does not happen by itself or solely with the hard work and good intentions of their proponents. The firm must have management and information systems, work practices, incentives, training, and other infrastructure elements with which to help define and impel sustainability-oriented behaviors and achieve ES&G performance improvement. Many companies, particularly larger ones, may have an existing array of EMSs, EHS management tools, procedures and processes, training materials, and other assets that can be drawn upon to establish the required sustainability program infrastructure. These existing assets may require expansion, updating, or even extensive retooling. But they offer the advantage of being familiar (and likely credible) to company staff, and they probably can be modified more quickly and at lower cost than starting anew. In other cases, it may be necessary to develop the required elements from scratch. In such cases, sustainability team members might want to perform some research on tools and resources developed by their industry/trade associations, consult relevant international standards and guidelines (discussed in Chapters 3 and 5), and examine resources available from public sector entities (including the EPA, OSHA, and state government agencies), NGOs, and educational institutions.

Leverage Capability Through Cross-Functional Teams

As suggested previously, ES&G issues are multifaceted and often complex. Successfully understanding them and optimizing the firm's activities to alleviate concerns and take advantage of opportunities requires the involvement of people having diverse knowledge, insight, capabilities, credibility, and authority. The only practical way in which the necessary diversity can be brought to bear throughout the preparation, launch, and ongoing operation of a sustainability program or initiative is to form a team collectively offering the perspectives and attributes required. The likely outcome is that the whole becomes greater than the sum of its parts, in terms of business-relevant insights, internal credibility, effectiveness in transforming ideas into action, and generating results efficiently and quickly. The likely outcomes if this is not done include some combination of internal resistance, hardening of organizational silos, thinking and improvement initiatives that are tactical rather than strategic, promotion of ideas that may not be operationally feasible, and unrecognized (and foregone) opportunities for improvement.

Measure and Report Performance

Just as it is important to establish long-term objectives and shorter-term goals toward their attainment, the firm must measure and document progress (or the lack thereof) at regular intervals. Only in this way is it possible to determine whether plans are taking shape as intended, tasks are being completed, and activities are achieving their desired ends. As suggested here and in Chapter 8, the team should carefully consider defining a set of metrics that address ES&G posture and performance concerns of external stakeholders and activity levels, investments, and operational and financial results generated by sustainability initiatives. Unfortunately, most corporate sustainability programs appear to currently focus almost exclusively on the former, that is, the conventional measures of ES&G performance described in Chapter 8. For companies to address sustainability in all of its dimensions, as suggested here, the focus needs to become broader and, in some ways, deeper, to address the value creation potential and results of sustainability activities. Another important decision to be made is how widely to report performance, and in what format(s). Clearly, regular reporting to senior management is essential. A variety of indications show that public reporting of at least key ES&G performance results will increasingly be required of public companies, whether through new mandates or in response to stakeholder demands. It would seem prudent for senior executives in many companies to consider their options and preferences now, while maximum flexibility regarding this important issue remains available to them.

Seek, Obtain, and Evaluate Feedback

Few people enjoy receiving criticism, whether from supervisors or others. But it is important to recognize that constructive criticism from one's management or from important stakeholders can provide important information and insights and can be the starting point for future improvements. Those involved in creating or improving a corporate sustainability program should ensure that it includes robust mechanisms to collect feedback from key internal and external stakeholders, whether or not such feedback is volunteered. They also should ensure that their program has a means by which reactions to the program and its results are factored into its deliberations and decision-making moving forward. In most companies, senior management and its views and preferences will receive adequate attention. But it also is important to "close the loop" with external parties by providing a response to their feedback. Even if the company's response is to not accept the requests(s) or recommendation(s) offered, it is important to keep the communication channel open as a means of ensuring that the relationship remains productive and respectful.

Continually Improve

As you probably know by now, sustainability should be viewed as a journey rather than a destination. The conditions confronting any company are continually changing, and ES&G issues are multidimensional and complex. Therefore, the leaders of any corporate sustainability team can be assured that the results of their efforts, no matter how insightful and effective, will position their company for success for only a limited time. In other words, as soon as (or before) the company reaps the rewards of its adept management of ES&G issues, the conditions that the team so skillfully addressed will have changed. And the firm will need to modify its positions, activities, and priorities in response. A realistic and reasonable expectation is that the firm, and its intellectual capital, brand value, relationships, and other intangible assets, will improve over time as it successfully addresses its substantial ES&G aspects. These improvements in the company's intangible assets will enable it to maintain and grow its revenue, increase earnings, and reduce and control its risks and liabilities. Accordingly, continual performance improvement along all relevant ES&G dimensions should be the stated goal and expectation of any coherent sustainability program or initiative.

By implementing this set of activities, companies and their leaders and managers can understand and optimize their collective responses to the important ES&G trends and challenges described in this book. Many of the recommended actions represent a distinct departure from the conditions and work practices that exist in many organizations today. Therefore, it should be unsurprising that those who are or would be involved in sustainability-oriented activities in corporations will need to exhibit some skills, behaviors, and attributes that may not be in common use today. This topic and its implications are explored in the next section.

Implications for Sustainability Professionals

From the foregoing, it should be clear that business as usual will be insufficient to meet the challenges and capture the opportunities presented by ES&G issues or to implement the steps needed to make corporations more sustainable. If you're involved in sustainability-related activities within a company, or you may become involved in the future, the trends and indicated actions discussed throughout this book suggest a number of implications.

The World, and Sustainability Challenges, Are Dynamic

The field of corporate sustainability, and all the business functions and external influences that affect it, are highly dynamic. This suggests that those involved in managing sustainability programs or initiatives, particularly those at executive levels (such as newly minted Chief Sustainability Officers), must be vigilant and inquisitive. They need to be able to perceive and understand changes in the business landscape as they occur. The dynamic nature of ES&G issues also implies that it is important to establish (or sharpen) a mechanism whereby corporate sustainability leaders can continually scan the horizon and identify emerging issues before they become acute concerns.

Another finding that emerges from examining ES&G issues and the trends that have unfolded over recent years is that the conventional wisdom is often incorrect. Any number of commonly, and often tightly, held assumptions about corporate sustainability have been upended or called into question. These include the nature and importance of EHS issues and their impact on the firm's financial success, the relationship of the firm to its employees and society, and the appropriate factors to consider when investing in corporate securities. Given recent trends, it is not unreasonable to expect further disruption of the consensus in relevant domains during the next several years.

As in so many other areas of business, ES&G issues and concerns are becoming more global. Notably, the trend runs in both directions. U.S. companies increasingly are being held responsible for their contributions to transboundary environmental problems, labor conditions used by offshore suppliers/manufacturers, and other issues. And major customers, national governments, and host societies are raising their level of expectations regarding acceptable corporate practices abroad. U.S. corporations having any substantial international involvement (virtually all large and mid-cap U.S. firms) and those who lead or seek to lead their sustainability efforts therefore must understand the reach of their companies (both the supply chain and customer markets). They also must remain abreast of the major ES&G concerns and trends in play in all relevant geographies.

In response to the nature and magnitude of several ES&G issues and growing public concern about them, there is significant potential for additional public sector activity across a number of domains relevant to the sustainability posture and programs of U.S. companies. Some of these activities may have important and unexpected impacts, and others are likely to have effects that are predictable but seem to be underappreciated at present. Examples (discussed in earlier chapters) include but by no means are limited to the following:

- The possibility of mandatory disclosure of corporate ES&G information imposed by the SEC
- A modified interpretation of ERISA by the U.S. Department of Labor
- Material/product restrictions under the REACH regulation of the EU
- More-restrictive product/process requirements issued by the EPA and/or GSA applied to goods and services sold to the U.S. federal government

Vigilance, on both a personal and systematic level, will be required to remain abreast of such developments. In addition, depending on the nature of the firm's lines of business and the prominence of particular issues or public sector entities in its operations, establishing and maintaining cooperative, respectful lines of bilateral communication with the relevant public sector organizations may be warranted.

One consequence of the dynamism created by the increasing prominence of ES&G issues and stakeholder expectations is that threats to and opportunities for the business may emerge from unexpected, even unfamiliar, places. This can occur in any number of ways. For example, a new EHS regulation (or natural resources use restriction) may impose short-term costs on either one's own firm or one or more major competitors. This might create a severe impact on production, pricing, or margins or, alternatively, an opportunity to price aggressively yet profitably to capture market share and build customer relationships. Lack of effective EHS management systems and controls can lead to accidents, incidents, and even disasters. These can create financial liabilities, damage public image and brand value, weaken the firm's competitive position, and, perversely, bring public pressure for new regulatory controls that affect all industry participants—even those with effective programs. Such wide-ranging effects also can create opportunities for firms with a track record of high-level performance and for those who bring to market new products and services that help alleviate the source(s) of concern.

Sustainability Must Be Viewed as a Core Requirement

As documented in numerous places throughout this book, the notion of sustainability as I have defined it (in Chapter 2) provides an accurate reflection of and appropriate response to external conditions. These conditions affect business enterprises of all types and sizes that are significant, growing, and more than likely to remain so during the next several decades. The question facing any business and its leadership, therefore, is not whether they need to accept and address the need for a coherent approach to sustainability, but when and how this work will be done. I have made the case that a disciplined, financially driven approach will be needed for such efforts to succeed and reach their full potential. And I have provided substantial evidence of how and why such an approach is justified and worthy of senior management support and involvement.

What It Takes

Assuming general agreement with these assertions, the key question then becomes, who should lead and be involved with sustainability program development, deployment, and operation (or, alternatively, refinement)? A growing number of companies are beginning to answer this question by appointing Chief Sustainability Officers (CSOs). Interestingly, however, there does not appear to be a common formula for how to fill this position, in terms of prior experience and qualifications. Some firms choose an EHS professional from their own ranks or from another company. Others select a member of the public relations staff. Still others broaden the responsibilities of an existing senior executive by adding the CSO title.

Every company is different, and there may be compelling reasons to place certain key employees in a multifaceted, challenging position such as the CSO. But I believe that the emerging realities described here suggest that what might be considered a general job description for a CSO is expanding. This means that certain attributes are important to success in this position and are likely to remain so for the foreseeable future. Among them are the attributes described in the following sections.

Strategic Thinking

Viewed through the appropriate lens, leading a coherent sustainability program or initiative in a company of substantial size is a major challenge that involves many moving parts. The relevant aspects of existing EHS compliance, employee development, philanthropy, and other corporate activities and functions must be brought together. And an effective way to manage multiple endpoints, people, and programs must be found. These tasks require the ability to think strategically. Moreover, existing programs must be woven together and expanded in scope to include active consideration of business-relevant opportunities. This implies the ability to look across functions, disciplines, programs, and issues, distill common themes, and develop effective strategies for satisfying multiple needs without substantially increasing the total effort and cost devoted to meeting these expectations.

Technical Expertise and Cross-Functional Understanding

CSOs and people in similar positions must be conversant in, at least on a conceptual level, the essence of EHS regulation and policy, energy management, pollution prevention, supply chain management, financial analysis, and operations management. This knowledge is essential to being able to "connect the dots" in the appropriate ways, make sound decisions about relative priorities, and plan, assign, and oversee work performed by company staff. A thorough grounding in at least one of these disciplines and some meaningful exposure to the others is now and always will be needed to effectively execute the duties of a CSO, at least as defined here.

A corollary to this point is that among the many EHS professionals currently doing sustainability work in corporations, a large percentage will need to gain a greater appreciation of and facility with financial concepts and financial market dynamics. These additional talents will be needed for them to make the right decisions and reach their full value-creation potential, whether or not they are chosen to fulfill the role of CSO. The following sidebar contains further perspective on these issues from some respected voices in the field.

Renaissance Men (and Women) Needed

"Professionals working in the EHS field in last few decades have been engineers and operational/manufacturing personnel for the most part. In the future, there will be more connections with customers and suppliers. This will mean that the capabilities needed will include being conversant in the language of business, and building skills for communication and negotiation."

—Mike Pisarcik, Sara Lee Corporation

"A cross-disciplinary background would be helpful, and this goes both ways. I'd like to see internal company EHS people spending some time working on the investment side, and also to have investment analysts (with an ESG background) going to work in corporate investor relations (IR) functions. One of my fears is that we will end up with degree programs and coursework that are focused on the soft edges of sustainability rather than on the hard science, engineering, and other technical disciplines underlying the real work of ESG performance improvement."

—Mark Bateman, IW Financial

"Higher education remains an issue. We have very few people trained using an interdisciplinary approach. Super-specialization is still very common and is often emphasized in many academic and professional fields, while a more generalist orientation is disparaged as being a 'jack-of-all-trades, master of none.'"

—Ira Feldman, greentrack strategies

Critical Thinking and Analysis Skills

As noted previously, emerging ES&G issues are raising many questions about widely held beliefs, attitudes, and practices. Therefore, it is important that CSOs and other senior professionals working on sustainability issues be able to parse and carefully evaluate competing claims and reach rational, fact-based conclusions and decisions. Executives and managers working on corporate sustainability issues therefore should cultivate the ability to think critically, ask probing questions, challenge assumptions and analytical methods, and generally bring a skeptical eye to claims based on or dependent on "what everyone knows."

Team Building and Leadership

Remaining abreast of the many ES&G issues and trends that are taking shape across multiple business functions and geographies necessarily involves forming and coordinating activities across a multidisciplinary team. Serving as team leader and, more generally, the focal point for internal sustainability efforts, the CSO needs to cultivate and maintain relationships with knowledgeable and reliable contacts in key roles across the company. The simple fact is that no one person has all the relevant knowledge, skills, and wherewithal to develop and implement an optimal sustainability strategy and program in a company of significant size. Nor can one person continually carry out the reconnaissance activities needed to remain informed about all relevant issues. Relationships across the organization are key to making things happen. The CSO needs to demonstrate (or quickly develop) the ability to get people of different backgrounds and with different immediate priorities to work together and pull in the same direction.

Sustainable Leadership

"An important success skill is to be able to lead through influence—that is, bring people to agreement on a common strategy without having formal authority. This requires 'softer skills,' and not everyone from the technical side of the business can do this well."

—Tim Mohin, AMD

Communication Skills

People who are assigned to develop, deploy, and explain a sustainability program or initiative to internal and external audiences must be able to communicate complex concepts in terms that can be readily understood by people with widely varying levels of education and sophistication. Being able to speak clearly and authoritatively, make oneself understood, and effectively respond to questions and even hostility under a variety of circumstances is and will become more important in the future as ES&G issues become more prominent for more companies. In addition, as in so many other aspects of the business world, the ability to write clearly and effectively is imperative. Increasing demands for corporate transparency inexorably lead to more disclosure, and the issues are complex and multifaceted.

For those companies, and the executives and aspiring sustainability leaders within them, it may be appropriate to seek opportunities to build or improve on existing skills in these areas. Partnerships or contractual arrangements with external stakeholders and product/service providers can accelerate progress. Many sources of guidance, training, tools, and other assistance are available. As discussed in Chapters 2 and 5, the availability of proven approaches, methods, data, and both formal and informal training is extensive. Hundreds of qualified consulting firms, NGOs, public sector programs, and educational institutions offer products and services ranging from EHS compliance training to facilitated team-building exercises. Finally, interested individuals might want to supplement their previous formal education by pursuing graduate-level study or working toward a certification.

As discussed in a number of places in this book (particularly in Chapters 3, 4, and 5), sustainability programs will be most effective if those leading them exhibit certain characteristics. I don't want to sound pejorative, but my experience suggests that by the time people enter the workforce, they either have these attributes or they don't. These qualities are not a function of formal education or on-the-job experience but instead are personality aspects that are shaped by an individual's life experiences and personal values. I suggest that having and using the personal attributes discussed next will distinguish those who are highly successful in the CSO role and the sustainability field more generally from those who are not.

Intellectual Curiosity

In my view, pursuing organizational sustainability is not concerned simply with demonstrating responsibility, satisfying external expectations, or controlling risk. Instead, it is fundamentally about continually asking yourself (and your colleagues) how the status quo can be improved upon. Viewed appropriately, ES&G issues are evaluated in terms of not only risk and liability exposure but also new opportunities for the business to grow and thrive. Finding and pursuing these opportunities requires a type of intellectual curiosity and impatience that are often absent (or suppressed) in many business organizations and functions. In my experience, these qualities are more common in corporate research and development departments. But they also can be found within the more creative NGOs, certain pockets of public sector organizations, and academia. Discovery is often an enlightening and empowering phenomenon. Those who would lead sustainability programs should be expected to either bring the intellectual firepower needed to drive discovery in their organizations or deploy and support others who can. The following sidebar offers some corporate perspectives on the importance of this attribute.

Continual Personal Improvement Through Learning

"To be successful in CSR, you must be curious. You will be exposed to a broad range of issues, many of which will be new to you. It is very important to be a lifelong learner, have an open mind, and take the risk of not being the 'smartest kid in the class.' Flexibility is incredibly important."

—Tim Mohin, AMD

"To be successful working in the sustainability field, you need to have an inherent interest in learning about issues outside of your core competency. You have to be able to ground yourself in areas outside your own expertise. I often rely on other subject-matter technical experts to better understand an issue, while at the same time educating them on sustainable business principles as related to their discipline."

—Marcella Thompson, ConAgra Foods

"Those working in sustainability need to be able to stay ahead of the curve—for example, by plugging into the CSR world. They also need to know their business and industry, and understand what drives the financials."

—Sandy Nessing, AEP

Personal Integrity

Working effectively with both colleagues and external stakeholders will be far easier and more productive if you display honesty, integrity, and fair dealing with others. People will willingly follow a leader who upholds their personal values (or aspirations), even if the work ahead is difficult and the outcomes are uncertain. People also will, under certain conditions, follow a leader who is unscrupulous, dishonest, or overly self-serving, particularly if they believe their employment or personal well-being are at risk if they do not. In the context of organizational sustainability, however, such people are poorly suited for leadership roles. Effectively managing the many ES&G issues that affect even moderately large companies requires the involvement of too many people and has too many moving parts for such an arrangement to be effective. And, importantly, putting someone who lacks personal integrity in charge of (or in a prominent role in) the firm's sustainability program(s) or initiatives puts at risk the company's social license to operate. Anyone who might become the face of the firm, even in a limited way, simply must embody its highest virtues and core values.

Courage of Convictions

Making sustainable business behavior happen within a company, particularly a large company, is intrinsically difficult. Those who take on the role of leading such efforts will inevitably face skepticism from some colleagues, employees, and external stakeholders. And because people are inherently resistant to change, it is not unlikely that CSOs and other sustainability leaders will encounter both active and passive resistance. To be effective in their roles, these people need to believe earnestly in what they are doing. They also must be willing to take a stand on important issues that may be unpopular, defy long-standing company custom, threaten the personal interests of internally powerful people, or otherwise upset the status quo and push people out of their comfort zones. Doing so involves taking on personal risk. Only those who are willing to face up to the possible consequences of taking an unpopular stand will be able to prevail. The CSO is an unsuitable position for company wallflowers, yes-men (or women), and those seeking tranquility, security, or popularity.

Open-Mindedness and Flexibility

By its nature, a coherent program or initiative focused on sustainable business practices will bring to light new issues and concerns, as well as possible solutions, ideas, and ways of doing things that are outside the firm's current normal operating practices. As discussed in Chapter 5, sustainability efforts will be greatly helped and, indeed, can only reach full flower, if it is widely understood that new ideas and ways of thinking are encouraged. Accordingly, the CSO must model the desired behavior by demonstrating open-mindedness and promoting experimentation and discovery. This may require the CSO and other senior leaders to set aside existing biases and beliefs, comfortable and widely accepted ways of looking at particular issues, and communication channels that provide only limited access from all employees to senior decision-makers. They also must show open-mindedness regarding the sources and types of ideas that are received and evaluated and make clear that good ideas are welcome and sought from all corners of the company, as well as from stakeholders. Similarly, the evaluation of potential improvements must be performed using criteria that are clear, reasonable, and consistently applied.

> ### Facilitation Is Key
>
> "The most gratifying part of my job is bringing people together with different points of view, and helping them reach a common understanding."
>
> —Sandy Nessing, AEP

Empathy

Finally, managing ES&G issues provides exposure to a wide array of different viewpoints, priorities, biases, and interests. Often it will be impossible to reconcile or harmonize all company and stakeholder positions on some issues. Nevertheless, it is important that any person serving as a CSO understand where others are coming from. Empathy is the ability to see an issue through another's eyes. Even if you disagree with the person's position on that issue, you can be reasonably confident that you understand why the other party sees the issue in the way he or she does. Being able to understand ES&G issues in this way is essential to the work of a CSO so that the firm can make decisions that are in its long-term interests. This includes maintaining productive relationships with all important stakeholders. Absent this understanding, the firm may make decisions that do not recognize or address legitimate stakeholder concerns (risking alienation or resistance), do not produce the desired and expected outcomes, or do not take advantage of potential win-win situations.

Closing Thoughts

In this book, I have attempted to show why and how sustainability is rapidly becoming a business imperative. I have provided extensive thoughts on what it will take for both businesses and the executives and managers working for them to respond to the challenges and opportunities presented by emerging environmental, health and safety, social, and governance issues. My greatest hope is that the information and ideas presented here will be of value to those who are dedicated to making their companies and communities as broadly successful, productive, and sustainable as possible. At the very least, I hope I have helped you look at some of these issues in a new light and to consider whether and how some of the concepts presented here can be of value to you in some small way. In either case, I wish you success in your endeavors.

Endnotes

1. As discussed at length in Chapter 5, when you begin a sustainability program in earnest, I strongly recommend the formation of a cross-functional team that includes high-ranking, respected members from across the organization. The following discussion assumes that such a team has been formed and is leading the sustainability program or initiative.

2. In the case of conglomerates, examining the few industries comprising the largest revenue shares and/or presenting the most prominent ES&G issues should suffice.

3. Note that in this context, I define "opportunity" to include elimination of risks and liabilities—that is, removing or diminishing the magnitude or likelihood of one or more negative outcomes.

4. As discussed in Chapters 3 and 4, firms can no longer truly control the information describing their operations and effects or, in a larger sense, their public image. But they can take steps to shape that image in constructive ways. However, doing so requires a degree of transparency that is beyond the current norm for many firms.

References

Bank Sarasin & Co., Inc., 2007. *Assessing corporate sustainability: Methodology of the Sarasin company rating.* August.

Bank Sarasin & Co., Inc., 2006. *The Sarasin Industry Rating: Methodology and results of sector sustainability analysis.* September.

Barth, M. and McNichols, M., 1994. "Estimation and Market Valuation of Environmental Liabilities Relating to Superfund Sites." *Journal of Accounting Research* 32, 177–208.

Bateman, M., 2011. Personal communication. 27 June.

Bauer, R. and Hann, D., 2010. *Corporate Environmental Management and Credit Risk.* Working paper. Maastricht University, European Centre for Corporate Engagement (ECCE). 30 June.

Berns, M., Townend, A., Khayat, Z., Balagopal, B., Reeves, M., Hopkins, M., and Kruschwitz, N., 2009. "The Business of Sustainability: Findings and Insights from the First Annual Business of Sustainability Survey and the Global Thought Leaders' Research Project." *MIT Sloan Management Review*, Cambridge, MA. Massachusetts Institute of Technology.

Berridge, R. and Cook, J., 2010. "Mutual Funds and Climate Change: Growing Support for Shareholder Resolutions," Appendix 4, *CERES*. June.

Blacconiere, W.G. and Northcut, W.D., 1997. "Environmental Information and Market Reactions to Environmental Legislation." *Auditing and Finance* 12(2): 149–178.

Blacconiere, W.G. and Patten, D.M., 1994. "Environmental Disclosures, Regulatory Costs, and Changes in Firm Value." *Journal of Accounting & Economics* 18: 357–377.

Bosch, J.C., Eckland, E.W., and Insup, L. 1998. "Environmental Regulation and Stockholder Wealth." *Managerial and Decision Economics* 19: 167-177.

Brooksbank, D., 2010. "Malaysian stock exchange to launch ESG index: Bursa Malaysia launches programme to promote ESG integration." *Responsible Investor*. 24 November.

Buc, L.G. and Soyka, P.A., 2009. "Bank of America, Mail, and the Environment," in Crew, M. and Kleindorfer, P. (Eds.). *Progress in the Competitive Agenda in the Postal and Delivery Sector*. Northampton, MA: Edward Elgar Publishing, Ltd. Pp. 298–308.

Business for Social Responsibility (BSR), 2003. *The Social License to Operate*. San Francisco.

Ciurea, C., 2010. *Sustainable Stock Exchanges: improving ESG standards among listed companies*. EIRIS. September.

Cohen, M., Fenn, S., and Naimon, J., 1995. *Environmental and Financial Performance: Are they related?* Investor Responsibility Research Center.

Cone, Inc., 2010. *Companies Fail to Engage Consumers on Environmental and Social Issues*. Cone Shared Responsibility Study. Boston.

Coyle, K., 2005. *Environmental Literacy in America*. National Environmental Education & Training Foundation. September.

Daicoff, C.L. and Wiemken, J.M., 2005. *Standard & Poor's Credit Market Services*. Presentation to U.S. EPA. 10 February.

Dhaliwal, D., Zhen Li, O., Tsang, A., and Yang, Y.G., 2009. *Voluntary Non-Financial Disclosure and the Cost of Equity Capital: The Case of Corporate Social Responsibility Reporting*. February.

Dowell, G., Hart, S., and Yeung, B., 2000. "Do Corporate Global Environmental Standards Create or Destroy Market Value?" *Management Science* 46: 1059–74.

Doyle, R., 1998. *Advisory Opinion*. U.S. Department of Labor, PWBA Office of Regulations and Interpretations. 28 May.

Dunlap, R.E., 2010. *At 40, Environmental Movement Endures, with Less Consensus*. Gallup, Inc. 22 April. Available from www.gallup.com/poll/127487/Environmental-Movement-Endures-Less-Consensus.aspx.

The Economist Intelligence Unit and Oracle Corporation, 2005. *The Importance of Corporate Responsibility*.

Edelman, Inc., 2011. *2011 Edelman Trust Barometer Findings: 2011 Annual Global Opinion Leaders Study*.

Edmans, A., 2011. "Does the Stock Market Fully Value Intangibles? Employee Satisfaction and Equity Prices." *Journal of Financial Economics* 101: 621-40.

El Ghoul, S., Guedhami, O., Kwok, C.C.Y, and Mishra, D., 2010. *Does Corporate Social Responsibility Affect the Cost of Capital?* Working paper. University of Alberta. July.

European Commission, 2006. *Environment Fact Sheet: REACH—A New Chemicals Policy for the EU*. Brussels. February.

Eurosif, 2010. *High Net Worth Individuals and Sustainable Investment*. Paris.

Federal Register, 2009. Vol. 74, No. 194. *Executive Order 13514—Federal Leadership in Environmental, Energy, and Economic Performance*. 8 October. Washington, D.C.

Federal Trade Commission, 2009. "It's Too Easy Being Green: Defining Fair Green Marketing Principles." Prepared statement presented to the Committee on Energy and Commerce, Subcommittee on Commerce, Trade, and Consumer Protection, U.S. House of Representatives. 9 June.

Feldman, I., 2011. Personal communication. 29 June.

Feldman, S., Soyka, P., and Ameer, P., 1997. "Does Improving a Firm's Environmental Management System and Environmental Performance Result in a Higher Stock Price?" *Journal of Investing* 6(4): 87–97.

Fortune, 2010. The Global 500. Fortune.com (web site). Available from http://money.cnn.com/magazines/fortune/global500/2010/full_list/. Accessed 28 January 2011.

FSC-US, 2010. *Forest Management Standard FSC-US (v1.0)*. Forest Stewardship Council–U.S. 8 July.

Garber, S. and Hammitt, J., 1998. "Risk Premiums for Environmental Liabilities: Superfund and the Cost of Capital." *Journal of Environmental Economics and Management* 36: 93–94.

Global Environmental Management Initiative (GEMI), 2004. *Clear Advantage: Building Shareholder Value*. Washington, D.C.

Global Environmental Management Initiative (GEMI), 1994. *Finding Cost-Effective Pollution Prevention Alternatives: Incorporating Environmental Costs into Business Decision Making*.

Global Reporting Initiative (GRI), 2011. *GRI launches its Focal Point USA* (press release). www.globalreporting.org.

Globescan, 2009. *Greendex 2009: Consumer Choice and the Environment: A Worldwide Tracking Survey*. Prepared for the National Geographic Society. Toronto.

Goldman Sachs, 2007. *Introducing GS Sustain*. Goldman Sachs Global Investment Research. 22 June.

Griffin, P.A., Lont, D.H., and Sun, Y., 2010. *The Relevance to Investors of Greenhouse Gas Emission Disclosures*. Working paper. University of California, Davis. 5 January.

Guenster, N., Derwall, J., Bauer, R., and Koeddijk, K., 2006. *The Economic Value of Corporate Eco-Efficiency*. Rotterdam. Erasmus University. August.

Hamilton, J., 1995. "Pollution as News: Media and Stock Market Reactions to the Toxic Release Inventory Data." *Journal of Environmental Economics and Management* 28: 98–113.

Hart, S. and Ahuja, G., 1996. "Does It Pay to Be Green? An Empirical Examination of the Relationship Between Emission Reduction and Firm Performance." *Business Strategy and the Environment* 5: 30–37.

Hartley, L.M., Wilke, B.J., Schramm, J.W., D'Avanzo, C., and Anderson, C.W., 2011. "College Students' Understanding of the Carbon Cycle: Contrasting Principle-based and Informal Reasoning." *BioScience* 61(1): 65–75.

Hawken, P., Lovins, A., and Lovins, L.H., 1999. *Natural Capitalism: Creating the Next Industrial Revolution*. Boston: Little, Brown and Company.

Hayles, L., 2010. "Mexico joins ESG index rush with Cancún launch: Sustainability benchmark will measure Mexican companies against international standards." *Responsible Investor* 2 December.

Hoepner, A.G.F., Yu, P.S., and Ferguson, J., 2010. *Corporate Social Responsibility Across Industries: When can who do well by doing good?* Working paper. School of Management, University of St. Andrews. March.

Hoepner, A.G.F., Yu, P.S., and Ferguson, J., 2008. *Industries, externalities, and asset prices*. Working paper, School of Management, University of St. Andrews.

ICCA and Responsible Care, 2008. *Responsible Care Status Report 2008*. International Council of Chemical Associations.

Internal Revenue Service (IRS), 2001. *Tax-Exempt Status for Your Organization*. Publication 557 (Rev. July 2001). July.

International Organization for Standardization (ISO), 2004. *International Standard ISO 14001: Environmental Management Systems—Requirements with Guidance for Use*. Second Edition. Geneva. 15 November.

Ioannou, I. and Serafeim, G., 2010. *The Impact of Corporate Social Responsibility on Investment Recommendations.* Working paper 11-017. Harvard Business School: Cambridge, MA. August.

Jones, J.M., 2011. *Americans Increasingly Prioritize Economy Over Environment Largest margin in favor of economy in nearly 30-year history of the trend.* Gallup, Inc. 17 March. Available from: www.gallup.com/poll/146681/Americans-Increasingly-Prioritize-Economy-Environment.aspx

Kempf, A. and Osthoff, P., 2007. "The effect of socially responsible investing on portfolio performance." *European Financial Management* 13(5): 908–922.

Klassen, R.D. and McLaughlin, C.P, 1996. "The Impact of Environmental Management on Firm Performance." *Management Science* 42(8): 1199-1214.

Knight, A., 2011. Personal communication. 21 April.

Konar, S. and Cohen, M., 2001. "Does the Market Value Environmental Performance?" *Rev. Econ & Statistics* 83(2): 281–309.

Lev, B., 2001. *Intangibles: Management, Measurement and Reporting.* Brookings Institution. Washington, D.C.

Makower, J., 2011. *Green Marketing Is Over. Let's Move On.* GreenBiz.com. 16 May.

Martin, M., 2011. *Green Marketing: It's Alive But Needs a Makeover.* GreenBiz.com. 23 May.

McKinsey Global Institute, 2008. *Mapping Global Capital Markets: Fourth Annual Report.*

Mercer Investment Consulting, 2006. *Fearless Forecast: Global Survey of Investment Managers.* Toronto.

Minami, H., 2008. "How Does Innovest Use EPA Data?" Innovest Strategic Value Advisors. Presented at *A Dialogue to Explore the Use of EPA Data in Financial and Investment Analysis.* New York, NY. 19 June.

Mining, Minerals and Sustainable Development Project (MMSD), 2002. *Breaking New Ground: The Report of the Mining, Minerals and Sustainable Development Project.* London: Earthscan Publications Ltd. May.

Mohin, T., 2011. Personal communication. 27 June.

Morales, R. and van Tichelen, E., 2010. *Sustainable Stock Exchanges: Real Obstacles, Real Opportunities.* Responsible Research: Geneva.

National Association for Environmental Management (NAEM), 2011. *Identifying Corporate EHS and Sustainability Metrics.* Washington, D.C. Forthcoming.

National Center for Education Statistics, 2011. *The Nation's Report Card: Science 2009.* Institute of Education Sciences, U.S. Department of Education, Washington, D.C. Document No. NCES 2011–451.

Nessing, S., 2011. Personal communication. 14 June.

Park, C. and Pavlovsky, K., 2010. *Sustainability in Business Today: A Cross-Industry View.* Deloitte Development, LLC.

Pisarcik, M., 2011. Personal communication. 8 March.

Plumlee, M., Brown, D., and Marshall, R.S., 2008. *The Impact of Voluntary Environmental Disclosure Quality on Firm Value.* Working paper, David Eccles School of Business, University of Utah. May.

Porter, M.E. and Kramer, M.R., 2011. "Creating Shared Value." *Harvard Business Review* Jan–Feb.

Principles for Responsible Investment (PRI), 2010. *PRI Report on Progress 2010: an Analysis of Signatory Progress and Guidance on Implementation.* UNEP Finance Initiative and UN Global Compact.

The Prince's Accounting for Sustainability Project and the Global Reporting Initiative, 2010. *Formation of the International Integrated Reporting Committee (IIRC) (Press Briefing).* 2 August.

Ray, J. and Pugliese, A., 2011a. *Fewer Americans, Europeans View Global Warming as a Threat: Worldwide, 42% see serious risk, similar to 2007–2008*. Gallup, Inc. 20 April. Available from www.gallup.com/poll/147203/Fewer-Americans-Europeans-View-Global-Warming-Threat.aspx.

Ray, J. and Pugliese, A., 2011b. *Worldwide, Blame for Climate Change Falls on Humans: Americans among least likely to attribute to human causes*. Gallup, Inc. 22 April. Available from www.gallup.com/poll/147242/Worldwide-Blame-Climate-Change-Falls-Humans.aspx.

Repetto, R. and Austin, D., 2000. "Coming Clean: Corporate Disclosure of Financially Significant Environmental Risks." Washington, D.C: World Resources Institute.

Responsible Investor, 2008. "Responsible Investment Landscape 2008: Asset Managers." June. p. 4.

Rohm, H., 2008. *Improve Financial Performance Using a Balanced Scorecard to Link Non-Financial Drivers to Financial Results*. Presentation to Financial Executives International-San Francisco Chapter. Balanced Scorecard Institute. October.

Russo, M. and Fouts, P., 1997. "A Resource-based Perspective on Corporate Environmental Performance and Profitability." *Academy of Management Journal* 40(3): 534–59.

Saad, L., 2011. *Water Issues Worry Americans Most, Global Warming Least: Environmental concerns are flat since 2010, but down over past decade*. Gallup, Inc. 28 March. Available from www.gallup.com/poll/146810/Water-Issues-Worry-Americans-Global-Warming-Least.aspx.

SAM Research, Inc., 2007. *Corporate Sustainability Assessment Questionnaire 2007*. Zurich.

SFI, 2010. *Requirements for the SFI 2010–2014 Program: Standards, Rules for Label Use, Procedures, and Guidance*. Washington, D.C. January.

Shapiro, I., 2011. *Tallying Up the Impact of New EPA Rules.* Washington, D.C. Environmental Policy Institute. EPI Briefing Paper #311. 31 May.

Smith, G.A. and Feldman, D., 2009. *Newmont Community Relationships Report: Global Summary Report.* March.

Smith, J., 2005. "Sarbanes-Oxley and EMS." Presentation given at U.S. Environmental Protection Agency. Cravath, Swain & Moore. 26 July.

Social Investment Forum (SIF) Foundation, 2010. *2010 Report on Socially Responsible Investing Trends in the United States* (Executive Summary). Washington, D.C.

Social Investment Forum (SIF) Foundation, 2009. *Investment consultants and responsible investing: Current Practice and Outlook in the United States.* Washington, D.C. December.

Soyka, P.A., 2009. "Do the U.S. Capital Markets Value Environmental Management Systems?: New Evidence," in Drury, E.K. and Pridgen, T.S. (Eds.). *Handbook on Environmental Quality.* Nova Science Publishers. pp. 223–263.

Soyka, P.A. and Bateman, M.E., 2010. *Benchmarking Analysis of Disclosed U.S. Corporate Environmental Practices.* Vienna, VA. May.

Soyka, P.A. and Bateman, M.E., 2009. *The Road Not Yet Taken: The State of U.S. Corporate Environmental Policy and Management.* Prepared for Sustainable Enterprise Institute. August.

Soyka, P. and Feldman, S., 1998. "Investor Attitudes Toward Corporate Environmentalism: New Survey Findings." *Environmental Quality Management* 8(1): 1–10.

Stanwick, P. and Stanwick, S., 1998. "The Relationship Between Corporate Social Performance and Size, Financial and Environmental Performance." *Journal of Business Ethics* 17(2): 195–204.

Statman, M., 2005. *Socially Responsible Indexes: Composition, Performance and Tracking Errors.* Santa Clara, CA: Santa Clara University, Leavey School of Business.

Statman, M. and Glushkov, D., 2009. "The Wages of Social Responsibility." *Financial Analysts Journal* 65: 20–29.

Terrachoice, 2010. *The Sins of Greenwashing: Home and Family Edition 2010: A report on environmental claims made in the North American consumer market.* Underwriters Laboratories.

Thompson, M., 2011. Personal communication. 29 June.

United Nations Environment Programme-Finance Initiative (UNEP-FI), 2009. Fiduciary Responsibility: Legal and Practical Aspects of Integrating Environmental, Social, and Governance Issues into Institutional Investment. UNEP-FI Asset Management Working Group. July.

UNEP-FI, 2004. *The Materiality of Social, Environmental, and Corporate Governance Issues to Equity Pricing.* New York: UNEP Finance Initiative.

UNEP-FI, Freshfields Bruckhaus Deringer, 2005. *A Legal Framework for the Integration of Environmental, Social and Governance Issues into Institutional Investment.* October.

United Nations Global Compact (UNGC), 2011. *The Ten Principles.* Available from www.unglobalcompact.org/AboutTheGC/TheTenPrinciples/index.html.

UNGC, 2011. "Number of Expelled Companies Reaches 2,000 as Global Compact Strengthens Disclosure Framework" (press release). New York. 20 January.

U.S. Environmental Protection Agency (USEPA), 2010. *The Benefits and Costs of the Clean Air Act from 1990 to 2020: Summary Report.* Office of Air and Radiation. March.

USEPA, 2006. *Financial Incentives for Environmental Management Systems: Project Findings from Phase I.* December.

USEPA, 1995. *An Introduction to Environmental Accounting as a Business Management Tool: Key Concepts and Terms.* Office of Pollution Prevention and Toxics. EPA 742-R-95-001. June.

USEPA/USDOE, 2008. *National Action Plan for Energy Efficiency—Vision for 2025: A Framework for Change (Executive Summary).* Washington, D.C. Available from www.epa.gov/cleanenergy/energy-programs/suca/resources.html.

U.S. Federal Reserve, 2011. *Flow of Funds Accounts of the United States.* Federal Reserve Statistical Release, Z.1 Release. Washington, D.C.

Watts, C., 2010. *Managing for Sustainability. The Economist* Intelligence Unit Limited. February.

White, A. (Ed.), 2009. *Paper Series on Restoring the Primacy of the Real Economy.* Proceedings of the Second Summit on the Future of the Corporation. Corporation 20/20. Boston. June.

World Business Council for Sustainable Development (WBCSD) and UNEP-FI, 2005. *Generation Lost: Young Financial Analysts and Environmental, Social and Governance Issues.* Young Managers Team: Geneva.

WBCSD/UNEP, 1996. *Eco-Efficiency and Cleaner Production: Charting the Course to Sustainability.* Geneva.

INDEX

Numbers

3M, 157-158

10-K, 203

2010 BP oil disaster, 11

A

absence of alignment with financial value drivers or endpoints considered by financial sector stakeholders

EHS, 32

accounting perspective, environment and finance, 270-271

activist investors, 44

AEP (American Electric Power), 86, 337-338

AMD, 49

analysts

ES&G information, 320-321

stakeholders, 124-125

influence on corporate behavior, *143-144*

antitrust laws, 190

applying life-cycle approaches and perspectives

KPIs, ES&G, 353-354

appropriate management approaches

needs, 322

aspects analysis, management systems, 169-170

assurance of compliant behavior

needs, 321

W-X

Y-Z

FINANCIAL TIMES

In an increasingly competitive world, it is quality
of thinking that gives an edge—an idea that opens new
doors, a technique that solves a problem, or an insight
that simply helps make sense of it all.

We work with leading authors in the various arenas
of business and finance to bring cutting-edge thinking
and best-learning practices to a global market.

It is our goal to create world-class print publications
and electronic products that give readers
knowledge and understanding that can then be
applied, whether studying or at work.

To find out more about our business
products, you can visit us at www.ftpress.com.